Odoo 15 Development Essentials

Fifth Edition

Enhance your Odoo development skills to create powerful business applications

Daniel Reis

BIRMINGHAM—MUMBAI

Odoo 15 Development Essentials

Fifth Edition

Group Product Manager: Alok Dhuri

Publishing Product Manager: Harshal Gundetty

Senior Editor: Ruvika Rao

Content Development Editor: Nithya Sadanandan

Technical Editor: Pradeep Sahu

Copy Editor: Safis Editing

Project Coordinator: Manisha Singh

Proofreader: Safis Editing

Indexer: Tejal Daruwale Soni

Production Designer: Ponraj Dhandapani

Marketing Coordinator: Teny Thomas

First published: November 2016
Fifth edition: February 2022
Production reference: 1030122

Published by Packt Publishing Ltd.
Livery Place
35 Livery Street
Birmingham
B3 2PB, UK.

ISBN 978-1-80020-006-7

www.packt.com

Thanks to Maria José Reis for all the companionship and support. This and the previous books are a joint achievement.

– Daniel Reis

Foreword

It is an easy time to be an Odoo developer…and that wasn't always the case. In 2010, when I first discovered OpenERP, the documentation was the code—and that was it. Knowledge was widely dispersed and shallow, and the Odoo community was just a mirage. Everything we all learned was through hard-won victories and transmitted as tribal lore between pioneers.

Fortunately, a few people started writing down these lessons, making it easier for all that followed. I must acknowledge the work that Fabien himself did in fostering this effort. Daniel, Holger, Alex, and others built on this foundation, and now, we all benefit from their largely unrecognized efforts.

The Odoo community has rocketed forward on a trajectory that all of us hoped for, but none of us were sure how it would be done. Out of many free or open source software projects, Odoo emerged as the most successful to tackle the enterprise resource planning market, solving business problems with freedom and flexibility.

I am consistently amazed at the creativity and productivity that Odoo developers demonstrate. Odoo attracts an especially curious, inspired sort of developer, and I think this book will be a great help to people at all levels.

Finally, there is a question—how do I use Odoo to solve my business goals? That is where the art is. This book does a good job of explaining how to build an application, but the trick is in how to build the *right application*. Development effort alone isn't enough to solve complex supply chain, manufacturing, or sales challenges. Thorough business analysis and optimization are key to a successful project—and one of the people that I think demonstrates this best is *Daniel Reis*. This book gives a few hints here and there that business process optimization is as important as good code.

Here's to Fabien, Odoo S.A., and to the community—may we continue to work together as friends and colleagues for decades to come.

Greg Mader

Founder and president of Open Source Integrators

Contributors

About the author

Daniel Reis has a degree in applied mathematics and an MBA. He has had a long career in the IT industry, mostly as a consultant implementing business applications in a variety of sectors.

He has been working with Odoo (OpenERP at the time) since 2010 and is an active contributor to the **Odoo Community Association (OCA)**, where he also serves as a board member.

He is the managing director of Open Source Integrators, a leading open source and Odoo consultancy firm.

About the reviewers

Bhavesh Odedra has been an innovative software developer since 2012 working on the open source ERP software development lifecycle – from concept through delivery of next-generation modules and customizable solutions. He started his journey with Odoo (formerly OpenERP) in 2012. He has been an active contributor to the Stack Overflow developer community and the Odoo Community Association since 2013 and is currently a delegate member of the Odoo Community Association. Currently, he works at Open Source Integrators in the United States as an implementation engineer.

Ashish Singh Bhatia is a reader and learner at his core. He has more than 13 years of rich experience in different IT sectors, encompassing training, development, and management. He has worked in many domains, such as software development, ERP, banking, and training. He is passionate about Python and Java and has recently been exploring R. He is mostly involved in web and mobile development in various capacities. He likes to explore new technologies and share his views and thoughts through various online media and magazines. He believes in sharing his experience with the new generation and also takes part in training and teaching. Currently, he is working with Odoo's India office.

Table of Contents

2
Preparing the Development Environment

3
Your First Odoo Application

4
Extending Modules

Section 2: Models

5
Importing, Exporting, and Module Data

6
Models – Structuring the Application Data

Section 3: Business Logic

7

Recordsets – Working with Model Data

8

Business Logic – Supporting Business Processes

9
External API – Integrating with Other Systems

12

Creating Printable PDF Reports with Server-Side QWeb

13
Creating Web and Portal Frontend Features

Section 5: Deployment and Maintenance

14
Understanding Odoo Built-In Models

15

Deploying and Maintaining Production Instances

Index

Other Books You May Enjoy

Preface

Odoo is a full-featured open source platform to build applications. Based on this core framework, a suite of integrated applications was built, covering all business areas from CRM and sales to inventory and accounting.

Beyond these out-of-the-box features, Odoo is an application development framework built with extensibility in mind. Extensions and modifications can be implemented as modules, to be applied over the module with the feature being changed. This avoids editing the original feature code and provides clean and easy-to-control customized applications.

This capability to combine several modules into feature-rich applications, along with the open source nature of Odoo, are important factors that explain the community that grew around Odoo. In fact, there are thousands of community modules available for Odoo, covering virtually every topic.

Odoo 15 Development Essentials provides a step-by-step guide to Odoo development, allowing you to quickly climb the learning curve and become productive on the Odoo application platform. At the same time, it provides good reference materials, to be kept nearby every time you are working with Odoo.

Who this book is for

This book was written keeping in mind developers with minimal programming knowledge but a strong will to learn. The Odoo server is implemented in Python, and basic knowledge of Python programming is expected before getting started with the book. The main platform used to run Odoo is an Ubuntu/Debian system, but little previous knowledge on it is assumed. The code examples are kept simple and clear, and they are accompanied by appropriate explanations to help build up knowledge on them.

Teachers, trainers, and Odoo development managers will also find the book useful for helping their students or trainees to learn Odoo development skills.

Experienced developers, already familiar with Odoo, should also be able to benefit from this book. Not only does it consolidate their knowledge, but it also provides an easy way to get up to date with all the details that changed in the last Odoo versions, which are highlighted whenever the changes are significant.

Finally, this book should provide a solid reference to be used daily, both by newcomers and experienced developers. The documentation of the relevant differences between the several Odoo versions should also be a good resource for any developer working with different Odoo versions at the same time or porting modules to other versions.

What this book covers

Chapter 1, *Quick Start Using the Developer Mode*, visually introduces the Odoo development concepts, creating an Odoo application directly from the user interface – a simple to-do tracking application. Instructions are given to get Odoo working on the work machine, but an existing Odoo installation, or an Odoo.com instance, can be used, so no local setup is required.

Chapter 2, *Preparing the Development Environment*, explains how to install Odoo from source code, and how to set up the development environment to be used throughout the book. We choose to install Odoo in an Ubuntu environment, and under Windows 10 the **Windows Subsystem for Linux** (**WSL**) can be used to achieve this.

Chapter 3, *Your First Odoo Application*, provides a step-by-step guide through the creation of our first Odoo module, a book catalog for a library app. While the example is kept simple, it covers all the different layers and components that can be involved in an Odoo application: models, business logic, backend views, and web frontend views.

Chapter 4, *Extending Modules*, explains the available inheritance mechanisms and how to use them to create extension modules, adding or modifying features from other existing add-on modules.

Chapter 5, *Importing, Exporting, and Module Data*, addresses the usage of data files in Odoo, and their role in modules to load data and configurations to the database. It covers the XML and CSV data file formats, the external identifier concept, how to use data files in modules, and data import/export operations.

Chapter 6, *Models – Structuring the Application Data*, discusses the model layer in detail, introducing the framework's **Object-Relational Mapping** (**ORM**), the different types of models available, and the field types, including relational and computed fields.

Chapter 7, *Recordsets – Working with Model Data*, introduces ORM concepts and features, how to query and browse data from models, how to manipulate recordsets, and how to write changes to model data.

Chapter 8, Business Logic – Supporting Business Processes, explores programming business logic on the server side to manipulate data and implement specific business rules. It also explains how to use wizards for more sophisticated user interaction. The built-in social features – messages, chatter, followers, and channels – are addressed, as well as testing and debugging techniques.

Chapter 9, External API – Integrating with Other Systems, shows how to implement Odoo external applications by implementing a command-line client that interacts with our Odoo server. There are several alternative client programming libraries available, which are introduced and used to implement our showcase client utility.

Chapter 10, Backend Views – Designing the User Interface, covers the web client's View layer, explaining the several types of views in detail and all the elements that can be used to create dynamic and intuitive user interfaces.

Chapter 11, Kanban Views and Client-Side QWeb, continues working with the web client, but introduces Kanban views and explains the QWeb templates used to design the Kanban board elements.

Chapter 12, Creating Printable PDF Reports with Server-Side QWeb, discusses using the QWeb-based report engine and everything needed to generate printer-friendly PDF reports.

Chapter 13, Creating Web and Portal Frontend Features, introduces Odoo website development, including web controller implementations and using QWeb templates to build frontend web pages.

Chapter 14, Understanding Odoo Built-In Models, provides an overview of the models provided by the Odoo base module, such as Partners, Users, and the Models and Fields definitions.

Chapter 15, Deploying and Maintaining Production Instances, shows how to prepare a server for production prime time, explaining what configuration should be taken care of and how to configure an nginx reverse proxy for improved security and scalability.

To get the most out of this book

Other than being familiar with programming, no particular knowledge is expected to be able to take advantage of this book.

Odoo is built using the Python programming language, so it is a good idea to have solid knowledge of it. We also chose to run Odoo on an Ubuntu host and will do some work on the command line, so it will help to be familiar with it.

To get the most out of this book, we recommend that you find complementary readings on the Python programming language, the Ubuntu/Debian Linux operating system, and the PostgreSQL database.

While we will run Odoo on an Ubuntu host (a popular cloud hosting option), we will provide guidance on how to set up our development environment on a Windows system using the WSL, available in Windows 10. Of course, working from an Ubuntu/Debian native system is also a good choice.

All the required software is freely available, and the instructions on where to find it will be given in the book's initial chapters.

Software/hardware covered in the book	Operating system requirements
Odoo 15	Windows, macOS, or Linux
Python 3.6 or later	

> **Note**
> If you are using the digital version of this book, we advise you to type the code yourself or access the code from the book's GitHub repository (a link is provided in the next section). Doing so will help you avoid any potential errors related to the copying and pasting of code.

Download the example code files

You can download the example code files for this book from GitHub at `https://github.com/PacktPublishing/Odoo-15-Development-Essentials`. If there's an update to the code, it will be updated in the GitHub repository.

We also have other code bundles from our rich catalog of books and videos available at `https://github.com/PacktPublishing/`. Check them out!

Download the color images

We also provide a PDF file that has color images of the screenshots and diagrams used in this book. You can download it here: `https://static.packt-cdn.com/downloads/9781800200067_ColorImages.pdf`.

Conventions used

There are a number of text conventions used throughout this book.

`Code in text`: Indicates code words in text, database table names, folder names, filenames, file extensions, pathnames, dummy URLs, user input, and Twitter handles. Here is an example: "At the top of the list, we can see the `library_app.action_library_book` complete identifier."

A block of code is set as follows:

```
"id","name"
"__export__.res_partner_43_f82d2ecc","Alexandre Fayolle"
"__export__.res_partner_41_30a5bc3c","Daniel Reis"
"__export__.res_partner_44_6be5a130","Holger Brunn"
"__export__.res_partner_42_38b48275","Packt Publishing"
```

When we wish to draw your attention to a particular part of a code block, the relevant lines or items are set in bold:

```
"id","name","date_published","publisher_id/id","author_ids/id"
library_book_ode11,"Odoo Development Essentials 11","2018-03-01",res_partner_packt,res_partner_daniel
library_book_odc11,"Odoo 11 Development Cookbook","2018-01-01",res_partner_packt,"res_partner_alexandre,res_partner_holger"
```

Any command-line input or output is written as follows:

```
$ sudo apt install git python3-dev python3-pip \
python3-wheel python3-venv -y
```

Bold: Indicates a new term, an important word, or words that you see onscreen. For instance, words in menus or dialog boxes appear in **bold**. Here is an example: "Bank data can be browsed at the **Contacts | Configuration | Bank Accounts | Banks** menu option."

Tips or Important Notes
Appear like this.

Get in touch

Feedback from our readers is always welcome.

General feedback: If you have questions about any aspect of this book, email us at customercare@packtpub.com and mention the book title in the subject of your message.

Errata: Although we have taken every care to ensure the accuracy of our content, mistakes do happen. If you have found a mistake in this book, we would be grateful if you would report this to us. Please visit www.packtpub.com/support/errata and fill in the form.

Piracy: If you come across any illegal copies of our works in any form on the internet, we would be grateful if you would provide us with the location address or website name. Please contact us at copyright@packt.com with a link to the material.

If you are interested in becoming an author: If there is a topic that you have expertise in and you are interested in either writing or contributing to a book, please visit authors.packtpub.com.

Share Your Thoughts

Once you've read *Odoo 15 Development Essentials*, we'd love to hear your thoughts! Scan the QR code below to go straight to the Amazon review page for this book and share your feedback.

https://packt.link/r/1800200064

Your review is important to us and the tech community and will help us make sure we're delivering excellent quality content.

Section 1: Introduction to Odoo Development

The first part helps in setting up the development environment and provides an overview of all the key components used to build Odoo applications, such as models and views. These will then be detailed in the rest of the book, organized following the Model-View-Controller pattern.

In this section, the following chapters are included:

- *Chapter 1, Quick Start Using the Developer Mode*
- *Chapter 2, Preparing the Development Environment*
- *Chapter 3, Your First Odoo Application*
- *Chapter 4, Extending Modules*

1
Quick Start Using the Developer Mode

Odoo provides a rapid application development framework that is particularly suited to building applications for business. Business applications usually focus on keeping business records and workflows. Odoo makes it easy to build this type of application and provides rich components to create compelling **user interfaces (UIs)**, such as a **kanban view**, as well as calendar and graph views.

In this chapter, we will jump straight into the action and start coding by exploring the Odoo internals directly from the web UI – even before we have to set up a local development environment. This will give you a hands-on understanding of the components involved in an Odoo app. At the same time, you will learn some essential tools for inspecting existing apps and building quick prototypes.

The topics discussed in this chapter are as follows:

- Introducing the to-do list project
- Understanding basic Odoo concepts
- Using an Odoo SaaS trial database
- Installing Odoo in your workstation
- Enabling the developer tools

- Adding a custom field to a model
- Creating a new model
- Creating menu items and actions
- Configuring access control security
- Creating views

By the end of this chapter, you will be familiar with the main components for Odoo customization and development.

Technical requirements

The minimum requirement for this chapter is to have a modern web browser, such as **Mozilla Firefox** or **Google Chrome**. With a browser and an internet connection, you can follow the chapter using an Odoo SaaS trial database, and no local installation is needed.

Of course, you can use a locally installed instance of Odoo if you want. In this case, you can follow the instructions in the *Installing Odoo in your workstation* section, which describes prepackaged installations for **Windows**, **Ubuntu**, and **Red Hat Enterprise Linux (RHEL)**. Alternatively, you can use **Docker**.

Introducing the to-do list project

Throughout this chapter, we will use an example project to illustrate the concepts being presented. The project will be to build a simple to-do list Odoo app.

We want the app to allow us to add new to-do items to a list and then mark them as completed. For example, we want to be able to add a *Buy eggs* to-do item to the list and then check an *Is done?* checkbox once the task is completed. Additionally, the to-do items should be private to each user – in other words, the current user should be able to access only their own to-do items. To make the project more interesting, we will introduce an additional complication – our to-do items should be able to include a list of the people involved in the task: the *work team*.

It is useful to think about our application by considering the tiers involved:

- **Data tier**: This tier is implemented through models.
- **Business Logic tier**: This tier is implemented through **Python** automation code.
- **Presentation tier**: This tier is implemented through views.

For the *Data* tier, we will create a *To-do Item* model. For the *work team* feature, we will make use of the built-in *Contact* model (also known as the *Partner* model). And we must not forget to configure the access control security for our new model.

The *Business Logic* tier will allow the basic **create**, **read**, **update**, and **delete** (**CRUD**) operations handled by the framework. In this case, we don't have additional automation requirements to support. We need to use Python code in developer modules to access the full power of the framework. We won't be doing that for developer modules yet, but the Technical menu provides access to the Automated Actions tool to implement business logic from the UI. We will look at an example of how to use this tool later in the chapter.

Finally, for the *Presentation* tier, we will add the menu option for our application and the views for the *To-do Item* model. The essential views for a business application are the *list* view (to browse the existing records) and the *form* view (to zoom in to a record and see all of its details). For user convenience, we can also add predefined filters to the list view's search box. The search box options are configured through a search view component.

We will follow these steps to build the to-do list app:

1. Create the new model for the to-do items.
2. Create the menu items to make them available to users.
3. Configure the access control security.
4. Create the list and form views for the to-do items.

The new *To-do Item* model should have these fields:

- A `Description` character field
- An `Is Done?` flag, which is a Boolean field

Our specification for the app includes a work team feature: that is, the ability to select a list of people that will be working on the task. So, we need a model to represent people. Odoo includes the *Contact* model (with the technical name of `res.partner`) to use for individual people, companies, and addresses.

The *To-do Item* model should include a *work team* field, which will allow us to select a list of people. We want to limit the people that can be selected to be part of work teams. For this, we will modify the *Contact* model to add a field for this: a `Is Work Team?` flag. Only people with this flag enabled can be added to a work team.

For the work team feature, we need to add a field to the Contact model and the form view.

Before we go into the actual implementation, we will first discuss a few basic concepts relating to the Odoo framework, and then learn how to prepare an environment to work with.

Understanding basic Odoo concepts

There are a few concepts that might not be obvious to people first learning about Odoo. Let's try to understand these before moving on.

About Odoo and the Odoo community

Odoo is a software product published by **Odoo SA**, a software company based in Belgium founded by Fabien Pinckaers. The Odoo software is company-driven, meaning that its roadmap and development are both tightly controlled by Odoo SA. However, it still follows open source principles, and community contributions to the code are welcome.

The Odoo software follows the **open core** business model, meaning that some parts of the software are open source and some parts are proprietary. As a result of this model, Odoo publishes two editions:

The **Community Edition** (**CE**) is publicly available, open source, and licensed under LGPL.

The **Enterprise Edition** (**EE**) is available only to official partners and customers and has a proprietary license requiring non-disclosure of the code.

The Odoo EE works as a layer of additional modules on top of the Odoo CE core, offering premium features that are expected to provide enough value to motivate users to upgrade. The revenue from the Odoo EE funds the development for both the Odoo CE and EE. The Odoo founder and CEO Fabien Pinckaers has repeatedly pledged a commitment to keeping 80% of the code as open source in the Odoo CE and 20% in the proprietary Odoo EE.

The biggest strength of any open source project is the community around it. Odoo has an active community of contributors. For the Odoo product, the community contributes with feature feedback, translations, security issue reports, bug fixes, and occasionally some technical improvements to the core product. The Odoo CE is developed at `https://github.com/odoo/odoo`.

Beyond the Odoo core product, the community publishes additional Odoo modules that add features. Many individuals and companies in the Odoo community make their Git repositories publicly available under open source licenses. They also publish them in **Odoo Apps** – which is the official Odoo app store: `apps.odoo.com`. The app store allows for both free and paid modules.

The Odoo core project does not offer a space to host these community module efforts, so they are developed in a dispersed way, with no common standards and quality controls. The **Odoo Community Association** (**OCA**) was created to address this issue. It provides the space to host community-contributed modules, along with common coding standards, guidelines, quality controls, and the tools for these workflows. The OCA code repositories can be found at `https://github.com/oca`, and the published modules can also be browsed at `https://odoo-community.org/shop`.

Odoo product versions

At the time of writing, Odoo's latest stable version is version 15, marked on **GitHub** as `branch 15.0`. This is the version we will work with throughout this book. Major stable versions of Odoo are released on a yearly basis at the annual **Odoo Experience** conference every October.

The last three stable versions are officially supported. With the release of version 15, versions 14 and 13 are still supported, but versions up to 12 have no official support. This means that they don't receive bug and security fixes anymore.

Odoo databases are incompatible between its major versions. If you run an Odoo 15 server against a database created for a previous major version of Odoo, it won't work. Non-trivial migration work is needed before a database can be used with a later version of Odoo.

The same is true for **addon modules**. As a general rule, an addon module developed for a major Odoo version will not work on other versions. When downloading a community module from the web, make sure it targets the Odoo version you are using.

Major releases – such as **15.0** – are expected to receive frequent updates, but these should be mostly bug fixes and not new features. They are guaranteed to be API-stable, meaning that model data structures and view element identifiers will remain stable. This is important because it means there will be no risk of custom modules breaking due to incompatible changes in the upstream core modules.

The Odoo Online SaaS edition may use intermediary versions, which are sometimes called the *SaaS versions*. These are also officially supported. The current list of supported versions can be checked at `https://www.odoo.com/documentation/user`, in the **Practical Information** section of the **Support** page.

The version in the `master` branch version will result in the next major stable version, but until then, it's not API-stable and you should not use it to build custom modules. Doing so is like moving on quicksand – you can't be sure when changes will be introduced and they could break your custom module. You have been warned.

The Odoo architecture

It's useful to understand the layers involved in the Odoo architecture and the role of each type of component we will use. So, we will now take a look at the Odoo application architecture and focus on how we can help application development by decomposing work into several component layers.

Odoo applications can be decomposed into three tiers: the **Data**, **Logic**, and **Presentation** tiers:

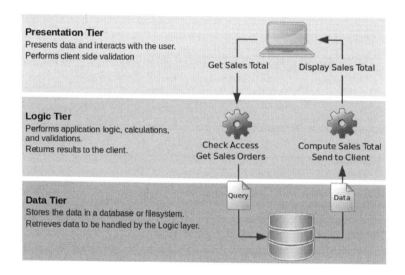

Figure 1.1 – The Odoo application layers

The *Data* tier is the lowest-level layer and is responsible for data storage and persistence. Odoo relies on a **PostgreSQL** server for this. PostgreSQL is the only supported database server in Odoo, and this is a design choice. Binary files – such as the attachments of documents or images – are stored in the filesystem in a directory referred to as `filestore`.

> **Note**
> This means that a full backup of an Odoo instance needs both a database dump and a copy of `filestore`.

We will rarely use SQL to interact directly with the database engine; however, this is possible and might be needed in particular cases.

Odoo relies on its **Object Relational Mapping (ORM)** engine as the interface between the apps and the database. The ORM provides the **application programming interface (API)** used by the addon modules to interact with the data. We implement the Data tier using **ORM models**. For example, the Partner data entity, which is used for data records such as customers or suppliers, is represented by a model.

As a general rule, the low-level database should only be accessed by this layer because it ensures secure access control and data consistency. ORM models are based on a Python object class that supports several interaction methods, such as the CRUD basic operations. In particular, these CRUD operations are implemented by the `create()`, `search()`, `write()`, and `unlink()` model methods.

The *Logic* tier is responsible for all of the interactions with the Data tier and is handled by the Odoo server. The basic CRUD operations can be extended to implement specific business logic. For example, the `create()` and `write()` methods might implement default values or some other automation. Other code methods can be added to enforce validation rules or automatically compute field values.

The *Presentation* tier is responsible for presenting data and interacting with the user. It is implemented by the client part of the software, which is responsible for end user interaction. The client software uses **remote procedure calls (RPCs)** to the Odoo service, running the ORM engine and the business logic. The ORM API calls are sent to the Odoo server for processing to read, write, verify, or perform any other action. Then, the results are sent back to the client for further handling.

Odoo provides a web client out of the box. The web client supports all of the features needed by a business application, such as login sessions, navigation menus, data lists, and forms.

A website framework is also available to use as a public frontend for external users. It provides CMS features, allowing us to create both static and dynamic web pages. The website framework uses **controller** components for the code implementing the presentation-specific logic, keeping it separate from the model's intrinsic logic. The page rendering uses **QWeb** as the templating engine. These are XML documents that contain HTML markup plus specific XML QWeb tags for operations such as loops, conditions, or calls to include other templates.

The Odoo server API is open, and all server functions are available through it. The server API used by the official web client is the same as the one available to any other application. So, other client implementations are possible and could be built in almost any platform or programming language. Desktop and smartphone applications can be built to provide specific user interfaces, leveraging the Odoo *Data* and *Logic* tiers for business logic and data persistence.

Using an Odoo SaaS trial database

The simplest way to get started with Odoo is to use an Odoo **software as a service (SaaS)** trial database. In this case, we don't need to install anything – just go to `https://odoo.com/` and click **Try it free** button.

You will be asked to select the first app to install in the new database. For the purpose of following this chapter, any choice will work for us, so feel free to choose any of the proposed apps. If you're unsure, the *CRM* app is a good choice.

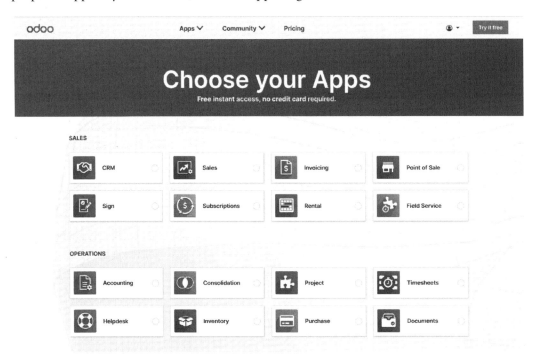

Figure 1.2 – The Odoo SaaS trial database initial app choice

New SaaS databases use the latest Odoo SaaS version – which is always based on the last stable Odoo EE version – but also have their own minor releases. So, it will not match the last stable Odoo EE version exactly.

The free trial will be valid for a period of 15 days. At the time of writing, the Odoo SaaS edition offers a free plan that allows you to keep this database running after this period (as long as you have more than one app installed).

Installing Odoo in your workstation

Using an Odoo SaaS trial database will be the default choice for this chapter. For the rest of the book, we will use a local Odoo installation, and in *Chapter 2, Preparing the Development Environment*, we will guide you through this process.

It is still worth noting that there are a few prepackaged installation alternatives for Odoo. We will briefly guide you through the available options in case you want to try any of them:

- **Install Odoo with a prepackaged installer for your operating system**: This is a good option if you're new to Odoo and want to quickly have a local environment running. Prepackaged installers are available for the following: **Windows** (EXE installer); **Debian/Ubuntu** (DEB package), and **CentOS/RHEL** (RPM package).

- **Install Odoo using a Docker container**: This could be a good option if you have experience with Docker and already have it installed on your system. If you're not confident with Docker, you might want to try another option so that learning Docker doesn't distract you from your current goal (learning Odoo development).

Odoo packages can be downloaded from `https://download.odoo.com`. They are available for all stable Odoo versions, as well as for the `master` branch corresponding to the latest development version. We will explain each of these options in the following sections.

For additional information on installing Odoo, you can refer to the official documentation at `https://www.odoo.com/documentation/15.0/setup/install.html`.

Installing on Windows using the all-in-one installer

Odoo provides an all-in-one installer for Windows, providing everything needed to run Odoo: a Python 3 runtime environment, a PostgreSQL database server, and the Odoo server with the required dependencies.

The installer can be downloaded from `https://download.odoo.com`. Select the desired version from the home page: **15 (stable) - Community Edition**. The daily builds should be in `15.0/nightly/windows`, and the latest build should be at the bottom of the list.

The installer is straightforward to follow. Odoo will be automatically started at the end of the installation.

It will also create a **Windows service** to automatically start the Odoo and PostgreSQL services when the machine starts. Remember this when you try other installation options such as the source code installation – port `8069` will already be used by the Windows installation, and this will prevent other installations from using the same port.

Installing on Linux using a pre-packaged installer

The Odoo download site (`https://download.odoo.com`) provides repositories with official packages for the Debian family (including Ubuntu) and for RHEL/CentOS.

Installation instructions for using the system-packed installers (`apt` or `yum`) are provided on the home page. Make sure that you replace the Odoo version used in the command line examples with your target one – for example, `15.0`.

Before installing Odoo 15 on our Linux system, you should install the PostgreSQL database. This way, Odoo will be able to create and configure its user.

Installing Odoo using Docker containers

Docker provides a convenient multi-platform solution to run applications. It can be used to run applications on Windows, Linux, and **macOS**. The container technology is simple to use and resource-efficient when compared to classic virtual machines.

You must first have Docker installed on your system. **Docker Desktop** is the community edition and is free to use. It can be downloaded from `https://www.docker.com`. It is worth referring to the Docker website for the latest installation details. Docker relies on virtualization hardware features, so make sure that your **basic input/output system** (**BIOS**) has these features enabled.

General guidance on how to install and run Docker can be found at `https://docs.docker.com/engine/install`.

For example, for Ubuntu systems, the detailed installation instructions point to `https://docs.docker.com/engine/install/ubuntu/`.

Important post-installation steps – such as running Docker with a non-root user – can be found at `https://docs.docker.com/engine/install/linux-postinstall/`.

Docker Desktop for Windows requires **Hyper-V**, which is only available in **Windows 10 Enterprise** or **Education** releases. Up-to-date details should be available at `https://docs.docker.com/desktop/windows/install/`.

Docker Desktop for Mac requires macOS 10.14 or later. Up-to-date details should be available at `https://docs.docker.com/desktop/mac/install/`.

> **Note**
>
> **Docker Toolbox** used to be available as an alternative for other Windows and macOS versions, but this distribution is now deprecated. Docker Toolbox bundles **VirtualBox** and provides a preconfigured shell that should be used as the command-line environment to operate Docker containers. See `https://docs.docker.com/toolbox/` for more details.

The Odoo Docker official images are available on **Docker Hub** at `https://hub.docker.com/_/odoo`. There, we can also find basic instructions to get started with the Odoo Docker images. To run Odoo, two Docker containers will be created: one for the PostgreSQL database and the other for the Odoo server.

The installation and operation are done from the command line. To install the PostgreSQL Docker container, run the following:

```
$ docker run -d -e POSTGRES_USER=odoo -e POSTGRES_PASSWORD=odoo
-e POSTGRES_DB=postgres --name db postgres:13
```

This will download the latest PostgreSQL image from the internet and start a container for it to run as a background job.

Next, install and run the Odoo server container, linking it to the PostgreSQL container we just started, and exposing it on port `8069`:

```
$ docker run -t -p 8069:8069 --name odoo --link db:db odoo:15.0
-d odoo15
```

With this, you will see the live Odoo server log in your terminal window, and you will be able to access the Odoo instance by opening `http://localhost:8069` with your chosen web browser.

> **Note**
>
> The Odoo server can fail to start if port 8069 is already in use. For instance, it could be in use by an already running Odoo server. In this case, you could look for and stop the running service (for example, by looking at the list of running services) or try to start this Odoo server on a different port by changing the `-p` option. For example, to use port 8070, use `-p 8070`. In that case, you can also use `-d <dbname>` to set the database name that this instance should use.

There are a few basic commands you should know to help manage these Docker containers:

- `docker stop <name>`: Stops a container
- `docker start <name>`: Starts a container
- `docker start -a <name>`: Starts a container and attaches the output – such as the server log – to the terminal window
- `docker attach <name>`: Reattaches a container's output to the current terminal window
- `docker ps`: Lists the current Docker containers

These are the basic commands needed to operate our Docker containers.

In case you get into trouble running the containers, here is a recipe to start over:

```
$ docker container stop db
$ docker container rm db
$ docker container stop odoo
$ docker container rm odoo
```

The Docker technology has more potential, and it might be interesting to learn more about it. The Docker website has good documentation to learn from, and a good place to get started is `https://www.docker.com/get-started`.

Enabling the developer tools

The Odoo **developer tools** are needed for us to implement our project. They are made available by enabling the developer mode.

The developer mode is useful for inspecting and modifying the current Odoo configurations. It allows us to customize Odoo apps directly from the UI and is a quick way to make changes and add features. It can be used for making small modifications, such as adding a custom field, or it can be used for larger customizations, such as creating an application with its own menus, views, and underlying data model.

> **Caution**
>
> The developer mode exposes internal configurations for Odoo apps and allows them to be changed. With great power comes great responsibility, so be careful with the changes made. Always try these changes on a copy database before making them in a live system. If things go wrong, there is a chance that an upgrade of the affected app – or the base module – can resolve the issues, but this is not guaranteed.

Making customizations through the developer tools has some limitations compared to the programming tools covered throughout the rest of the book. For example, the developer tools can't add or extend the default ORM methods.

The customizations made with the developer mode (and with the **Odoo Studio** app, for that matter) can't be easily integrated into a structured development workflow with version control, automated tests, and QA/staging/production code promotion workflows.

The developer mode features will be used in this chapter as a way to introduce how the application configuration data is organized in the Odoo framework and how the developer mode can be leveraged for simple customizations or prototyping solutions.

Enabling the developer mode

For Odoo 13 and later, the developer mode is enabled on the **Settings | General Settings** page. Near the bottom, you will find a **Developer Tools** section. There, you will find the **Activate the developer mode** link. Clicking on this enables the developer mode features for the current browser window, as shown in the following screenshot:

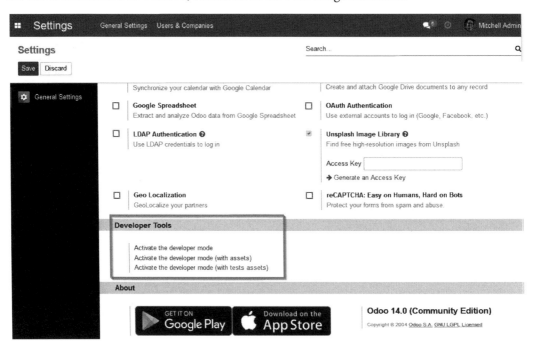

Figure 1.3 – The Developer Tools options section on the Settings page

Note that the **General Settings** menu option is only visible if there is at least one app installed. If it is not available, install an app such as *Contacts* or *CRM* (or any other of your choice).

> **Changes in Odoo 13**
>
> In Odoo versions 10 to 12, the developer mode is enabled on the **Settings | Dashboard** page in the lower-right corner. For Odoo 9 and before, the developer mode is activated in the **About** dialog window, which is available from the **User** menu in the upper-right corner of the web client.

Once the developer mode is enabled, we will see the following menus made available:

- On the top menu bar, the developer tools bug icon will be on the right-hand side next to the **Conversations** and **Activities** icons.

- On the **Settings** app, the **Technical** and **Translations** menu items will be visible on the top bar.

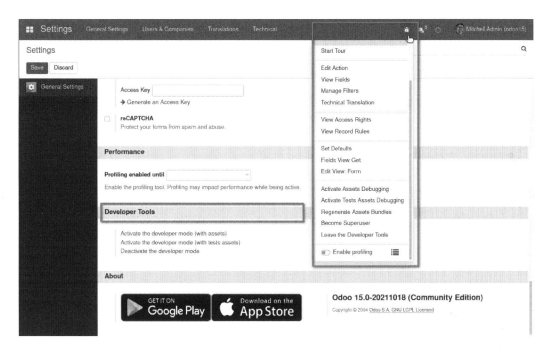

Figure 1.4 – The Settings page with the developer mode enabled

The developer mode also enables additional information on the web client views – when hovering the mouse pointer over a field, a tooltip will display technical information relating to it.

> **Note**
>
> The developer mode can also be enabled by directly editing the current URL without having to leave the current page to open the settings. Edit the URL to change the .../web#... part to insert .../web?debug=1#... in its place. For example, `http://localhost:8069/web#home` would become `http://localhost_8069/web?debug=1#home`.

Using the developer mode with assets

For faster load times, the web client *minifies* the **JavaScript** and **CSS** assets into compact files. Unfortunately, that makes web client debugging nearly impossible.

The **Activate the developer mode (with assets)** option prevents this minification and loads the web assets in individual, non-minified files. This is useful to debug the web client itself, but it comes at the expense of making the web client navigation slower.

> **Tip**
>
> Both Firefox and Chrome browsers have extensions available providing a button to conveniently enable and disable the developer mode in Odoo. Search for Odoo Debug in their extension stores.

About Odoo Studio

It is also worth noting that both the Odoo EE and the Odoo SaaS edition offer the Odoo Studio app – an interactive application builder. We won't be using it because it's not available for the Odoo CE that is used as the example edition in this book.

Odoo Studio provides a user-friendly UI for the same interactive development features introduced in this chapter – along with a few extra features, such as the ability to export our customizations to a file.

Here, we will be using the developer mode (sometimes referred to as the debug mode) and the Technical menu, which are both available in all Odoo editions. Most of what can be built using Odoo Studio can also be built with these tools – albeit in a more technical way that is not as easy for non-developers.

Adding a custom field to a model

Adding a **custom field** to an existing form is a common customization, and it can be done from the UI without the need to create a custom module.

For our *to-do list* app, we want to select a group of people that will be able to collaborate on to-do items. We will identify them by setting a flag on their partner form. To do that, we will add an Is Work Team? flag to the Contact model.

The Contact model is part of the Odoo core and is available even if you haven't installed any apps yet. However, you may not have a menu option available to visit it.

If the *Contacts* app is not available in the main menu, you should install it now. To do this, open the **Apps** item in the top menu, look up this application, and install it.

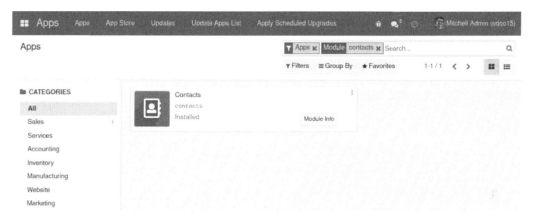

Figure 1.5 – The Contacts app listed in the Apps menu

Once the app is installed, the **Contacts** application top menu option will be available.

Adding a field to a model

We will start by adding a custom field to the data model.

To do this, click the **Contacts** app menu item to see the Contacts main view. Click the developer tools bug icon and select the **View Fields** option.

> **Changes in Odoo 12**
>
> The **View Fields** option in the developer menu was added in Odoo 12. For earlier versions, fields can be added and edited in the **Settings | Technical | Database Structure** menu. You can either use the **Models** or the **Fields** option.

Now, you will see a list with all the existing fields for the current model: *Contact*. Click the **Create** button in the top left and fill in the details for this new field:

- **Field Name**: x_is_work_team
- **Field Label**: Is Work Team?
- **Field Type**: **boolean**

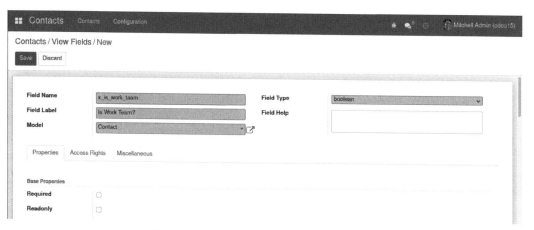

Figure 1.6 – Creating the Is Work Team? field

The **Field Name** field entry must start with the x_ prefix. This is mandatory for models and fields created from the developer tools. Customizations made through addon modules don't have this limitation.

Click **Save**, and our new field should have been added to the fields list. By default, the list view is limited to 80 records, so you will need to use the right arrow in the upper-left corner to navigate to the next page to see the new field, or you can edit the number of records to present next to the page navigation arrows.

Adding a field to a form view

Our new field is now available in the *Contact* model (as noted previously, this is also known as the *Partner* model). But it is not visible in the UI. It now needs to be given a *view*. We will add it to the contact's form view.

Go back to the **Contacts** list and open the form view, either by selecting one of the existing contacts or by clicking on the **Create** button.

We should now decide where in the form we want to add the field. For example, we could add it after the **Tags** field. This will be the extension point to use.

Hovering the mouse pointer over the field shows us useful technical details for it, as shown in the following screenshot:

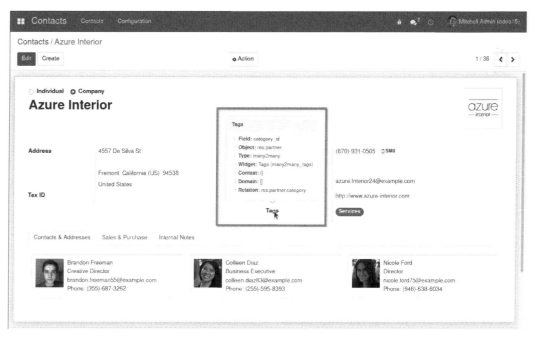

Figure 1.7 – The Tags field tooltip with technical details

Next, we need to find out the technical name of that field. We can find this by hovering the mouse pointer over the field's label. By doing so, we can see that the field name is `category_id`.

We can now extend the form view to add that field. Click the developer tools bug icon and select the **Edit View: Form** option. This will open a window with the form's definition.

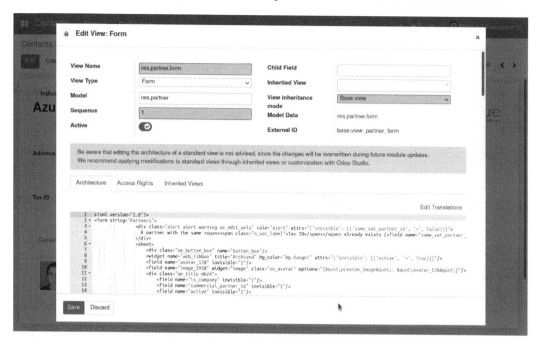

Figure 1.8 – The Edit View: Form window

In the **Architecture** tab, we can see the XML for the base view. We could edit this directly, but this is not a good idea because those changes will be lost in the case that the module adding it is upgraded. The correct way to edit it is by creating an extension view.

When additional modules are installed, they can add more fields and visual elements to the base view. This is done using extension views, and we can see them in the **Inherited Views** tab. This is where we will be adding our own extension to the contacts form view.

On the **Inherited Views** list, click **Add a line** at the bottom and create the extension view using these values:

- **View Name**: Add some short description such as `Contacts Form extensions for To-do App`.

- **Architecture**: This requires an XML fragment specifying an extension point and the content to add. Use `<field name="category_id" position="after"><field name="x_is_work_team"/></field>`.

The extension view should look like the following figure:

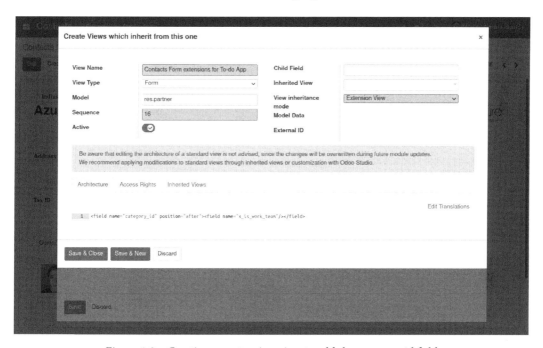

Figure 1.9 – Creating an extension view to add the category_id field

Now, click **Save & Close** – if your XML is correct, you get back to the **Inherited Views** list, where our extension will also be included. Click **Save** to finalize the form changes, and close the **Edit Form: View** window by clicking the **x** button in the top right.

The change is made, but the form needs to be reloaded for us to see it. Reload the page, and the **Is Work Team?** field should now be visible below the **Tags** field, as shown in the following figure:

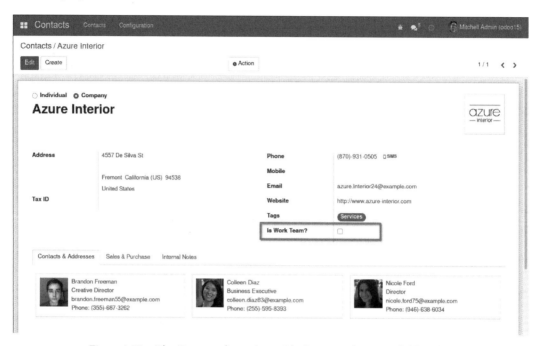

Figure 1.10 – The Contacts form view with the Is Work Team? field visible

This completes the steps needed to add a custom field to a form view. Forms are one of the view types available. The following section discusses view types in more detail.

Understanding view types

We just interacted with a particular view type, the *form view*. But the user interface also uses other view types.

The initial view type for Contacts is a **kanban view**, showing the records in data cards. Kanban views can also group the cards in columns. For example, the CRM app uses this in the initial view, the **Pipeline** view. In a kanban view, the developer menu will show an **Edit View: Kanban** option.

The *list view* (sometimes referred to as the *tree view*) displays the records as a list. In a list view, the developer menu will show an **Edit View: List** option.

Finally, the *search view* controls the behavior of the search box on the top-right of the kanban and list views, as well as the buttons under it: **Filters** and **Group By**. When a search box is visible, the developer menu will show an **Edit View: ControlPanelView** option.

The view types available are not limited to these; there are others available that will be explored in *Chapter 10, Backend Views – Designing the User Interface.*

We can see all the view definitions via the **Settings | Technical | User Interface | Views** menu option.

A more focused alternative is to use **Settings | Technical | Database Structure | Models** to find the model we want (in this case, res.partner, alternatively known as *Contact*), and open the **Views** tab.

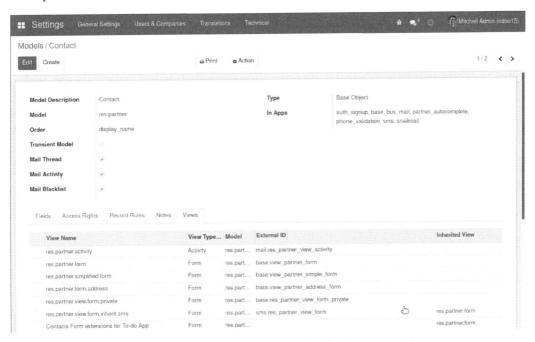

Figure 1.11 – The database structure for the Contact model

Here, we can see all the view definitions for the selected model. We can see records for the different view types – identified by the **View Type** column – and for base views and their extensions. Changing or adding view records is immediately effective, and the changes will be visible the next time the view is reloaded.

Sorting the list by view type is helpful to see all the extensions related to the same view type together.

The base view is the one with an empty **Inherited View** field. A view type is not limited to a single base view. For example, the *Contact* model (`res.partner`) has multiple base views available for the form view, such as `base.view_partner_form` and `base.view_partner_simple_form`.

Views also have a **Sequence** field. The base view with the lowest **Sequence** number is the one displayed by default. When visiting the form for the view definition, we will see a field with this **Sequence** value. Window actions, which are used in menu items, can specify a particular base view to use. As mentioned, if no specific view is defined, the one with the lowest sequence will be used.

Creating a new model

Models are the basic components for building applications and provide the data structures and storage to be used. Next, we will create the model for our *to-do list* app with three fields:

- Description text
- The `Is Done?` flag
- Work team (that is, a list of people collaborating in this item)

Model names should use the singular form, so the new model should be named *To-do Item*. The model technical name must be a valid database object identifier, so we should use letters and underscores and avoid other symbols. Since the models created through the Technical menu must have an `x_` prefix, the technical name for the new model will be `x_todo_item`.

Model definitions are accessed in the **Settings** app in the **Technical | Database Structure | Models** menu.

To create a new model, click the **Create** button on the **Models** list:

1. Fill in the basic definition values for it – enter `To-do Item` in the **Model Description** field and `x_todo_item` for the **Model** field.
2. By default, the model will include in the fields list the `x_name` field. This is a title that represents the record in lists or when it is referenced in other records. It can be used for the **To-do Item** title, so edit it to change the **Field Label** column accordingly.

3. Next, add the `Is Done?` field. This should be straightforward. On the **Fields** list, click **Add a line** at the bottom of the list to open the new field form, and then, enter these values:

    -   **Field Name**: `x_is_done`

    -   **Field Label**: `Is Done?`

    -   **Field Type**: **boolean**

    Then, click the **Save & Close** button and click **Save** on the model form.

Figure 1.12 – The Create Fields form

4.   Now, adding the **Work Team** field should be a little more challenging. Not only is this a relation field that refers to records in the *Contact* (`res.partner`) model, but it is also a multiple-value selection field.

Fortunately, Odoo supports many-to-many relations. This is the case here since a *to-do item* can be related to many *contacts*, and each *contact* can be related to many *to-do items*.

To add the **Work Team** field on the **Fields** list, click again on the form **Edit** button, then click **Add a line** to open the new field form. Then, enter these values:

- **Field Name**: `x_work_team_ids`
- **Field Label**: `Work Team`
- **Field Type**: `many2many`
- **Related Model**: `res.partner`
- **Domain**: `[('x_is_work_team', '=', True)]`

Many-to-many fields have a few specific base properties: **Relation Table**, **Column 1**, and **Column 2**. These are automatically filled out for you, and the defaults work for most cases. These properties are discussed in more detail in *Chapter 6, Models – Structuring the Application Data*.

The `Domain` attribute is optional and defines a filter for the records to be presented. We are using it to limit the selectable contacts to the ones that have the `Is Work Team?` flag checked on them. Otherwise, all contacts would be available for selection.

The domain expression to use follows an Odoo-specific syntax – it is a list of triplets, where each triplet is a filter condition, indicating the field name to filter, the filter operator to use, and the value to filter against. A detailed explanation of domain expressions is given in *Chapter 7, Recordsets – Working with Model Data*.

Tip
Odoo has an interactive domain filter wizard that can be used as a helper to generate domain expressions. To use it, select the **Settings | Technical | User Interface | User-defined Filters** menu option. Once a target model is selected in the form, the **Domain** field will display an **+ Add filter** button to add filter conditions. When doing so, the textbox below it will dynamically show the corresponding domain expression code.

---

5. When we are done, click the model form **Save** button. When the new model is created, a few fields are automatically added. The ORM engine includes them in all models, and they can be useful for audit purposes:

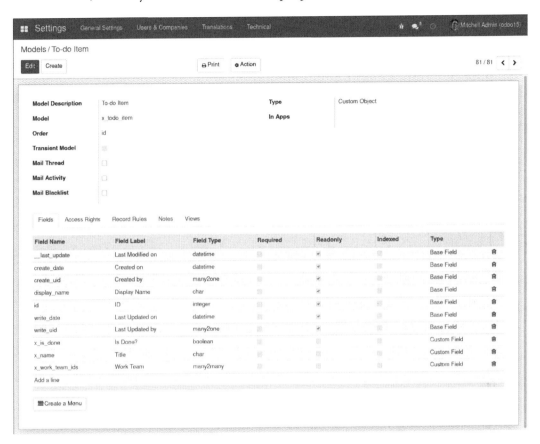

Figure 1.13 – The database structure for the To-do Item model

We now have the underlying model for the *to-do list* app, but it is still not accessible by users. For that, access security needs to be configured. So, let's look at that in the next section.

Creating menu items and actions

We now have a model to store the to-do items and want to have it available in the UI. This is done by adding menu items to the UI.

We will create a top-level menu item that directly opens the to-do list. Some apps (such as *Contacts*) work like this, while others have submenu items shown in the top bar.

Menu definitions can be found in the **Settings** app in the **Technical | User Interface | Menu Items** option:

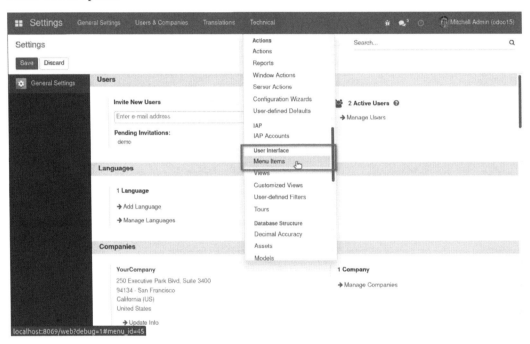

Figure 1.14 – The Technical menu Menu Items option

We'll perform the following steps to create menu items:

1. Navigate there, click on **Create**, and enter the following values:

    -   **Menu**: To-do.

    -   **Parent Menu**: [leave empty].

    -   **Action**: Select the **ir.actions.act_window** option.

    -   In the selection box next to the **Action** field, type To-do Items, and in the drop-down list, select **Create and Edit....** This will open a **Create: Action** form.

2. In the **Create: Action** form, set the following values:

- **Action Name**: To-do Items
- **External ID Object**: x_todo_item (the technical name of the target model).
- At this point, the action definition should look like this:

Figure 1.15 – The Create: Action form

3. Click **Save** in the **Create: Action** form. Then, click **Save** in the **Menu Items** form, and the menu item for the *to-do list* application should be almost ready to use.

Changes to menus require a full browser page reload to be visible. In most browsers, the F5 key can be used for this. But if we try that now, we won't be able to see the **To-do** menu option yet. *Why?* The reason we won't be able to see the menu yet is that our user wasn't given access to it.

Access security needs to be configured before the menu item can be presented to the users. We will take care of that in this chapter, but before that, it is worth discussing a few more details about *window actions*.

Understanding window actions

In our case, an action was added directly to a top-level menu item with no child menu items. But menus can be a tree of menu items with parent/child relations. The leaf menu items have a related action that defines what happens when it is selected. This *action name* is what will be used as the title of the presented view.

There are several *action types* available, and the most important ones are *window*, *report*, and *server* actions. *Window* actions are the most frequent ones and are used to present views in the web client. *Report* actions are used to run reports and *server* actions are used to define automated tasks.

At this point, we are concerned with window actions that are used to display views. The menu item we just created for the *to-do item* uses a window action that was created directly from the **Menu Item** form. We can also view and edit this window action from the **Settings | Technical | Actions** menu options. In this particular case, we are interested in the window actions menu option.

> **Tip**
>
> In many cases, it is more convenient to use the **Edit Action** option in the **Developer Tools** menu, providing a convenient shortcut to edit the window action that was used to access the current view.

Configuring access control security

Odoo includes built-in access control mechanisms. A user will only be able to use the features they were granted access to. This means that the *To-do Item* model we created is not accessible by the users.

> **Changes in Odoo 12**
>
> The admin user is now subject to access control like any other user. In previous Odoo versions, the admin user was special and bypassed security rules. This is no longer true, and admin must be granted access privileges to be able to access model data.

Access security is defined using *user groups*. *Groups*, which are sometimes called **access control lists** (**ACLs**), define the access permissions for models. Users belong to groups. So, each user's access depends on the group they belong to.

For our project, we will create a to-do group to be assigned to the users that should have access to this feature.

Furthermore, we can also define *record rules* (sometimes called row-level security), restricting the records each user can access.

For our project, we want the to-do items to be private for each user, so users should only be able to access the records they created.

Security groups

Access control is based on *groups*. A *security group* is given access privileges on models, and this will determine the menu items available to the users belonging to that group. For more fine-grained control, we can also give access to specific menu items, views, fields, and even data records by using record rules, which we will explain in the next section.

Security groups are also organized around apps, and typically, each app provides at least two groups: User, with permissions for performing daily tasks, and Manager, with permissions for performing all configurations for that app.

We will now create a new security group for the *to-do list* app.

In the **Settings** top menu, navigate to **Users & Companies | Groups** and create a new record using the following values:

- **Application**: [leave empty] .
- **Name**: To-Do User.
- **Inherited tab**: Add a line and select **User types / Internal User**.

This is how it should look:

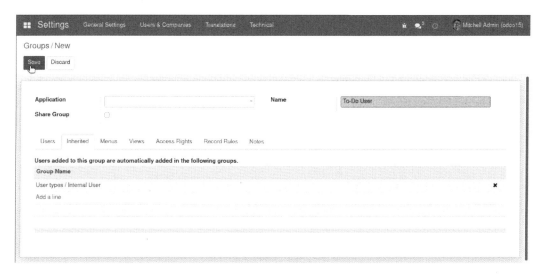

Figure 1.16 – The To-Do User security group

Our security group inherits the `Internal User` group. Group inheritance means that members of this group will also be members of the inherited groups and will accumulate the permissions granted to all of them. The `Internal User` group is the basic access group, and app security groups usually inherit it.

> **Changes in Odoo 12**
>
> Before Odoo 12, the `Internal User` group was called `Employee`. This was just a cosmetic change, and the technical identifier (that is, the XML ID) is still the same as in previous versions: `base.group_user`.

Security access control lists

Now, we can grant the group/`to-do` user access to specific models.

The simplest way to do this is to use the **Access Rights** tab in the **Groups** form. Add a line there using these values:

- **Name**: `To-do Item User Access`.
- **Object**: Select **To-do Item** from the list.
- **Read Access**, **Write Access**, **Create Access**, and **Delete Access**: Check all of these checkboxes to grant the respective privileges.

It is useful to know that these model ACLs can also be managed from the **Technical | Security | Access Rights** menu item.

Notice that we don't need to specifically add access to the Contact model since we are inheriting the `Internal User` group that already grants access to it.

Assigning security groups to users

Now, we can try these new security settings by adding the `admin` user to this new security group:

1. Select the **Users & Companies | Users** menu item, open the **Mitchell Admin** user form, and click **Edit**.

2. In the **Other** section in the **Access Rights** tab, we will see a **To-do User** checkbox to enable the security group for this user. Select it and save the form.

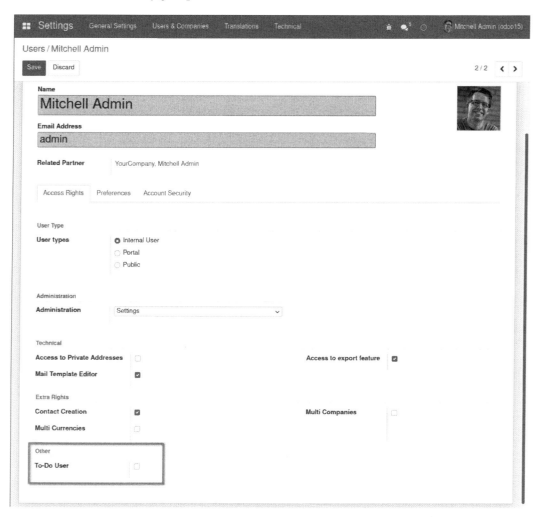

Figure 1.17 – The Mitchel Admin user form

If everything went as expected, you should be able to see the **To-do** app top menu. A browser page reload should be needed to force a refresh of the menu items.

We haven't created any views for it yet, but the Odoo framework is nice enough to automatically generate some basic views for us:

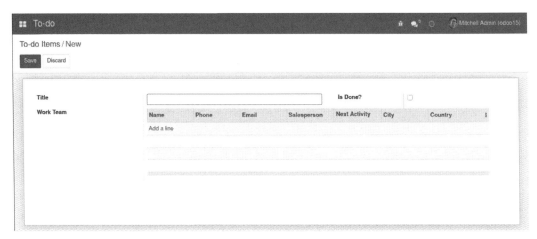

Figure 1.18 – The To-do Items default form view

Security record rules

When given access to a model, users will be able to access all of its records by default. But in some cases, we need to restrict what records each user can access. This can be done using **record rules**.

Record rules set domain filters on models that will be enforced when read or write operations are made on them.

For example, in our *to-do list* app, the to-do items are expected to be private to each user, so we want each user to only see their own items. So, we should create a record rule with a filter to show only the records created by the current user, taking the following into consideration:

- Records have a `create_uid` field – which is automatically added by the framework – that stores the user that created the record. So, we can use it to know who owns each record.

- The domain evaluation context includes a `user` variable that contains a browser record for the current user. So, we can use dot notation on it to access its attributes, such as the `user.id` value.

We can use this in a domain expression to achieve our goal:

```
[('create_uid', '=', user.id)]
```

Record rules are available in the **Settings | Technical | Security | Record Rules** menu, or in the **View Record Rules** option in the developer menu. Navigate there and create a new record rule with the following values:

- **Name**: Enter a descriptive title such as `To-do User Own Items`.
- **Model**: Select the model from the drop-down list (in our case, **To-do Item**).
- **Access Rights**: These checkboxes control the actions where the rule will be applied. Keep all of them checked.
- **Rule Definition (Domain Filter)**: Enter `[('create_uid', '=', user.id)]`.
- **Groups**: This section contains the security groups the rule will apply to. Click **Add a line** and select the **To-do User** group option.

Now, this is what the record rules definition will look like:

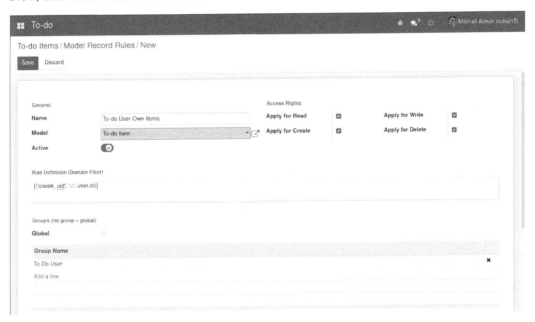

Figure 1.19 – The To-do User Own Items record rule

And we're done. You can now try this new rule by creating a couple of to-do items with both the `Admin` and `Demo` users. Each should be able to see only their own items.

Understanding the superuser account

Odoo includes an internal root-like superuser that has special privileges and bypasses security controls. It is used for internal operations or actions that need to ignore security controls. This superuser is named `OdooBot` – it is automatically created upon database creation and has the database ID 1.

> **Changes in Odoo 12**
>
> Before Odoo 12, the default `admin` user used for system setups was also the superuser. So, the `admin` user bypassed access controls by default. This is no longer the case since Odoo 12. Now, the default `admin` user is a regular user, but it is set as the manager on all Odoo apps by default.

The superuser has no login password, but it is possible to enable one. When logged in as a user with the `Admin \ Setting` group, the **Become Superuser** option is then available in the developer menu.

It is also possible to go directly into superuser mode from the login screen. For this, you need to enable the developer mode by editing the URL to add `?debug=1` (for example, `http://localhost:8069/web/login?debug=1`). Then, the **Login as superuser** option will be available below the **Login** button.

When the superuser is enabled, in the upper-right corner, the current user is shown as `OdooBot`, and the colors in the upper-right area change to yellow and black stripes to make it clear the superuser is enabled.

> **Caution**
>
> Using the superuser should be done only if absolutely necessary. The fact that the superuser bypasses access security can lead to data inconsistencies – for example, in a multi-company context – and should be avoided.

Creating views

We created the *To-do Item* model and made it available in the UI with a menu item. Next, we will be creating the two essential views for it: the *list* and *form* views.

The list view is the most basic way for users to browse the existing records. In some cases, records can be edited directly in the list view, but the most common case is to navigate to a form view when clicking on a record to edit the record data.

Creating a list view

We can manage views in **Settings | Technical | User Interface | Views**. There, click the **Create** button and enter the following values:

- **View Name**: To-do List View.

- **View Type**: **Tree**.

- **Model**: x_todo_item.

- **Architecture**: This tab should contain the XML for the view structure. Use the following XML code:

```
<tree>
    <field name="x_name" />
    <field name="x_is_done" />
</tree>
```

This is what the view definition is expected to look like:

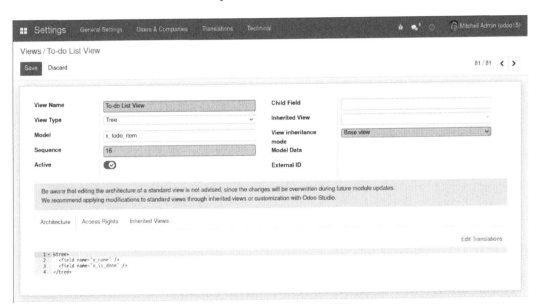

Figure 1.20 – The To-do List View definition

The basic structure of a list view is quite simple – it contains a `<tree>` element containing one or more `<field>` elements for each of the columns to display in the list view.

We can do a few more interesting things with list views, and we will explore them in more detail in *Chapter 10, Backend Views – Designing the User Interface.*

Creating a form view

Form views can also be created in **Settings | Technical | User Interface | Views**. Create another view record by clicking the **Create** button and enter the following values:

- **View Name:** `To-do Form View`.

- **View Type:** **Form**.

- **Model:** `x_todo_item`.

- **Architecture:** In this tab, add the following XML code:

```
<form>
  <group>
    <field name="x_name" />
    <field name="x_is_done" />
    <field name="x_work_team_ids"
           widget="many2many_tags"
           context="{'default_x_is_work_team': True}" />
  </group>
</form>
```

> **Note**
>
> If we don't specify the view type, it will be auto-detected from the view definition.

The form view structure has a root `<form>` element, which contains elements such as `<field>` among others. We will learn about these other elements in *Chapter 10, Backend Views – Designing the User Interface*. For the `x_work_team_ids` work team field, we chose to use a specific widget – `many2many_tags` – that presents the related records as button-line tags instead of the usual list.

You can also see that a `context` attribute is being used in the `x_work_team_ids` work team field. By default, relational fields allow us to directly create a new record to be used in the relation. So, users can create a new **Partner** record directly from the **Work Team** field. Since only partners with the `Is Work Team?` flag set are selectable, we want any created partners to have this flag enabled by default. This is what the `default_x_is_work_team` context key is doing – setting a default value for the records created from this field.

And with that, we have our new form view. If we now try the **To-Do** menu option and create a new item or open an existing one from the list, we will see the form view we just added.

Creating search views

We can find a search box in the top left of the Odoo views screen. The search box allows us to search in particular fields. The **Filters** and **Group By** buttons are available under the search box and offer some predefined options.

The **Search** view is the UI element controlling these behaviors. It defines the searches made when typing in the search box and the options available in the **Filters** and **Group By** buttons.

Views can be edited either in the **Settings | Technical | User Interface** menu or from the **Edit ControlPanelView** option in the developer tools menu in Odoo 13, or **Edit Search View** in previous Odoo versions.

The *To-do Item* model has no search view yet, so we should create a new one. We will add an option to filter the outstanding to-do items to the filters menu.

Fill in the following values in the new **View** form and click **Save**:

- **View Name**: To-do Search View.
- **View Type**: **Search**.
- **Model**: x_todo_item.
- **Architecture**: In this tab, add this XML code:

```
<search>
  <filter name="item_not_done"
          string="Not Done"
          domain="[('x_is_done', '=', False)]" />
</search>
```

After this, and when reopening or reloading the to-do list view, the **Not Done** option should be available in the **Filters** option list.

Enabling default filters on views

It would be nice to have this filter enabled by default and remove it when needed.

When we click the **To-do** menu option, it runs a window action to open the **To-do** list view. The window action `context` object can be used to set default filters in a similar way to how default values can be set on fields.

Let's try this:

1. Open the **To-do** menu option to navigate to the **To-do** list view.
2. Open the developer tools menu and select the **Edit Action** option. This will open a form with the window action used to open the current views. In the **General Settings** tab, in the **Filters** section, we have the **Context Value** field, along with a **Domain Value** field.
3. In the **Context Value** field, enter the following: `{'search_default_item_not_done': True}`

The `search_default_` prefix instructs a particular filter – `item_not_done` in this case – to be selected by default. Now, if we click on the **To-do** menu option, we should see the **Not Done** filter enabled by default on the search box, and the user is free to disable it.

The **Domain Value** field can also be used to set a filter on the records to present, but it will be a fixed filter that can't be removed by the user.

Summary

In this chapter, we presented an overview of Odoo's components, and we also made use of the developer mode to dive into Odoo's internals and understand how the components work together to create applications.

We used these tools to build a simple application with models, views, and the corresponding menu. We also learned how to use the developer tools to inspect existing applications or make quick customizations directly from the UI.

In the next chapter, we will learn how to install Odoo from source and to prepare the development environment to be used for Odoo module development.

2
Preparing the Development Environment

Before we dive into Odoo development, we need to set up our development environment and learn about the basic administration tasks for it.

In this chapter, we will learn how to set up the working environment where we will build our Odoo applications. We will set up an Ubuntu system to host the development server instance. This can be a cloud server, a local network server, or a subsystem on your Windows 10 computer.

By the end of this chapter, you will know how to prepare a development working environment, run Odoo from source code, and have several projects and versions of Odoo on the same machine. You will also know how Odoo server instances operate, as well as how to work with them during your development work.

The following topics will be covered in this chapter:

- Setting up a host for the Odoo server

- Installing Odoo from source

- Managing Odoo databases

- Configuring the Odoo server options

- Finding and installing community modules

- Using the server development options

The first steps of this chapter involve checking that we have met the technical requirements for this chapter and setting up a host to install Odoo on later.

Technical requirements

In this chapter, we will install Odoo from source on an Ubuntu 20.04 operating system. We only need a terminal environment; the Ubuntu graphical user interface is not needed.

If you don't have an Ubuntu 20.04 system available, a Windows 10 workstation will also work. We will be using the **Windows Subsystem for Linux** (**WSL**) to ensure you have a working Ubuntu environment on your Windows system.

The reference code for this chapter can be found in this book's GitHub repository at `https://github.com/PacktPublishing/Odoo-15-Development-Essentials`, in the `ch02/` directory.

Setting up a host for the Odoo server

A Debian/Ubuntu system is recommended to run Odoo and is considered the reference deployment platform. Odoo's own SaaS operations are known to be Debian-based and are also the most popular choice in the community. This means that it will be easier to find help or advice if you use Debian or Ubuntu.

> **Note**
>
> An option for developing and running Odoo is the Odoo.sh service. It provides Git-based development workflows and provides all the complementary services needed to run a production system, such as inbound and outbound email. If this is your preference, the Odoo official documentation does a good job of introducing it. It can be found at `https://www.odoo.com/documentation/user/15.0/odoo_sh/documentation.html`.

If you already have an Ubuntu 20.04 system, you might be good to go. You just need to check whether you have elevated access to perform the necessary installation steps. To check this, try to run the following command on a terminal. If it is successful, you can move on to the next section:

```
$ sudo apt list
```

If you are using Windows, the simplest solution is to use WSL. We will guide you through doing that next.

If this doesn't work for you, an alternative is to use a virtual machine. We won't be providing details for that, but these pointers might be useful:

- VirtualBox is a free cross-platform virtualization software, available at `https://www.virtualbox.org`.
- Ubuntu Server ISO images can be downloaded from `https://www.ubuntu.com/server`. It is recommended to use the latest **long-term support** (**LTS**) version available.

TurnKey Linux provides easy-to-use preinstalled images in several formats, including ISO. The ISO format will work with any virtualization software you choose, even on a bare-metal machine you might have. A good option might be the LAPP image, which includes Python and PostgreSQL. It can be found at `http://www.turnkeylinux.org/lapp`.

Installing the Windows Subsystem for Linux

The more robust **Windows Subsystem for Linux 2** (**WSL 2**) was made generally available starting from Windows 10 version 2004, in March 2020. With it, we can have an Ubuntu system running inside Windows, capable of performing everything we need for Odoo development. More information on WSL 2 can be found at `https://docs.microsoft.com/en-us/windows/wsl/wsl2-index`.

WSL is a Windows 10 optional feature and must be enabled first. After that, we should install Ubuntu from the Windows Store. The official instructions for that can be found at `https://docs.microsoft.com/en-us/windows/wsl/install`.

After this, we should install the Ubuntu Windows app. Open the Windows Store and search for Ubuntu. At the time of writing, the latest Ubuntu **LTS** release is 20.04. Follow the installation process, including setting up a user account and corresponding password.

Running the Ubuntu application will open the Linux command-line window, where we can run Ubuntu commands. Take note of the username and password that were configured during the Ubuntu installation, since you will be prompted for this information whenever actions need to be performed with elevated privileges, such as when using `sudo`.

Now that we have a Debian-based operating system to work with, we are ready to install Odoo and its dependencies, including the PostgreSQL database.

Installing Odoo from source

Odoo uses the Python programming language to run and uses the PostgreSQL database for data storage. To run Odoo from source, we will need to install the Python libraries it depends on. The Odoo source code can then be downloaded from GitHub. Using a Git repository should be preferred over downloading the source code ZIP or tarball file. Using Git gives us control over the code versions and is a good tool for our release process.

> **Note**
>
> The exact dependency installation may vary, depending on your operating system and on the Odoo version you are installing. If you have trouble with any of the previous steps, make sure you check the official documentation at `https://www.odoo.com/documentation/15.0/setup/install.html`. Instructions for previous editions are also available there.

Installing the PostgreSQL database

Odoo needs a PostgreSQL server to work with. The typical development setup is to have PostgreSQL installed on the same machine as Odoo.

To install the PostgreSQL database on your Debian/Ubuntu system, run the following commands:

```
$ sudo apt update
$ sudo apt install postgresql # Installs PostgreSQL
$ sudo su -c "createuser -s $USER" postgres # Creates db
superuser
```

The last command creates a PostgreSQL user for the current system user. This is needed for your system user to be able to create and drop databases that are used by Odoo instances.

If you are running Ubuntu inside WSL, note that system services are not automatically started. This means that the PostgreSQL service must be manually started for the database to be available. To manually start the PostgreSQL service, run the following command:

```
$ sudo service postgresql start
```

Installing the Odoo system dependencies

Odoo requires some system libraries to run. Git is needed to get the version-controlled source code, and Python 3.6 or later is needed to run Odoo 13. The following are the basic system dependencies that are needed:

```
$ sudo apt update
$ sudo apt upgrade
$ sudo apt install git  # Install Git
$ sudo apt install python3-dev python3-pip python3-wheel \
python3-venv # Python 3 for dev
$ sudo apt install build-essential libpq-dev libxslt-dev \
libzip-dev libldap2-dev libsasl2-dev libssl-dev
```

> **Changes in Odoo 12**
>
> The CSS preprocessor changed from **less** to **SASS**. This means that less is no longer required to run Odoo. Odoo versions 9 to 11 require the less CSS preprocessor.

If you need to work on Odoo versions up to 11, you will also need to install the less CSS preprocessor:

```
$ sudo apt install npm  # Install Node.js and its package
manager
$ sudo ln -s /usr/bin/nodejs /usr/bin/node  # node runs Node.js
$ sudo npm install -g less less-plugin-clean-css  # Install
less
```

Installing Odoo from source

To keep things organized, we will work in a /work15 directory inside our home directory. Throughout this book, we will assume that this is where all our Odoo code is.

Odoo 15 uses Python 3, specifically 3.6 or later. This means that on the system command line, we should use python3 and pip3, instead of python and pip.

Changes in Odoo 11

Starting from version 11, Odoo runs on Python 3. Odoo 11 also works with Python 2.7, but Odoo 12 only runs on Python 3.5+. Up to Odoo 10 only runs on Python 2.7.

To install Odoo from source, we must start by cloning the Odoo source code directly from GitHub:

```
$ mkdir ~/work15  # Create a directory to work in
$ cd ~/work15  # Go into our work directory
$ git clone https://github.com/odoo/odoo.git -b 15.0 \
--depth=1  # Get Odoo sources
```

The ~ symbol is a shortcut for the user's home directory, such as /home/daniel. If you're using WSL on Windows 10, you can find this directory with the **File Explorer** by opening \\wsl$. The full path to the working directory should be similar to \\wsl$\ Ubuntu-20.04\home\daniel\work15.

The -b 15.0 option in the Git command explicitly downloads the 15.0 branch of Odoo. At the time of writing, this is redundant, since it is the default branch, but this may change.

The --depth=1 option tells Git to download only the last revision, instead of the full change history, making the download significantly smaller.

Tip

To download the missing commit history later, you can run git fetch --unshallow. We can also just fetch the recent history. The git fetch --depth=100 command will get the last 100 commits, while git fetch --shallow-since=2020-01-01 will get all the commits since January 1, 2020.

Next, we should install the Python dependencies that are declared in the requirements.txt file. The recommended approach is to do this inside a Python virtual environment. Doing so protects your Odoo environment from possible changes in the system-wide Python libraries. Another benefit is to be able to keep several virtual environments, according to the particular needs of the projects you are working on, such as using older versions of Odoo. Let's get started:

1. To create a new virtual environment, run the following command:

    ```
    $ python3 -m venv ~/work15/env15
    ```

    This will create a Python environment in ~/work15/env15.

2. We want to run all the Python code using ~/work15/env15/bin/python. This command can confirm this, displaying the Python version that's been installed there:

    ```
    $ ~/work15/env15/bin/python -V
    Python 3.8.10
    ```

3. It will be much more comfortable for us if we set this as the current default Python interpreter. This can be achieved by activating the virtual environment:

    ```
    $ source ~/work15/env15/bin/activate
    ```

Once we have activated the virtual environment, the prompt will change to include the information of the active environment. In this case, it will change from $ to (env15) $.

We can run the which command to confirm that the correct Python interpreter is being used:

```
(env15) $ which python
/home/daniel/work15/env15/bin/python
```

To deactivate the virtual environment, simply run `deactivate`; the Python interpreter will be the system default here as well:

```
$ deactivate
$ which python3
/usr/bin/python3
```

Make sure that you reactivate the virtual environment to continue with the following instructions.

With the virtual environment activated, we can now install the Python dependencies inside it:

```
$ source ~/work15/env15/bin/activate
(env15) $ pip install -U pip  # Update pip
(env15) $ pip install -r ~/work15/odoo/requirements.txt
```

> **Note**
>
> Inside a virtual environment, the `python` and `pip` commands will point to the correct version. This is not the case for your operating system, where `pip` will point to Python 2 and `pip3` will point to Python 3. If you need to run these commands at the system-wide level, make sure to replace `pip` with `pip3`, since Odoo uses Python 3.

Some of the Python libraries require system binaries to be installed. If some libraries refuse to install, please confirm that the system dependencies are installed, as described in the *Installing the Odoo system dependencies* section, earlier in this chapter.

We now have the Python library dependencies installed. However, we still need to install Odoo itself. You can use `pip` for this:

```
(env15) $ pip install -e ~/work15/odoo
```

The -e option is used to make a **Python editable install**. With this, the source code files in the ~/work15/odoo directory will be used to run Odoo. Without this option, the installation process would copy the code files from the source directory into an internal site-packages/ directory and run from those copies; they won't reflect changes or updates to the source code.

Running Odoo

To run Odoo, first, make sure you have the corresponding virtual environment activated:

```
$ source ~/work15/env15/bin/activate
```

Inside a virtual environment, simply run Odoo to start an instance:

```
(env15) $ odoo --version
Odoo Server 15.0
```

The odoo command is a convenient shortcut, and we will use it throughout this book. It is still worth knowing that we can start an Odoo server instance by calling the corresponding executable directly:

```
(env15) $ ~/work15/odoo/odoo-bin --version
```

For full control, we can run Odoo from a specific source, using a specific Python executable, without depending on virtual environment activation:

```
$ ~/work15/env15/bin/python ~/work15/odoo/odoo-bin --version
```

If we run Odoo without the --version option, it will keep running, waiting for client calls.

The Odoo default listening port is 8069. To reach the Odoo service from a web browser, we should use the URL http://localhost:8069.

To stop the server and return to the command prompt, press *Ctrl + C*.

Creating a new database from the web client

When we access Odoo for the first time, since there are no databases available yet, we should go to an assistant to create a new database. Under the default configuration, Odoo should be available at `http://localhost:8069`:

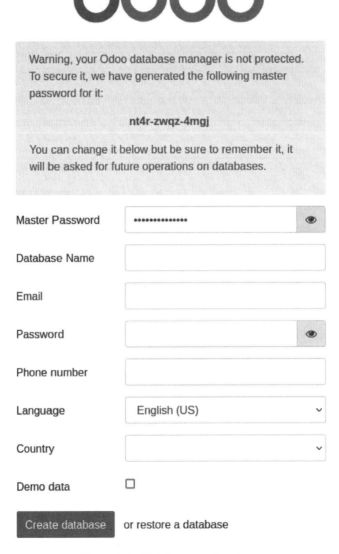

Figure 2.1 – Database creation form

The information that's been requested for this database creation form is as follows:

- **Master Password** is the database manager password and is stored in the Odoo configuration file. Recent Odoo versions generate one automatically, as shown in the preceding screenshot.

- **Database Name** is the identifier name to use for the database. The same database server may host several Odoo databases, each with a unique identifier name.

- **Email** is the login username to use for the default administrator user. It doesn't have to be an actual email address. The default value is `admin`.

- **Password** is the secret password to log in as an administrator.

- **Language** is the default language to use for the database.

- **Country** is the country to use for the company's default settings. It is optional and is relevant for localization features in some apps, such as Invoicing and Accounting.

- The **Demo data** checkbox, when enabled, also installs the demonstration data, instead of starting with an empty database. This is usually desirable for development and test environments.

A master password field might also be asked for if one was set in the Odoo server configuration. This allows you to prevent unauthorized people from performing these administrative tasks. But it is not set by default, so you probably won't be asked for it.

> **Note**
>
> Be aware that the `admin` and `master` passwords are different concepts. The `master` password gives access to the database manager features, allowing you to back up, restore, and duplicate Odoo databases. The `admin` password is for the admin default user login, giving them access to the Odoo database settings and user management.

After clicking the **Create database** button, the new database will be created and initialized, a process that can take a couple of minutes. Once it's ready, you will be redirected to the login screen.

The database manager can be accessed from the login screen, from **Manage databases** at the bottom. The database manager shows the list of available databases and options to back up, duplicate, or delete them, as well as the ability to create new ones.

The database manager can also be directly accessed at `http://localhost:8069/web/database/manager`.

> **Note**
>
> The database manager allows for privileged administration operations, and by default, it is enabled and unprotected by a password. While convenient, this can be a security risk. Consider setting a strong master password, or even better, disabling the database manager feature. The master password is set in the Odoo configuration file, with an entry of `admin_passwd = <your-complex-password>`. To disable the database manager, add the `list_db = False` setting. See the *Configuring the Odoo server options* section for more details on configuration files.

Creating a new database from the command line

As developers, we will need to work with several databases. It is more convenient to create them from the command line.

If the terminal window has Odoo running, press *Ctrl + C* to stop it and go back to the command prompt.

To create and initialize an Odoo database, run the Odoo server using the `-d` option:

```
(env15) $ odoo -d 15-demo --stop-after-init
```

It may take a minute to initialize the `15-demo` database; it will return to the command prompt once finished.

If we omit the `--stop-after-init` option, the Odoo service will keep running once the database is ready. In this case, have a close look at the log messages to find an `INFO` log line with the `Modules loaded` message. This signals that the database startup was completed and that it is now ready to accept client calls. Note that it might not be the last log message and that it can be in the last three or four lines.

By default, new databases are initialized with demonstration data, which is often useful for development databases. This is the equivalent of having the **Load demonstration data** checkbox ticked when creating a new database from the user interface.

To initialize a database without demonstration data, add the `--without-demo=all` option to the `odoo` command.

To be able to create a new database, the user running Odoo must be a PostgreSQL superuser. If this is not the case, check the PostgreSQL setup script in the *Installing Odoo from source* section.

> **Tip**
>
> For a development environment, it is fine for the user running the Odoo instance to be a database superuser. But for a production environment, Odoo security best practices state running the Odoo service with a user that is not a database superuser.

We now have a running Odoo instance and a database to work with. Opening the `http://localhost:8069` URL with a web browser should present us with the Odoo login screen.

If you're not sure about the server name and port to use in the URL, look that up in the Odoo service log messages. One of the first log messages in the startup sequence contains that information. It should look like this:

```
INFO ? odoo.service.server: HTTP service (werkzeug) running on
MYMACHINE:8069
```

On Linux, you can also use the `hostname` command to find the server's name, or use the `ifconfig` command to find the IP address.

The default Odoo administrator account is `admin`, with a password of `admin`. Once logged in, if no application has been installed in the database yet, we will be presented with the **Apps** menu, displaying the applications available for installation.

To stop the Odoo server instance and return to the command line, press *Ctrl + C* on the terminal window running the server. Pressing the up arrow key will bring up the previous shell command, so it's a quick way to start Odoo again with the same options. The *Ctrl + C* keys, followed by the up arrow key and *Enter*, is a frequently used combination to restart the Odoo server during development.

At this point, Odoo should be installed on our system and ready to work, and we even have a database with an Odoo instance ready to work with. Next, we will learn how to manage databases, create new ones, and remove those we don't need anymore.

Managing Odoo databases

In the previous section, we learned how to create and initialize new Odoo databases from the command line. There are more commands worth knowing about to manage Odoo databases.

The Odoo server automatically creates the new PostgreSQL database for us. But we can also do that manually using the following command:

```
$ createdb MyDBName
```

This command can be used with the `--template` option to copy a database. The copied database can't have open connections for this to work. So, make sure that any Odoo instance using it has been stopped.

> **Tip**
>
> When running PostgreSQL in WSL, it may be the case that some operations display a message such as `WARNING: could not flush dirty data: Function not implemented`. A workaround for this is to modify the PostgreSQL configuration file. For version 12, it should be at `/etc/postgresql/12/main/postgresql.conf`. Edit it at add two lines, `fsync = off` and `data_sync_retry = true`. Then, restart the PostgreSQL server using `sudo server posgresql restart`.

To copy a `MyDBName` original database to a `MyDBCopy` database, use the following command:

```
$ createdb --template=MyDBName MyDBCopy
```

To list the existing databases, use the PostgreSQL `psql` utility with the `-l` option:

```
$ psql -l
```

This lists the databases we have created so far. If you followed the previous commands, you should see `MyDBName` and `MyDBCopy` listed. The list will also display the encodings that were used in each database. The default is `UTF-8`, which is the encoding that's needed for Odoo databases.

To remove a database you no longer need (or want to recreate), use the `dropdb` command:

```
$ dropdb MyDBCopy
```

These are the basics of working with databases. To learn more about PostgreSQL, refer to the official documentation at `http://www.postgresql.org/docs/`. The `psql` documentation page can be found at `https://www.postgresql.org/docs/12/app-psql.html`.

> **Warning**
>
> The dropdb command will irrevocably destroy your data. Be careful when using it and always keep backups of important databases before using this command.

We now have Odoo running and know how to manage database instances for our project or experiment needs. However, we still need to learn about the most relevant Odoo server configuration options, and how to conveniently store them in configuration files.

Configuring the Odoo server options

The Odoo server supports several options. To see all the available options, use --help:

```
(env15) $ odoo --help
```

We will review the most relevant options in the following sections. Let's start by looking at how to use configuration files.

Odoo server configuration files

Most of the options can be saved in a configuration file. By default, Odoo will use the .odoorc file. In Linux systems, the default location is in the home directory ($HOME), while in the Windows distribution, it is in the same directory as the Odoo executable.

> **Note**
>
> In older Odoo/OpenERP versions, the name for the default configuration file was .openerp-serverrc. For backward compatibility, Odoo will still use this if it's present and no .odoorc file is found.

In a clean installation, the .odoorc configuration file is not automatically created. We should use the --save option to create the default configuration file, if it doesn't exist yet, and store the current instance configuration in it:

```
(env15) $ odoo --save --stop-after-init
```

The --stop-after-init option we've used here stops the Odoo server after it finishes running through its actions.

> **Note**
>
> Command options can be shortened, so long as they remain unambiguous. For example, the --stop-after-init option can be shortened to --stop.

Now, we can inspect what was saved in this default configuration file:

```
$ cat ~/.odoorc  # show the configuration file
```

This will show all the available configuration options, along with their default values. Editing them will be effective the next time you start an Odoo instance. Type q to quit and go back to the prompt.

To start Odoo using a specific configuration file, use the --conf=<filepath> option or the equivalent -c <filepath> short notation.

For example, the following command creates a new 15-demo.conf configuration file in the ~/work15 directory:

```
(env15) $ odoo -c ~/work15/15-demo.conf --save --stop
```

The following command starts an Odoo server using it:

```
(env15) $ odoo -c ~/work15/15-demo.conf
```

Changing the listening port

The Odoo server uses the 8069 port by default. To use a different port, we can use the --http-port=<port> option, or just the -p <port> short form. This is useful for running more than one instance at the same time, on the same machine.

> **Changed since Odoo 11**
>
> The --http-port server option was introduced in Odoo 11 and replaces the old --xmlrpc-port option, which was used in previous versions.

Let's try this out. Open two terminal windows. In the first, run the following command:

```
$ source ~/work15/env15/bin/activate
(env15) $ odoo --http-port=8070
```

In the second terminal, run the following command:

```
$ source ~/work15/env15/bin/activate
(env15) $ odoo --http-port=8071
```

Now, there are two Odoo instances in the same server, listening on different ports. These two instances can use the same or different databases, depending on the configuration parameters used, and the two could be running the same or different versions of Odoo.

> **Tip**
>
> Different Odoo versions must work with different databases. Trying to use the same database with different Odoo versions won't work, since major versions have incompatible database schemas.

Filtering the list of accessible databases

The `--database`, or `-d`, option sets the database to use by the Odoo server instance. All the calls for that server will use that database, and any calls destined for a different database will be rejected. This can happen when the Odoo server is restarted to use a different database, and there are web browser windows open still with sessions using the previous database.

The same Odoo server can serve several databases. This is the default behavior when no database is selected (the `--database` option is not set, neither in the command options, the configuration file, nor the default `~/.odoorc` configuration). In this case, a new web browser session will open the database manager page, allowing us to select the database we want to work with.

If we don't set a specific database to work with, then all the existing databases will be available. Using the `--db-filter` option limits the databases that are made available by the Odoo server.

The `--db-filter` value can either be a comma-separated list of database names or a regular expression. For example, the expression for filtering to the `15-demo` name is as follows:

```
(env15) $ odoo --db-filter=^15-demo$
```

The following are some examples of useful regular expressions:

- To filter names starting with some text, use the ^ prefix. For example, ^15 filters all names starting with 15.

- To filter names ending with some text, use the $ suffix. For example, demo$ filters all names ending with demo.

- To filter exact matches, combine the ^ prefix with the $ suffix. For example, ^15-demo$ matches only the 15-demo database name.

- To filter an optional single character, use .. For example, ^15-demo.$ matches 15-demo, 15-demo1, 15-demo2, and so on.

- To filter an optional sequence of characters, use .*. For example, ^15.*demo$ matches 15-emo, 15-demo, or 15-this-is-a-demo.

Managing server log messages

By default, Odoo prints the server log messages to standard output, so they are printed out to the terminal window.

Here is an example log line:

```
2021-11-08 08:06:57,786 18592 INFO 15-demo odoo.modules.
loading: Modules loaded.
```

Each log line follows a structure containing these columns:

- 2021-11-08 08:06:57,786: Date and time timestamp of the log message, using UTC, not local time.

- 18592: PID, the system process ID.

- INFO: Message log level.

- 15-demo: Database name. It is ? for actions that have not been performed in the context of a particular database.

- werkzeug: Odoo module posting the message. For example, odoo.modules.loading is used for the module loading actions.

The remaining text is the log message's content.

The message text has a particular structure for HTTP requests and is handled by the
werkzeug module. Here is an example:

```
2021-11-08 08:06:57,786 18592 INFO 15-demo werkzeug: 127.0.0.1
- - [08/Apr/2020 08:06:57] "POST /web/dataset/call_kw/res.
partner/read HTTP/1.1" 200 - 213 0.135 0.092
```

Here, we can see the details about the HTTP request that was made, including its source
IP address, the endpoint that was called, and the HTTP status code.

We can also see performance information, which was added to the end of the text
message: the three last numbers. In this example, this is 213 0.135 0.092. These
performance numbers tell us the following:

- The query count, which is the number of SQL queries that have been executed
- The time spent running SQL queries
- The remaining time spent on anything except SQL (this should mainly be Python
  code)

For logging, there are two settings we can control – where the log output should be
printed to and what the log verbosity should be.

The --log-level option allows us to set the log verbosity. By default, it is set to the
info level.

To lower the log verbosity, set the log level to any of the following:

- warn to display only warnings and errors
- error to display only errors
- critical to display only errors that prevent the server from functioning

Increasing the log level can be helpful to understand some issues with the server. The
following more verbose log levels are available:

- debug enables debug-level log messages.
- debug_sql displays the SQL queries that have been executed.
- debug_rpc shows the details of the RPC requests that have been received.

debug_rpc_answer shows details about the RPC answers that have been sent back to
the client.

Try out these different log levels by adding the parameter to the server start command, as in the following example:

```
(env15) $ odoo --log-level=debug_sql
```

Then, browse through the web client and check the server log's output to see the differences.

The `--log-handler` option allows you to refine the logging verbosity for specific modules. Its usage follows the format of `--log-handler=MODULE1:LEVEL,MODULE2:LEVEL,....` One way to find or confirm the module's name to use is to check existing messages that have been written to the log. The log level can be either `DEBUG`, `INFO`, `WARN`, `ERROR`, or `CRITICAL` (in uppercase).

For example, to increase the module loading log messages to debug, use this command:

```
(env15) $ odoo --log-handler=odoo.modules:DEBUG
```

To reduce the HTTP request handling verbosity, use this command:

```
(env15) $ odoo --log-handler=werkzeug:WARN
```

Regarding where the log output is sent, by default, it is directed to standard output (your console screen), but it can be directed to a log file. For this, the `--logfile=<filepath>` option can be used, like so:

```
(env15) $ odoo --logfile=~/work15/odoo.log
```

> **Note**
>
> In Linux systems, the expected location of a log file is inside `/var/log`. So, Odoo log files can be frequently found inside `/var/log/odoo/`.

We now know how to control our Odoo instances and the most important server options, which means we can start doing some serious work with it. We can benefit from the many community-provided Odoo modules available, so a key skill to learn is how to make these modules available in our Odoo instances.

Finding and installing additional modules

The Odoo ecosystem has a rich community where many modules are available. Installing new modules in an Odoo instance is something that newcomers frequently find confusing. But it doesn't have to be.

Finding community modules

The **Odoo Apps** store at `https://apps.odoo.com` is a catalog of modules that can be downloaded and installed on your system.

Another important resource is the **Odoo Community Association (OCA)**, which hosts community-maintained modules. These modules are hosted on GitHub, at `https://github.com/OCA`, and a searchable index is also provided at `https://odoo-community.org/shop`.

The OCA is a non-profit organization that was created to coordinate community contributions, promote software quality, development best practices, and open source values. You can learn more about the OCA at `https://odoo-community.org`.

To add a module to an Odoo installation, we could just copy it into the `addons` directory, alongside the official modules. In our case, the add-ons directory would be located at `~/work15/odoo/addons/`. However, this is not a good idea. Our Odoo installation is a Git version-controlled code repository, and we want to keep it synchronized with the upstream GitHub repository. Polluting it with foreign modules will make it hard to manage.

Instead, we can select additional locations for modules, which the Odoo server will also look into. Not only can custom modules be separated from the Odoo add-ons directory, but they can also be organized into several directories.

Let's try this now with this book's code, available in GitHub, by making those add-on modules available in our Odoo installation. To get the source code from GitHub, run the following commands:

```
$ cd ~/work15
$ git clone https://github.com/PacktPublishing/Odoo-15-
  Development-Essentials.git library
```

This changes the working directory to `~/work15` and downloads the code from this book's GitHub repository into the `library/` subdirectory. Next, Odoo needs to know about this new module directory.

Configuring the add-ons path

The Odoo `addons_path` configuration option lists the directories where the server should look for modules. By default, this points to two directories – one for the server's internal code, containing the base module, and the other for the add-ons directory, which contains the standard modules and apps. For the setup followed in this chapter, this is `~/work15/odoo/odoo/addons,~/work15/odoo/addons`.

Let's start the server with an add-ons path that includes our new module directory:

```
$ cd ~/work15
$ source env15/bin/activate
(env15) $ odoo -d 15-library --addons-path="./library,../odoo/addons"
```

did it work?
no manifest.

Here, we are making sure that we are in our work directory and that the Python virtual environment is activated. Then, Odoo is started with two options – the database name to be used by Odoo, `15-library`, and the add-ons directories to use. For shorter notations, we use relative paths.

When the server starts, have a close look at the first few lines of the log. There should be a log message reporting the add-ons path being used, similar to `INFO ? odoo: addons paths: [...]`. Confirm that it contains the `library/` directory:

```
(env15) ~/work15
20:20 $ odoo -d 15-library --addons-path="./library,../odoo/addons"
2021-11-01 20:20:53,477 817742 INFO ? odoo: Odoo version 15.0
2021-11-01 20:20:53,477 817742 INFO ? odoo: Using configuration file at /home/daniel/.odoorc
2021-11-01 20:20:53,477 817742 INFO ? odoo: addons paths: ['/home/daniel/work15/odoo/odoo/addons', '/home/daniel/.local/share/Odoo/addons/15.0', '/home/daniel/work15/library', '/home/daniel/work15/odoo/addons']
2021-11-01 20:20:53,477 817742 INFO ? odoo: database: default@default:default
2021-11-01 20:20:53,597 817742 INFO ? odoo.addons.base.models.ir_actions_report: Will use the Wkhtmltopdf binary at /usr/local/bin/wkhtmltopdf
2021-11-01 20:20:53,692 817742 INFO ? odoo.service.server: HTTP service (werkzeug) running on daniel-Lenovo-ideapad-720S-14IKB:8069
2021-11-01 20:20:53,698 817742 INFO 15-library odoo.modules.loading: loading 1 modules...
2021-11-01 20:20:53,766 817742 INFO 15-library odoo.modules.loading: 1 modules loaded in 0.01s, 0 queries (+0 extra)
2021-11-01 20:20:53,711 817742 INFO 15-library odoo.modules.loading: loading 6 modules...
2021-11-01 20:20:53,729 817742 INFO 15-library odoo.modules.loading: 6 modules loaded in 0.02s, 0 queries (+0 extra)
2021-11-01 20:20:53,750 817742 INFO 15-library odoo.modules.loading: Modules loaded.
2021-11-01 20:20:53,752 817742 INFO 15-library odoo.modules.registry: Registry loaded in 0.060s
```

Figure 2.2 – The Odoo startup sequence log messages with the add-ons path used

We now know how to add third-party modules to our Odoo instances, and want to start developing our own modules. There are a few Odoo server options aimed at making development easier. It's good to know about them before we start coding.

Using the server development options

Odoo also provides a server-side development mode, which can be enabled by using the `--dev=all` option.

Development mode enables features to speed up the development cycle:

- Changes to Python code are automatically reloaded when a code file is saved, avoiding a manual server restart.
- Changes to `View` definitions have an instant effect, avoiding manual module upgrades (note that a browser page reload is still needed).

The `--dev=all` option will bring up the `pdb` Python debugger when an exception is raised. It is useful for doing a postmortem analysis of a server error. More details on the Python debugger commands can be found at `https://docs.python.org/3/library/pdb.html#debugger-commands`.

The `--dev` option accepts a comma-separated list of options, although the `all` option will be suitable most of the time. By default, the Python debugger, `pdb`, is used. This debugger is a bit terse, and other options are available. The supported external debuggers are `ipdb`, `pudb`, and `wpdb`.

To use the automatic reload feature, when changes to code files are detected, the `watchdog` Python package must be installed:

```
(env15) $ pip install watchdog
```

The use of debuggers will be addressed in detail in *Chapter 8, Business Logic – Supporting Business Processes*.

Odoo commands quick reference

Here is a quick reference for the most important Odoo commands:

- `-c, --conf=my.conf`: Sets the configuration file to use.
- `--save`: Saves the config file.
- `--stop, --stop-after-init`: Stops after module loading.
- `-d, --database=mydb`: Uses this database.
- `--db-filter=^mydb$`: Filters the databases that are available using a regular expression.
- `-p, --http-port=8069`: The database port to use for HTTP.
- `-i, --init=MODULES`: Installs the modules in a comma-separated list.
- `-u, --update=MODULES`: Updates the modules in a comma-separated list.

- `--log-level=debug`: The log level. Examples include `debug`, `debug_sql`, `debug_rpc`, `debug_rpc_answer`, and `warn`. Alternatives for debugging specific core components are as follows:

  - `--log-sql`: Debugs `SQL` calls
  - `--log-request`: Debugs HTTP request calls
  - `--log-response`: Debugs responses to HTTP calls
  - `--log-web`: Debugs HTTP request responses

- `--log-handler=MODULE:LEVEL`: Sets the log level for a specific module. The following are examples:

  - `--log-handler=werkzeug:WARN`
  - `--log-handler=odoo.addons:DEBUG`

- `--logfile=<filepath>`: Sends the log to a file.
- `--dev=OPTIONS`: Options include `all`, [`pudb`|`wdb`|`ipdb`|`pdb`], `reload`, `qweb`, `werkzeug`, and `xml`.

Summary

In this chapter, we learned how to set up an Ubuntu system to host Odoo and install it from the GitHub source code. We also learned how to create Odoo databases and run Odoo instances.

You should now have a functioning Odoo environment to work with and be comfortable with managing databases and instances.

With this in place, we're ready to jump straight into the action. In the next chapter, we will create our first Odoo module from scratch and understand the main elements it involves.

3
Your First Odoo Application

Developing in Odoo usually means creating our own modules. In this chapter, we will create our first Odoo application, learn the steps needed to make it available to Odoo, and install it.

We will get started by learning the basics of the development workflow—we'll create and install a new module and update it to apply the changes we make throughout the development iterations.

Odoo follows a **Model-View-Controller** (**MVC**)-like architecture, and we will go through the different layers to implement a library application.

In this chapter, we will cover the following topics:

- Overview of the library project
- Step 1 – Creating a new `addon` module
- Step 2 – Creating a new application
- Step 3 – Adding automated tests
- Step 4 – Implementing the model layer
- Step 5 – Setting up access security

- Step 6 – Implementing the backend view layer
- Step 7 – Implementing the business logic layer
- Step 8 – Implementing the website **user interface (UI)**

With this approach, you will be able to gradually learn about the basic building blocks that make up an application and experience the iterative process of building an Odoo module from scratch.

Technical requirements

This chapter requires you to have an Odoo server installed and be able to start it from the command line to perform actions such as installing modules or running tests. If you don't have a working Odoo development environment, make sure you review *Chapter 2, Preparing the Development Environment*.

In this chapter, we will create our first Odoo application from a blank slate, so we won't need any additional code to get started.

The code for this chapter can be found in the book's GitHub repository at `https://github.com/PacktPublishing/Odoo-15-Development-Essentials`, in the `ch03` directory.

Overview of the library project

We will use a learning project to better explore the topics explained in this chapter, and see them work in practice. We will create a new Odoo app to manage a book library. We will use this project in all the following chapters, where each chapter will be an iteration, adding features to the app. Here, we will create a first iteration of the library app.

The first feature we will implement will be the book catalog. The catalog allows us to keep records of the books in our library, with their relevant details. We also want to make this catalog available through a public website, where the available books can be seen.

Library books should have the following data:

- Title
- Authors
- Publishing company
- Date published
- Cover image

- **International Standard Book Number** (**ISBN**), with check digit validation
- Active flag, indicating the books that should be publicly available on the website

As is usual for the Odoo base apps, the Library app will have two user groups, the Library User and the Library Manager. The User level is expected to be able to perform all daily operations, and the Manager level is expected to additionally be able to edit the app's configurations.

For the book catalog feature, we will keep editing book records as a reserved feature for Managers. The following should apply:

- Library Managers should be able to edit books.
- Library users and Public users using the website should be able to only view books.

This simple project will allow us to cover all the main components involved in building an Odoo app. The first step is to create a module directory that will host the code and components for our app.

Step 1 – Creating a new addon module

An addon module is a directory containing files that implement some Odoo features. It can add new features or modify existing ones. The addon module directory must contain a manifest file—or descriptor file—named `__manifest__.py`.

Some module addons are featured as an **app**. Apps are the top-level module for a feature area in Odoo, and we expect our module to be featured in the top-level **Apps** menu. Examples of apps in base Odoo include **CRM**, **Project**, and **HR**. A non-app **module addon** is expected to depend on an app, adding or extending features to it.

If a new module adds new or major functionality to Odoo, it probably should be an app. If the module just makes changes to an existing app, it probably should be a regular addon module.

To develop a new module, we will do the following:

1. Ensure that the directory where we will work is in the Odoo server addons path.
2. Create the module's directory, containing the manifest file.
3. Choose a license for the module, if we intend to distribute it.
4. Add a module description.
5. Optionally, add an icon to represent the module.

After this, we can install the module to confirm that it is available to the Odoo server and that it installs correctly.

Preparing the addons path

An **addon module** is a directory containing an Odoo **manifest** file providing features, such as a new app or additional features for an existing app. An **addons directory** contains several addon modules. The **addons path** is an Odoo configuration, with a list of directories where the Odoo server will look for available addons.

By default, the addons path includes the base apps bundled with Odoo, in the odoo/ addons directory, and the base module providing the core features, in the odoo/odoo/ addons directory. The addons path is usually modified to add one or more directories for the custom-developed and community modules we want to use.

The Library project will be composed of several modules. Doing so is a good practice since it promotes smaller more focused modules, helping reduce complexity. We will create an addons directory for the project's modules.

If the instructions in *Chapter 2, Preparing the Development Environment,* were followed, the Odoo server code should be at ~/work15/odoo/. Custom addon modules should be kept in their own directory, separate from the Odoo code.

For the Library, we will create a ~/work15/library directory and include it in the addons path. We can do this by editing the configuration file directly or by using the Odoo **command-line interface (CLI)**. Here is how to do the latter:

```
$ mkdir ~/work15/library
$ source ~/work15/env15/bin/activate
(env15) $ odoo \
--addons-path="~/work15/library,~/work15/odoo/addons" \
-d library -c ~/work15/library.conf --save --stop
```

Right now, the Odoo command will return an error such as this: odoo: error: option --addons-path: no such directory: '/home/daniel/work15/ library'. This is because the directory is still empty, and Odoo is not able to find any addon module inside it. We won't have this problem as soon as the skeleton for the first Library app module is created.

Here's an explanation of the options used in the Odoo command:

- The `--addons-path` option sets a list of all the directories to use for Odoo modules.

- The `--d` or `--database` option sets the database name to use. If the database doesn't exist, it will be created and initialized with Odoo's basic database schema.

- The `--c` or `--config` option sets the configuration file to use.

- The `--save` option used along with `-c` saves the options used in the configuration file.

- The `--stop` option, short for `--stop-after-init`, stops the Odoo server and returns to the command line once all actions are done and the start sequence is done.

If relative paths are used for the addons path option, Odoo will convert them to absolute paths before storing them in the configuration file.

> **Changes in Odoo 15**
>
> The configuration file created will use the default configuration as a template.
> In Linux systems, the default configuration file is the one at `~/.odoorc`.

The Odoo `scaffold` command provides a quick way to create a new module skeleton. We can use it to populate the `library` addons directory with a valid module. To scaffold the `library_app` module directory, execute this code:

```
(env15) $ odoo scaffold library_app ~/work15/library
```

The `scaffold` command expects two arguments—the module directory name and the path where to create it. For more details on the `scaffold` command, run `odoo scaffold --help`.

Now, we can retry the command to save the configuration file, including the `~/work15/library/` addons directory, and it should run successfully now.

The startup sequence's first log messages summarize the settings being used. They include an `INFO ? odoo: Using configuration file at...` line identifying the configuration file being used and an `INFO ? odoo: addons paths: [...]` line listing the addons directories being considered. These are the first things to check when troubleshooting why Odoo is not discovering your custom module.

Creating a module directory

Following the previous section, we should now have the ~/work15/library directory for our Odoo modules and have included it in the Odoo addons path so that the Odoo server will be able to find modules in it.

In the previous section, we also used the Odoo scaffold command to automatically create a skeleton structure for the new library_app module directory, with a basic structure already in place. Remembering the scaffold command, it looks like this: odoo scaffold <module> <addons-directory>. The module directory created looks like this:

```
library_app/
├── __init__.py
├── __manifest__.py
├── controllers
│   ├── __init__.py
│   └── controllers.py
├── demo
│   └── demo.xml
├── models
│   ├── __init__.py
│   └── models.py
├── security
│   └── ir.model.access.csv
└── views
    ├── templates.xml
    └── views.xml
```

The module directory name is its technical name. In this case, we used library_app for it. The technical name must be a valid Python **identifier** (**ID**)—it should begin with a letter and can only contain letters, numbers, and the underscore character.

It contains several subdirectories for the different components of the module. This subdirectory structure is not required, but it is a widely used convention.

A valid Odoo addon module directory must contain a __manifest__.py descriptor file. It also needs to be Python-importable, so it must also have an __init__.py file. These are the two first files we see in the directory tree.

Tip

In older Odoo versions, the module manifest file was named __
openerp__.py. This filename is still supported but is deprecated.

The manifest file contains a Python dictionary, with the attributes describing the module. The scaffold's automatically generated manifest file should be similar to this:

```python
{
    'name': "library_app",
    'summary': """
        Short (1 phrase/line) summary of the module's
        purpose, used as subtitle on modules listing or
        apps.openerp.com""",
    'description': """
        Long description of module's purpose
    """,
    'author': "My Company",
    'website': "http://www.yourcompany.com",
    # Categories can be used to filter modules in modules
    # listing
    # Check https://github.com/odoo/odoo/blob/15.0/
    #    odoo/addons/base/data/ir_module_category_data.xml
    # for the full list
    'category': 'Uncategorized',
    'version': '0.1',
    # any module necessary for this one to work correctly
    'depends': ['base'],
    # always loaded
    'data': [
        # 'security/ir.model.access.csv',
        'views/views.xml',
        'views/templates.xml',
    ],
    # only loaded in demonstration mode
    'demo': [
        'demo/demo.xml',
    ],
}
```

The next section will discuss the manifest file in more detail.

The __init__.py module file should trigger the import of all the module's Python files. More specifically, it should import the Python files at the module top level and import the subdirectories also containing Python files. Similarly, each of these subdirectories should also contain an __init__.py file, importing the Python assets in that subdirectory.

This is the top __init__.py file generated by the scaffold command:

```
from . import controllers
from . import models
```

There are no Python files at the top level, and two subdirectories with Python files, controllers, and models. Reviewing the module tree, we can see that these two directories contain Python files and an __init__.py file each.

Creating a manifest file

The scaffold command prepared a manifest file that can be used as a guideline, or we can create a manifest file from an empty file.

The manifest file should be a valid Python file containing a dictionary. None of the possible dictionary keys is required, so an empty dictionary, { }, would be a valid content for the file. In practice, we want to at least provide some basic description of the module, assert authorship, and choose a distribution license.

The following should be a good starting point:

```
{
    "name": "Library Management",
    "summary": "Manage library catalog and book lending.",
    "author": "Daniel Reis",
    "license": "AGPL-3",
    "website": "https://github.com/PacktPublishing"
                "/Odoo-15-Development-Essentials",
    "version": "15.0.1.0.0",
    "depends": ["base"],
    "application": True,
}
```

The keys used here provide all the data presented in the main tab of the app form, as illustrated in the following screenshot:

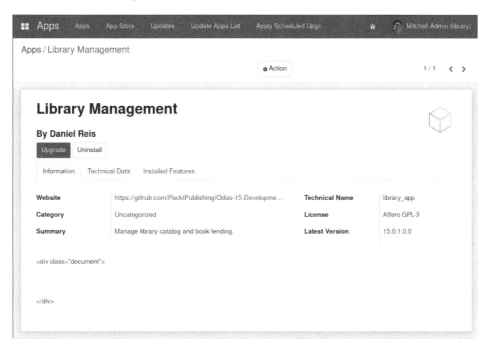

Figure 3.1 – Library Management module app form

We used the following keys:

- `name`: For the module title.

- `summary`: For a one-line summary of the purpose of the module.

- `author`: For the name of the copyright author. It is a string but can contain a comma-separated list of names.

- `license`: This identifies the license under which the author allows the module to be distributed. `AGPL-3` and `LGPL-3` are popular open source choices. Proprietary modules sold through the Odoo Apps Store usually use the `OPL-1` Odoo proprietary license. Licenses are discussed in more detail later in this chapter.

- `website`: A **Uniform Resource Locator** (**URL**) to get more information about the module. This can help people find more documentation or the issue tracker to file bugs and suggestions.

- version: The version of the module. It should follow semantic versioning rules (see `http://semver.org/` for details). It is a good practice to use the Odoo version before our module version since it helps identify the Odoo version the module targets. For example, a `1.0.0` module built for Odoo 15.0 should carry version `15.0.1.0.0`.

- depends: A list of the addon modules it depends on. The installation of this module will trigger the installation of these dependencies. If the module has no particular dependencies, it is a common practice to have it depend on the `base` module, but this is not required.

- application: A flag, declaring whether the module should be featured as an app in the apps list. Most extension modules, adding features to existing apps, will have this set to `False`. The Library management module is a new app, so we used `True`.

The dependencies list is something to be careful about. We should ensure all dependencies are explicitly set here; otherwise, the module may fail to install in a clean database install due to missing dependencies or have loading errors if, by chance, the other required modules are loaded later than ours, in the Odoo startup sequence. Both these cases can happen when deploying your work on other machines and can be time-consuming to identify and solve.

The `<div class="document">` line seen in *Figure 3.1* is for the long module description, now empty. Adding a description is discussed in a later section, *Adding a description*.

These other descriptor keys are also available, and used less often:

- installable: Indicates if this module is available for installation. The default value is `True`, so we don't need to explicitly set it. It can be set to `False` if for some reason we need to disable it but still keep its files in the addon directory.

- auto_install: This can be set to `True`, and is used for **glue** modules. A glue module installation is triggered once all the dependencies are installed. For example, this can be used to automatically provide features that bridge two apps, once they are both installed in the same instance.

Setting the module category

Modules are grouped into categories, representing the function areas they relate to. These categories are used to group addon modules, and also the security groups.

If no category is set on the addon, the **Uncategorized** value will be assigned. This is right now the category for the Library app.

We can see several categories on Odoo in the **Apps** menu, on the left side panel. There, we can see the categories that can be used for our modules, as illustrated in the following screenshot:

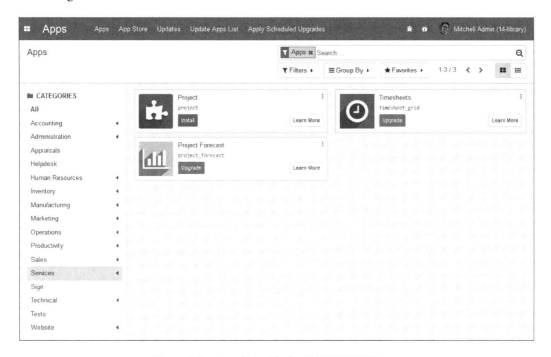

Figure 3.2 – Apps list with the CATEGORIES pane

The categories can have a hierarchy—for example, the **Project** apps belong to the **Services/Project** category.

If a non-existent category is used on an addon module, Odoo will automatically create it and make it available. We will take advantage of this to create a new category for the Library app: **Services/Library**.

Edit the __manifest__.py file thus to add a category key:

```
    "category": "Services/Library",
```

Categories are also relevant for organizing security groups, and to reference them in **Extensible Markup Language** (**XML**) data files, we will need to use the corresponding XML ID.

The XML ID assigned to a module category is automatically generated from the base. module_category_ prefix plus the category name. For example, for **Services/Library**, the generated XML ID is base.module_category_services_library.

We can confirm the XML ID for app categories by navigating to the corresponding form view and then using the **View Metadata** option in the developer menu.

There is no menu item for app categories, but the category form can be accessed from the security **Groups** form, as follows:

1. Open the **Settings | User | Groups** menu option and create a new test record.

2. Select an option from the **Application** field drop-down list, and save. The process is illustrated in the following screenshot:

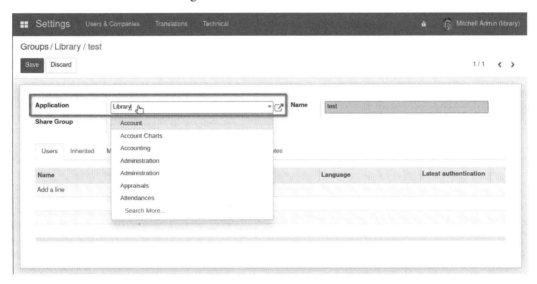

Figure 3.3 – Application selection list, in the User Group form

3. Click on the **Application** link to open the selected category's corresponding details form.

4. On the category form, select the **View Metadata** option in the developer menu to see the XML ID assigned to it.

5. You may want to delete the test group if it is no longer of use to you.

Alternatively, the list of built-in categories and their XML IDs can be found in the Odoo source code. The GitHub URL is provided here: `https://github.com/odoo/odoo/blob/15.0/odoo/addons/base/data/ir_module_category_data.xml`.

Choosing a license

Choosing a license for your work is important, and you should carefully consider which is the best choice for you, and its implications.

Software code is covered by copyright law, reserving to the authors the rights to use or modify the work. This will usually mean you individually or the company you are working for. For other parties to safely be allowed to use the work, they must have a license agreement with the code authors.

If you want to make your code freely available, it needs to carry a license, stating what other people are allowed to do with your code. Different licenses will state different terms.

The most-used licenses for Odoo modules are version 3 of the **GNU's Not Unix (GNU) Lesser General Public License (LGPL-3)** and the **Affero General Public License (AGPL-3)**. Both allow you to freely distribute and modify the work, as long as the authors are credited and the derived works are distributed under the same license conditions.

The AGPL is a strong open source license and requires online services using the code to share the source code with their users. This license is popular among the community because it forces derivative works to also be distributed under the AGPL terms. So, the open sourced code can't be incorporated in a closed commercial solution, and the original authors can benefit from the improvements made by other people.

The LGPL is more permissive than AGPL and also allows commercial modifications, without the need to share the corresponding source code. This license is usually chosen for web and system integration components, where solutions might contain components under private licenses, or under terms incompatible with AGPL.

You can learn more about the GNU licenses at `https://www.gnu.org/licenses/`.

While you can sell GPL licensed apps, this is not a popular business model since the license allows people to freely copy and distribute the code. For this reason, many modules sold in the Odoo App Store prefer to use a proprietary license. Odoo proposes the Odoo proprietary license, `OPL-1`, for this.

More details on Odoo licenses can be found at `https://www.odoo.com/documentation/user/legal/licenses/licenses.html`.

Adding a description

A description is a long text presenting the module features. The description text supports the **reStructuredText (RST)** format to produce a rich text document.

You can learn more about RST here: `https://docutils.sourceforge.io/rst.html`. The page includes a quick reference link that is worth bookmarking: `https://docutils.sourceforge.io/docs/user/rst/quickstart.html`.

Here is a short sample of an RST document:

```
Title
=====

Subtitle
--------

This is *emphasis*, rendered in italics.
This is **strong emphasis**, rendered in bold.

This is a bullet list:

- Item one.
- Item two.
```

One way to add a description is to use the `description` key in the module manifest. Since chances are the description text will span multiple lines, it is best added inside triple quotes, `"""`, the Python syntax for multiline strings.

Source code published on websites such as GitHub is expected to include a README file, for visitors to easily find an introduction to the module. So, instead of the `description` manifest key, Odoo modules can have a `README.rst` or `README.md` file for the same purpose. This file should be placed at the root of the module directory, alongside the `__manifest__.py` file.

Another alternative is to provide a **HyperText Markup Language (HTML)** document description file. Many modules distributed in the Odoo Apps Store choose to use this for a richer visual presentation of the app's features. The `index.html` HTML file should be located in the `static/description/` module subdirectory. Page assets, such as images and **Cascading Style Sheets (CSS)**, should also be located in that same directory.

> **Note**
>
> For modules with the `application` key set to `True`, only the `index.html` description will be used, and the description key is ignored.

Adding an icon

Modules can optionally have an icon representing them. In the case of modules creating a new app, this is particularly important, since the app is expected to have an icon in the **Apps** menu.

To add an icon, we need to add a `static/description/icon.png` file to the module, with the icon to be used.

For the Library app project, we will reuse an icon from the **Notes** existing Odoo app and copy it into the `library_app/static/description` directory.

From the command line, we would run the following:

```
$ cd ~/work15/library/library_app
$ mkdir -p ./static/description
$ cp ~/work15/odoo/addons/note/static/description/\
icon.png ./static/description/
```

Installing a new module

We now have a minimal `addon` module. It doesn't implement any features yet, but we can install it to confirm that it is working properly so far.

To install a new module, we should start the server using both the `-d` and `-i` options. The `-d` or `--database` option ensures that we are working with the correct Odoo database. The `-i` or `--init` option accepts a comma-separated list of modules to install.

> **Changes in Odoo 11**
>
> When installing a new module, Odoo will automatically update the list of available modules from the currently configured addons paths. This was not so up to Odoo 10, where the module list needed to be manually updated before a new addon module could be installed. The modules list is updated in the web client, from the menu option in the **Apps** list.

For the Odoo environment prepared earlier in this chapter and having activated the Python virtual environment, the following command installs the library_app module:

```
(env15)$ odoo -c ~/work15/library.conf -d library -i \
library_app
```

We added the -d library option to make sure that the correct database is selected for the installation. It could be the case that this option was already defined in the configuration file and is thus redundant. Even if that is the case, it is best to play safe and explicitly declare the database to install on in the command.

> **Tip**
> Pay close attention to the server log messages to confirm that the module was correctly found and installed. You should see an odoo.addons.base. models.ir_module: ALLOW access to module.button_ install message and no warnings.

For the module installation to be possible, the addons directory where the module is in should be known to the Odoo server. This can be confirmed by stopping and starting the Odoo server and looking at the odoo: addons paths: log message printed during the Odoo startup sequence.

If the module is not found, that is often because the addons path is incorrect. Double-check that by taking a close look at the addons path being used.

Upgrading modules

Developing a module is an iterative process, with changes made on source files that are then to be applied to Odoo.

This can be done from the **graphical UI (GUI)** by looking up the module in the **Apps** list and clicking on the **Upgrade** button. This reloads the data files, applying the changes made, and updates the database schema definitions. However, when the changes are only in Python logic, the upgrade may not be sufficient. An Odoo server restart may be needed to reload the changed Python code. When the module changes are both data files and Python logic, both operations might be needed.

In summary, the following applies:

- When modifying models or their fields, an upgrade is needed to apply the database schema changes.

- When changing logic Python code, a restart is needed to reload the code files.

- When changing XML or **comma-separated values** (**CSV**) files, an upgrade is needed to reapply the data in the files.

To avoid any confusion or frustration related to having code changes applied to Odoo, the simplest solution is to restart the Odoo service with the module upgrade command after the code changes are made.

In the terminal where the server instance is running, use *Ctrl + C* to stop it. Then, start the server and upgrade the library_app module using the following command:

```
(env15)$ odoo -c ~/work15/library.conf -d library \
 -u library_app
```

The -u option, --update in the long format, requires the -d option and accepts a comma-separated list of modules to update. For example, we could use -u library_app,mail. When a module is updated, all other installed modules depending on it are also updated.

Pressing the up arrow key brings to you the previous command that was used. So, most of the time, when repeating this action, you will find yourself using the *Ctrl + C*, up arrow, and *Enter* key combination.

In recent Odoo versions, the --dev=all developer-friendly mode is available, automating this workflow. When this option is used, changes to data files will instantly be available to the running Odoo service, and Python code changes will trigger an Odoo code reload. For more details on this option, please refer to the *Using the server development options* section of *Chapter 2, Preparing the Development Environment*.

We now have a module directory ready to host the components that implement the app. Since this is an app, and not a technical module adding a feature, we will start by adding a few basic components expected for apps.

Step 2 – Creating a new application

Some Odoo modules create new applications, and others add features or modify existing applications. While the technical components involved are about the same, an app is expected to include a few characteristic elements. Since the Library module is a new app, we should include them in our module.

An app is expected to have the following:

- An icon, to be presented in the app list
- A top-level menu item, under which all the app's menu items will be placed
- Security groups for the app so that it can be enabled only for users that need it, and where access security will be set

The app icon is an `icon.png` file in the module's `static/description/` subdirectory. This was done earlier, in the *Adding an icon* section.

Next, we will take care of the app's top-level menu.

Adding a top menu item

Since we are creating a new app, it should have a main menu item. On the **Community Edition (CE)**, this is shown as a new entry in the top-left drop-down menu. On the **Enterprise Edition (EE)**, it is shown as an additional icon in the **App Switcher** main menu.

Menu items are view components added using XML data files. To define a menu item, create a `views/library_menu.xml` file with the following content:

```
<odoo>
  <!-- Library App Menu -->
  <menuitem id="menu_library" name="Library" />
</odoo>
```

The UI, including menu options and actions, has database stored records read and interpreted by the web client in real time.

The aforementioned file describes records to load into the Odoo database. The `<menuitem>` element is an instruction to write a record on the `ir.ui.menu` model, where Odoo menu items are stored.

The id attribute is also known as an **XML ID** and is used to uniquely identify each data element, providing a way for other elements to reference it. For example, library submenu items added later will need to reference their parent menu item, using the menu_ library XML ID.

The menu item added here is very simple and is using only one attribute: name. There are other attributes available that we didn't use here. We will learn more about them later in this chapter, in the *Implementing the backend view layer* section.

The Library module does not know about this new XML data file yet. To be known and loaded into the Odoo instance, it needs to be declared in the data attribute of the manifest file. Edit the __manifest__.py file dictionary to add this key, as follows:

```
"data": [
    "views/library_menu.xml",
],
```

The data manifest key is a list of the data files to be loaded by the module upon installation or upgrade. The file paths are relative to the module's root directory, where the manifest file is.

To load these menu configurations into our Odoo database, we need to upgrade the module. Doing that at this point won't have any visible effects. This menu item has no actionable submenu yet, and so won't be shown. It will be visible later, once we add submenus and the corresponding access permissions.

> **Tip**
> Items in the menu tree are only shown if there are any visible submenu items. The lower-level menu items that open views will only be visible if the user has access to the corresponding model.

Adding security groups

Before features can be used by regular users, access must be granted to them. In Odoo, this is done using security **groups**. Access privileges are granted to security groups, and users are assigned security groups.

Odoo apps typically provide two groups for two levels of access, as follows:

- A user access level, for users performing daily operations
- A manager access level, with full access to all features, including configurations

The Library app will feature these two security groups. We will work on this next.

Access-security-related files are usually kept in a `security/` module subdirectory, so we should create a `security/library_security.xml` file for these definitions.

Security groups are organized in the same categories used for addon modules. To assign a category to a security group, we should find the corresponding XML ID. The way this XML ID can be found was discussed earlier in this chapter, in the *Setting the module category* section. There, we can learn that the XML ID for the **Services/Library** category is `base.module_category_services_library`.

Next, we will add the Library User security group. It belongs to the **Library** category defined previously, with an XML ID of `module_library_category`, and it will inherit the internal user security permissions, building on top of them. If we open that group's form and use the developer menu **View Metadata** option, we can see that its XML ID is `base.group_user`.

Now, add to the `security/library_security.xml` file with the following XML:

```xml
<odoo>
  <data>
    <!-- Library User Group -->
    <record id="library_group_user" model="res.groups">
      <field name="name">User</field>
      <field name="category_id"
             ref="base.module_category_services_library "/>
      <field name="implied_ids"
             eval="[(4, ref('base.group_user'))]"/>
    </record>
  </data>
</odoo>
```

We have a lot going on here, so let's slowly go through each of the elements here. This XML is adding one record to the groups model, `res.groups`. This record has values for three fields, as follows:

- `name` is the group title. This is a simple string value.
- `category_id` is the related app. It is a relational field, so the `ref` attribute is used to link it to the category created before, using its XML ID.

- `implied_ids` is a one-to-many relational field and contains a list of groups that will also apply to users belonging to this group. To-many fields use a special syntax that is detailed in *Chapter 5, Importing, Exporting, and Module Data*. In this case, we are using code 4 to add a link to the existing internal user XML ID, `base.group_user`.

Changes in Odoo 12

The **User** form has a **User Type** section, only visible when the Developer Mode is enabled. It allows us to select between the mutually exclusive options— **Internal User**, **Portal** (external users, such as customers), and **Public** (website anonymous visitors). This was changed to avoid misconfigurations found in previous Odoo versions, where internal users could accidentally be included in the **Portal** or **Public** groups, effectively reducing their access privileges.

Next, we will create a manager group. It should give us all the privileges of the user group, plus some additional access reserved to the manager. So, we want it to inherit from the `library_group_user` library user.

Editing the `security/library_security.xml` file, add the following XML inside the `<odoo>` element:

```xml
<!-- Library Manager Group -->
<record id="library_group_manager" model="res.groups">
    <field name="name">Manager</field>
    <field name="category_id"
            ref="base.module_category_services_library "/>
    <field name="implied_ids"
            eval="[(4, ref('library_group_user'))]"/>
    <field name="users"
            eval="[(4, ref('base.user_root')),
                   (4, ref('base.user_admin'))]"/>
</record>
```

Here, we also see the `name`, `category_id`, and `implied_ids` fields, as before. The `implied_ids` field is set with a link to the **Library** user group, to inherit its privileges.

It is also setting values on the `users` field. This has this group assigned to the Administrator (`admin`) and the Odoobot users.

> **Changes in Odoo 12**
>
> Since Odoo 12, we have a system root user, which is not shown in the user list and is used internally by the framework when privilege elevation is needed (`sudo`). The `admin` user can be used to log in to the server and should have full access to all features but does bypass access security, as the system root does. On Odoo versions up to 11, the `admin` user was also the internal root superuser.

We also need to have this additional XML data file in the manifest file:

```
"data": [
        "security/library_security.xml",
        "views/library_menu.xml",
    ],
```

Notice that the `library_security.xml` file was added before `library_menu.xml`. The order used to load data files is important since references can only use IDs that have already been defined. It is common for menu items to reference security groups, and so it is a good practice to add security definitions before menu and view definitions.

The next step is to add the Python code defining the app models. But before that, we will add some test cases, following a **test-driven development (TDD)** approach.

Step 3 – Adding automated tests

Programming best practices include having automated tests for your code. This is even more important for dynamic languages such as Python—since there is no compilation step, you can't be sure there are no syntactic errors until the interpreter runs the code. A good editor can help us detect some of these problems ahead of time but can't help us ensure the code performs as intended, as automated tests can.

The TDD method states that we should write tests upfront, check that they fail, then develop code that, in the end, should pass the tests. Inspired by this approach, we will add our module tests now before we add the actual features.

Odoo supports automated tests, based on Python's built-in `unittest` library. Here, we will have a quick introduction to automated tests, and a longer explanation is provided in *Chapter 8, Business Logic – Supporting Business Processes*.

Changes in Odoo 12

Until Odoo 11, tests could also be described using **YAML Ain't Markup Language** (**YAML**) data files. YAML data-file support was removed in Odoo 12, so this kind of test is not available anymore.

The tests need to meet a few requirements to be found and executed by the test runner, as follows:

1. Tests are placed in the `tests/` subdirectory. Unlike regular module Python code, this directory does not need to be imported into the top level `__init__.py` file. The test-running engine will look for these test directories in modules, and then run them.

2. The test code files should have a name starting with `test_` and should be imported from `tests/__init__.py`. The test code will be in classes derived from one of the several test objects available in the Odoo framework, imported from `odoo.tests.common`. The most frequently used test class is `TransactionCase`. The test objects use the `setUp()` method to initialize the data used by the test cases.

3. Each test case is a method with a name starting with `test_`. For the `TrasactionCase` test object, each test is an independent transaction, running the setup step before, and rolling it back at the end. So, the next step won't see the changes made by the previous test.

Tip

Tests can use demonstration data for an easier setup phase, but this is not a good practice since test cases can then only run in databases with demo data installed. If all the test data is prepared in the test setup, then the test can run in any database, including empty databases or copies of production databases.

We plan for our app to have a `library.book` model. Let's add a simple test to confirm that a new book has been created correctly.

Adding test cases

We will add a simple test to check book creation. For this, we need to add some setup data and add a test case. The test case will just confirm that the `active` field has the expected default value, `True`.

To do this, follow these steps:

1. Add a `tests/__init__.py` file with the following code:

```
from . import test_book
```

2. Then, add the actual test code, available in the `tests/test_book.py` file, as follows:

```
from odoo.tests.common import import TransactionCase


class TestBook(TransactionCase):

    def setUp(self, *args, **kwargs):
        super().setUp(*args, **kwargs)
        self.Book = self.env["library.book"]
        self.book1 = self.Book.create({
            "name": "Odoo Development Essentials",
            "isbn": "879-1-78439-279-6"})


    def test_book_create(self):
        "New Books are active by default"
        self.assertEqual(
            self.book1.active, True
        )
```

The `setUp()` function gets a pointer to the `Book` model object and uses it to create a new book.

The `test_book_create` test case adds a simple test case, checking that the created book has the expected default value for the `active` field. It would make sense for the book to be created in the test case, instead of in the setup method. The reason we chose not to do this is that we want to also use this book for other test cases, and having it created in the setup avoids duplicating that code.

Running tests

Tests are run starting the server with the `--test-enable` option while installing or upgrading the module, as follows:

```
(env15) $ odoo -c ~/work15/library.conf -u library_app \
--test-enable
```

The Odoo server will look for a `tests/` subdirectory in the upgraded modules and will run them. At this point, the tests are expected to throw an error, so you should see ERROR messages related to the tests in the server log. This should change once we add the book model to the module.

Now, we should add tests for the business logic. Ideally, we want every line of code to be covered by at least one test case.

Testing business logic

We plan to have logic checking for a valid ISBN. So, we will add a test case to check that the method correctly validates the ISBN for the *Odoo Development Essentials* first edition book. The check will be implemented by a `_check_isbn()` method, returning `True` or `False`.

In `tests/test_book.py`, add a few more lines of code after the `test_create()` method, as follows:

```
    def test_check_isbn(self):
        "Check valid ISBN"
        self.assertTrue(self.book1._check_isbn)
```

It is recommended to write a different test case for each action to check. Remember that when using the `TransactionCase` test, each test will run independently from the others, and the data created or changed during one test case is rolled back when it ends.

Note that if we run the tests now they should fail, since the tested features have not been implemented yet.

Testing access security

Access security can also be checked to confirm that users have the correct privileges granted.

By default, tests are executed with the Odoo internal user, __system__, which bypasses access security. So, we need to change the user running the tests, to check whether the right access security has been given to them. This is done by modifying the execution environment, self.env, setting the user attribute to the user we want to run the tests with.

We can modify our tests to take this into account. Edit the tests/test_book.py file to add a setUp method, as follows:

```
def setUp(self, *args, **kwargs):
    super().setUp(*args, **kwargs)
    user_admin = self.env.ref("base.user_admin")
    self.env = self.env(user=user_admin)
    self.Book = self.env["library.book"]
    self.book_ode = self.Book.create({
        "name": "Odoo Development Essentials",
        "isbn": "879-1-78439-279-6"})
```

We added two lines to the setUp method. This first one finds the admin user record, using its XML ID. The second line modifies the environment used to run the tests, self.env, changing the active user to the admin user.

No further changes are needed for the tests we already wrote. They will run in the same way, but now using the admin user, because of the modified environment.

The Library app now has a couple of basic tests, but they are failing. Next, we should add the code implementing the features, to make the tests pass.

Step 4 – Implementing the model layer

Models describe and store business object data, such as a **customer relationship management (CRM)** opportunity, sales order, or a partner (customer, supplier, and so on). A **model** describes a list of **fields** and can also have specific business logic attached to it.

Model data structure and attached business logic are described with Python code, using an object class derived from an Odoo template class. A model maps to a database table, and the Odoo framework takes care of all the database interactions, both in keeping the database structure in sync with the object and in translating all transactions to database instructions. The framework component responsible for this is the **object-relational mapping** (**ORM**) component.

Our application will be used to manage a library, and we need a model for the book catalog.

Creating a data model

Following the Odoo development guidelines, the Python files for models should be placed inside a `models` subdirectory, and there should be one file for each model. So, we will create a `models/library_book.py` file in the `library_app` module.

> **Tip**
> The Odoo official coding guidelines can be found at `http://www.odoo.com/documentation/15.0/reference/guidelines.html`. Another relevant coding standards document is the **Odoo Community Association** (**OCA**) coding guidelines, which can be found at `https://odoo-community.org/page/contributing`.

The first thing is to have the `models/` directory used by our module. This means that it should be imported by Python when the module is loaded by Odoo. For this, edit the module's main `__init__.py` file so that it contains this line:

```
from . import models
```

Similarly, the `models/` subdirectory should contain an `__init__.py` file importing the code file to use. Add a `models/__init__.py` file containing the following code:

```
from . import library_book
```

Next, we can create a `models/library_book.py` file with the following content:

```
from odoo import fields, models


class Book(models.Model):
    _name = "library.book"
    _description = "Book"
    name = fields.Char("Title", required=True)
```

```
isbn = fields.Char("ISBN")
active = fields.Boolean("Active?", default=True)
date_published = fields.Date()
image = fields.Binary("Cover")
publisher_id = fields.Many2one("res.partner",
    string="Publisher")
author_ids = fields.Many2many("res.partner",
    string="Authors")
```

The first line is a Python code `import` statement, to make the `models` and `fields` Odoo core objects available.

The second line declares the new `library.book` model. This is a Python class derived from `models.Model`.

The next lines are indented. Python code blocks are defined by indentation levels, so this means that these next lines are part of the `Book` class definition. The class name uses CamelCase, as that is the usual convention for Python. The actual Python class name used is irrelevant for the Odoo framework. The model ID relevant for Odoo is the `_name` attribute, declared in the next line.

The two next lines start with an underscore and declare some Odoo class attributes. The `_name` attribute defines the **unique ID (UID)** that will be used throughout Odoo to refer to this model. Model IDs use dots (.) to separate their keywords.

> **Tip**
> Model IDs use dot-separated words. Everything else uses underscores (_):
> addon module names, XML IDs, table names, and so on.

Then, we have the `_description` model attribute. This is a display name for the model records that can be used in some user messages to refer to a record. It is not mandatory but will display a warning message in the server log if it is missing.

The last seven lines declare model fields. We can see a sample of the most frequently used field types. For scalar values, we can see the `Char`, `Boolean`, `Date`, and `Binary` field types being used. For relational fields, we can see `Many2one` and `Many2many`.

The `name` field is used for the data record title—in this case, the book title.

The `active` field is used for active records. By default, only active records are shown, and inactive records are automatically hidden. This is useful on master data models to hide away records that are no longer in use but, for historical reasons, need to be kept in the database.

> **Tip**
>
> `name` and `active` are special field names. By default, the Odoo framework makes special use of them. The `name` field is used by default for the record display name the text shows when a record is referenced from another model. The `active` field is used to filter out inactive records from the UI.

`publisher_id` is a **many-to-one** relation field—in database jargon, a **foreign key** (**FK**). It stores a link to a record in another model—the `res.partner` partner model in this case. It is used to reference the publishing company. The convention is for many-to-one field names to end with `_id`.

`author_ids` is a **many-to-many** relation field. It can store links to one or more records in another model. It is used for the book authors and can reference several records in the `res.partner` partner model. At the database level, this data is not actually stored in a table field but in a helper table, automatically created to store the relations between records in the two tables. The convention is for to-many field names to end with `_ids`.

These are two different relations, both between the book and the partner models. The partner model is built into the Odoo framework and is where people, companies, and addresses should be stored. We are using it to store both our publishers and authors.

Now, we make these changes effective in Odoo by upgrading the Library app module. Again, this is the command we can run to update the `library_app` module on the `library` database:

```
(env15)$ odoo -c ~/work15/library.conf -d library \
 -u library_app
```

There are no menu items yet to access the book model. These will be added later in the chapter. Still, to inspect the newly created model and confirm it was properly created in the database, we can use the **Technical** menu. In the **Settings** top menu, go to **Technical | Database Structure | Models**, search the list for the `library.book` model and click on it to see its definition, as illustrated in the following screenshot:

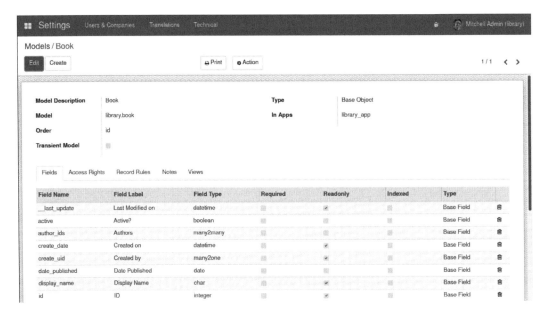

Figure 3.4 – The library.book model view in the Technical menu

We should be able to see the model listed, and confirm that it contains the fields we defined in the Python file. If you can't see this, try again a server restart with a module upgrade, and pay close attention to the server log, looking for the messages loading the Library app, and for any warnings reporting issues with the Odoo database.

On the `library.book` field list, we can see some additional fields that we didn't declare. These are special fields that Odoo automatically adds to every model. They are listed as follows:

- `id` is a unique numeric database ID for each record.
- `create_date` and `create_uid` are the record creation timestamp and the user who created the record.

- `display_name` provides a textual representation for the record used—for example, when it is referenced in other records. It is a computed field and, by default, just uses the text in the `name` field, if available.

- `write_date` and `write_uid` are the record's last modification timestamp and the user who did that update.

- `__last_update` is a computed field not stored in the database and is used for concurrency checks.

The book model is now created in the database, but it is not yet available to users. We need a menu item for that, but that won't be enough. For the menu item to be visible, users first need to be granted access to the new model.

Step 5 – Setting up access security

The `library.book` model was created as the database, but you might have noticed that when it is loaded, it prints this warning message to the server log:

```
The model library.book has no access rules, consider adding
one.
```

The message is pretty clear—the new model has no access rules, and so it can't be used by anyone yet. Earlier, we created the security groups for this app, and we now need to give them access to the app's models.

Changes in Odoo 12

The `admin` user follows access security rules, just as with any other user, except for the root-like internal superuser. We need to grant it access to new models before it can use them. This was not the case up to Odoo 11. In these earlier Odoo versions, the `admin` user was also the internal superuser and bypassed access security rules. This means that newly created models were automatically available and usable to it.

Adding access control security

To get a picture of what information is needed to add access rules to a model, on the web client, navigate to **Settings | Technical | Security | Access Rights**, as illustrated in the following screenshot:

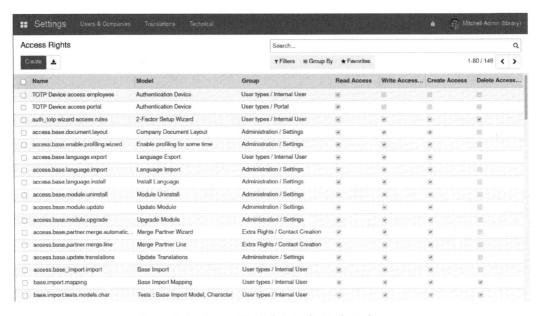

Figure 3.5 – Access Rights list, in the Technical menu

These access rights are also referred to as an **access control list** or **ACL**. In the previous screenshot, we can see the ACL for some models. It indicates, for a security group, what kinds of actions are allowed on records: read, write, create, and delete.

Changes in Odoo 14

Transient models, used for interactive wizards, now also need to be provided access rights to user groups. In previous Odoo versions, this was not so, and users had access to these models by default. The recommendation is to grant read, write and create rights and not grant delete/unlink rights (1, 1, 1, 0 on CSV files).

For the Library app, we will grant library users access to read, write, and create book records, and grant full access to library managers, including deleting records.

This data can be provided by a module data file, loading records into the `ir.model.access` model. The filename for CSV data files must match the model ID we are loading data into.

So we should add the `security/ir.model.access.csv` file, with the following content:

```
id,name,model_id:id,group_id:id,perm_read,perm_write,perm_
create,perm_unlink
access_book_user,BookUser,model_library_book,library_group_
user,1,1,1,0
access_book_manager,BookManager,model_library_book,library_
group_manager,1,1,1,1
```

The first line of the file has the field names. These are the columns provided in our CSV file:

- `id` is the record's external ID (also known as XML ID). It should be unique in our module.

- `name` is a descriptive title. It is informative and it is recommended for it to be unique.

- `model_id` is the external ID for the model we are giving access to. Models have XML IDs automatically generated by the ORM; for `library.book`, the ID is `model_library_book`.

- `group_id` identifies the security group to give permissions to. We grant access to the security groups created before: `library_group_user` and `library_group_manager`.

- The `perm_...` fields grant access to the `read`, `write`, `create`, or `unlink` (delete) operations. We used `1` for yes/`true` and `0` for no/`false`.

We must not forget to reference this new file in the `data` key in the `__manifest__.py` file. It should look like this:

```
    "data": [
        "security/library_security.xml",
        "security/ir.model.access.csv",
        "views/library_menu.xml",
    ],
```

As before, upgrade the module to make these changes effective in the Odoo database. The warning message should be gone.

At this point, the books model is available and should be accessible to the admin user. So, the first of our tests should be passing. Let's run it now, as follows:

```
(env15) $ odoo -c ~/work15/library.conf -u library_app --test-
enable
```

We should see one test pass and one test fail.

The ACL **Access Rights** option grants permissions at the model level, but Odoo also supports row-level access security, through **Record Rules**. This feature is explained in the following section.

Row-level access rules

Record rules define filters limiting the records a security group can access. For example, a salesperson could be limited to seeing only their own quotations, or an accounting user could be limited to seeing only accounting entries for the company they were given access to.

To showcase this feature, we will limit library users to not be able to see inactive books. It is true that by default these are hidden, but they are still accessible if we filter the records with an active equals True condition.

Record Rules can be found in the **Technical** menu, alongside the **Access Rights** option. They are stored in the ir.rule model.

Record rule definition fields needed are outlined here:

- name: A distinctive title, preferably unique.
- model_id: A reference to the model that the rule applies to.
- groups: A reference to the security group the rule applies to. This field is optional, and if not set it is considered a global rule (the global field is automatically set to True). Global rules behave differently—they impose restrictions that non-global rules can't override. It uses a specific syntax to write on to-many fields.
- domain_force: The domain filter to use for the access restriction, using a list of tuples syntax for filter expressions used by Odoo.

To add a record rule to the Library app, edit the security/library_security.xml file to add a second <data> section, just before the </odoo> final tag, as follows:

```
<data noupdate="1">
    <record id="book_user_rule" model="ir.rule">
        <field name="name">Library Book User Access</field>
        <field name="model_id" ref="model_library_book"/>
```

```
<field name="domain_force">
    [('active', '=', True)]
</field>
<field name="groups" eval="[(4,
    ref('library_group_user'))]"/>
</record>
</data>
```

The record rule is inside a `<data noupdate="1">` element, meaning that those records will be created on module install but won't be rewritten on module updates. The point is to allow these rules to be later customized without the risk of those customizations having a module upgrade.

> **Tip**
>
> While developing, `noupdate="1"` data sections can be a nuisance since later fixes and changes won't be updated on module upgrade. There are two ways to work around this. One is to temporarily work with `noupdate="0"` during development, and change it to the final `noupdate="1"` when you're finished. The second way is to reinstall the module instead of upgrading. This is possible in the command line, using `-i` instead of `-u` on an already installed module.

The `groups` field is a many-to-many relation and uses a special syntax needed for the to-many fields. It is a list of tuples, where each tuple is a command. In this case, a `(4, x)` command was used, and the code 4 means that the record referenced next is to be appended to the values. The referenced record is `library_group_user`, the Library user group. The to-many field write syntax is discussed in more detail in *Chapter 6, Models – Structuring the Application Data*.

The domain expression also uses a special syntax, with a list of triples, each specifying a filter condition. The domain filter syntax is explained in *Chapter 7, Recordsets — Working with Model Data*.

Now that users can access the book model, we can go ahead with adding the UI, starting with the menu items.

Step 6 – Implementing the backend view layer

The view layer describes the UI. Views are defined using XML, which is used by the web client framework to dynamically generate data-aware HTML views.

Menu items can execute **window actions** to render **views**. For example, the **Users** menu item processes a window action, also called **Users**, that in turn renders a **view** composition, with a **list** and a **form**.

Several view types are available. The three most commonly used views are the **List** (sometimes called **tree** for historical reasons), the **Form**, and the **Search** options available in the top-right search box.

Throughout the next sections, we will make gradual improvements and will need frequent module upgrades to make them available, or we can use the --dev=all server option, which spares us from module upgrades while developing. Using it, the view definitions are read directly from the XML files, and the changes made are immediately available to Odoo without the need for a module upgrade. In *Chapter 2, Preparing the Development Environment*, more details are given on the --dev server option.

> **Tip**
>
> If a module upgrade fails because of an XML error, don't panic! Carefully read the error message in the server log. It should point you to where the problem is. If you feel in trouble, just comment out the last edited XML portions or remove the XML file from __manifest__.py and repeat the upgrade. The server should then start correctly.

Following the Odoo development guidelines, the XML files for the UI should be inside a views/ subdirectory.

Let's start creating a UI for our to-do application.

Adding menu items

The Library app now has the model to store book data, and we want to have it available on the UI. The first thing to do is add the corresponding menu options.

Edit the views/library_menu.xml file and add the records for the window action and the menu item for the books model, as follows:

```xml
<!-- Action to open the Book list -->
<record id="action_library_book" model=
    "ir.actions.act_window">
    <field name="name">Library Books</field>
```

```
    <field name="res_model">library.book</field>
    <field name="view_mode">tree,form</field>
  </record>
  <!-- Menu item to open the Book list -->
  <menuitem id="menu_library_book"
    name="Books"
    parent="menu_library"
    action="action_library_book"
  />
```

This data file describes two records to add to Odoo, as follows:

- The <record> element defines a client-side window action, to open the library.book model with the tree and form views enabled, in that order.

- The <menuitem> for Books, running the action_library_book action, defined before.

Upgrading the Library app now will make these changes available. A browser page reload might be needed to see the new menu items. Once this is done, the **Library** top menu should be available in Odoo, having a **Books** submenu option.

Even though we haven't defined our UI view, Odoo provides automatically generated views, allowing us to start browsing and editing data right away.

Clicking on the **Library | Books** menu item will display a basic list view, and clicking on the **Create** button will show a form like this:

Figure 3.6 – Automatically generated form view for Library Books

Odoo provides automatically generated views for us, but they're not that great. We might take this into our own hands and create our views, starting with the book form view.

Creating a form view

Views are data records stored in the database, in the `ir.ui.view` model. So, we need to add a data file, with a `<record>` element describing the view.

Add this new `views/book_view.xml` file to define the form view:

```
<odoo>
    <record id="view_form_book" model="ir.ui.view">
        <field name="name">Book Form</field>
        <field name="model">library.book</field>
        <field name="arch" type="xml">
            <form string="Book">
                <group>
                    <field name="name" />
                    <field name="author_ids"
                        widget="many2many_tags" />
                    <field name="publisher_id" />
                    <field name="date_published" />
                    <field name="isbn" />
                    <field name="active" />
                    <field name="image" widget="image" />
                </group>
            </form>
        </field>
    </record>
</odoo>
```

The `ir.ui.view` record has a record `id` field that defines an XML ID that can be used for other records to reference it. The view record sets values for three fields: `name`, `model`, and `arch`.

The view is for the `library.book` model and is named `Book Form`. The name is just for information purposes. It does not have to be unique, but it should allow you to easily identify which record it refers to. In fact, the name can be entirely omitted; in that case, it will be automatically generated from the model name and the view type.

The most important field is `arch` as it contains the actual view definition, and this needs closer examination.

The first element of the view definition is the `<form>` tag. It declares the type of view we are defining and the remaining elements that should be contained in it.

Next, we define sections inside the form, using `<group>` elements. These may contain can contain `<field>` elements or other elements, including nested group elements. A group adds an invisible grid with two columns, perfect for fields because, by default, they occupy two columns, one for the label text, and another for the input field.

Our simple form contains a single `<group>` element, and inside it, we added a `<field>` element for each of the fields to be presented. The fields automatically use an appropriate default widget, such as a date selection widget for date fields. In some cases, we might want to use a specific widget, adding the `widget` attribute. That was the case for `author_ids`, using a widget to display the authors as a list of tags, and the `image` field, using a widget appropriate for handling images. A detailed explanation of view elements is provided in *Chapter 10, Backend Views – Designing the User Interface*.

Remember to add this new file to the `data` key in the manifest file; otherwise, our module won't know about it and it won't be loaded. Here's the code you'll need to do this:

```
"data": [
    "security/library_security.xml",
    "security/ir.model.access.csv",
    "views/book_view.xml",
    "views/library_menu.xml",
],
```

The views will usually go after the security files, and before the menu file.

Remember that for the changes to be loaded to our Odoo database, a module upgrade is needed. To see the changes in the web client, the form needs to be reloaded. Either click again on the menu option that opens it or reload the browser page (*F5* in most browsers).

Business document form views

The preceding section provided a basic form view, but we can make some improvements to it. For document models, Odoo has a presentation style that mimics a paper page. This form contains two top elements: a `<header>` element, to contain action buttons, and a `<sheet>` element, to contain data fields.

We can use this and modify the basic `<form>` element defined in the previous section with this one:

```
<form>
  <header>
    <!-- Buttons will go here -->
  </header>
  <sheet>
    <!-- Content goes here: -->
    <group>
      <field name="name" />
      <field name="author_ids" widget="many2many_tags" />
      <field name="publisher_id" />
      <field name="date_published" />
      <field name="isbn" />
      <field name="active" />
      <field name="image" widget="image" />
    </group>
  </sheet>
</form>
```

Forms can feature buttons, used to perform actions. These buttons can run a window action, usually opening another form, or run a Python class method. Buttons can be placed inside a `<header>` section at the top, or anywhere inside a form. Let's see how.

Adding action buttons

We will showcase a button in the header that checks if the book ISBN is valid. The code for this will be in a method of the book model that we will name `button_check_isbn()`.

We haven't added the method, but we can already add the corresponding button to the form, as follows:

```
<header>
  <button name="button_check_isbn" type="object"
          string="Check ISBN" />
</header>
```

The basic attributes of a button are listed as follows:

- string: The UI text to display on the button

- type: The type of action it performs, object or action.

- name: This is the ID of the action that is run. For object, type is the method name; for action, this is the action record ID.

- class: This is an optional attribute to apply CSS styles, as in regular HTML.

Using groups to organize forms

The <group> tag allows us to organize the form content. A <group> element creates an invisible grid with two columns. Field elements added inside it will be vertically stacked, as each field takes up two cells—one for the label and another for the input box. Adding two <group> elements inside a <group> element creates a layout with two columns of fields.

We will use this to organize the book form. We will change the <sheet> content to match this:

```
<sheet>
  <group name="group_top">
    <group name="group_left">
      <field name="name" />
      <field name="author_ids" widget="many2many_tags" />
      <field name="publisher_id" />
      <field name="date_published" />
    </group>
    <group name="group_right">
      <field name="isbn" />
      <field name="active" />
```

```
      <field name="image" widget="image" />
    </group>
  </group>
</sheet>
```

The `<group>` elements used have a `name` attribute assigning an ID to them. This is not required but is advised, since it makes it easier for them to be referenced by extension views.

The complete form view

At this point, the XML definition for the book form view should look like this:

```
<form>
  <header>
    <button name="check_isbn" type="object"
      string="Check ISBN" />
  </header>
  <sheet>
    <group name="group_top">
      <group name="group_left">
        <field name="name" />
        <field name="author_ids" widget="many2many_tags" />
        <field name="publisher_id" />
        <field name="date_published" />
      </group>
      <group name="group_right">
        <field name="isbn" />
        <field name="active" />
        <field name="image" widget="image" />
      </group>
    </group>
  </sheet>
</form>
```

The action buttons don't work yet, since we still need to add their business logic. This will be done later in this chapter.

Adding list and search views

List views are defined using a `<tree>` view type. Their structure is quite straightforward. The `<tree>` top element should include the fields to present as columns.

We can add the following `<tree>` view definition to `book_view.xml`:

```xml
<record id="view_tree_book" model="ir.ui.view">
  <field name="name">Book List</field>
  <field name="model">library.book</field>
  <field name="arch" type="xml">
    <tree>
      <field name="name"/>
      <field name="author_ids" widget="many2many_tags" />
      <field name="publisher_id"/>
      <field name="date_published"/>
    </tree>
  </field>
</record>
```

This defines a list with four columns: `name`, `author_ids`, `publisher_id`, and `date_published`.

At the top-right corner of the list, Odoo displays a search box. The fields it searches in and the available filters are defined by a `<search>` view.

As before, we will add this to `book_view.xml`, as follows:

```xml
<record id="view_search_book" model="ir.ui.view">
  <field name="name">Book Filters</field>
  <field name="model">library.book</field>
  <field name="arch" type="xml">
    <search>
      <field name="publisher_id"/>
      <filter name="filter_inactive"
              string="Inactive"
              domain="[('active','=',True)]"/>
      <filter name="filter_active"
              string="Active"
```

```
                    domain="[('active','=',False)]"/>
        </search>
    </field>
</record>
```

This search view is using two different elements, `<field>` and `<filter>`.

The `<field>` elements define fields that are automatically searched when the user is typing in the search box. We added `publisher_id` to automatically show search results for the publisher field. The `<filter>` elements add predefined filter conditions, which can be toggled with a user click. The filter condition uses the Odoo domain filter syntax. Domain filters are addressed in more detail in *Chapter 10, Backend Views — Designing the User Interface*.

> **Changes in Odoo 12**
>
> `<filter>` elements are now required to have a `name="..."` attribute, uniquely identifying each filter definition. If it's missing, the XML validation will fail and the module will not install or upgrade.

We now have the Library app's basic components in place—the model and the view layers. Next, we add the business logic layer, adding the code that will make the **Check ISBN** button work.

Step 7 – Implementing the business logic layer

The business logic layer supports the application's business rules, such as validations and automation. We will now add the logic for the **Check ISBN** button. This is done using Python code, adding a method to the Python class representing the `library.book` model.

Adding business logic

Modern ISBNs have 13 digits, the last of which is a check digit computed from the first 12. If `digits` contains the first 12 digits, this Python code returns the corresponding check digit:

```
ponderations = [1, 3] * 6
terms = [a * b for a, b in zip(digits, ponderations)]
remain = sum(terms) % 10
check = 10 - remain if remain != 0 else 0
return digits[-1]
```

The preceding code, with some adjustments, will be at the heart of our validation function. It should be a method in the class Book(...) object. We will add a method that checks a record's ISBN and returns True or False, as follows:

```
def _check_isbn(self):
    self.ensure_one()
    digits = [int(x) for x in self.isbn if x.isdigit()]
    if len(digits) == 13:
        ponderations = [1, 3] * 6
        terms = [a * b for a, b in zip(digits[:12],
            ponderations)]
        remain = sum(terms) % 10
        check = 10 - remain if remain != 0 else 0
        return digits[-1] == check
```

Note that this method is not directly usable from the **Form** button, because it doesn't provide any visual cue of the result. Next, we will add a second method for that.

Changes in Odoo 13

The @api.multi decorator was removed from the Odoo **application programming interface** (**API**) and can't be used. Note that for previous Odoo versions, this decorator was available, but not necessary. Adding it or not would have the exact same effect.

To report validation issues to the user, we will use the Odoo ValidationError exception, so the first thing to do is to make it available by importing it. Edit the models/library_book.py Python file to add this at the top of the file, as follows:

```
from odoo.exceptions import ValidationError
```

Next, still in the models/library_book.py file, add the following code to the Book class:

```
def button_check_isbn(self):
    for book in self:
        if not book.isbn:
            raise ValidationError("Please provide an ISBN
                for %s" % book.name)
```

```
        if book.isbn and not book._check_isbn():
            raise ValidationError("%s ISBN is invalid" %
                book.isbn)
    return True
```

Here, `self` represents a recordset, and we can loop through each record and perform a check on each.

This method is used in a **Form** button, so it would be reasonable to expect `self` to be a single record and have no need to use the `for` loop. In fact, we did something similar with the `_check_isbn()` helper method. If you're going this way, it is recommended to add `self.ensure_one()` at the beginning of the method, to fail early if for some reason `self` is not a single record.

But we chose to use a `for` loop to support multiple records, making our code capable of performing mass validations if we want to have that feature later on.

The code loops through all the selected book task records and, for each one, if the book ISBN has a value, it checks if it is valid. If not, a warning message is raised for the user.

The `Model` method does not need to return anything, but we should have it at least return a `True` value. The reason is that not all client implementations of the XML-**Remote Procedure Call** (**RPC**) protocol support None/Null values, and may raise errors when such a value is returned by a method.

This is a good moment to upgrade the module and run the tests again, adding the `--test-enable` option to confirm that tests are now passing. You can also try it live, going into a book form and trying the button with both correct and incorrect ISBNs.

The Library app has all the backend features we wanted to add for its first iteration, and we implemented the Odoo components at the several layers: model, view, and business logic. But Odoo also supports creating external-facing web pages. In the next section, we will create our first Odoo website page.

Step 8 – Implementing the website UI

Odoo also provides a web development framework, to develop website features closely integrated with the backend apps. We will take our first steps toward this by creating a simple web page to display a list of active books in our library.

The book catalog page will respond to web requests at the `http://my-server/library/books` address, so `/library/books` is the URL endpoint we want to implement.

Web **controllers** are the components responsible for rendering web pages. A controller is a Python method in an `http.Controller` derived class. The method is bound to one or more URL endpoints using the `@http.route` controller. When any of these URL endpoints are accessed, the controller code executes and returns the HTML to be presented to the user. The HTML rendering will usually be done using the QWeb templating engine.

Adding the endpoint controller

Code for controllers is expected to be inside a `/controllers` subdirectory. To add a controller, first edit the `library_app/__init__.py` file to have it also import the `controllers` subdirectory, as follows:

```
from . import models
from . import controllers
```

Then, add a `library_app/controllers/__init__.py` file so that this directory can be Python-imported, and add an `import` statement to it for the `main.py` Python file we will implement the controller with, as follows:

```
from . import main
```

Now, add the actual file for the controller, `library_app/controllers/main.py`, with the following code:

```python
from odoo import http


class Books(http.Controller):

    @http.route("/library/books")
    def list(self, **kwargs):
        Book = http.request.env["library.book"]
        books = Book.search([])
        return http.request.render(
            "library_app.book_list_template",
            {"book"': books}
        )
```

The first line imports the `odoo.http` module, the core framework component providing web-related features. Next, we create a controller object class, derived from `http.Controller`.

The particular ID name we choose for the class and for its methods is not relevant. The @http.route decorator is important since it declares the URL endpoint to be bound—/books in this case. For now, the web page is using the default access control and requires a user login.

Inside the controller method, we can access the run environment using http.request.env. We use it to get a recordset with all active books in the catalog.

The final step is to use http.request.render() to process the library_app.index_template QWeb template and generate the output HTML. We can make values available to the template through a dictionary, and this was used to pass the books recordset.

If we now restart the Odoo server to reload the Python code and try accessing the /library/books URL, we should get an error message in the server log: ValueError: External ID not found in the system: library_app.book_list_template. This is expected since we haven't defined that template yet. That should be our next step.

Adding a QWeb template

QWeb templates are also stored along with the other Odoo views, and the corresponding data files are usually stored in the /views subdirectory. Let's add the views/book_list_template.xml file, as follows:

```xml
<odoo>


<template id="book_list_template" name="Book List">
  <div id="wrap" class="container">
    <h1>Books</h1>
      <t t-foreach="books" t-as="book">
        <div class="row">
          <span t-field="book.name" />,
          <span t-field="book.date_published" />,
          <span t-field="book.publisher_id" />
        </div>
      </t>
  </div>
</template>


</odoo>
```

The `<template>` element declares a QWeb template. In fact, it is a shortcut for an `ir.ui.view` record, the base model where templates are stored. The template contains the HTML to use and uses QWeb-specific tags and attributes.

The `t-foreach` attribute is used to loop through the items in the `books` variable that was made available to the template by the controller's `http.request.render()` call. The `t-field` attribute takes care of properly rendering the content of an Odoo record field.

The QWeb template data file needs to be declared in the module manifest, as with any other XML data file, so that it gets loaded and can be made available. So, the __ manifest__.py file should be edited to add it, as shown next:

```
"data": [
    "security/library_security.xml",
    "security/ir.model.access.csv",
    "views/book_view.xml",
    "views/library_menu.xml",
    "views/book_list_template.xml",
],
```

After declaring the XML file in the manifest and performing a module upgrade, the web page should be working. Opening the `http://<my-server>:8069/library/books` URL with an active Odoo login should show us a simple list of the available books, as shown in the next screenshot:

Figure 3.7 – Web page with a book list

This is a short overview of the Odoo web page features. These features are discussed in more depth in *Chapter 13, Creating Web and Portal Frontend Features*.

Quick reference

Most of the components are discussed in more detail in other chapters, and quick references are provided there, as follows:

- *Chapter 2*, *Preparing the Development Environment*, for the CLI `install` and `upgrade` modules

- *Chapter 5*, *Importing, Exporting, and Module Data*, for creating XML and CSV data files

- *Chapter 6*, *Models – Structuring the Application Data*, for the model layer, defining models and fields

- *Chapter 7*, *Recordsets – Working with Model Data*, for domain filter syntax and recordset manipulation

- *Chapter 8*, *Business Logic – Supporting Business Processes*, for Python method business logic

- *Chapter 10*, *Backend Views – Designing the User Interface*, for views, including window actions, menu items, forms, lists, and searches

- *Chapter 13*, *Creating Web and Portal Frontend Features*, for web controllers and QWeb syntax

Not explained further elsewhere is access security, and we provide here a quick reference for those components.

Access security

Internal system models are listed here:

- `res.groups`: **groups**—relevant fields: `name`, `implied_ids`, `users`

- `res.users`: **users**—relevant fields: `name`, `groups_id`

- `ir.model.access`: **Access Control**—relevant fields: `name`, `model_id`, `group_id`, `perm_read`, `perm_write`, `perm_create`, `perm_unlink`

- `ir.access.rule`: **Record Rules**—relevant fields: `name`, `model_id`, `groups`, `domain_force`

XML IDs for the most relevant security groups are listed here:

- `base.group_user`: **internal user**—any backend user
- `base.group_system`: **Settings**—the Administrator belongs to this group
- `base.group_no_one`: **technical feature**, usually used to make features not visible to users
- `base.group_public`: **Public**, used to make features accessible to web anonymous users

XML IDs for the default users provided by Odoo are listed here:

- `base.user_root`: The root system superuser, also known as `OdooBot`.
- `base.user_admin`: The default user, by default named `Administrator`.
- `base.default_user`: The template used for new backend users. It is a template and is inactive, but can be duplicated to create new users.
- `base.default_public user`: The template used to create new portal users.

Summary

We created a new module from scratch, covering the essential components involved in a module—models, access security, menus, the three basic types of views (form, list, and search), and business logic in model methods. We also learned how to create web pages using web controllers and QWeb templates.

In the process, we got familiar with the module-development process, which involves module upgrades and application-server restarts to make gradual changes effective in Odoo.

Always remember, when adding model fields, an upgrade is needed. When changing Python code, including the manifest file, a restart is needed. When changing XML or CSV files, an upgrade is needed; also, when in doubt, do both: restart the server and upgrade the modules.

We've gone through the essential elements and steps to create a new Odoo app. But in most cases, our modules will be extending existing apps to add features. This is what we will learn about in the next chapter.

Further reading

All of the Odoo-specific topics presented here will be covered in more depth in the remaining chapters of this book.

The official documentation offers some relevant resources that make good complementary reading, as listed here:

- The *Building a Module* tutorial: `https://www.odoo.com/documentation/15.0/howtos/backend.html`

- The *Odoo Guidelines* provide a list of code conventions and guidelines for module development: `https://www.odoo.com/documentation/15.0/reference/guidelines.html`

- The *Odoo Community Association Guidelines* provide a good resource for Odoo development best practices: `https://odoo-community.org/page/contributing`

Learning Python is important for Odoo development. There are some good Python books from the *Packt* catalog, such as *Learn Python Programming – Second Edition*: `https://www.packtpub.com/application-development/learn-python-programming-second-edition`.

4
Extending Modules

One of Odoo's most powerful capabilities is being able to add features without directly touching the code of the extended modules. This allows for clean feature extensions that are isolated in their own code components. Extending modules can be achieved through inheritance mechanisms, which work as modification layers on top of existing objects. These modifications can happen at every level – including the model, view, and business logic levels. Instead of directly modifying an existing module, we will create a new module by adding a layer on top of the existing one with the intended modifications.

The previous chapter guided us through creating a new app from scratch. In this chapter, we will learn how to create modules that extend existing apps or modules and use existing core or community features.

To achieve this, we will cover the following topics:

- Learning project – extending the Library app
- Adding a new field to an existing model
- Extending models using classic in-place extension
- More model inheritance mechanisms
- Extending views and data
- Extending web pages

By the end of this chapter, you should be able to create Odoo modules that extend existing apps. You will be able to add modifications to any of the several application components: models, views, business logic code, web page controllers, and web page templates.

Technical requirements

For this chapter, you will need an Odoo server that you can command from a terminal session.

The code in this chapter depends on the code that we created in *Chapter 3*, *Your First Odoo Application*. You should have that code in your add-ons path and have a database with the `library_app` module installed.

This chapter adds the `library_member` add-on module to our project. The corresponding code can be found in this book's GitHub repository, `https://github.com/PacktPublishing/Odoo-15-Development-Essentials`, in the `ch04` directory.

Learning project – extending the Library app

In *Chapter 3*, *Your First Odoo Application*, we created the initial module for the **Library** app and provided a book catalog. Now, we will extend the application to add library members and allow them to borrow books. For this, we will create an extension module called `library_member`.

These are the features we must provide:

- Library books can be available to be borrowed or not. This information should be shown in the book form and on the website's catalog page.

- Some library member master data, along with the library card number, plus personal data, such as name, address, and email.

- We would like to provide members with the messaging and social features that are available on the borrowing form, including the planned activities widget, to allow for better collaboration.

Later, we plan to introduce a feature that allows members to borrow books from the library, but this is outside our scope for now. This will happen gradually throughout the next few chapters.

Books

The following is a summary of the technical changes we must introduce to books:

- Add an `Is Available?` field. For now, it will be managed manually, but this can be automated later.

- Extend the ISBN validation logic to also support the older 10-digit ISBN format.

- Extend the web catalog page to identify unavailable books and to allow the user to only filter through available books.

Members

The following is a summary of the technical changes to introduce to library members:

- Add a new model to store the person's name, card number, and contact information, such as email and address.

- Add the social discussion and planned activities features.

To start working on this extension module, we should create the `library_member` directory alongside `library_app` and add two files—an empty `__init__.py` file and a `__manifest__.py` file with the following content:

```
{
    "name": "Library Members",
    "license": "AGPL-3",
    "description": "Manage members borrowing books.",
    "author": "Daniel Reis",
    "depends": ["library_app"],
    "application": False,
}
```

Now, we are ready to start working on the features. Our first task is a frequent and simple request – adding a new field to an existing model. This happens to be a great way to introduce Odoo's inheritance mechanisms.

Adding a new field to an existing model

Our first task is to add the `is_available` Boolean field to the book model. For now, this will be a simple editable field, but at a later stage, we can imagine changing it to be automatic, based on books that have been borrowed and returned.

To extend an existing model, we must use a Python class with the `_inherit` attribute, identifying the model being extended. The new class inherits all of the features of the parent Odoo model, and we only need to declare the modifications to introduce. We can think of this type of inheritance as getting a reference for the existing model and making in-place changes to it.

Adding new fields with the in-place model extension

Extending models is done through Python classes by using the Odoo-specific inheritance mechanism that's declared using the `_inherit` class attribute. This `_inherit` class attribute identifies the model to be extended. The declared calls capture all the features of the inherited Odoo model and are ready for the modifications to introduce to be declared.

The coding style guidelines recommend having a Python file for each model, so we will add a `library_member/models/library_book.py` file that extends the original model. Let's start by adding the `__init__.py` code files that are needed for that file to be included in the module:

1. Add the `library_member/__init__.py` file, making the code that's in the `models` subdirectory known:

    ```
    from . import models
    ```

2. Add the `library_member/models/__init__.py` file, importing the used code files inside that subdirectory:

    ```
    from . import library_book
    ```

3. Create the `library_member/models/library_book.py` file by extending the `library.book` model:

    ```
    from odoo import fields, models


    class Book(models.Model):
        _inherit = "library.book"
        is_available = fields.Boolean("Is Available?")
    ```

Here, we used the `_inherit` class attribute to declare the model to extend. Notice that we didn't use any other class attributes, not even `_name`. This is not needed unless we want to make changes to any of them.

> **Tip**
> `_name` is the model identifier; what happens if we try to change it? This is allowed, and doing so creates a new model that is a copy of the inherited one. This is called **prototype inheritance** and it will be discussed later in this chapter, in the *Copying models with prototype inheritance* section.

We can think of this as getting a reference to a model definition living in a central registry and making in-place changes to it. This can include adding fields, modifying existing fields, modifying model class attributes, or adding methods with new business logic.

To add the new model fields to the database tables, we must install the add-on module. If everything goes as expected, the newly added fields should be visible if we go to the **Technical | Database Structure | Models** menu option and inspect the `library.book` model.

Adding a field to the Form view

Forms, lists, and search views are defined using XML data structures. To extend views, we need a way to modify the XML. This means locating XML elements and then introducing modifications at those points.

The XML data record for inherited views is similar to the ones for regular views, with an additional `inherit_id` attribute for referring to the view being extended.

We are going to extend the book view to add the `is_available` field.

The first thing we need to do is find the XML ID for the view to be extended. We can find that by looking up the view in the **Settings** app, in the **Technical | User Interface | Views** menu. The XML ID for the book form is `library_app.view_form_book`.

While we're there, we should also locate the XML element to insert the changes. We will choose to add the `Is Available?` field after the `ISBN` field. The element to use can usually be identified by its `name` attribute. In this case, it's `<field name="isbn" />`.

When adding the XML file to extend the `Partner` views, `views/book_view.xml`, it should have the following content:

```xml
<odoo>
  <record id="view_form_book_extend" model="ir.ui.view">
    <field name="name">Book: add Is Available?
       field</field>
    <field name="model">library.book</field>
    <field name="inherit_id" ref=
      "library_app.view_form_book"/>
    <field name="arch" type="xml">

      <field name="isbn" position="after">
        <field name="is_available" />
      </field>

    </field>
  </record>
</odoo>
```

The inheritance-specific elements are highlighted in the preceding code. The `inherit_id` record field identifies the view to be extended while using the `ref` attribute to refer to its external identifier.

The `arch` field contains the element for declaring the extension point to use, the `<field>` element with `name="isbn"`, and the position of the new elements to add, which is `position="after"` in this case. Inside the extension elements, we have the XML to add, which is the `is_available` field in this case.

This is what the book form will look like after creating this extension:

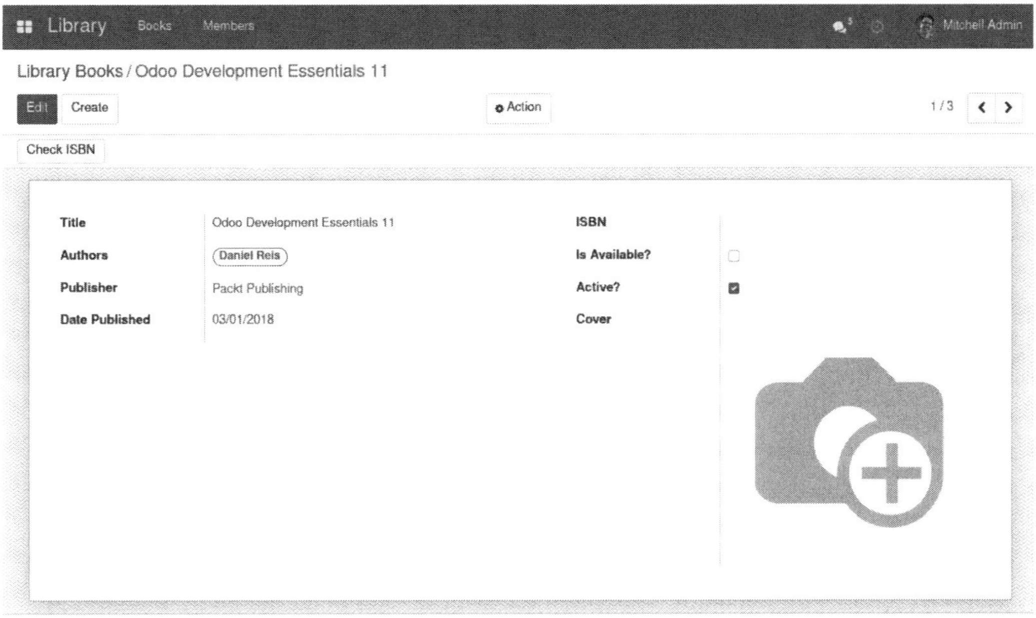

Figure 4.1 – The book form with the "Is Available?" field added

We just went through the inheritance basics and added a new field for the model and view layers. Next, we will learn more about the model extension approach we used; that is, classic inheritance.

Extending models using classic in-place extension

We can think of the classic model inheritance as an in-place extension. When a Python class with the `_inherit` attribute is declared, it gets a reference to the corresponding model definition, to then add extensions to it. The model definition is stored in the Odoo model registry and is available for us to add further modifications to it.

Now, let's learn how to use this for frequent extension use cases: modifying the attributes of an existing field and extending Python methods to add or modify business logic.

Incrementally modifying existing fields

When we're extending a model, existing fields can be modified incrementally. This means that we only need to define the field attributes to change or add.

We will make two changes to the book fields that were created in the library_app module:

- On the isbn field, add a help tooltip explaining that we support both 10- and 13-digit ISBNs, with the latter being implemented in the following section.

- On the publisher_id field, add a database index to it to make searching on it more efficient.

We should edit the library_member/models/library_book.py file and add the following lines to the library.book model:

```
# class Book(models.Model):
    isbn = fields.Char(help="Use a valid ISBN-13 or
        ISBN-10.")
    publisher_id = fields.Many2one(index=True)
```

This modifies the fields with the specified attributes, leaving all the other attributes that were not explicitly mentioned unmodified.

Once we upgrade the module, going to the book form and hovering the mouse pointer over the ISBN field will show the tooltip message that was added to the field. The effect of `index=True` is harder to notice, but it can be seen in the field definition, which can be accessed from the **Developer Tools** menu by choosing the **View Fields** option, or from the **Settings** | **Technical** | **Database Structure** | **Models** menu:

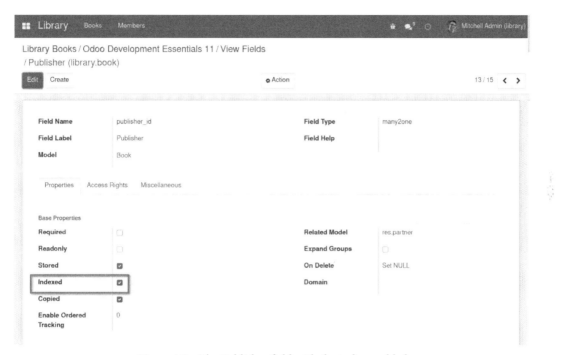

Figure 4.2 – The Publisher field with the index enabled

Extending Python methods to add features to the business logic

The business logic that's coded in Python methods can also be extended. For this, Odoo uses the Python object inheritance mechanism to extend the inherited class behavior.

As a practical example, we will extend the library book ISBN validation logic. The logic provided by the base Library app validates modern 13-digit ISBNs. But some older titles might come with a 10-digit ISBN. The `_check_isbn()` method should be extended to also validate these cases.

Edit the `library_member/models/library_book.py` file by adding the following code:

```python
# class Book(models.Model):

    def _check_isbn(self):
        self.ensure_one()
        digits = [int(x) for x in self.isbn if x.isdigit()]
        if len(digits) == 10:
            ponderators = [1, 2, 3, 4, 5, 6, 7, 8, 9]
            total = sum(
                a * b for a, b in zip(digits[:9],
                ponderators)
            )
            check = total % 11
            return digits[-1] == check
        else:
            return super()._check_isbn()
```

To extend a method, in the inherited class, we define a method with the same name – `_check_isbn()`, in this case. This method should, at some point, use `super()` to call the corresponding method that was implemented in the parent class. In this example, the particular code that was used was `super()._check_isbn()`.

In this method extension, we added our logic before the `super()` call, running the parent class code. It checks whether the ISBN is 10 digits long. In that case, the added ISBN-10 validation logic is executed. Otherwise, it falls back to the original ISBN checking logic, handling the 13-digit case.

We can try this, or even better, write a test case. Here is an example of a 10-digit ISBN: the original ISBN of William Golding's *Lord of the Flies* is 0-571-05686-5.

> **Changes in Odoo 11**
>
> In Odoo 11, the Python version that was used changed from *2.7* to *3.5* or later. Python 3 has breaking changes and is not fully compatible with Python 2. In particular, the `super()` syntax was simplified in Python 3. For previous Odoo versions that use Python 2, `super()` needs two arguments – the class name and `self`; for example, `super(Book, self)._check_isbn()`.

Classic inheritance is the most frequently used extension mechanism. But Odoo provides additional extension approaches that are useful in other cases. We will explore those next.

More model inheritance mechanisms

The previous section discussed **classic inheritance**, which can be seen as an *in-place extension*. This is the most frequently used approach, but the Odoo framework also supports a few other extension mechanisms that are useful in other cases.

These are delegation inheritance, prototype inheritance, and the use of mixins:

- **Delegation inheritance** embeds another model in the inheriting one. For example, a User record embeds a Partner record, so that a User record has all the fields available for the Partner records, plus the fields specific to the User records. It is used through the _inherits attribute.

- **Prototype inheritance** creates a new model by copying the features from the inherited model and has a database table and data. It is not used often and it is never used in the Odoo-included add-on modules. It is used to set _inherit with the model to copy and the _name attribute with the identifier for the new model to be created.

- **Mixin classes** are abstract models that implement generic features that are to be reused in other models. They are like feature containers, ready to be added to other models, and are not expected to be used alone. An example is the mail.thread model, which is provided by the mail add-on module. It implements the chatter and messaging features that are available in several models throughout Odoo, such as *Partners* and *Sales Quotations*. A mixin class is constructed from Models. abstract, instead of Models.model, and is used with _inherit.

The next few sections explore these possibilities in more detail.

Embedding models using delegation inheritance

Delegation inheritance allows us to reuse data structures, without duplication in the database. It embeds an instance of the delegated model inside the inheriting model.

> **Note**
> To be technically precise, delegation inheritance is not real object inheritance; instead, it is object composition, where some features of an object are delegated to, or provided by, a second object.

Note the following about delegation:

- Creating a new model record also creates and links a delegated model record.
- Fields from the delegated model that don't exist in the inheriting model are available for read and write operations, behaving like related computed fields.

For example, for the User model, each record contains a Partner record, so the fields you find on a Partner will be available, plus a few fields that are specific to users.

For the Library project, we want to add a **Library Members** model. Members will be able to borrow books and have a library card to be used when borrowing. Member master data should include the card number, plus some personal information, such as email and address. The Partner model already supports contact and address information, so it's best to reuse it, rather than duplicating the data structures.

To add the Partner fields to the Library Member model using delegation inheritance, follow these steps:

1. The Python file that will be used to implement inheritance must be imported. Edit `library_member/model/__init__.py` by adding the following highlighted line:

```
from . import library_book
from . import library_member
```

2. Next, add the Python file describing the new Library Member model, `library_member/models/library_member.py`, which contains the following code:

```
from odoo import fields, models


class Member(models.Model):
    _name = "library.member"
    _description = "Library Member"

    card_number = fields.Char()
    partner_id = fields.Many2one(
        "res.partner",
        delegate=True,
        ondelete="cascade",
        required=True)
```

With delegation inheritance, the `library.member` model embeds the inherited model, `res.partner`, so that when a new Member record is created, a related Partner is automatically created and referenced in the `partner_id` field.

Through the delegation mechanism, all the fields of the embedded model are automatically made available as if they were fields of the parent model fields. In this case, the Library Member model has all of the Partner fields available for use, such as `name`, `address`, and `email`, plus the ones specific to members, such as `card_ number`. Behind the scenes, the Partner fields are stored in the linked Partner record, and no data structure duplication occurs.

Delegation inheritance works only at the data level, not at the logic level. No methods from the inherited model are inherited. They are still accessible using the **dot operator**, which is used to access an object's attributes, also known as **dot notation**. For example, for the Library Member model, `partner_id.open_ parent()` runs the `open_parent()` method of the embedded Partner record.

There is an alternative syntax for delegation inheritance that's available through the `_inherits` model attribute. It comes from the pre-Odoo 8 old API, and it is still widely used. The Library Model example with the same effect as earlier looks like this:

```
from odoo import fields, models


class Member(models.Model):
    _name = "library.member"
    _description = "Library Member"
    _inherits = {"res.partner": "partner_id"}

    card_number = fields.Char()
    partner_id = fields.Many2one(
        "res.partner",
        ondelete="cascade",
        required=True)
```

To finish adding this new model, a few additional steps are needed – add the security ACLs, a menu item, and some view3.

3. To add the security ACLs, create the `library_member/security/ir.model.access.csv` file with this content:

```
id,name,model_id:id,group_id:id,perm_read,perm_
write,perm_create,perm_unlink
access_member_user,Member User Access,model_library_
member,library_app.library_group_user,1,1,1,0
access_member_manager,Member Manager Access,model_
library_member,library_app.library_group_manager,1,1,1,4
```

4. To add the menu item, create the `library_member/views/library_menu.xml` file with the following code:

```
<odoo>
    <act_window id="action_library_member"
      name="Library Members"
      res_model="library.member"
      view_mode="tree,form" />
    <menuitem id="menu_library_member"
      name="Members"
      action="action_library_member"
      parent="library_app.menu_library" />
</odoo5
```

5. To add the views, create the `library_member/views/member_view.xml` file with the following code:

```
<odoo>
  <record id="view_form_member" model="ir.ui.view">
    <field name="name">Library Member Form
      View</field>
    <field name="model">library.member</field>
    <field name="arch" type="xml">
      <form>
        <group>
          <field name="name" />
          <field name="email" />
          <field name="card_number" />
        </group>
      </form>
```

```
        </field>
    </record>

    <record id="view_tree_member" model="ir.ui.view">
        <field name="name">Library Member List
          View</field>
        <field name="model">library.member</field>
        <field name="arch" type="xml">
          <tree>
              <field name="name" />
              <field name="card_number" />
          </tree>
        </field>
    </record>
</odoo6
```

6. Finally, we should edit the manifest to declare these three new files:

```
"data": [
    "security/ir.model.access.csv",
    "views/book_view.xml",
    "views/member_view.xml",
    "views/library_menu.xml",
],
```

If everything was entered correctly, after a module upgrade, we should be able to work with the new Library Member model.

Copying models with prototype inheritance

Classic inheritance uses the _inherit attribute to extend a model. Since the _name attribute is not modified, it effectively performs an in-place modification on the same model.

If the _name attribute is also modified, along with _inherit, we get a new model that is a copy of the inherited one. This new model can then have features added to it that are specific to it and won't be added to the parent model. The copied model is independent of the parent model, which will be unaffected by its modifications. It has its own database table and data. The official documentation calls this **prototype inheritance**.

In practice, there is little benefit in using _inherit to copy a model. Instead, delegation inheritance is preferred, since it reuses data structures without duplicating them.

Things become more interesting when we use inheritance from multiple parents. For this, _inherit will be a list of model names, instead of a single name.

This can be used to mix several models into one. It allows us to have a model proposing features to be reused several times. This pattern is widely used with abstract mixin classes. This will be discussed in detail in the next section.

Reusing model features using mixin classes

Setting the _inherit attribute with a list of model names will inherit the features from those models. Most of the time, this is done to leverage mixin classes.

A **mixin class** is like a container of features, meant to be reused. They implement generic features, ready to be added to other models. They are not expected to stand alone and be used directly. So, they are abstract models, based on models.AbstractModel, with no actual representation in the database, instead of models.Model.

The Odoo standard add-ons propose several useful mixins. Searching the code for models.AbstractModel will reveal them. What's noteworthy, and probably the two most widely used, are these mixins, which are provided by the Discuss app (the mail add-on module):

- The mail.thread mixin provides features for the message board, also known as **chatter**, which can be found at the bottom or right-hand side of many document forms, along with the logic regarding messages and notifications.

- The mail.activity.mixin mixin provides *activities*, which are also exposed through the chatter discussion widget, to define and plan to-do tasks.

> **Changes in Odoo 11**
>
> The *activities* mixin is a new feature that was introduced in Odoo 11 and is not available in earlier versions.

Chatter and activities are widely used features, and in the next section, we will take a moment to demonstrate how to add them.

Adding message chatter and activities to a model

We will now add the message chatter and activity mixins to the **Library Members** model. This is what is needed to add them:

1. Add the dependency to the add-on module that's providing the mixin models; that is, `mail`.

2. Inherit the `mail.thread` and `mail.activity.mixin` mixin classes.

3. Add fields to the `Form` view.

Let's check the preceding steps in detail:

1. To add the dependency to the `mail` add-on, edit the `__manifest__.py` file:

   ```
   "depends": ["library_app", "mail"],
   ```

2. To inherit the mixin classes, edit the `library_member/models/library_member.py` file to add the following highlighted text:

   ```
   class Member(models.Model):
       _name = "library.member"
       _description = "Library Member"
       _inherits = {"res.partner": "partner_id"}
       _inherit = ["mail.thread", "mail.activity.mixin"]
   ```

   With this extra line of code, our model will include all the additional fields and methods provided by these mixins.

   > **Tip**
   >
   > In this example, the mixins are being added to a new model that is being created now. If we were adding these mixins to an already existing model, which had been created in another module, then the parent model should also be included in the inherited list; for example,
   >
   > `_inherit = ["library.member", "mail.thread", "mail.activity.mixin"].`

3. Finally, we must add the relevant fields to Library Member Form. Edit the library_member/views/member_view.xml file by adding the following highlighted code:

```xml
<record id="view_form_member" model="ir.ui.view">
    <field name="name">Library Member Form
    View</field>
    <field name="model">library.member</field>
    <field name="arch" type="xml">
        <form>
            <group>
                <field name="name" />
                <field name="email" />
                <field name="card_number" />
            </group>
            <!-- mail mixin fields -->
            <div class="oe_chatter">
                <field name="message_follower_ids"
                        widget="mail_followers"/>
                <field name="activity_ids"
                        widget="mail_activity"/>
                <field name="message_ids"
                        widget="mail_thread"/>
            </div>
        </form>
    </field>
</record>
```

As we can see, the mail module not only provides fields for the followers, activities, and messages, but it also provides specific web client widgets for them, all of which are being used here.

Once the module has been upgraded, the **Library Members** form should look like this:

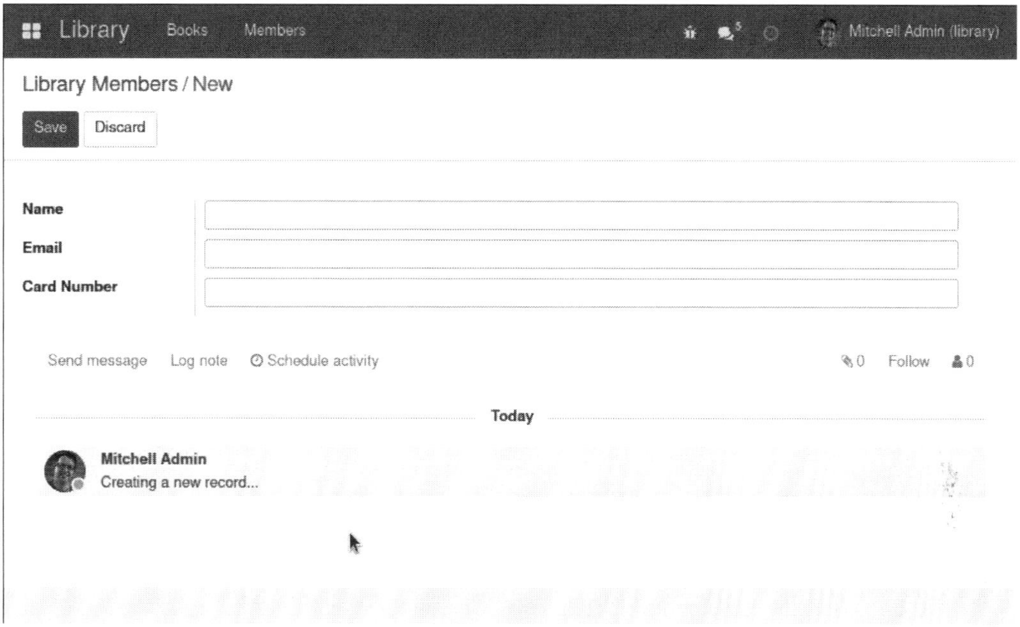

Figure 4.3 – The Library Members form view

Note that the mixins alone don't cause any changes to be made to access security, including record rules. In some cases, there are record rules in place, limiting what records are accessible to each user. For example, if we want users to only view records they are followers of, a record rule for that must be explicitly added.

The `mail.thread` model includes a field for listing the follower **Partners**, called `message_partner_ids`. To implement the followers' access rules, a **record rule** should be added, with a **domain** expression including a condition similar to `[('message_partner_ids', 'in', [user.partner_id.id])]`.

With that, we've seen how to extend modules at the model and logic layers. The next step is to extend the views to reflect the changes that were made in the model layer.

Extending views and data

Views and other data components can also be modified by an extension module. For views, the case is usually to add features. The view presentation structure is defined with XML. To extend this XML, we must locate the node to extend and then declare the action to perform there, such as inserting additional XML elements.

The other data elements represent records that were written to the database. Extension modules can write on them to change some values.

Extending views

Views are defined using XML and are stored in the architecture field, `arch`. To extend a view, we must locate the node where the extension will take place, and then perform the intended change, such as adding XML elements.

Odoo provides a simplified notation to extend XML by using the XML tag we want to match – `<field>`, for example – with one or more distinctive attributes to match, such as `name`. Then, we must add the `position` attribute to declare the kind of modification to make.

Recovering the example we used earlier in this chapter, to add additional content after the `isbn` field, we can use the following code:

```
<field name="isbn" position="after">
    <!-- Changed content goes here -->
</field>
```

Any XML element and attribute can be used to select the node to use as the extension point, except for `string` attributes. The values of string attributes are translated into the user's active language during view generation, so they can't be reliably used as node selectors.

The extension operation to perform is declared with the `position` attribute. Several operations are allowed, as follows:

- `inside` (the default): Appends the content inside the selected node. The node should be a container, such as `<group>` or `<page>`.
- `after`: Adds the content after the selected node.
- `before`: Adds the content before the selected node.

- `replace`: Replaces the selected node. If it's used with empty content, it deletes the element. Since Odoo 10, it also allows you to wrap an element with other markups by using `$0` in the content to represent the element being replaced; for example, `<field name="name" position="replace"><h1>$0</h1></field>`.

- `attributes`: Modifies the attribute values for the matched element. The content should have one or more `<attribute name="attr-name">value<attribute>` elements, such as `<attribute name="invisible">True></attribute>`. If it's used with no body, such as in `<attribute name="invisible"/>`, the attribute is removed from the selected element.

> **Tip**
>
> While `position="replace"` allows us to delete XML elements, this should be avoided. It can break based on modules that may be using the deleted node as an extension point to add other elements. As an alternative, consider leaving the element and making it invisible instead.

Moving XML nodes to a different location

Except for the `attributes` operation, the preceding locators can be combined with a child element with `position="move"`. The effect is to move the child locator target node to the parent locator's target position.

> **Changes in Odoo 12**
>
> The `position="move"` child locator is new in Odoo 12 and is not available in previous versions.

Here is an example of moving `my_field` from its current location to the position after `target_field`:

```
<field name="target_field" position="after">
    <field name="my_field" position="move"/>
</field>
```

The other view types, such as list and search views, also have an `arch` field and can be extended in the same way as form views can.

Using XPath to select XML extension points

In some cases, we may not have an attribute with a unique value to use as the XML node selector. This can happen when the element to select does not have a `name` attribute, as is often the case for `<group>`, `<notebook>`, or `<page>` view elements. Another case is when there are several elements with the same `name` attribute, as in the case of Kanban QWeb views, where the same field can be included more than once in the same XML template.

For these cases, we need a more sophisticated way to locate the XML element to extend. Being XML, **XPath expressions** are the natural way to locate elements.

For example, taking the book form view we defined in the previous chapter, an XPath expression for locating the `<field name="isbn">` element is `//field[@name]='isbn'`. This expression finds `<field>` elements with a `name` attribute equal to `isbn`.

The XPath equivalent to the book form view extension that we created in the previous section would be as follows:

```
<xpath expr="//field[@name='isbn']" position="after">
    <field name="is_available" />
</xpath>
```

More information on the supported XPath syntax can be found in the official Python documentation: `https://docs.python.org/3/library/xml.etree.elementtree.html#supported-xpath-syntax`.

If an XPath expression matches multiple elements, only the first one will be selected as the target for an extension. Therefore, they should be made as specific as possible using unique attributes. Using the `name` attribute is the easiest way to ensure that we find the elements we want to use as an extension point. Thus, it is important to have these unique identifiers in the XML elements of the views we create.

Modifying existing data

Regular data records can also be *extended*, which, in practice, means writing over existing values. For this, we just need to identify the record to write on, as well as the fields and values to update. XPath expressions are not needed since we are not modifying XML `arch` structures, as we do for views.

The `<record id="x" model="y">` data loading elements perform an insert or update operation on model `y`: if record `x` does not exist, it is created; otherwise, it is updated/written over.

Records in other modules can be accessed using the `<module>.<identifier>` global identifier, so a module can update a record that's been created by another module.

> **Tip**
> The dot (.) is reserved to separate the module name from the object identifier.
> So, it can't be used in identifier names. Instead, use the underscore (_) character.

As an example, we will change the name of the User security group to `Librarian`. The record to modify was created in the `library_app` module, with the `library_app.library_group_user` identifier.

To do this, we will add the `library_member/security/library_security.xml` file, along with the following code:

```xml
<odoo>
  <!-- Modify Group name -->
  <record id="library_app.library_group_user"
    model="res.groups">
    <field name="name">Librarian</field>
  </record>
</odoo>
```

Note that we used a `<record>` element, writing only to the `name` field. You can think of this as a write operation in this field.

> **Tip**
> When using a `<record>` element, we can select the fields we want to write on, but the same is not true for shortcut elements, such as `<menuitem>` and `<act_window>`. These need all of the attributes to be provided and missing any of them will set the corresponding field to an empty value. However, you can use `<record>` to set a value on a field that was created through a shortcut element.

Don't forget to add the `library_member/security/library_security.xml` file to the `data` key in the manifest file. Having done this and upgraded the module, we should see the name change in the user groups.

Extending views allows you to introduce modifications to the backend presentation layer. But the same can be done to the frontend web presentation layer. This is what we will address in the next section.

Extending web pages

Extensibility is a key design choice for the Odoo framework, and the Odoo web components are no exception. So, Odoo web controllers and templates can be also extended.

The Library app that we created in the previous *Chapter 3*, *Your First Odoo Application*, provided a book catalog page that now needs to be improved.

We will extend it to leverage the book availability information that was added by the Library Members module:

- On the controller side, we will add support to a query string parameter to filter only the available books; that is, /library/books?available=1.

- On the template side, we will specify the books that are not available.

Let's start extending the web controller.

Extending the web controllers

Web controllers are responsible for handling web requests and rendering the page to return as a response. They should focus on presentation logic, not deal with business logic, which should be incorporated into model methods instead.

Supporting additional parameters or even URL routes is web presentation-specific and something appropriate for a web controller to deal with.

The /library/books endpoint will be extended here to support a query string parameter, available=1, which we will use to filter the catalog of books so that it only displays the available titles.

To extend an existing controller, we need to import the original object that created it, declare a Python class based on it, and then implement the class method holding the additional logic.

The code to extend the controller should be added to the library_member/controllers/main.py file, as follows:

```python
from odoo import http
from odoo.addons.library_app.controllers.main import Books


class BooksExtended(Books):

    @http.route()
    def list(self, **kwargs):
```

```
    response = super().list(**kwargs)
    if kwargs.get("available"):
        all_books = response.qcontext["books"]
        available_books = all_books.filtered(
          "is_available")
        response.qcontext["books"] = available_books
    return response
```

The steps to add the controller code are as follows:

1. Add the `library_member/controllers/main.py` file, ensuring it contains the preceding code.

2. Make this new Python file known to the module by adding the controller's subdirectory to the `library_member/__init__.py` file:

```
from . import models
from . import controllers
```

3. Add the `library_member/controllers/__init__.py` file with the following line of code:

```
from . import main
```

4. After this, accessing `http://localhost:8069/library/books?available=1` should only show us the books with the `Is Available?` field checked.

Now, let's review the controller extension code to understand how it works.

The controller to extend, `Books`, was originally declared by the `library_app` module, in the `controllers/main.py` file. So, to get a reference to it, we need to import `odoo.addons.library_app.controllers.main`.

This is different from models, where we have a central registry available where we can get a reference to any model class, such as `self.env['library.book']`, without knowing the particular file that's implementing it. We don't have such a registry for controllers, and we need to know the module and file implementing the controller to be able to extend it.

Then, the `BooksExtended` class is declared based on the original one, `Books`. The identifier name that's used for this class is not relevant. It is used as a vehicle to reference the original class and extend it.

Next, we (re)define the controller method to be extended, which is `list()` in this case. It needs to be decorated with at least the simple `@http.route()` for its route to be kept active. If it's used like this, with no arguments, it will preserve the routes that are defined by the parent class. But we could also add parameters to this `@http.route()` decorator to replace and redefine the class routes.

The `list()` method has a `**kwargs` argument, which captures all the parameters in the `kwargs` dictionary. These are the parameters that are given in the URL, such as `?available=1`.

> **Tip**
>
> Using a `**kwargs` argument that sweeps all the given arguments is not required, but it makes our URL tolerant to unexpected URL arguments. If we choose to specify particular arguments, if different ones are set, the page will fail immediately and return an **internal error** when trying to call the corresponding controller.

The code for the `list()` method starts by calling the corresponding parent class method using `super()`. This returns the `Response` object that was computed by the parent method, including the attributes and the template to render, `template`, and the context to use when rendering, `qcontext`. But the HTML is yet to be generated. This will only happen when the controller finishes running. So, it is possible to change the `Response` attributes before the final rendering is done.

The method checks `kwargs` for a non-empty value in the `available` key. If it is found, the non-available books are filtered out, and `qcontext` is updated with this recordset. So, when the controller's processing completes, the HTML will be rendered using the updated book's recordset, which will only include available books.

Extending QWeb templates

Web page templates are XML documents, just like the other Odoo view types, and selector expressions can be used, as we do for other view types, such as forms. QWeb templates are usually more complex since they include more HTML elements, so most of the time, the more versatile XPath expressions are needed.

To modify the actual presentation of the web page, we should extend the QWeb template being used. As an example of this, we will extend `library_app.book_list_template` to add visual information about the books that are not available.

A QWeb extension is a `<template>` element that uses the additional `inherit_id` attribute to identify the QWeb template to extend. It is `library_app.book_list_template` in this case.

Follow these steps:

1. Add the `library_member/views/book_list_template.xml` file, along with the following code:

```
<odoo>
    <template id="book_list_extended"
              name="Extended Book List"
              inherit_id=
                "library_app.book_list_template">

        <xpath expr="//span[@t-field='book.publisher_id']"
               position="after">
          <t t-if="not book.is_available">
            <b>(Not Available)</b>
          </t>
        </xpath>

    </template>
</odoo>
```

The preceding example uses an `xpath` notation. Note that in this case, we could have also used the equivalent simplified notation; that is, `<span t-field="book.publisher_id" position=after>`.

2. Declare this additional data file in the add-on manifest; that is, `library_member/__manifest__.py`:

```
"data": [
    "security/library_security.xml",
    "security/ir.model.access.csv",
    "views/book_view.xml",
    "views/member_view.xml",
    "views/library_menu.xml",
    "views/book_list_template.xml",
],
```

After this, accessing `http://localhost:8069/library/books` should show the additional (not available) visual information on the books that are not available. Here is what the web page will look like:

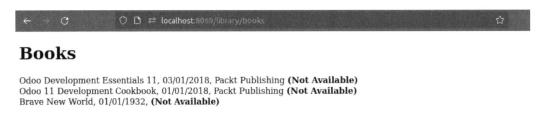

Books

Odoo Development Essentials 11, 03/01/2018, Packt Publishing **(Not Available)**
Odoo 11 Development Cookbook, 01/01/2018, Packt Publishing **(Not Available)**
Brave New World, 01/01/1932, **(Not Available)**

Figure 4.4 – Books list web page with availability information

This completes our review of how to extend each type of Odoo component, from the data model to the user interface elements.

Summary

Extensibility is a key feature of the Odoo framework. We can build add-on modules that change or add features to other existing add-ons at the several layers needed to implement features in Odoo. With this, our projects will be able to reuse and extend third-party add-on modules in a clean and modular way.

At the model layer, we use the `_inherit` model attribute to get a reference to an existing model and then make in-place modifications to it. The field objects inside the model also support incremental definitions so that we can *redeclare* an existing field, providing only the attributes to change.

Additional model inheritance mechanisms allow you to reuse data structures and business logic. Delegation inheritance, which is activated with the `delegate=True` attribute on a many-to-one relationship field (or the old-style `inherits` model attribute), makes all the fields from the related model available and reuses its data structure. Prototype inheritance, which uses `_inherit` with additional models, allows you to copy features (data structure definitions and methods) from other models and enables the use of abstract mixin classes, providing a set of reusable features, such as document discussion messages and followers.

At the view layer, the view structures are defined using XML, and extensions can be made by locating an XML element (using XPath or the Odoo simplified syntax) and providing the XML fragment to add. Other data records that are created by a module can also be modified by extension modules by simply referencing the corresponding complete XML ID and performing a write operation on the intended fields.

At the business logic layer, extensions can be made with the same mechanism that's used for model extension and redeclaring the methods to extend. Inside them, the `super()` Python function is used to call the code of the inherited method, and our additional code can run before or after that.

For the frontend web pages, the presentation logic in controllers can be extended in a similar way to model methods, and the web templates are also views with XML structures, so these can be extended in the same way as the other view types.

In the next chapter, we will dive deeper into models and explore everything they can offer us.

Further reading

The following are some additional references to the official documentation, which can provide useful information regarding module extensions and inheritance mechanisms:

- Model inheritance: `https://www.odoo.com/documentation/15.0/developer/reference/backend/orm.html`

- View inheritance: `https://www.odoo.com/documentation/15.0/developer/reference/backend/views.html`

- Web controllers: `https://www.odoo.com/documentation/15.0/developer/reference/backend/http.html`

Section 2: Models

The second part introduces models, which are responsible for the data model structures around which the application is built. Closely related to models, data loading techniques and access control are also discussed.

The following chapters are included in this section:

- *Chapter 5, Importing, Exporting, and Module Data*
- *Chapter 6, Models – Structuring the Application Data*

5
Importing, Exporting, and Module Data

Most Odoo module definitions, such as **user interfaces** and **security rules**, are data records that are stored in specific **database tables**. The XML and CSV files that are found in modules are not used by Odoo applications at runtime. They are a means of loading those definitions into database tables.

Because of this, an important part of Odoo modules is representing data in files so that it can be loaded into a database upon module installation. Modules can also contain initial data and demonstration data. Data files allow us to add that to our modules.

Additionally, understanding Odoo data representation formats is important for exporting and importing business data within the context of a project's implementation.

The following topics will be covered in this chapter:

- Understanding the external identifier concept
- Exporting and importing data files
- Using CSV files
- Adding module data
- Using XML data files

By the end of this chapter, you will be able to perform data exports and imports to populate initial data into a database and automate the creation of default and demonstration data in modules that have been created.

Technical requirements

This chapter requires you to have an Odoo server running, with the library app base module installed.

The code for this chapter can be found in this book's GitHub repository, `https://github.com/PacktPublishing/Odoo-15-Development-Essentials`, in the `ch05/` directory. It contains a copy of the original `library_app` that we created in *Chapter 3*, *Your First Odoo Application*, with additional files added for this chapter.

Understanding the external identifier concept

An **external identifier**, also called an **XML ID**, is a *human-readable string identifier* that uniquely identifies a particular record in Odoo. They are important for loading data into Odoo, allowing us to modify an existing data record or reference it in other data records.

First, we will introduce how external identifiers work, and how we can inspect them. Then, we will learn how to use the web client to find the external identifiers for particular data records, since this is frequently needed when creating add-on modules, thus extending existing features.

How external identifiers work

Let's begin by understanding how identifiers work. The actual database identifier for a record is an automatically assigned sequential number, and there is no way to know ahead of time what ID will be assigned to each record during module installation. External identifiers let us reference a related record without the need to know the actual database ID that's been assigned to it. The XML ID provides a convenient alias for the database ID so that we can use it whenever we need to reference a particular record.

Records defined in Odoo module data files use *XML IDs*. One reason for this is to avoid creating duplicate records when upgrading a module. The module upgrade will load the data files into the database again. We want it to detect pre-existing records for them to be updated, instead of creating duplicate records.

Another reason to use XML IDs is to support interrelated data: data records that need to reference other data records. Since we can't know the actual database ID, we can use the XML ID, so the translation will be transparently handled by the **Odoo framework**.

Odoo takes care of translating the external identifier names into the actual database IDs that have been assigned to them. The mechanism behind this is quite simple: Odoo keeps a table with the mapping between the named external identifiers and their corresponding numeric database IDs: the `ir.model.data` model.

We must have **Developer mode** enabled to have the menu option available. Check whether you have the *Developer mode* bug icon in the top right, next to the user's avatar icon. If not, you should enable it now in the **Settings** top menu. Please refer to *Chapter 1, Quick Start Using the Developer Mode*, for more details.

We can inspect the existing mappings using the **Settings | Technical | Sequences & Identifiers | External Identifiers** menu item. For example, if we visit the external identifiers list and filter it by the `library_app` module, we will see the external identifiers that have been generated by the module we created, as shown in the following screenshot:

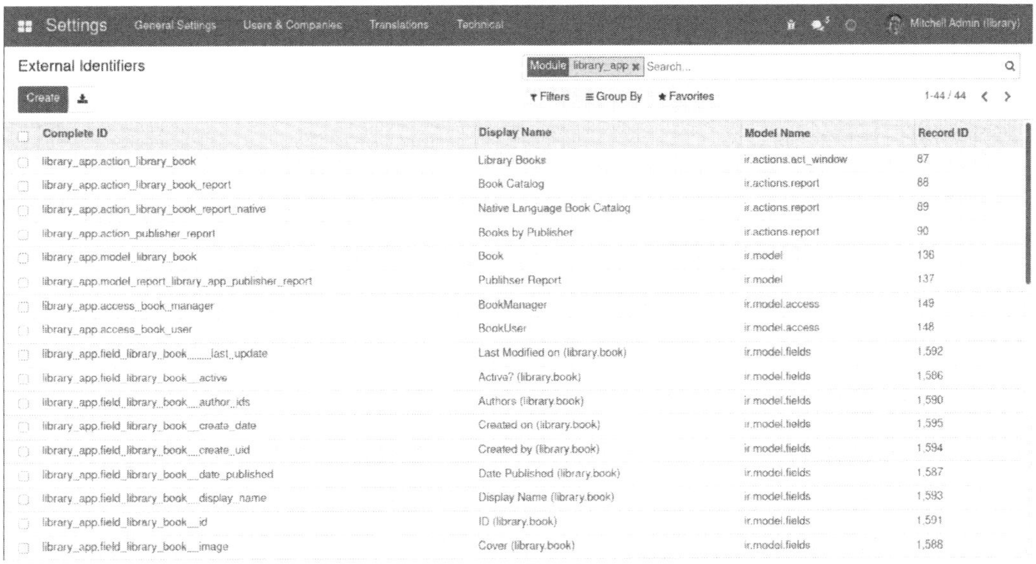

Figure 5.1 – External identifiers generated by the library_app module

Here, we can see that the external identifiers have **Complete ID** labels. Notice how they are composed of the module name and the identifier name, joined with a dot; for example, `library_app.action_library_book`.

External identifiers only need to be unique inside an Odoo module so that there is no risk of two modules conflicting because of accidentally choosing the same identifier name. The globally unique identifier is built by joining the module name with the actual external identifier name. This is what you can see in the **Complete ID** field.

When using an external identifier in a data file, we can choose to use either the complete identifier or just the external identifier name. Usually, it's simpler to just use the external identifier name, but the complete identifier enables us to reference data records from other modules. When doing so, make sure that those modules are included in the module dependencies to ensure that those records are loaded before ours.

There are some cases where the complete ID is needed, even if we're referring to an XML ID from the same module.

At the top of the list, we can see the `library_app.action_library_book` complete identifier. This is the menu action we created for the module, which is also referenced in the corresponding menu item. By clicking on it, we go to the form view, which contains its details. There, we can see that the `action_library_book` external identifier in the `library_app` module maps to a specific record ID in the `ir.actions.act_window` model, which is `87` in this case.

By clicking on the record's line, the information can be seen in a form view, as shown in the following screenshot:

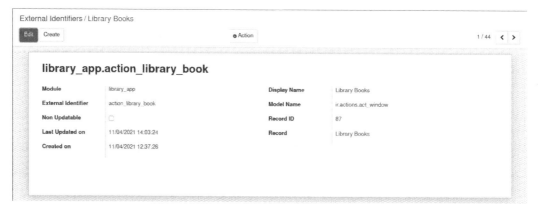

Figure 5.2 – Form view for the library_app.action_library_book external identifier

Besides providing a way for records to easily reference other records, external identifiers also allow you to avoid data duplication on repeated imports. If the external identifier is already present, the existing record will be updated, avoiding a new, duplicate record being created.

Finding external identifiers

When we're writing data records for our modules, we frequently need to look up the existing external identifiers to use for our reference. So, it is important to know how to find these identifiers.

One way to do this is to use the **Settings | Technical | Sequences & Identifiers | External Identifiers** menu, which was shown earlier in *Figure 5.1*. We can also use the **Developer** menu for this. As you may recall from *Chapter 1, Quick Start Using the Developer Mode*, the **Developer** menu can be activated in the **Settings** dashboard, at the bottom right.

To find the external identifier for a data record, we should open the corresponding form view, select the **Developer** menu, and then choose the **View Metadata** option. This will display a dialog containing the record's database ID and external identifier (also known as the XML ID).

For example, to look up the demo user ID, we should navigate to the users form view at **Settings | Users**, open the demo user form, and then select the **View Metadata** option from the **Developer Tools** menu. In the following screenshot, we can see that the XML ID is base.user_demo and that the database ID is 6:

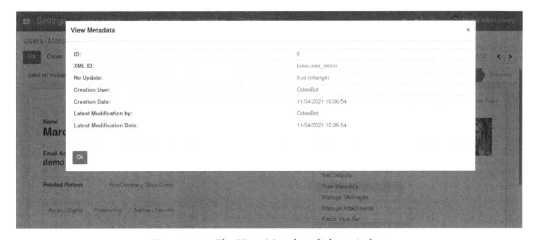

Figure 5.3 – The View Metadata dialog window

To find the external identifier for view elements, such as **form**, **tree**, **search**, or **action**, the **Developer** menu is also a good source of help. For this, we can use the appropriate **Edit View** option to open a form containing the details of the corresponding view. There, we will find an **External ID** field, which provides the information we are looking for.

For example, in the following screenshot, we can see that the **External ID** property for the user's form view is `base.view_users_form`:

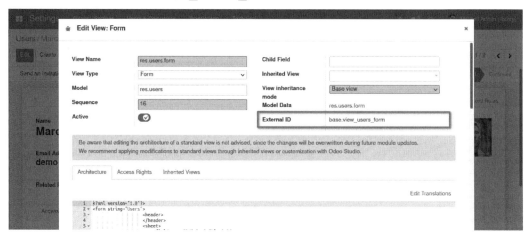

Figure 5.4 – The Edit View window showing the External ID property for a form view

With that, we have learned about **External IDs** and how they can be used as aliases to reference database records. We have also looked at several ways to find the **XML IDs** that will be needed to reference records in the data files. Next, we will learn how to create data files where these **XML IDs** will be useful.

Exporting and importing CSV data files

An easy way to generate data files and get insight into what structure the files should have is to use the built-in export feature.

With generated CSV files, we can learn about the format that's needed to import data manually into the system, edit them to perform mass updates, or even use them to produce demo data for our add-on modules.

In this section, we will learn about the basics of exporting and importing data from Odoo's user interface.

Exporting data

Data exporting is a standard feature that's available in any list view. To use it, we must pick the rows to export by selecting the corresponding checkboxes, on the far left, and then selecting the **Export** option from the **Action** button at the top of the list.

First, we should add a couple of Odoo books to the **Library** app, along with their publishers and authors. For this example, we created `Odoo Development Essentials 11` and `Odoo 11 Development Cookbook`.

We also need to have the **Contacts** app installed so that we can see a **Partner** list view and can export those records from there. Notice that the default view is **Kanban** for the contact cards, so we need to switch to the **list** view:

Figure 5.5 – The Export option in the Action menu

We can also tick the checkbox in the header of the column to select all of the available records that match the current search criteria.

The **Export** option takes us to the **Export Data** dialog form, where we can choose what and how to export. We are concerned with exporting in a way that allows us to import that file later, either manually or as part of an add-on module:

Figure 5.6 – The Export Data dialog window

At the top of the dialog form, we have two selections available:

- **I want to update data (import-compatible export)**: Enable this checkbox so that the data is exported in a format-friendly manner for a later import.

- **Export format**: You can choose between **CSV** or **XLSX** here. We will choose a **CSV** file to get a better understanding of the raw export format, which is still understood by any spreadsheet application.

Next, pick the columns to export. In this example, a very simple export was done by choosing only the **Name** field. By clicking on the **Export** button, an exported data file will be available. The exported CSV file should look like this:

```
"id","name"
"__export__.res_partner_43_f82d2ecc","Alexandre Fayolle"
"__export__.res_partner_41_30a5bc3c","Daniel Reis"
"__export__.res_partner_44_6be5a130","Holger Brunn"
"__export__.res_partner_42_38b48275","Packt Publishing"
```

The first row contains the **field names**, which will be used during the import to automatically map the columns to their destination.

The first row has the selected name column, as expected. An initial ID column was automatically added because the import-compatible export option was selected.

The automatically added id column has the external ID assigned to each record. This allows the exported data file to be edited and reimported later, to update the records, instead of creating duplicated ones.

Missing external identifiers are automatically generated using the __export__ prefix, as shown in the previous file export example.

> **Tip**
> Because of the automatically generated record identifiers, the export or import features can be used to mass edit Odoo data – export the data to CSV, use spreadsheet software to mass edit it, and then import it back into Odoo.

Importing data

Once we have a properly formatted data file ready, we want to import it into Odoo. Let's learn how this is can be done through the web client user interface.

First, we have to make sure that the import feature is *enabled*. It should be enabled by default. If not, the option is available in the **Settings** app, under the **General Settings** menu item. Under the **Permissions** section, the **Import & Export** option should be checked.

With this option enabled, the list view search widget will show an **Import records** option in the **Favorites** menu, next to the **Filters** and **Group By** menus.

> **Note**
>
> The **Import & Export** setting installs the `base_import` module, which is responsible for providing this feature.

Let's try performing a bulk edit on our *Contact* or *Partner* data. Open the CSV file we just downloaded in a spreadsheet or a text editor and change a few values. We can also add some new rows, leaving the `id` column blank for them.

As we mentioned previously, the first column, `id`, provides a unique identifier for each row. This allows pre-existing records to be updated instead of us needing to duplicate them when we import the data back to Odoo. If we edit any of the names in the exported file, the corresponding record will be updated when we import the file.

For the new rows that have been added to the CSV file, we can choose to either provide an external identifier of our choice or we can leave the `id` column blank. Either way, a new record will be created for them. As an example, we added a line with no `id` and the name `Phillip K. Dick` to be created in the database:

```
,Phillip K. Dick
```

After saving these changes to the **CSV** file, click on the **Import** option, in the **Favorites** menu. The next page allows us to upload the data file. Then, the import assistant will be presented:

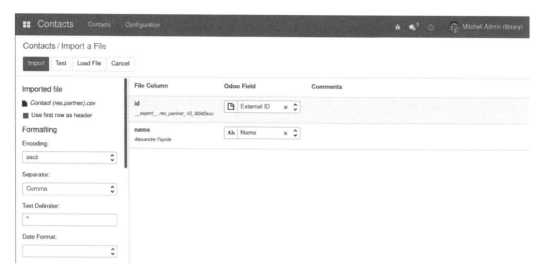

Figure 5.7 – The Import a File assistant

Here, we should select the CSV file's location on the disk and then click on the **Test** button, at the top left, to check it for correctness.

Since the file to import is based on an Odoo export, there is a good chance that it will be valid and that the columns will be automatically mapped to their proper destination in the database. Depending on the application that's used to edit the data file, you may have to play with the separator and encoding options to get the best results.

Now, click on **Import**, and there you go – the modifications and new records should have been loaded into Odoo!

Related records in CSV data files

The examples in the previous section were quite simple, but the data files can become more complex once we start using relational fields, linking records from several tables.

Previously, we handled *Partner* records that were used in *Books*. We will now look at how we can represent the reference for these Partners in a CSV file for book data. In particular, we have a many-to-one (or a foreign key) relationship for the Publisher (the `publisher_id` field) and a many-to-many relationship for the Authors (the `author_ids` field).

In the CSV file header line, relationship columns should have `/id` appended to their names. It will reference the related records using external identifiers. In our example, we will load the book publisher into a `publisher_id/id` field, using the external ID for the related partner as a value.

It is possible to use `/.id` instead so that we can use the actual database IDs (the real numeric identifier that's been assigned), but this is rarely what we need. Unless you have good reason to do otherwise, always use external IDs instead of database IDs. Also, remember that database IDs are specific to a particular Odoo database, so, most of the time, it won't work correctly if it's imported into a database other than the original one.

Many-to-many fields can also be imported through CSV data files. It's as easy as providing a comma-separated list of external IDs, surrounded by double quotes. For example, to load the book authors, we would have an `author_ids/id` column, where we would use a comma-separated list of the external IDs of the Partners to link as values. Here is an example of what a to-many field would look like in a CSV file:

```
id, name, author_ids/id
book_odc11, "Odoo 11 Development Cookbook", "__export__.res_
partner_43_f82d2ecc,__export__.res_partner_44_6be5a130"
```

One-to-many fields often represent headers or lines, or parent or child relationships, and there is special support to import these types of relationships – for the same parent record, we can have several related lines.

Here, we have an example of a one-to-many field in the *Partners* model: a company partner can have several child contacts. If we export the data from the *Partner* model and include the **Contacts/Name** field, we will see the structure that can be used to import this type of data:

id	name	child_ids/id	child_ids/name
base.res_partner_12	Azure Interior	base.res_partner_address_15	Brandon Freeman
		base.res_partner_address_28	Colleen Diaz
		base.res_partner_address_16	Nicole Ford

Figure 5.8 – Data file example importing to-many related records

The `id` and `name` columns are for the parent records, while the `child_ids` columns are for the child records. Notice how the parent record columns are left blank for the child records after the first one.

The preceding table, which is represented as a CSV file, looks as follows:

```
"id","name","child_ids/id","child_ids/name"
"base.res_partner_12","Azure Interior","base.res_partner_
address_15","Brandon Freeman"
"","","base.res_partner_address_28","Colleen Diaz"
"","","base.res_partner_address_16","Nicole Ford"
```

Here, we can see that the first two columns, `id` and `name`, have values in the first line and are empty in the next two lines. They have data for the parent record, which is the *Contact's Company*.

The other two columns are both prefixed with `child_ids/` and have values on all three lines. They contain data for the contacts related to the parent company. The first line contains data for both the company and the first contact, while the lines that follow contain data for the columns of the child contacts.

Adding module data

Modules use data files to load their default data, demonstration data, user interface definitions, and other configurations into the database. For this, we can use both CSV and XML files.

> **Changes in Odoo 12**
>
> The YAML file format was also supported until Odoo 11 and was removed in Odoo 12. Still, for a usage example, you can look at the `l10n_be` official module in Odoo 11, and for information on the YAML format, you can visit `http://yaml.org/`.

CSV files that are used by modules are the same as those we have seen and used for the import feature. When using them in modules, the filename must match the name of the model that the data will be loaded into. For example, a CSV file for loading data into the `library.book` model must be named `library.book.csv`.

A common usage of data CSV files is for accessing security definitions that have been loaded into the `ir.model.access` model. They usually use CSV files in a `security/` subdirectory, named `ir.model.access.csv`.

Demonstration data

Odoo add-on modules may install demonstration data, and it is considered good practice to do so. This is useful for providing usage examples for a module and the datasets to be used in tests. Demonstration data for a module is declared using the demo attribute of the __manifest__.py manifest file. Just like the data attribute, it is a list of filenames with the corresponding relative paths inside the module.

Some demonstration data should be added to the library.book module. An easy way to do this is to export some data from the development database with the module installed.

The convention is to place data files in a data/ subdirectory. We should save these data files in the library_app add-on module as data/library.book.csv. Since this data will be owned by our module, we should edit the id values to remove the __export__ prefix in the identifiers that are generated by the export feature.

As an example, our res.partner.csv data file might look as follows:

```
id,name
res_partner_alexandre,"Alexandre Fayolle"
res_partner_daniel,"Daniel Reis"
res_partner_holger,"Holger Brunn"
res_partner_packt,"Packt Publishing"
```

The library.book.csv data file containing the Book demo data will look as follows:

```
"id","name","date_published","publisher_id/id","author_ids/id"
library_book_ode11,"Odoo Development Essentials 11","2018-03-
01",res_partner_packt,res_partner_daniel
library_book_odc11,"Odoo 11 Development Cookbook","2018-01-
01",res_partner_packt,"res_partner_alexandre,res_partner_
holger"
```

Do not forget to add these data files to the __manifest__.py manifest's demo attribute:

```
"demo": [
    "data/res.partner.csv",
    "data/library.book.csv",
],
```

The files are loaded in the order they are declared. This is important since records in a file cannot reference other records that haven't been created yet.

The next time the module is updated, the content of the file will be imported, so long as it is installed with the demo data enabled.

> **Note**
>
> While data files are also re-imported on module upgrades, this is not the case for the demo data files: these are only imported upon module installation.

Of course, XML files can also be used to load or initialize data, leveraging the additional features they provide, compared to plain CSV files. In the next section, we will discuss using data files in XML format.

Using XML data files

While CSV files provide a simple and compact format to represent data, XML files are more powerful and give more control over the loading process. For example, their filenames are not required to match the model to be loaded. This is because the XML format is much richer and more information regarding what to load can be provided through the XML elements inside the file.

We used XML data files in the previous chapters. The user interface components, such as the views and menu items, are, in fact, records that are stored in system models. The XML files in the modules are used to load these records into the instance database.

To showcase this, a second data file will be added to the `library_app` module, `data/book_demo.xml`, with the following content:

```xml
<?xml version="1.0"?>
<odoo noupdate="1">
  <!-- Data to load -->
  <record model="res.partner" id="res_partner_huxley">
    <field name="name">Aldous Huxley</field>
  </record>
  <record model="library.book" id="library_book_bnw">
    <field name="name">Brave New World</field>
    <field name="author_ids"
        eval="[(4, ref('res_partner_huxley'))]" />
    <field name="date_published">1932-01-01</field>
```

```
    </record>
</odoo>
```

As usual, the new data file must be declared in the `__manifest__.py` file:

```
"demo": [
    "data/res.partner.csv",
    "data/library.book.csv",
    "data/book_demo.xml",
],
```

Similar to the CSV data file we saw in the previous section, this file also loads data into the *Library Books* model.

XML data files have an `<odoo>` top element, inside of which there can be several `<record>` elements, which are the equivalent to data rows in CSV files.

> **Note**
>
> The `<odoo>` top element in data files was introduced in version 9.0 and replaces the former `<openerp>` tag. A `<data>` section inside the top element is still supported, but it's now optional. In fact, now, `<odoo>` and `<data>` are equivalent, so we could use either one as the top element for our XML data files.

A `<record>` element has two mandatory attributes, `model` and `id`, for the external identifier for the record, and contains a `<field>` tag for each field to write on.

Note that the slash notation in the field names is not available here; we can't use `<field name="publisher_id/id">`. Instead, the `ref` special attribute is used to reference external identifiers. We'll discuss the values of the relational to-many fields in a moment.

You may have noticed the `noupdate="1"` attribute in the top `<odoo>` element. This prevents the data records from being loaded on module upgrades so that any later edits that are made to them are not lost.

The noupdate data attribute

When a module is upgraded, the data file loading is repeated, and the module's records are rewritten. This means that upgrading a module will overwrite any manual changes that might have been made to the module's data.

> **Tip**
>
> Notably, if views were manually modified to add quick customizations, these changes will be lost with the next module upgrade. To avoid this, the correct approach is to create inherited views with the changes we want to introduce.

This rewrite behavior is the default, but it can be changed so that some of the data is only imported at install time, and is ignored in later module upgrades. This can be done using the noupdate="1" attribute in the <odoo> or <data> elements.

This is useful for data that is to be used for the initial configuration but is expected to be customized later since these manually made customizations will be safe from module upgrades. For example, it is frequently used for record access rules, allowing them to be adapted to implementation-specific needs.

It is possible to have more than one <data> section in the same XML file. We can take advantage of this to separate data to import only once, with noupdate="1", and data that can be re-imported on each upgrade, with noupdate="0". noupdate="0" is the default, so we can just omit it if we prefer. Note that we need to have a top-level XML element, so in this case, we will use two <data> sections. They must be inside a top-level <odoo> or <data> element.

> **Tip**
>
> The noupdate attribute can be tricky when we're developing modules because changes that are made to the data later will be ignored. One solution is to, instead of upgrading the module with the -u option, reinstall it using the -i option. Reinstalling from the command line using the -i option ignores the noupdate flags on data records.

The noupdate flag is stored in the **External Identifier** information for each record. It's possible to manually edit it directly using the **External Identifier** form, which is available in the **Technical** menu, by using the **Non Updatable** checkbox.

> **Changes in Odoo 12**
>
> In **Developer Menu**, when accessing **View Metadata**, the dialog box now also shows the value for the **No Update** flag, along with the record's **XML ID**. Furthermore, **No Update flag** can be changed there by clicking on it.

Defining records in XML

In an XML data file, each `<record>` element has two basic attributes, id and model, and contains `<field>` elements that assign values to each column. The id attribute corresponds to the record's external identifier, while the model attribute corresponds to the target model. The `<field>` elements have a few different ways to assign values. Let's look at them in detail.

Setting field values directly

The name attribute of a `<field>` element identifies the field to write on.

The value to write is the element's content: the text between the field's opening and closing tag. For dates and date-times, eval attributes with expressions that return date or datetime objects will work. Returning strings with "YYYY-mm-dd" and "YYYY-mm-dd HH:MM:SS" will be converted properly. For boolean fields, the "0" and "False" values are converted into False, and any other non-empty values will be converted into True.

> **Changes in Odoo 10**
>
> The way Boolean False values are read from data files has been improved in Odoo 10. In previous versions, any non-empty values, including "0" and "False", were converted into True. Until Odoo 9, Boolean values should be set using the eval attribute, such as eval="False".

Setting values using expressions

A more elaborate alternative for setting a field value is using the eval attribute. It evaluates a Python expression and assigns the result to the field.

The expression is evaluated in a context that, besides Python built-ins, also has some additional identifiers that are available to build the expression to evaluate.

To handle dates, the following Python modules are available: time, datetime, timedelta, and relativedelta. They allow you to calculate date values, something that is frequently used in demonstrations and test data so that the dates used are close to the module installation date. For more information about these Python modules, see the documentation at https://docs.python.org/3/library/datatypes.html.

For example, to set a value to yesterday, we can use the following code:

```
<field name="date_published"
       eval="(datetime.now() + timedelta(-1))" />
```

Also available in the evaluation context is the `ref()` function, which is used to translate an external identifier into the corresponding database ID. This can be used to set values for relational fields. Here is an example:

```
<field name="publisher_id" eval="ref('res_partner_packt')" />
```

This example sets a value for the `publisher_id` field using the `eval` attribute. The evaluated expression is Python code that uses the special `ref()` function, which is used to translate an *XML ID* into the corresponding database ID.

Setting values on many-to-one relationship fields

For many-to-one relationship fields, the value to write is the database ID for the linked record. In XML files, we usually know the *XML ID* for the record, and we need to have it translated into the actual database ID.

One way to do this is to use the `eval` attribute with a `ref()` function, like we just did in the previous section.

A simpler alternative is to use the `ref` attribute, which is available for `<field>` elements; for example:

```
<field name="publisher_id" ref="res_partner_packt" />
```

This example sets a value for the `publisher_id` many-to-one field, referencing the database record with an *XML ID* of `res_partner_packt`.

Setting values on to-many relationship fields

For one-to-many and many-to-many fields, instead of a single ID, a list of related IDs is expected. Furthermore, several operations can be performed – we may want to replace the current list of related records with a new one, or append a few records to it, or even unlink some records.

To support write operations on to-many fields, we can use a special syntax in the `eval` attribute. To write to a to-many field, we can use a *list* of *triples*. Each *triple* is a `write` command that does different things based on the code that was used in the first element.

To overwrite the list of authors of a book, we would use the following code:

```
<field name="author_ids"
       eval="[(6, 0,
            [ref('res_partner_alexandre'),
             ref('res_partner_holger')]
```

```
            )]"
/>
```

To append a linked record to the current list of the authors of a book, we would use the following code:

```
<field name="author_ids"
        eval="[(4, ref('res_partner_daniel'))]"
/>
```

The preceding examples are the most common. In both cases, we used just one command, but we could chain several commands in the outer list. The append (4) and replace (6) commands are the most used. In the case of append (4), the last value of the triple is not used and is not needed, so it can be omitted, as we did in the preceding code sample.

The complete list of available **to-many write commands** is as follows:

- (0, _ , {'field': value}) creates a new record and links it to this one.
- (1, id, {'field': value}) updates the values on an already linked record.
- (2, id, _) removes the link to and deletes the id-related record.
- (3, id, _) removes the link to, but does not delete, the id-related record. This is usually what you will use to delete related records on many-to-many fields.
- (4, id, _) links an already existing record. This can only be used for many-to-many fields.
- (5, _, _) removes all the links, without deleting the linked records.
- (6, _, [ids]) replaces the list of linked records with the provided list.

The _ underscore symbol that was used in the preceding list represents irrelevant values, usually filled with 0 or False.

Tip

The trailing irrelevant values can be safely omitted. For example, (4, id, _) can be used as (4, id).

In this section, we learned how to use the <record> tag to load records into the database. As an alternative, there are a few shortcut tags that can be used in place of a regular <record> tag. The next section will introduce these to us.

Shortcuts for frequently used models

If we go back to *Chapter 3*, *Your First Odoo Application*, we will find elements other than `<record>` in the XML files, such as `<menuitem>`.

These are convenient shortcuts for frequently used models, with a more compact notation compared to the regular `<record>` elements. They are used to load data into base models that support the user interface, and they will be explored in more detail later, in *Chapter 10*, *Backend Views – Designing the User Interface*.

For reference, these are the shortcut elements available, along with the corresponding models they load data into:

- `<menuitem>` is for the menu items model, `ir.ui.menu`.

- `<template>` is for *QWeb* templates stored in the `ir.ui.view` model.

> **Changes in Odoo 14**
>
> Past versions of Odoo used to support additional shortcut tags, which are not supported anymore. There was an `<act_window>` for the window action model, `ir.actions.act_window`, and a `<report>` for the report action model, `ir.actions.report.xml`.

It is important to note that, when used to modify existing records, the shortcut elements overwrite all the fields. This differs from the `<record>` basic element, which only writes to the fields provided. So, for cases where we need to modify just a particular field of a user interface element, we should do so using a `<record>` element instead.

Using other actions in XML data files

So far, we have seen how to add or update data using XML files. But XML files also allow you to delete data and execute arbitrary model methods. This can be useful for more complex data setups. In the following sections, we will learn how the delete and function call XML features can be used.

Deleting records

To delete a data record, we can use the `<delete>` element, providing it with either an ID or a search domain to find the target records.

For example, using a search domain to find the record to delete looks as follows:

```
<delete
  model="res.partner"
```

```
    search="[('id','=',ref(
        'library_app.res_partner_daniel'))]"
/>
```

If we know the specific ID to delete, we can use it with the `id` attribute instead. This was the case for the previous example, so it could also be written like this:

```
<delete model="res.partner" id="library_app.res_partner_daniel"
/>
```

This has the same effect as the previous example. Since we know the ID to look for, instead of using the `search` attribute with a domain expression, we can simply use the `id` attribute with the *XML ID*.

Calling model methods

An XML file can also execute arbitrary methods during its load process through the `<function>` element. This can be used to set up demo and test data.

For example, the **Notes** app, which is bundled with Odoo, uses it to set up demonstration data:

```
<data noupdate="1">
<function
    model="res.users"
    name="_init_data_user_note_stages"
    eval="[]" />
</data>
```

This calls the `_init_data_user_note_stages` method of the `res.users` model, passing no arguments. The argument list is provided by the `eval` attribute, which is an empty list in this case.

This completes everything we need to know to use XML data files. We provided an overview of `<data>` elements and the `noupdate` flag. We then learned how to use the `<record>` element to load data records, as well as how to set values on related fields. We also learned about record shortcuts, such as `<menuitem>` and `<template>`. Finally, we learned how to delete records and make arbitrary function calls with the `<delete>` and `<function>` elements.

With this, we should be prepared to use XML data files for whatever data needs our project might have.

Summary

In this chapter, we learned how to represent data in text files. These can be used to manually import data into Odoo or include it in add-on modules as default or *demonstration data*.

At this point, we should be able to export and import CSV data files from the web interface and leverage *external IDs* to detect and update records that already exist in the database. They can also be used to perform a mass edit on data, by editing and reimporting a CSV file that has been exported from Odoo.

We also learned about how XML data files are structured, and all the features they provide, in more detail. These were not only set values on fields but also actions such as deleting records and calling model methods.

In the next chapter, we will focus on how to use *records* to work with the data contained in models. This will give us the necessary tools to then implement our application's business logic and rules.

Further reading

The official Odoo documentation provides additional resources on data files: `https://www.odoo.com/documentation/15.0/developer/reference/backend/data.html`.

6
Models – Structuring the Application Data

In this chapter, we will learn more about the model layer and how to use models to design the data structures that support applications. We will explore the available model types, when each should be used, and how to define constraints that enforce data validations.

Models are composed of data fields that support several data types, and some field types support defining relationships between models. More advanced usage of fields involves having values automatically computed using specific business logic.

The following topics will be covered in this chapter:

- Learning project – improving the Library app
- Creating models
- Creating fields
- Relationships between models
- Computed fields
- Model constraints
- Overview of the Odoo base models

Throughout these topics, you will learn how to create non-trivial data structures for your Odoo projects. By the end of this chapter, you should have a clear overview of all the relevant features needed to structure data models.

Technical requirements

This chapter is based on the code we created in *Chapter 3*, *Your First Odoo Application*. This code can be found in the `ch06/` directory of this book's GitHub repository at `https://github.com/PacktPublishing/Odoo-15-Development-Essentials`.

You should have it in your add-ons path. Make sure that you install the `library_app` module.

Learning project – improving the Library app

In *Chapter 3*, *Your First Odoo Application*, we created the `library_app` add-on module and implemented the simple `library.book` model to represent a book catalog. In this chapter, we will revisit that module to enrich the data that we can store for each book.

We will add a category hierarchy to use for book categorization with the following structure:

- **Name**: The category title
- **Parent**: The parent category that it belongs to
- **Subcategories**: The categories that have this one as the parent
- **Featured book or author**: A selected book or author that represents this category

A few more fields will be added to showcase the different data types available for Odoo fields. We will also use model constraints to implement a few validations on the Books model:

- The title and publication date should be unique.
- ISBNs entered should be valid.

We will start by revisiting Odoo models, now in more depth, to learn about all the options that are available for us.

Creating models

Models are at the heart of the Odoo framework. They describe the application data structures and are the bridge between the application server and the database storage. Business logic can be implemented around models to provide application features, and user interfaces are created on top of them to provide the user experience.

In the following subsections, we will learn about the model's generic attributes, which are used to influence their behavior, and the several types we have available – **regular models**, **transient models**, and **abstract models**.

Model attributes

Model classes can use additional attributes to control some behaviors. These are the most commonly used attributes:

- `_name`: This is the internal identifier for the Odoo model we are creating. This is mandatory when creating a new model.

- `_description`: This is a user-friendly title that can be used to refer to a single `Model` record, such as `Book`. This is optional but recommended. If this is not set, a server log warning will be displayed during the loading sequence.

- `_order`: This sets the default order to use when the model's records are browsed, or shown in a list view. It is a text string to be used as the SQL order by clause, so it can be anything you could use there, although it has smart behavior and supports translatable and many-to-one field names.

Our `Book` model is already using the `_name` and `_description` attributes. The following code adds the `_order` attribute to have the default order by book title, and then by reverse order of publication date (from newest to oldest):

```
class Book(models.Model):
    _name = "library.book"
    _description = "Book"
    _order = "name, date_published desc"
```

There are a few more advanced attributes available that can be helpful in advanced cases:

- `_rec_name`: This sets the field to use for the record's display name. By default, it is the `name` field, which is why we usually choose this particular field name for the records title field.

- _table: This is the name of the database table supporting the model. Usually, it is left to be automatically set by the ORM, which will use the model name after replacing the dots with underscores. However, we are free to choose a specific database table name to be used.

- _log_access=False: This can be used to prevent audit tracking fields from being automatically created; that is, create_uid, create_date, write_uid, and write_date.

- _auto=False: This prevents the underlying database table from being automatically created. In this case, we should use the init() method to provide our specific logic for creating the supporting database object, a table, or a view. This is usually used for views that support read-only reports.

As an example, the following code sets the default values on the library.book model:

```
_recname = "name"
_table = "library_book"
_log_access = True
_auto = True
```

> **Note**
>
> There are also the _inherit and _inherits attributes, which are used for module extension. These were explained in detail in *Chapter 4, Extending Modules.*

When using _auto = False, we are overriding the process of creating the database object, so we should provide the logic for that. A frequent application of this is models to use for reports, based on a database view that gathers all the data needed for the report.

Here is an example taken from the sale core module, in the sale/report/sale_report.py file:

```
def init(self):
    tools.drop_view_if_exists(self.env.cr, self._table)
    self.env.cr.execute(
        "CREATE or REPLACE VIEW %s as (%s)"
        % (self._table, self._query())
    )
```

The preceding code uses a tools Python module, which needs to be imported using odoo import tools.

Models and Python classes

Odoo models use Python classes. In the preceding code, we can see a Python class, `Book`, based on the `models.Model` class, being used to define an Odoo model named `library.book`.

Odoo models are kept in a *central registry*, available through the *environment object*, which is usually accessed using `self.env`. The central registry keeps references to all the models available, and they can be accessed with a dictionary-like syntax.

For example, to get a reference to the library book model inside a method, we could use `self.env["library.book"]` or `self.env.get(["library.book"])`.

As you can see, model names are important and are the key to accessing the model registry.

Model names must be globally unique. Because of this, it is a good practice to use the first word of the application the module belongs to as the first word in the model's name. In the case of the `Library` app, all model names should have `library` as a prefix. Other examples from the core modules are `project`, `crm`, or `sale`.

> **Tip**
>
> Model names should use the singular form, `library.book`, rather than `library.books`. The convention is to use a list of lowercase words joined with dots. The first word should identify the main app the model belongs to, such as `library.book` or `library.book.category`. Other examples that have been taken from official add-ons include `project.project`, `project.task`, and `project.task.type`.

On the other hand, Python class identifiers are local to the Python file where they are declared and are not relevant to the Odoo framework. The identifier that's used for them is only significant for the code in that file and is rarely relevant. The Python convention for class identifiers is to use *CamelCase*, following the standards defined by the PEP8 coding conventions.

There are several types of models available. The most frequently used one is the `models.Model` class, for persistent database stored models. Next, we will learn about the other available model types.

Transient and abstract models

For most Odoo models, the Python class is based on `models.Model`. This type of model has permanent database persistence, which means that database tables are created for them and their records are stored until they're explicitly deleted. And most of the time, this is what you need.

But in some cases, we don't need permanent database persistence, and hence these two other model types can be useful:

- **Transient models**, based on `models.TransientModel`, are used for wizard-style user interaction. Their data is still stored in the database, but it is expected to be temporary. A vacuum job periodically clears old data from these tables. For example, the **Settings | Translations | Import Translation** menu option opens a dialog window that uses a transient model to store the user selections and implement the wizard logic. An example of using a transient model will be discussed in *Chapter 8, Business Logic – Supporting Business Processes*.

- **Abstract models** are based on the `models.AbstractModel` class and have no data storage attached to them. They can be used as reusable feature sets, to be mixed in with other models using Odoo's inheritance capabilities. For example, `mail.thread` is an abstract model provided by the **Discuss** app, which is used to add messages and follower features to other models. Mixin classes that use abstract models and the `mail.thread` example mentioned previously were discussed in *Chapter 4, Extending Modules*.

Inspecting existing models

The models and fields that are created by Python classes can be inspected through the user interface. With **Developer Mode** enabled, via the **Settings** top menu, navigate to the **Technical | Database Structure | Models** menu item. Here, you will find a list of all the models available in the database.

Clicking on a model in the list will open a form showing its details, as shown in the following screenshot:

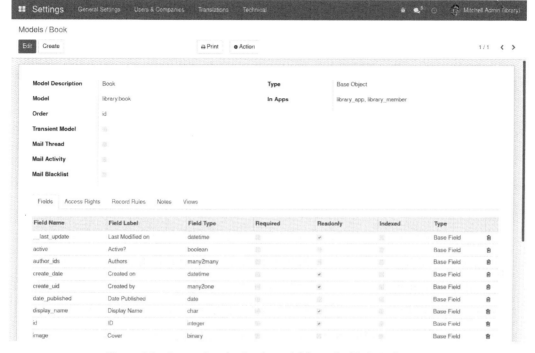

Figure 6.1 – Inspecting the Book model from the Technical menu

This is a good tool for inspecting a model since it shows the results of all the modifications made by different modules. At the top right of the form, in the **In Apps** field, we can see the list of modules affecting it. In this example, we can see that `library.book` is affected by the `library_app` and `library_member` modules.

> **Tip**
>
> As seen in *Chapter 1, Quick Start Using Developer Mode*, the **Models** form is editable! It is possible to create and modify models, fields, and views from here. You can use this to build prototypes that will be implemented as add-on modules later.

In the lower area, we have some tabs with additional information available:

- **Fields** lists the model fields.
- **Access Rights** lists the access control rules granted to security groups.
- **Record Rules** lists the record rules applying filters to records.
- **Notes** is the model definition docstring.
- **Views** lists the views available for the model.

To find the model's external identifier or XML ID, we can use the **Developer** menu's **View Metadata** option. Model external identifiers are automatically generated by the ORM and follow a simple rule – the model name, replacing dots with underscores, prefixed with model_. As an example, the identifier that's generated for the library.book model, as created by the library_app module, is library_app.model_library_book. These XML IDs are usually needed for the CSV files defining the security ACLs.

We are now familiar with the options we have for defining the model. The next step is to understand the several field types, as well as the options available to configure them.

Creating fields

Having created a new model, the next step is to add fields to it. Odoo supports all the basic data types that are expected, such as text strings, integers, floating-point numbers, Booleans, dates and time, and image or binary data.

Let's explore the several types of fields available in Odoo.

Basic field types

We will go back to the book model to present the several available field types.

In the library_app/models/library_book.py file, edit the Book class, replacing the current field definitions with this one:

```python
class Book(models.Model):
    _name = "library.book"
    _description = "Book"

    # String fields:
    name = fields.Char("Title")
    isbn = fields.Char("ISBN")
    book_type = fields.Selection(
        [("paper","Paperback"),
         ("hard","Hardcover"),
         ("electronic","Electronic"),
         ("other", "Other")],
        "Type")
```

```
notes = fields.Text("Internal Notes")
descr = fields.Html("Description")

# Numeric fields:
copies = fields.Integer(default=1)
avg_rating = fields.Float("Average Rating", (3, 2))
price = fields.Monetary("Price", "currency_id")
# price helper
currency_id = fields.Many2one("res.currency")

# Date and time fields:
date_published = fields.Date()
last_borrow_date = fields.Datetime(
    "Last Borrowed On",
     default=lambda self: fields.Datetime.now())

# Other fields:
active = fields.Boolean("Active?")
image = fields.Binary("Cover")

# Relational Fields        Books
publisher_id = fields.Many2one(
    "res.partner", string="Publisher")
author_ids = fields.Many2many(
    "res.partner", string="Authors")
```

These are examples of the non-relational field types that are available in Odoo with the positional arguments expected by each one. Next, we will explain all these field types and options.

> **Tip**
>
> Python functions can have two types of arguments: positional and keyword.
>
> **Positional arguments** are expected to be used in a specific order. For example, the call to `fn(x, y)` should be something such as `f(1, 2)`.
>
> **Keyword arguments** are passed with the name of the argument. For this same function, we could also use `f(x=1, y=2)`, or even mix both styles, with something such as `f(1, y=2)`.
>
> However, note that positional arguments must come before keyword arguments, so `f(x=1, 2)` is not allowed. More information on keyword arguments can be found in the Python official documentation at `https://docs.python.org/3/tutorial/controlflow.html#keyword-arguments`.

As a general rule, the first positional argument is the field title, which corresponds to the `string` keyword argument. The exception to this rule is the **Selection** fields and all the relational fields.

The `string` attribute is used as the default text for the user interface labels. If the `string` attribute is not provided, it will be automatically generated from the field name, replacing underscores with spaces and capitalizing the first letter in each word. For example, the `date_published` default label is **Date Published**.

For reference, this is the list of all the non-relational field types that are available, along with the positional arguments expected by each:

- `Char(string)` is a simple text field. The only positional argument that's expected is the field label.

- `Text(string)` is a multiline text field. The only positional argument is also the field label.

- `Selection(selection, string)` is a drop-down selection list. The selection positional arguments is a `[("value", "Description"),]` list of tuples. For each pair, the first element is the value stored in the database, and the second element is the description presented in the user interface. Extension modules can add options to this list using the `selection_add` keyword argument.

- `Html(string)` is stored as a text field but has specific handling for the user interface for HTML content presentation. For security reasons, it is sanitized by default, but this behavior can be overridden using the `sanitize=False` attribute.

- `Integer(string)` is for integer numbers and expects a string argument for the field label.

- `Float(string, digits)` stores floating-point numbers and has a second optional argument for the precision to use. This is an `(n, d)` tuple, where `n` is the total number of digits, and `d` is the number of those digits used for decimals.

- `Monetary(string, currency_field)` is similar to a `float` field but has specific handling for currency values. The `currency_field` second argument is for the name of the currency field. By default, it is set to `currency_field="currency_id"`.

- The `Date(string)` and `Datetime(string)` fields are for dates and date-time values. They only expect the label text as a positional argument.

- `Boolean(string)` stores True or False values and has one positional argument for the label text.

- `Binary(string)` stores binary data, including images, and expects the string label positional argument.

These field definitions provide the basic parameters that are usually used. Note that there are no required arguments, and Odoo will use reasonable defaults for the missing ones.

> **Changes in Odoo 12**
>
> The `Date` and `Datetime` fields are now handled in the ORM as Python date objects. In previous versions, they were handled as text representations. Because of this, when manipulated, an explicit conversion into a Python date object was needed, which would have to be converted back into a text string after.

Text-based fields, including `Char`, `Text`, and `Html`, have a few specific attributes:

- `size` (only for `Char` fields) sets the maximum allowed size. It is recommended to not use it unless there is a good reason for it; for example, a social security number with a maximum length allowed.

- `translate=True` makes the field contents translatable, holding different values for different languages.

- `trim` is set to `True` by default and automatically trims the surrounding white space, which is performed by the web client. This can be explicitly disabled by setting `trim=False`.

> **Changes in Odoo 12**
>
> The `trim` field attribute was introduced in Odoo 12. In previous versions, text fields were saved along with the white space.

Additionally, we also have relational field types available. These will be explained later in this chapter, in the *Relationships between models* section.

Before we get to that, however, there is still more to know about the attributes of the basic field types, as explained in the next section.

Common field attributes

So far, we have looked at the basic positional arguments available for several basic field types. However, there are more attributes available to us.

The following keyword argument attributes are generally available to all field types:

- `string` is the field's default label, to be used in the user interface. Except for `Selection` and relational fields, it is available as the first positional argument, so most of the time, it is not used as a keyword argument. If it's not provided, it is automatically generated from the field name.

- `default` sets a default value for the field. It can be a fixed value (such as `default=True` in the `active` field), or a callable reference, either the named function reference or a `lambda` anonymous function.

- `help` provides the text for tooltips that are displayed to users when hovering the mouse over the field in the UI.

- `readonly=True` makes the field not editable in the user interface by default. This is not enforced at the API level: code in model methods will still be capable of writing to it, and a view definition can override this. It is only a user interface setting.

- `required=True` makes the field mandatory in the user interface by default. This is enforced at the database level by adding a `NOT NULL` constraint to the database column.

- `index=True` adds a database index to the field, for faster search operations at the expense of disk space usage and slower write operations.

- `copy=False` has the field ignored when duplicating a record via the `copy()` ORM method. Field values are copied by default, except for to-many relational fields, which are not copied by default.

- `deprecated=True` marks the field as deprecated. It will still work as usual, but any access to it will write a warning message to the server log.

- `groups` allows you to limit the field's access and visibility to only some groups. It expects a comma-separated list of XML IDs for security groups; for example, `groups="base.group_user,base.group_system"`.

- `states` expects dictionary mapping values for UI attributes, depending on the values of the `state` field. The attributes that can be used are `readonly`, `required`, and `invisible`; for example, `states={'done':[('readonly',True)]}`.

> **Tip**
>
> Note that the `states` field attribute is equivalent to the `attrs` attribute in views. Also, views support a `states` attribute that has a different use: it is a comma-separated list of states in which the view element should be visible.

Here is an example of the `name` field with all the available keyword arguments spelled out:

```
name = fields.Char(
    "Title",
    default=None,
    help="Book cover title.",
    readonly=False,
    required=True,
    index=True,
    copy=False,
    deprecated=True,
    groups="",
    states={},
)
```

Previous Odoo versions supported the `oldname="field"` attribute, which is used when a field is renamed in a newer version. It enabled the data in the old field to be automatically copied into the new field during the module upgrade process.

> **Changes in Odoo 13**
>
> The `oldname` field attribute was removed and is no longer available. The alternative is to use migration scripts.

The preceding field attributes are generic and apply to all field types. Next, we will learn how to set default values on fields.

Setting default values

As we mentioned previously, the `default` attribute can have a fixed value or a reference to a function to dynamically compute the default value.

For trivial computations, we can use a `lambda` function to avoid the overhead of creating a named method function. Here is a common example of computing a default value with the current date and time:

```
last_borrow_date = fields.Datetime(
    "Last Borrowed On",
    default=lambda self: fields.Datetime.now(),
)
```

The `default` value can also be a function reference. This can be a name reference or a string with the function name.

The following example uses a name reference to the `_default_last_borrow_date` function method:

```
def _default_last_borrow_date(self):
    return fields.Datetime.now()


last_borrow_date = fields.Datetime(
    "Last Borrowed On",
    default=_default_last_borrow_date,
)
```

And this example does the same, but uses a string with the function name:

```
last_borrow_date = fields.Datetime(
    "Last Borrowed On",
    default="_default_last_borrow_date",
)


def _default_last_borrow_date(self):
    return fields.Datetime.now()
```

With this latter method, the function name resolution is delayed at runtime, rather than Python file loading time. So, in the second example, we can reference a function declared later in the code, while in the first example, the function must be declared before the function declaration.

Still, the general code convention here is to have the default value function defined before the field's definitions. Another argument for preferring the first approach, using the function name reference, is that code editors can detect typing errors if they support static code analysis.

Automatic field names

Some field names are special, either because they are reserved by the ORM for special purposes, or because some built-in features make use of some default field names.

The `id` field is reserved to be used as an automatic number, uniquely identifying each record, and is used as the database's primary key. It is automatically added to every model.

The following fields are automatically created on new models unless the `_log_access=False` model attribute is set:

- `create_uid` is for the user who created the record.
- `create_date` is for the date and time when the record is created.
- `write_uid` is for the last user to modify the record.
- `write_date` is for the last date and time when the record was modified.

The information in these fields is available in the web client when in a form view if you go to the **Developer Mode** menu and then click the **View Metadata** option.

The preceding field names have a special meaning for the Odoo framework. Other than these, there are a few more field names that are used as defaults for some Odoo features. The next section describes them.

Reserved field names

Some built-in API features expect specific field names by default. These are considered reserved field names, and we should avoid using them for purposes other than the expected ones.

These are the reserved fields:

- `name` or `x_name` of the `Char` type: These are used by default as the display name for the record. But a different field can be used for the display name by setting the `_rec_name` model attribute. Non-character field types are also known to work for this, and a number to text conversion will be forced for this.

- `active` or `x_active` of the `Boolean` type: These allow you to deactivate records, making them invisible. Records with `active=False` are automatically excluded from queries unless the `{'active_test': False}` key is added to the environmental context. It can be used as a record *archive* or *soft delete* feature.

- `state` of the `Selection` type: This represents basic states for the record life cycle. It enables the usage of the `states` field attribute to dynamically set the `readonly`, `required`, or `invisible` attributes; for example, `states={'draft': [('readonly', False)]}`.

- `parent_id` of the `Many2one` type: This is used to define tree-like hierarchical structures, and enables the usage of the `child_of` and `parent_of` operators in domain expressions. The field to use as `parent_id` can be set to a different one using the `_parent_name` model attribute.

- `parent_path` of the `Char` type: This can be used to optimize the usage of the `child_of` and `parent_of` operators in domain expressions. For proper operation, use `add index=True` to use a database index. We will discuss hierarchical relations later in this chapter, in the *Hierarchical relationships* section.

- `company_id` of the `Many2one` type: This is used to identify the company that the record belongs to. An empty value means that the record is shared between companies. It is used by internal checks on company data consistency via the `_check_company` function.

Changes in Odoo 14

`x_active` is now recognized as an equivalent to the `active` field and can be used for the same effect. This was introduced for better support for customizations using **Developer Mode** or the **Odoo Studio** app.

So far, we have discussed non-relational fields. But a good part of an application data structure is about describing the relationships between entities. Let's look at that now.

Relationships between models

Non-trivial business applications need to use relationships between the different entities involved. To do this, we need to use relational fields.

Looking at the `Library` app, the `Book` model has the following relationships:

- Each book can have one publisher, and each publisher can have many books. From the book's point of view, this is a *many-to-one relationship*. It is implemented in the database as an integer field, holding the ID of the related publisher record, and a database foreign key in it, enforcing referential integrity.

- The reverse of this, from the publisher's point of view, is a **one-to-many relation**, meaning that each publisher can have many books. While this is also a field type in Odoo, its database representation relies on the many-to-one relationship. We know the books related to a publisher running a query on books, filtered by the publisher ID.

- Each book can have many authors, and each author can have many books. This is a **many-to-many** relationship. The inverse relationship is also a many-to-many relationship. In relational databases, many-to-many relationships are represented through a helper database table. Odoo will automatically take care of this, although we can have some control over the technical details if we want.

We will explore each of these relationships in the following sections.

A particular case is hierarchical relations, where records in a model are related to other records in the same model. We will introduce a book category model to explain this.

Finally, the Odoo framework also supports flexible relationships, where the same field is capable of representing relationships with several different models. These are called `Reference` fields.

Many-to-one relationships

A **many-to-one relationship** is a reference to a record in another model. For example, in the library book model, the `publisher_id` field represents a reference to the book publisher – a record in the **Partner** model.

As a reminder, this is the publisher field definition using positional arguments only:

```
publisher_id = fields.Many2one(
        "res.partner", "Publisher")
```

The preceding `Many2one` field definition uses positional arguments:

- The first positional argument is the related model, corresponding to the `comodel` keyword argument, which is `res.partner` in this case.

- The second positional argument is the field label, corresponding to the `string` keyword argument. This is not the case for the other relational fields, so the preferred option is to always use `string` as a keyword argument.

A many-to-one model field creates a column in the database table, with a foreign key to the related table, and holds the database ID of the related record.

Keyword arguments can be used instead of, or to complement, the positional argument. These are the keyword arguments that are supported by many-to-one fields:

- `ondelete`: This defines what happens when the related record is deleted. The possible behaviors are as follows:

  `set null` (the default): An empty value is set when the related record is deleted.

  `restricted`: This raises an error, preventing the deletion.

  `cascade`: This will also delete this record when the related record is deleted.

- `context`: This is a dictionary of data that's meaningful for the web client views to carry information when navigating through the relationship, such as to set default values. This will be explained in more detail in *Chapter 8*, *Business Logic – Supporting Business Processes*.

- `domain`: This is a domain expression – a list of tuples used to filter the records made available for selection on the relationship field. See *Chapter 8*, *Business Logic – Supporting Business Processes*, for more details.

- `auto_join=True`: This allows the ORM to use SQL joins when doing searches using this relationship. If used, the access security rules will be bypassed, and the user could have access to related records that the security rules would not allow, but the SQL queries will run faster.

- `delegate=True`: This creates a delegation inheritance with the related model. When used, the `required=True` and `ondelete="cascade"` attributes must also be set. See *Chapter 4*, *Extending Modules*, for more information on delegation inheritance.

One-to-many inverse relationships

A **one-to-many relationship** is the inverse of the many-to-one relationship. It lists the records that have a relationship with this record.

For example, in the library book model, the `publisher_id` field has a many-to-one relationship with the partner model. This means that the partner model can have a one-to-many inverse relationship with the book model, listing the books published by each partner.

Before a one-to-many relationship field can be created, the inverse many-to-one field should be added to the related model. For this, create the `library_app/models/res_partner.py` file with the following code:

```python
from odoo import fields, models


class Partner(models.Model):
    _inherit = "res.partner"

    published_book_ids = fields.One2many(
        "library.book",
        "publisher_id",
        string="Published Books")
```

partner → books (handwritten annotation)

Since this is a new code file for the module, it must also be added to the `library_app/models/__init__.py` file:

```python
from . import library_book
from . import res_partner
```

The `One2many` fields expect three positional arguments:

- The related model, which corresponds to the `comodel_name` keyword argument
- The related model field that's used to refer to this record, which corresponds to the `inverse_name` keyword argument
- The field label, which corresponds to the `string` keyword argument

The additional keyword arguments that are available are the same as those for the many-to-one fields: `context`, `domain`, `auto_join`, and `ondelete` (here, these act on the **many** sides of the relationship).

Many-to-many relationships

A **many-to-many relationship** is used when both entities have a to-many relationship between them. Using the library books example, there is a many-to-many relationship between books and authors: each book can have many authors, and each author can have many books.

On the book's side – that is, the `library.book` model – we have the following:

```
class Book(models.Model)
    _name = "library.book"

    author_ids = fields.Many2many(
        "res.partner",
        string="Authors")
```

On the author's side, we can have the `res.partner` model inverse relationship:

```
class Partner(models.Model):
    _inherit = "res.partner"

    book_ids = fields.Many2many(
        "library.book",
        string="Authored Books")
```

The `Many2many` minimal signature expects one positional argument for the related model – the `comodel_name` keyword argument – and it is recommended to also provide the `string` argument with the field label.

At the database level, many-to-many relationships don't add any columns to the existing tables. Instead, a special relationship table is automatically created to store the relationships between records. This special table has only two ID fields, with foreign keys for each of the two related tables.

By default, the relationship table's name is the two table names joined with an underscore and `_rel` appended at the end. In the case of our books or authors relationship, it should be named `library_book_res_partner_rel`.

On some occasions, we may need to override these automatic defaults. One such case is when the related models have long names, and the name for the automatically generated relationship table is too long, exceeding the 63-character PostgreSQL limit. In these cases, we need to manually choose a name for the relationship table to conform to the table name size limit.

Another case is when we need a second many-to-many relationship between the same models. In these cases, a relationship table name must be manually provided so that it doesn't collide with the table name already being used for the first relationship.

There are two alternatives to manually override these values: either use positional arguments or keyword arguments.

When using positional arguments for the field definition, the field definition looks like this:

```
# Book <-> Authors relation (using positional args)
author_ids = fields.Many2many(
    "res.partner",
    "library_book_res_partner_rel",
    "a_id",
    "b_id",
    "Authors")
```

Keyword arguments can be used instead, which may be preferred for readability:

```
# Book <-> Authors relation (using keyword args)
author_ids = fields.Many2many(
    comodel_name="res.partner",
    relation="library_book_res_partner_rel",
    column1="a_id",
    column2="b_id",
    string="Authors")
```

The following arguments were used here:

- `comodel_name` is the name of the related model.
- `relation` is the database table name supporting the relationship data.
- `column1` is the column name referring to the model records.
- `column2` is the column name referring to the related model records.
- `string` is the field label in the user interface.

Similar to one-to-many relational fields, many-to-many fields can also use the `context`, `domain`, and `auto_join` keyword arguments.

> **Tip**
>
> On abstract models, don't use the many-to-many field `column1` and `column2` attributes. There is a limitation in the ORM design regarding abstract models, and when you force the names of the relationship columns, they cannot be cleanly inherited anymore.

Parent-child relationships are a particular case that is worth looking into in more detail. We will do this in the next section.

Hierarchical relationships

Parent-child tree relationships are represented using a many-to-one relationship with the same model, where each record holds a reference to its parent. The inverse one-to-many relationship represents the record's direct children.

Odoo provides improved support for these hierarchical data structures, making the `child_of` and `parent_of` operators available in domain expressions. These operators are available so long as the model has a `parent_id` field (or the model has a `_parent_name` valid definition, setting an alternative field name to use for this purpose).

Optimized hierarchy tree searching can be enabled by setting the `_parent_store=True` model attribute and adding the `parent_path` helper field. This helper field stores additional information about the hierarchy tree structure, which is used to run faster queries.

> **Changes in Odoo 12**
>
> The `parent_path` hierarchy helper field was introduced in Odoo 12. Previous versions used the `parent_left` and `parent_right` integer fields for the same purpose, but these were deprecated as of Odoo 12.

As an example of a hierarchical structure, we will add a category tree to the **Library** app to be used to categorize books.

Let's add the `library_app/models/library_book_category.py` file, along with the following code:

```python
from odoo import api, fields, models


class BookCategory(models.Model):
    _name = "library.book.category"
    _description = "Book Category"
    _parent_store = True

    name = fields.Char(translate=True, required=True)
    # Hierarchy fields
    parent_id = fields.Many2one(
        "library.book.category",
        "Parent Category",
        ondelete="restrict")
    parent_path = fields.Char(index=True)

    # Optional, but nice to have:
    child_ids = fields.One2many(
        "library.book.category",
        "parent_id",
        "Subcategories")
```

Here, we have a basic model with a `parent_id` field to reference the parent record.

To enable a faster tree search, we added the `_parent_store=True` model attribute. When doing so, the `parent_path` field must also be added, and it must be indexed. The field that's used to refer to the parent is expected to be named `parent_id`, but any other field name can be used, so long as we declare that in the `_parent_name` optional model attribute.

It is often convenient to add a field to list the direct children. This is the one-to-many inverse relationship shown in the previous code.

For the previous code to be used by our module, remember to add a reference to its file in `library_app/models/__init__.py`:

```
from . import library_book_category
from . import library_book
from . import res_partner
```

Be aware that these additional operations come with storage and execution time penalties, so they are best used when you expect to read more frequently than write, such as in the case of category trees. This is only necessary when optimizing deep hierarchies with many nodes; this can be misused for small or shallow hierarchies.

Flexible relationships using Reference fields

Regular relational fields can only reference one fixed co-model. The `Reference` field type does not have this limitation and supports flexible relationships, and the same field can reference records from different destination models.

As an example, we will add a `Reference` field to the book category model, to indicate a highlighted book or author. This field can link to either a book or a partner record:

```
highlighted_id = fields.Reference(
    [("library.book", "Book"), ("res.partner",
        "Author")],
    "Category Highlight",
)
```

The field definition is similar to a `Selection` field, but here, the selection list holds the models that can be used on the field. In the user interface, the user will pick a model from the available list, and then pick a specific record from that model.

Reference fields are stored in the database as a character field, containing a `<model>,<id>` string.

> **Changes in Odoo 12**
>
> Previous Odoo versions featured a referenceable model configuration that could be used to pick the models used in `Reference` fields from the **Settings | Technical | Database Structure** menu. These configurations could be used in the `Reference` field, by adding the `odoo.addons.res.res_request.referenceable_models` function in place of the model selection list. This feature was removed in Odoo 12.

With that, we've seen the field types that are supported by Odoo. Not only can fields store user-provided data, but they are also capable of presenting computed values. The next section introduces this feature.

Computed fields

Fields can have their values automatically calculated by a function, instead of simply reading a database stored value. A computed field is declared just like a regular field but has the additional `compute` argument to define the function that's used for the computation.

Computed fields involve writing some business logic. So, to take full advantage of this feature, we should be comfortable with the topics that will be explained in *Chapter 8, Business Logic – Supporting Business Processes*. Computed fields will still be explained here, but we will keep the business logic as simple as possible.

As an example, we will add a computed field to the `Books` model, displaying the publisher's country. This will allow the country to be displayed in the form view.

The code that's needed to find the value is simple: if `book` represents a book record, we can use object dot notation to get the publisher's country using `book.publisher_id.country_id`.

Edit the book model in the `library_app/models/library_book.py` file by adding the following code:

```
publisher_country_id = fields.Many2one(
    "res.country", string="Publisher Country",
    compute="_compute_publisher_country",
)


@api.depends("publisher_id.country_id")
def _compute_publisher_country(self):
    for book in self:
        book.publisher_country_id = \
            book.publisher_id.country_id
```

First, this code adds the `publisher_country_id` field and sets the compute attribute with the name of the method function to use for its computation, `_compute_publisher_country`.

The function name was passed to the field as a string argument, but it may also be passed as a callable reference (the function identifier, without the surrounding quotes). In this case, we need to make sure the function is defined in the Python file before the field is.

The coding convention for computation method names is to append the `_compute_` prefix to the computed field name.

The `_compute_publisher_country` method receives a `self` record set to operate on and is expected to set the computed field values for all of those records. The code should iterate on the `self` recordset, to act on each record.

The computed value is set using the usual assignment (write) operation. In our case, the computation is quite simple: we assign it to the current book's `publisher_id.country_id` value.

> **Tip**
>
> The same computation method can be used to compute two or more fields. In this case, the method should be used on the `compute` attribute of the computed fields, and the computation method should assign values to all of them.

The computation function must always assign a value to the field, or fields, to compute. If your computation method has `if` conditions, make sure that all the run paths assign values to the computed fields. Computation methods will error if it misses assigning a value to some computed field(s).

> **Changes in Odoo 13**
>
> Odoo 13 introduced **computed writeable** fields, intended to replace the **onchange** mechanism in the future. Computed writeable fields have a computation logic, triggered by changes on the dependencies, and also allow for the value to be directly set by users. This mechanism will be discussed alongside **onchange** in *Chapter 8, Business Logic – Supporting Business Processes*.

The `@api.depends` decorator is needed to specify the fields the computation depends on. It is used by the ORM to know when the computation needs to be triggered to update stored or cached values. One or more field names are accepted as arguments and dot-notation can be used to follow field relationships. In this example, the `publisher_country_id` field should be recomputed when `publisher_id.country_id` changes.

> **Warning**
>
> Forgetting to add the @api.depends decorator to a computation method, or adding it but failing to add all the dependency fields used for the computation, will prevent the computed field from being recalculated when it is supposed to. This can lead to hard-to-identify bugs.

We can see the result of our work by adding the publisher_country_id field to the book form view, in the library_app/views/library_book.xml file. Make sure that the selected publishers have the country set on them when trying this with a web client.

Searching and writing on computed fields

The computed field we created can be read, but it cannot be searched or written to. By default, computed field values are computed immediately when read, and their values are not stored in the database. That's why they can't be searched like regular stored fields can.

One way to work around this limitation is to have the computed values stored in the database by adding the store = True attribute. They will be recomputed when any of their dependencies change. Since the values are now stored, they can be searched just like regular fields, and a search function is not needed.

Computed fields also support search and write operations without being stored in the database. This can be enabled by implementing specialized functions for these operations, alongside the compute function:

- A search function to implement the search logic
- An inverse function to implement the write logic

Using these, our computed field declaration will look as follows:

```
publisher_country_id = fields.Many2one(
    "res.country",
    string="Publisher Country",
    compute="_compute_publisher_country",
    inverse="_inverse_publisher_country",
    search="_search_publisher_country",
)
```

To write on a computed field, we must implement the *inverse* logic of the value computation. This is why the function in charge of handling the write operation is called `inverse`.

In this example, setting a value on `publisher_country_id` is expected to change the publisher's country.

Note that this will also change the value that's seen in all the books with this publisher. Regular access controls apply to these write operations, so this action will only be successful if the current user also has to write access to the partner model.

This inverse function implementation uses the values set on the computed field to perform the actual write operations needed to make this change persistent:

```
def _inverse_publisher_country(self):
    for book in self:
        book.publisher_id.country_id = \
            book.publisher_country_id
```

The original value computation copies the `book.publisher_id.country_id` value to the `book.publisher_country_id` field. The inverse implementation, shown previously, does the opposite. It reads the value set on `book.publisher_country_id` and writes it to the `book.publisher_id.country_id` field.

To enable search operations on a computed field, its `search` function must be implemented. The `search` function intercepts domain expressions operating on the computed field, and then replaces them with an alternative domain expression, using only regular stored fields.

In the `publisher_country_id` example, the actual search should be done on the `country_id` field of the linked `publisher_id` partner record. Here is the function implementation for this translation:

```
def _search_publisher_country(self, operator, value):
    return [
        ("publisher_id.country_id", operator, value)
    ]
"
```

When we perform a search on a model, a domain expression tuple is used as an argument, giving the details of the operator and the value that was used in the domain expression.

The `search` function is triggered whenever this computed field is found in conditions of a domain expression. It receives `operator` and `value` for the search and is expected to translate the original search element into an alternative domain search expression. The `country_id` field is stored in the related partner model, so our search implementation just alters the original search expression to use the `publisher_id.country_id` field instead.

For reference, domain expressions will be explained in more detail in *Chapter 8, Business Logic – Supporting Business Processes*.

Related fields

The computed field we implemented in the previous section simply copies a value from a related record to a field of the model. This is a common use case and is needed when we want to present a field in a form from a related record. The Odoo framework provides a shortcut for this: the **related field** feature.

Related fields make fields that belong to a related model available in a model and are accessible using a *dot notation chain*. This makes them available in cases where dot notation can't be used, such as UI form views.

To create a related field, a field of the required type must be declared, and the `related` attribute must be used, with the dot notation field chain needed to reach the target-related field.

A `related` field can be used to get the same effect as in the previous `publisher_country_id` computed field example.

Here is the alternative implementation, now using a `related` field:

```
publisher_country_id = fields.Many2one(
    "res.country",
    string="Publisher Country",
    related="publisher_id.country_id",
)
```

Behind the scenes, related fields are just computed fields, and they also conveniently implement `search` and `inverse` methods. So, they can be searched and written on.

By default, related fields are read-only, so the inverse write operation won't be available. To enable it, set the `readonly=False` field attribute.

Changes in Odoo 12

In previous Odoo versions, related fields were writable by default, but it was proven to be a dangerous default since it could allow changes to setup or master data in cases where that was not expected to be allowed. Because of this, starting with Odoo 12, the `related` fields are now read-only by default: `readonly=True`.

It's also worth noting that `related` fields can also be stored in a database using `store=True`, just like any other computed field.

With that, we've learned about the features supported by Odoo fields, including computed fields. Another important element regarding data structures is constraints that enforce data quality and integrity. This is what the next section will discuss.

Model constraints

Often, applications need to ensure data integrity and enforce validations to ensure that the data is complete and correct.

The PostgreSQL database manager supports many useful validations, such as avoiding duplicates or checking that values meet certain simple conditions. Odoo models can use the PostgreSQL constraints capabilities for this.

Some checks require more sophisticated logic and are better implemented as Python code. For these cases, we can use specific model methods that implement that Python constraint logic.

Let's learn more about these two possibilities.

SQL model constraints

SQL constraints are added to the database table definition and are enforced directly by PostgreSQL. They are declared using the `_sql_constraints` class attribute.

It is a list of tuples, and each tuple has a format of (`name`, `sql`, `message`):

- `name` is the constraint identifier name.
- `sql` is the PostgreSQL syntax for the constraint.

- `message` is the error message to present to users when the constraint is not verified.

The most used SQL constraints are `UNIQUE` constraints, which are used to prevent data duplication, and `CHECK` constraints, which are used to test a SQL expression on the data.

As an example, we will add two constraints to the `Book` model:

- Ensure that there are repeated books with the same title and publication date.

- Ensure that the publication date is not in the future.

Edit the `library_app/models/library_book.py` file by adding the following code, which implements these two constraints. Usually, this goes after a section of the code with the field declarations:

```
_sql_constraints = [
    ("library_book_name_date_uq",
     "UNIQUE (name, date_published)",
    "Title and publication date must be unique."),
    ("library_book_check_date",
     "CHECK (date_published <= current_date)",
     "Publication date must not be in the future."),
]
```

For more information on the PostgreSQL constraint syntax, see the official documentation at `https://www.postgresql.org/docs/current/ddl-constraints.html`.

Python model constraints

Python constraints can use arbitrary code to perform validations. The validation function should be decorated with `@api.constrains` and the list of fields involved in the check. The validation is triggered when any of those fields are modified and should raise an exception if the condition fails – usually, `ValidationError`.

In the case of the Library app, an obvious example is to prevent inserting incorrect ISBNs. We already have the logic to check that an ISBN is correct in the `_check_isbn()` method. We can use this in a model constraint to prevent saving incorrect data.

Edit the `library_app/models/library_book.py` file by going to the top of the file and adding the following `import` statement:

```
from odoo.exceptions import ValidationError
```

Now, in the same file, add the following code to the `Book` class:

```
    @api.constrains("isbn")
    def _constrain_isbn_valid(self):
        for book in self:
            if book.isbn and not book._check_isbn():
                raise ValidationError(
                    "%s is an invalid ISBN" % book.isbn)
```

Python SQL constraints are usually added before the code section containing the field declaration.

Overview of the Odoo base models

In the previous chapters, we had the chance to create new models, such as the **Book** model, but we also made use of the already existing models, such as the **Partner** model, provided by the Odoo base module. In this section, we will provide a short introduction to these built-in models.

The Odoo core framework includes the `base` add-on module. It provides the essential features needed for Odoo apps to work. It can be found in the Odoo repository, in the `./odoo/addons/base` subdirectory.

The standard add-on modules, which provide the official apps and features made available with Odoo, depend on and build on top of the `base` module. The standard add-ons can be found in the Odoo repository, in the `./addons` subdirectory.

The `base` module provides two kinds of models:

- Information repository, `ir.*`, models
- Resources, `res.*`, models

The **information repository** models are used to store basic data needed for the Odoo framework, such as Menus, Views, Models, and Actions. The data we find in the **Technical** menu is usually stored in information repository models.

Some relevant examples are as follows:

- `ir.actions.act_window` for **Windows Actions**
- `ir.config_parameter` for global configuration options
- `ir.ui.menu` for **Menu Items**
- `ir.ui.view` for **Views**
- `ir.model` for **Models**
- `ir.model.fields` for model **Fields**
- `ir.model.data` for **XML IDs**

The **resources** models store basic master data that can be used by any module.

These are the most important resource models:

- `res.partner` for business partners, such as customers and suppliers, and addresses
- `res.company` for company data
- `res.country` for countries
- `res.country.state` for states or regions inside countries
- `res.currency` for currencies
- `res.groups` for application security groups
- `res.users` for application users

This should provide useful context to help you understand the origin of these models.

Summary

In this chapter, we learned about the different model types, such as transient and abstract models, and why these are useful for user interface wizards and mixins, respectively. Other relevant model features include Python and SQL constraints, which can be used to prevent data entry errors.

We also learned about the available field types, as well as all the attributes they support, to be able to represent the business data in the most accurate way possible. We also learned about relationships fields, and how to use them to create relationships between the different entities that are used by our applications.

After that, we saw that models are usually based on the `models.Model` class, but that we can also use `models.Abstract` for reusable mixin models and `models.Transient` for wizards or advanced user interaction dialogs. We saw the general model attributes that are available, such as `_order` for default sort order and `_rec_name` for the default field to use for record representation.

The fields in a model define all the data they will store. We have also seen the non-relational field types that are available and the attributes they support. We also learned about the several types of relational fields – many-to-one, one-to-many, and many-to-many – and how they define relationships between models, including hierarchical parent/child relationships.

Most fields store user input in databases, but fields can have values automatically computed by Python code. We saw how to implement computed fields and some advanced possibilities we have, such as making them writable and searchable.

Also part of model definitions is constraints, enforcing data consistency, and validation. These can be implemented either using PostgreSQL or Python code.

Now that we have created the data model, we should populate it with some default and demonstration data. In the next chapter, we will learn how to use data files to export, import, and load data using our system.

Further reading

The official documentation for models can be found at `https://www.odoo.com/documentation/15.0/developer/reference/backend/orm.html`.

Section 3: Business Logic

In the third part, we explain how to write the business logic layer around the models, corresponding to the controller component of the architecture. This includes the built-in **Object-Relational Mapping (ORM)** functions, used to manipulate the data in the models, and social features used for messages and notifications.

In this section, the following chapters are included:

- *Chapter 7, Recordsets – Working with Model Data*
- *Chapter 8, Business Logic – Supporting Business Processes*
- *Chapter 9, External APIs – Integrating with Other Systems*

7
Recordsets – Working with Model Data

In the previous chapters, we gave an overview of model creation and loading data into models. Now that we have a data model and some data to work with, it's time to learn more about how to programmatically interact with it.

A business application needs business logic to compute data, perform validations, or automate operations. The **Odoo** framework API provides the tools for a developer to implement this business logic. Most of the time, this means querying, transforming, and writing data.

Odoo implements an **Object-Relational Mapping** (**ORM**) layer on top of the lower level database. The ORM objects provide the **Application Programming Interface** (**API**) to be used to interact with the data. This API provides an execution environment and the creation of **recordsets**, that are objects used to work the data stored in the database.

This chapter explains how to use the execution environment and recordsets so that you have all the tools needed to implement the business processes.

In this chapter, we'll cover the following topics:

- Using the shell command to interactively explore the ORM API
- Understanding the execution environment and context
- Querying data using recordsets and domains
- Accessing data in recordsets
- Writing to records
- Working with date and time
- Working with recordsets
- Transactions and low-level SQL

By the end of this chapter, you should be able to use Odoo code to perform all of these actions, and you will also be ready to use these tools to implement your own business processes.

Technical requirements

The code examples in this chapter will be executed in an interactive shell and do not require any code from the previous chapters. A copy of the code can be found in the **GitHub** repository for this book (`https://github.com/PacktPublishing/Odoo-15-Development-Essentials`) in the `ch07/ch07_recorsets_code.py` file.

Using the shell command

Python includes a command-line interface that is a great way to explore the language. Odoo includes a similar feature through the `shell` command option. These commands can be executed interactively to better understand how they work.

To use it, add the `shell` command when starting Odoo, plus any Odoo options that we would usually use when starting Odoo:

```
(env15) $ odoo shell -c library.conf
```

This will initiate the usual server startup sequence in the terminal, but instead of launching an HTTP server listening for requests, it will start a Python prompt waiting for input.

This interactive command interface simulates the environment found inside a `class` method, running under the `OdooBot` superuser. The `self` variable is available and is set to the `OdooBot` superuser record object.

For example, these commands inspect the `self` recordset:

```
>>> self
res.users(1,)
>>> self._name
'res.users'
>>> self.name
'OdooBot'
>>> self.login
'__system__'
```

The previous commands print out the following:

- The `self` variable contains a `res.users` recordset containing a record with `ID 1`.

- The recordset model name, inspecting `self._name`, is `res.users`, as expected.

- The value for the record `name` field is `OdooBot`.

- The value for the record `login` field is `__system__`.

> **Changes in Odoo 12**
>
> The `ID 1` superuser changed from `admin` to the internal `__system__` user. The `admin` user is now the `ID 2` user, and not a superuser, although the Odoo standard apps are careful to automatically grant it full access to them. The main reason for this change was to avoid having users perform day-to-day activities with the superuser account. Doing so is dangerous because this change bypasses all access rules and may cause inconsistent data, such as cross-company relationships. It's now meant to be used only for troubleshooting or very specific cross-company operations.

As with Python, to exit the prompt, press *Ctrl + D*. This will also close the server process and return to the system shell prompt.

We now know how to start an Odoo shell session. This is important for us to discover the Odoo API features. So, let's use it to explore the execution environment.

The execution environment

Odoo recordsets operate in an **environment** context, providing relevant information about the context where the operation was triggered. For example, the database cursor being used, the current Odoo user, and more.

Python code running inside a model method has access to the `self` recordset variable, and the local environment can be accessed with `self.env`. The server shell environment also provides a `self` reference in a similar way to what is found inside a method.

In this section, we will learn about the attributes made available by the execution environment and how to use them.

Environment attributes

As we have seen, `self` is a recordset. Recordsets carry environment information with them such as the user browsing the data and additional context-related information (for example, the active language and time zone).

The current environment can be accessed using the `env` attribute of a recordset, as shown in this example:

```
>>> self.env
<odoo.api.Environment object at 0x7f6882f7df40>
```

The execution environment in `self.env` has the following attributes available:

- The `env.cr` attribute is the database cursor being used.
- The `env.user` attribute is the record for the current user.
- The `env.uid` attribute is the ID for the session user. It is the same as `env.user.id`.
- The `env.context` attribute is an immutable dictionary containing the session context data.
- The `env.company` attribute is the active company.
- The `env.companies` attributes are the user's allowed companies.

> **Changes in Odoo 13**
>
> The `env.company` and `env.companies` attributes were introduced in Odoo 13. In previous versions, this information was read from the user record by using `env.user.company_id` and `env.user.company_ids`.

The environment also provides access to the registry where all installed models are available. For example, self.env["res.partner"] returns a reference to the partner model. We can then use search() or browse() on it to create recordsets:

```
>>> self.env["res.partner"].search([("display_name", "like",
"Azure")])
res.partner(14, 26, 33, 27)
```

In this example, the returned recordset for the res.partner model contains three records, with IDs 14, 26, 33, and 27. The recordset is not ordered by ID, as the default order for the corresponding model was used. In the case of the partner model, the default object _order is display_name.

The environment context

The context object is a dictionary carrying session data that can be used on both the client-side user interface and the server-side ORM and business logic.

From the client side, it can carry information from one view to the next—such as the ID of the record active on the previous view after following a link or a button—or it can provide default values to be used in the next view.

On the server side, some recordset field values can depend on the locale settings provided by the context. In particular, the lang key affects the value of the translatable fields.

Context can also provide signals for server-side code. For example, the active_test key, when set to False, changes the behavior of the ORM search() method so that it does not apply the automatic filter on inactive records, ignoring the active record field.

An initial context from the web client looks like this:

```
>>> self.env.context
{'lang': 'en_US', 'tz': 'Europe/Brussels'}
```

Here, you can see the lang key with the user language and tz with the time zone information. The content in records might be different depending on the current context:

- Translated fields can have different values depending on the active lang language.
- Datetime fields, when returned to clients, can show different times depending on the active tz timezone.

When opening a view from a link or a button in a previous view, the web client will automatically add a few keys to the context, providing information on the record we are navigating from:

- `active_model` is the previous model name.
- `active_id` is the ID of the original record the user was positioned at.
- `active_ids` is a list of the IDs selected in cases where the user is navigating from a list view.

Wizard assistants frequently use these keys to find the records they are expected to act on.

The context can be used to set default values and activate default filters on the target web client view by using keys with these specific prefixes:

- The `default_` prefix added to a field name sets a default value for that field. For example, `{'default_user_id': uid}` sets the current user as a default value.
- The `default_search_` prefix added to a filter name will automatically enable that filter. For example, `{'default_search_filter_my_tasks': 1}` activates the filter with name `filter_my_books`.

These prefixes are frequently used in **window actions** and in views in `<field context="{...}">` elements.

Modifying the recordset execution environment and context

The recordset execution context can be modified to take advantage of the behaviors described in the previous section or to add information to be used in methods called on that recordset.

The environment and its context can be modified through the following methods. Each of these returns a new recordset, along with a copy of the original with a modified environment:

- The `<recordset>.with_context(<dictionary>)` method replaces the context with the one provided in the dictionary.
- The `<recordset>.with_context(key=value, ...)` method modifies the context by setting the provided attributes on it.

- The `<recordset>.sudo([flag=True])` method enables or disables the superuser mode, allowing it to bypass security rules. The context user is kept the same.

- The `<recordset>.with_user(<user>)` method modifies the user to the one provided, which is either a user record or an ID number.

- The `<recordset>.with_company(<company>)` method modifies the company to the one provided, which is either a company record or an ID number.

- The `<recordset>.with_env(<env>)` method modifies the full environment of the recordset to the one provided.

> **Changes in Odoo 13**
>
> The `with_user()` and `with_company()` methods were introduced in Odoo 13. To switch users, previous versions used the `sudo([<user>])` method, which could be provided to a specific user to switch to the superuser context. To switch companies, previous versions used `with_context(force=company=<id>)`, setting a `context` key that was checked in the relevant business logic.

Additionally, the environment object provides the `env.ref()` function, taking a string with an external identifier and returning the corresponding record, as shown in the following example:

```
>>> self.env.ref('base.user_root')
res.users(1,)
```

If the external identifier does not exist, a `ValueError` exception is raised.

We learned more about the execution environments when running Python code in the Odoo server. The next step is to interact with data. In this case, the first thing to learn is how to query data and create recordsets, which is discussed in the next section.

Querying data with recordsets and domains

Odoo business logic will need to read data from the database to perform actions based on it. This is done through *recordsets*, which query the raw data and expose it as Python objects we can manipulate.

Odoo Python will usually be running in a class method, where `self` represents the recordset to work with. In some cases, we need to create recordsets for other models. For that, we should get a reference to the models and then query it to create the recordset.

The environment object, usually accessible as `self.env`, holds references to all the models available, and these can be accessed using dictionary-like syntax. For example, to get a reference to the `partner` model, use `self.env['res.partner']` or `self.env.get('res.partner')`. This model reference can then be used to create recordsets, as we will see next.

Creating recordsets

The `search()` method takes a domain expression and returns a recordset with the records matching those conditions. For example, `[('name', 'like', 'Azure')]` will return all records with a `name` field containing `Azure`.

If the model has the `active` special field then by default, only the records with `active=True` will be considered.

The following keyword arguments can also be used:

- The `order` keyword is a string to be used as the `ORDER BY` clause in the database query. This is usually a comma-separated list of field names. Each field name may be followed by the `DESC` keyword to indicate a descending order.
- The `limit` keyword sets a maximum number of records to retrieve.
- The `offset` keyword ignores the first n results; it can be used with `limit` to query blocks of records at a time.

Sometimes, we just need to know the number of records meeting certain conditions. For that, we can use `search_count()`, which returns the record count instead of a recordset in a more efficient way.

The `browse()` method takes a list of IDs or a single ID and returns a recordset with those records. This can be convenient in cases where we already know the IDs of the records we want.

For example, to get all the partner records containing `Lumber` in the display name, use the following `search()` call:

```
>>> self.env['res.partner'].search([('display_name', 'like',
'Lumber')])
res.partner(15, 34)
```

In the case the IDs to query are known, use a `browse()` call, as in the following example:

```
>>> self.env['res.partner'].browse([15, 34])
res.partner(15, 34)
```

Most of the time the IDs are not known, so the `search()` method is used more often than `browse()`.

To make good use of `search()`, a good understanding of the domain filter syntax is needed. So, we will focus on this in the next section.

Domain expressions

A **domain** is used to filter data records. It uses a specific syntax that the Odoo ORM parses to produce the SQL WHERE expressions that are used to query the database. A **domain expression** is a list of conditions, and each condition is a (`'<field>'`, `'<operator>'`, `<value>`) tuple. For example, the following is a valid domain expression, with a single condition: `[('is_done', '=', False)]`. A domain expression with no conditions is also allowed. This translates to an empty list (`[]`) and the result is a query returning all records.

There are actually two possible evaluation contexts for domains: on the client side, such as in *window actions* and web client *views*, and on the server side, such as in security *record rules* and model method Python code. What can be used in the `<field>` and `<value>` elements may depend on the evaluation context.

Next, we will look at a detailed explanation for each element of a domain condition: **field**, **operator**, and **value**.

The field element of a domain condition

The first condition element is a string with the name of the field being filtered. When the domain expression is used on the server side, the field element can use dot-notation to access the values of related models. For example, we could use something like `'publisher_id.name'`, or even `'publisher_id.country_id.name'`.

On the client side, dot-notation is not allowed, and only simple field names can be used.

> **Tip**
> In cases where a related record value is needed for a client-side domain expression because dot-notation can't be used, the solution is to add to the model a related field by using a `related=` attribute. This way, the value is accessible as a directly accessible model field.

The operator element of a domain condition

The second condition element is the operator to apply on the field being filtered. What follows is a list of the allowed operators:

Operator	Description
=	Is equal to.
!=	Is not equal to.
<	Is lower than. In XML files, use the alternative syntax of <.
<=	Is lower than or equal to. In XML files, use the alternative syntax of <=.
>	Is greater than. In XML files, use the alternative syntax of >.
>=	Is greater or equal than. In XML files, use the alternative syntax of >=.
Like	Contains the value string. This is similar to a string using wildcards (_). This matches any single character, and % matches any sequence of characters. It is the same as =like with % appended around the value to search for.
ilike	This is the same as like, but case insensitive.
=like	This searches for the value using the database like operator, applying _ and % wildcards in the value. It does not append % around the searched value in the way ilike does.
=ilike	This is the same as ilike, but case insensitive.
in	This checks if the field value is equal to any of the items in the value list. The value is expected to be a list, but a single value will be handled as a one-element list.
not in	This is the opposite of in. It checks if the field value is not in the items in the value list.
child_of	When the searched field defines a hierarchical relation, child_of checks if the record is a child of the record identified by the value.
parent_of	When the searched field defines a hierarchical relation, parent_of checks if the record is a parent of the record identified by the value.

These operators are applied to the field provided in the first element, using the value provided in the third element. For example, (`'shipping_address_id'`, `'child_ of'`, `partner_id`) checks the evaluation context for a `partner_id` variable and reads its value. The database is queried on the `shipping_address_id` field, selecting the records where that address is a child of the one identified in the `partner_id` value.

The value element of a domain condition

The third element is evaluated as a Python expression. It can use literal values, such as numbers, Booleans, strings, or lists, and can use fields and identifiers available in the evaluation context.

Record objects are not accepted values. Instead, the corresponding ID values should be used. For example, don't use [(`'user_id'`, `'='`, `user`)] – instead, use [(`'user_ id'`, `'='`, `user.id`)].

For record rules, the evaluation context has the following names available:

- `user`: A record for the current user (equivalent to `self.env.user`). Use `user. id` to get the corresponding ID.

- `company_id`: The ID of a record for the active company (equivalent to `self. env.company.id`).

- `company_ids`: A list of IDs for the allowed companies (equivalent to `self.env. companies.ids`).

- `time`: The Python time module, exposing date and time functions. The official reference can be found at `https://docs.python.org/3/library/time. html`.

> **Changes in Odoo 13**
>
> The `company_id` and `company_ids` context values are available for record rule evaluation since Odoo 13, and the approach from the previous version, using `user.company_id.id`, should not be used anymore. For example, the previously frequently used [`'|'`, (`'company_id'`, `'='`, `False`), (`'company_id'`, `'child_of'`, [`user. company_id.id`])] domain should now be written as [(`'company_ id'`, `'in'`, `company_ids`)].

Searching on to-many fields

When the searched field is a *to-many*, the operator is applied to each of the field values, and the evaluated record is included in the result if any of the field values match the domain condition.

The = and in operators behave like a *contains* operation. They both check if *any* of the field values match any of the list of values searched for. Symmetrically, the != and not in operators check that *none* of the field values match any of the list of values searched for.

Composing a domain expression with multiple conditions

A domain expression is a list of items and can contain several condition tuples. By default, these conditions will implicitly be combined using the AND logical operator. This means that it will only return records meeting all of the conditions.

Explicit logic operators can also be used – for example, the ampersand symbol (&) for AND operations (the default) and the pipe symbol (|) for OR operations. These will operate on the next two items, working in a recursive way. We'll look at this in more detail in a moment.

For a slightly more formal definition, a domain expression uses prefix notation, also known as **Polish notation** (**PN**), where operators precede operands. The AND and OR operators are binary operators, while NOT is a unary operator.

The exclamation point (!) represents the NOT operator and it operates on the following item. So, it should be placed before the item to be negated. For example, the ['!', ('is_done', '=',True)] expression will filter all *not done* records.

Operator items, such as (!) or (|), can be nested, allowing the definition of AND/OR/NOT complex conditions. Let's illustrate this with an example.

In server-side record rules, we can find domain expressions similar to this one:

```
['|',
    ('message_follower_ids', 'in', [user.partner_id.id]),
    '|',
        ('user_id', '=', user.id),
        ('user_id', '=', False)
]
```

This domain filters all of the records where:

- the current user is a follower, or

- the current user is the record's responsible (user_id), or

- the record has no responsible user set.

The following diagram illustrates the abstract syntax tree repr
domain expression example:

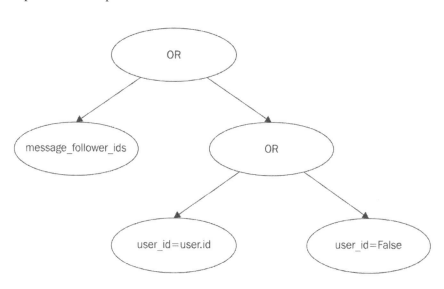

Figure 7.1 – A diagram illustrating a composed domain expression

The first | (*OR*) operator acts on the follower's condition plus the result of the next condition. The next condition is again the union of two other conditions - records where either the user ID is set to the current user, or the user ID is not set.

Special domain conditions

Some special domain conditions are also supported for the cases where an *always true* or *always false* expression is needed.

The (1, "=", 1) condition represents an *always true* expression. It can be used on record rules to give a higher user group access to all records, previously limited by a lower user group. For example, it is used on the User: All Documents group, to override the record access limitation in the inherited User: Own Documents only group. For an example of this, see addons/sales_team/security/sales_team_security.xml in the Odoo source code.

, 1) condition is also supported and represents an *always false* expression.

ping by fields and aggregate data

times, we need to group records by their data field. Odoo can do this using the `ad_group()` method. The method arguments are as follows:

- The `domain` argument is a list with a domain expression to filter the records to retrieve.

- The `fields` argument is a list of field names, along with an aggregation function to apply in the format of `field:aggr`. Aggregation functions are the ones allowed by **PostgreSQL**, such as `sum`, `avg`, `min`, `max`, `count`, and `count_distinct`. For example: `["subtotal:sum"]`.

- The `groupby` argument is a list with the data field names to group by.

- The `limit` argument is an optional maximum number of groups to return.

- The `offset` argument is an optional number of records to skip.

- The `orderby` argument is an optional string with an *order by* clause to apply to the result (similar to what `search()` supports).

- The `lazy` argument, if set to `True`, only groups by the first field, and adds the remaining group of fields to the `__context` result. This argument defaults to `True`, so set it to `False` to have all *group by fields* immediately applied.

Here is an example grouping partner record by country, and count the number of different states found:

```
>>> self.env["res.partner"].read_group([("display_name",
"like", "Azure")], fields=["state_id:count_distinct",],
groupby=["country_id"], lazy=False)
[{'__count': 4, 'state_id': 1, 'country_id': (233, <odoo.
tools.func.lazy object at 0x7f197b65fc00>), '__domain': ['&',
('country_id', '=', 233), ('display_name', 'like', 'Azure')]}]
```

This returned a list with a single group result for the 233 country ID. Running `self.env["res.country"].browse(233).name`, we can see that the country is United Sates. The `__count` key shows that there are 4 partners in the 233 country ID, and the `state_id` object shows the count distinct aggregation results: 1 distinct state is used by these partners.

We now know how to create recordsets. Next, we will want to read the data in them. In many cases, this is a trivial operation, but for some field types, there are a few details involved that are worth noting. The next section will help us with that.

Accessing data in recordsets

Once we have a recordset, we want to inspect the data contained in it. So, in the following sections, we will explore how to access data in recordsets.

We can get field values for individual records called *singletons*. Relational fields have special properties, and we can use dot-notation to navigate through linked records. Finally, we will discuss some considerations for when we need to handle date and time records and convert them between different formats.

Accessing individual record data

When a recordset has only one record it is called a **singleton**. Singletons are still recordsets and can be used wherever a recordset is expected.

But unlike multi-element recordsets, singletons can access their fields using dot-notation, as follows:

```
>>> print(self.name)
OdooBot
```

In the next example, we can see that the same `self` singleton recordset also behaves as a recordset, and we can iterate it. It has only one record, so only one name is printed out:

```
>>> for rec in self: print(rec.name)
...
OdooBot
```

Trying to access field values in recordsets with more than one record will result in an error, so this can be an issue in cases where we are not sure if we are working with a singleton recordset.

> **Tip**
> Although using dot-notation to access fields won't work on multiple records, it is possible to access them in bulk by mapping the values to a recordset. This is done using `mapped()`. For example, `rset.mapped("name")` returns a list with the `name` values.

For methods designed to work only with a singleton, we can check this using `self.ensure_one()` at the beginning. It will raise an error if `self` is not a singleton.

> **Tip**
>
> The `ensure_one()` function also raises an error if the record is empty.
> To check if a `rset` has one or zero records, you can use `rset or rset.ensure_one()`.

An empty record is also a singleton. This is convenient because accessing field values will return a `None` value instead of raising an error. This is also true for relational fields, and accessing related records using dot notation won't raise errors.

So, in practice, there is no need to check for an empty recordset before accessing their field values. For example, instead of `if record: print(record.name)`, we can safely write the simpler `print(record.name)` method. A default value for an empty value can also be provided by using an `or` condition: `print(record.name or "None")`.

Accessing relational fields

As we saw earlier, models can have relational fields—**many-to-one**, **one-to-many**, and **many-to-many**. These field types have recordsets as values.

In the case of many-to-one fields, the value can be a singleton or an empty recordset. In both cases, we can directly access their field values. As an example, the following instructions are correct and safe:

```
>>> self.company_id
res.company(1,)
>>> self.company_id.name
'YourCompany'
>>> self.company_id.currency_id
res.currency(1,)
>>> self.company_id.currency_id.name
'EUR'
```

An empty recordset conveniently also behaves like a singleton, and accessing its fields does not return an error but just returns `False`. Because of this, we can traverse records using dot-notation without worrying about errors from empty values, as shown here:

```
>>> self.company_id.parent_id
res.company()
>>> self.company_id.parent_id.name
False
```

Accessing date and time values

In recordsets, `date` and `datetime` values are represented as native Python objects. For example, when we look up the last login date for the `admin` user:

```
>>> self.browse(2).login_date
datetime.datetime(2021, 11, 2, 16, 47, 57, 327756)
```

Since the `date` and `datetime` values are Python objects, they have all of the manipulation features available for these objects.

> **Changes in Odoo 12**
>
> The `date` and `datetime` field values are now represented as Python objects, unlike previous Odoo versions, where the `date` and `datetime` values were represented as text strings. These field type values can still be set using text representations in the same way as previous Odoo versions.

Dates and times are stored in the database in a native **Coordinated Universal Time** (**UTC**) format, which is not time zone-aware. The `datetime` values seen on recordsets are also in UTC. When presented to the user by the web client, the `datetime` values are converted into the user's time zone by using the current session's time zone setting that is stored in the context `tz` key, for example, `{'tz': 'Europe/Brussels'}`. This conversion is a web client responsibility, as it isn't done by the server.

For example, an 11:00 AM datetime value entered by a Brussels (UTC+1) user is stored in the database as 10:00 AM UTC, and will be seen by a New York (UTC-4) user as 06:00 AM. The Odoo server log message timestamps use the UTC time and not the local server time.

The opposite conversion—from the session time zone to UTC—also needs to be done by the web client when sending the user's `datetime` input back to the server.

> **Tip**
>
> Remember that the date and time data stored in the database and handled by the server code is always represented in UTC. Even the server log message timestamps are represented in UTC.

We have now reviewed the details of how to access record data. However, our application will provide some automation for business processes, so inevitably we will also need to write to recordsets. Let's look at this in detail in the next section.

Writing to records

We have two different ways to write to records: using the object-style direct assignment or using the `write()` method. The `write()` method is the low-level method in charge of performing write operations, and it is still used directly when using the external API or when loading XML records. The object-style direct assignment was added later into the ORM model. It implements the **active record** pattern and can be used in Python code logic.

> **Changes in Odoo 13**
>
> In Odoo 13, the ORM model introduced a new database writing approach called **in-memory ORM**. In previous Odoo versions, every write would immediately generate the corresponding database SQL command, and this came with a performance penalty, especially when complex interdependencies caused repeated updates on the same records. Since Odoo 13, these operations are instead saved in a memory cache, and at the end of the transaction, the new `flush()` method is automatically called to perform the corresponding database operations in a single go.

Next, we will look at both of these methods and their differences.

Using object-style value assignments

Recordsets implement the **active record pattern**. This means that we can assign values to them and these changes will be made persistent in the database. This is an intuitive and convenient way to manipulate data.

> Changes in Odoo 13
>
> Assigning values to a recordset with more than one record is supported as of Odoo 13. Up to Odoo 12, only writing values to single records was supported, and the `write()` method had to be used to write to multiple records.

Here is an example:

```
>>> root = self.env["res.users"].browse(1)
>>> print(root.name)
System
>>> root.name = "Superuser"
>>> print(root.name)
Superuser
```

When using the *active record* pattern, the value of relational fields can be set by assigning a recordset.

Date and time fields can be assigned values as either Python native objects or string representations in the Odoo default format:

```
>>> from datetime import date
>>> self.date = date(2020, 12, 1)
>>> self.date
datetime.date(2020, 12, 1)
>>> self.date = "2020-12-02"
>>> self.date
datetime.date(2020, 12, 2)
```

Binary fields should be assigned `base64` encoded values. For example, when having raw binary data read from a file, that value must be converted using `base64.b64encode()` before being assigned to a field:

```
>>> import base64
>>> blackdot_binary = b"\x89PNG\r\n\x1a\n\x00\x00\x00\rIHDR\
x00\x00\x00\x01\x00\x00\x00\x01\x08\x04\x00\x00\x00\xb5\x1c\
x0c\x02\x00\x00\x00\x0bIDATx\xdacd\xf8\x0f\x00\x01\x05\x01\
x01'\x18\xe3f\x00\x00\x00\x00IEND\xaeB'\x82"
>>> self.image_1920 = base64.b64encode(blackdot_binary).
decode("utf-8")
```

When assigning values on many-to-one fields, the value assigned must be a single record (that is, a **singleton recordset**).

For to-many fields, the value can also be assigned with a recordset, replacing the list of linked records (if any) with a new one. Here, a recordset of any size is allowed.

To set an empty value on a relational field, set it with None or False:

```
>>> self.child_ids = None
>>> self.child_ids
res.partner()
```

To append or remove a record on the assigned list, use the record manipulation operations.

For example, imagine a company record also has a related partner record that is used to hold address details. Suppose that we want to add the current user as a company child contact. This can be done with the following:

```
>>> mycompany_partner = self.company_id.partner_id
>>> myaddress = self.partner_id
>>> mycompany_partner.child_ids = mycompany_partner.child_ids | myaddress
```

Here, the pipe operator (|) was used to join a record to obtain a larger recordset.

The compact append and assign operator (| =) could have been used for the same effect:

```
>>> mycompany_partner.child_ids |= myaddress
```

More details on record manipulation operations are given later in this chapter in the *Composing recordsets* section.

Using the write() method

The write() method can also be used to update data in records. It accepts a dictionary with the field names and values to assign. It can be more convenient to use in some cases, for example, where the dictionary is prepared first, and the assignment is performed later. It is also useful in older versions of Odoo (up to Odoo 12) for cases where direct assignment can't be used.

The write() method receives a dictionary with the fields and values to assign and updates the recordset with them:

```
>>> Partner = self.env['res.partner']
>>> recs = Partner.search( [("name", "ilike", "Azure")])
>>> recs.write({"comment": "Hello!"})
True
```

Date and time fields can be assigned with values of the corresponding Python objects or by using string text representations, just like with object-style assignments.

Since Odoo 13, write() can use recordsets to set values on to-one and to-many relational fields, just like with object-style assignments.

> **Changes in Odoo 13**
>
> The write() method can use recordsets to assign values on relational fields. Up to Odoo 12, many-to-one fields were set using an ID value, and to-many fields were set using a special syntax, for example, (4, <id>, _) to add a record and (6, 0, [<ids>]) to set the full record list. This syntax is discussed in more detail in *Chapter 5*, *Importing, Exporting, and Module Data*.

For example, suppose we have two Partner records, address1 and address2, and we want to set them on the self.child_ids field.

Using the write() method, we would use the following:

```
self.write({ 'child_ids': address1 | address2})
```

Another option (needed for versions before Odoo 13) is as follows:

```
self.write({ 'child_ids': [(6, 0, [address1.id, address2.
id])]})
```

The write() method is used to write dates on existing records. But we also need to create and delete records, which we will discuss in the next section.

Creating and deleting records

The create() and unlink() model methods allow us to create and delete existing records, respectively.

The create() method takes a dictionary with the fields and values for the record to be created, using the same syntax as write(). Default values are automatically applied as expected, as shown in this example:

```
>>> Partner = self.env['res.partner']
>>> new = Partner.create({'name': 'ACME', 'is_company': True})
>>> print(new)
res.partner(59,)
```

The unlink() method deletes the records in the recordset, as done in the next example:

```
>>> rec = Partner.search([('name', '=', 'ACME')])
>>> rec.unlink()
2021-11-15 18:40:10,090 3756 INFO library odoo.models.unlink:
User #1 deleted mail.message records with IDs: [20]
2021-11-15 18:40:10,146 3756 INFO library odoo.models.unlink:
User #1 deleted res.partner records with IDs: [59]
2021-11-15 18:40:10,160 3756 INFO library odoo.models.unlink:
User #1 deleted mail.followers records with IDs: [9]
True
```

The unlink() method returns a True value. Also, during the delete operation, it triggers log messages informing the cascade deletion of related records, such as Chatter messages and followers.

Another way to create a record is to duplicate an existing one. The copy() model method is available for this. It accepts an optional argument with a dictionary, which contains values to override when creating the new record.

For example, to create a new user from the demo user, we could use the following:

```
>>> demo = self.env.ref("base.user_demo")
>>> new = demo.copy({"name": "John", "login": "john@example.com"})
```

The fields with the copy=False attribute won't be automatically copied. To-many relational fields have this flag disabled by default, so they won't be copied.

In the previous sections, we have learned how to access data in re
write to recordsets. However, there are some field types that deserve n
next section, we will discuss specific techniques for working with date an

Working with date and time fields

In the *Accessing data in recordsets* section, we saw how to read date and time values from
records. It is common to also need to perform date calculations and to convert dates
between their native format and string representations. Here, we will see how to perform
these kinds of operations.

Odoo provides a few useful functions to create new date and time objects.

The `odoo.fields.Date` object provides these helper functions:

- The `fields.Date.today()` function returns a string with the current date in
  the format expected by the server, using UTC as a reference. This is adequate to
  compute default values. It can be used directly in a date field definition by using
  `default=fields.Date.today`.

- The `fields.Date.context_today(record, timestamp=None)` function
  returns a string with the current date in the session's context. The time zone
  value is taken from the record's context. The optional `timestamp` parameter is a
  `datetime` object and will be used instead of the current time if provided.

The `odoo.fields.Datetime` objects provide these datetime creation functions:

- The `fields.Datetime.now()` function returns a string with the current
  `datetime` in the format expected by the server, using UTC as a reference. This
  is adequate to compute default values. It can be used directly in a `datetime` field
  definition by using `default=fields.Datetime.now`.

- The `fields.Datetime.context_timestamp(record, timestamp)`
  function converts a naive `datetime` value (without time zone) into a time zone-
  aware `datetime` value. The time zone is extracted from the record's context, hence
  the name of the function.

ing with date and time fields

rdsets and create and
re attention. In the
ime fields.   231

:ime

racted to find the time elapsed between both
ta object. A `timedelta` object can be added to or
e objects, performing date arithmetic.

thon standard library `datetime` module. Here is a
e can do with them:

```
: date


, 3)
rt timedelta
+ timedelta(days=7)
1, 10)
```

A full reference for the `date`, `datetime`, and `timedelta` data types can be found at https://docs.python.org/3/library/datetime.html.

The `timedelta` object supports weeks, days, hours, seconds, and more. But it doesn't support years or months.

To perform date arithmetic using months or years, we should use the `relativedelta` object. Here is an example of adding one year and one month:

```
>>> from dateutil.relativedelta import relativedelta
>>> date(2021, 11, 3) + relativedelta(years=1, months=1)
datetime.date(2022, 12, 3)
```

The `relativedelta` object supports advanced date arithmetic, including leap years and Easter calculations. The documentation for it can be found at https://dateutil.readthedocs.io.

Odoo also provides a few additional functions in the `odoo.tools.date_utils` module:

- The `start_of(value, granularity)` function returns the start of a time period with the specified granularity, which is a string value with one of `year`, `quarter`, `month`, `week`, `day`, or `hour`.

- The `end_of(value, granularity)` function returns the end of a time period with the specified granularity.

- The add(value, **kwargs) function adds a time interval to the given value. The **kwargs arguments are to be used by a relativedelta object to define the time interval. These arguments can be years, months, weeks, days, hours, minutes, and so on.

- The subtract(value, **kwargs) function subtracts a time interval from the given value.

These utility functions are also exposed in the odoo.fields.Date and the odoo.fields.Datetime objects.

Here are a few examples using the previous functions:

```
>>> from odoo.tools import date_utils
>>> from datetime import datetime
>>> now = datetime(2020, 11, 3, 0, 0, 0)
>>> date_utils.start_of(now, 'week')
datetime.datetime(2020, 11, 2, 0, 0)
>>> date_utils.end_of(now, 'week')
datetime.datetime(2020, 11, 8, 23, 59, 59, 999999)
>>> today = date(2020, 11, 3)
>>> date_utils.add(today, months=2)
datetime.date(2021, 1, 3)
>>> date_utils.subtract(today, months=2)
datetime.date(2020, 9, 3)
```

Converting date and time objects to text representations

There will be cases where we need to convert a Python date object into a text representation. This may be needed, for example, to prepare a user message or to format data to send to another system.

The Odoo field objects provide helper functions to convert the native Python objects to string representations:

- The fields.Date.to_string(value) function converts a date object into a string in the format expected by the Odoo server.

- The fields.Datetime.to_string(value) function converts a datetime object into a string in the format expected by the Odoo server.

These use the Odoo server predefined defaults, which are defined in the following constants:

- `odoo.tools.DEFAULT_SERVER_DATE_FORMAT`
- `odoo.tools.DEFAULT_SERVER_DATETIME_FORMAT`

These map to `%Y-%m-%d` and `%Y-%m-%d  %H:%M:%S`, respectively.

The `date.strftime` and `datetime.strftime` functions accept a format string parameter that can be used for other conversions to text.

For example, consider the following:

```
>>> from datetime import date
>>> date(2020, 11, 3).strftime("%d/%m/%Y")
'03/11/2020'
```

Further details on the available format codes can be found at `https://docs.python.org/3/library/datetime.html#strftime-and-strptime-behavior`.

Converting text-represented dates and times

There are cases where dates arrive formatted as text strings and need to be converted to Python `date` or `datetime` objects. This was frequently needed up to Odoo 11, where stored dates were read as text representations. Some tools are provided to help with this conversion from text into native data types and then back into text.

To facilitate this conversion between formats, the `fields.Date` and `fields.Datetime` objects provide these functions:

- The `fields.Date.to_date` function converts a string into a `date` object.
- The `fields.Datetime.to_datetime(value)` function converts a string into a `datetime` object.

An example of a usage of `to_datetime` is as follows:

```
>>> from odoo import fields
>>> fields.Datetime.to_datetime("2020-11-21 23:11:55")
datetime.datetime(2020, 11, 21, 23, 11, 55)
```

The preceding example uses the Odoo internal date format to parse the provided string and convert it into a Python `datetime` object.

For other date and time formats, the `strptime` method from the `date` and `datetime` object can be used:

```
>>> from datetime import datetime
>>> datetime.strptime("03/11/2020", "%d/%m/%Y")
datetime.datetime(2020, 11, 3, 0, 0)
```

In most cases, the text-represented time will not be in UTC, as expected by the Odoo server. The time must be converted to UTC before it can be stored in the Odoo database.

For example, if the user is in the Europe/Brussels timezone (at +1:00 hours from UTC) the `2020-12-01 00:30:00` user time should be stored in UTC as `2020-11-30 23:30:00`. Here is the code recipe for this:

```
>>> from datetime import datetime
>>> import pytz
>>> naive_date = datetime(2020, 12, 1, 0, 30, 0)
>>> client_tz = self.env.context["tz"]
>>> client_date = pytz.timezone(client_tz).localize(naive_date)
>>> utc_date = client_date.astimezone(pytz.utc)
>>> print(utc_date)
2020-11-30 23:30:00+00:00
```

This code gets the user time zone name from the context and then uses it to convert the naive date to a time zone-aware date. The final step is to convert the client time zone date to a UTC date by using `astimezone(pytz.utc)`.

We've now learned specific techniques to work with date and time in Odoo. There are also specific techniques to work with recordsets and the values stored in relational fields, which we'll discuss in the next section.

Working with recordsets

A **recordset** is a collection of records, and Python business logic frequently needs to use them. There are several operations that can be performed on recordsets, such as mapping and filtering. We can also compose new recordsets by adding or removing records. Other common operations are inspecting the contents of a recordset to check if a particular record is there or not, for example.

> **Changes in Odoo 10**
>
> Since Odoo 10, recordset manipulation has preserved the record order. This is unlike previous Odoo versions, where recordset manipulation was not guaranteed to preserve the record order, although addition and slicing maintained the record order.

Recordset operations

Recordsets have a few functions available to perform useful actions on them, such as **sorting** or **filtering records**.

These are the supported functions and attributes:

- The `recordset.ids` attribute returns a list with the IDs of the recordset elements.

- The `recordset.ensure_one()` function checks whether it's a single record (that is, a singleton); if it's not, a `ValueError` exception is raised.

- The `recordset.filtered(<function or str>)` function returns a filtered recordset, and this function is a test function to filter records. The argument can instead be a string containing a dot-separated sequence of fields to evaluate. The records evaluating to a truthy value are selected.

- The `recordset.mapped(<function or str>)` function returns a list of values, and the function returns a value for each record. The argument can instead be a string containing a dot-separated sequence of fields to evaluate to reach the field to return. To-many relations are safe to use in the field sequence.

- The `recordset.sorted(<function ot str>)` function returns the recordset with a specific element order. The function returns a value for each record, which are used to sort the recordset. The argument can instead be a string with the name of the field to sort by. Note that a dot-notation sequence of fields is not allowed. An optional `reverse=True` argument is also available.

Here are some usage examples for these functions:

```
>>> rs0 = self.env["res.partner"].search([("display_name",
"like", "Azure")])
>>> len(rs0)  # how many records?
4
>>> rs0.filtered(lambda r: r.name.startswith("Nicole"))
res.partner(27,)
>>> rs0.filtered("is_company")
res.partner(14,)
>>> rs0.mapped("name")
['Azure Interior', 'Brandon Freeman', 'Colleen Diaz', 'Nicole
Ford']
>>> rs0.sorted("name", reverse=True).mapped("name")
['Nicole Ford', 'Colleen Diaz', 'Brandon Freeman', 'Azure
Interior']
>>> rs0.mapped(lambda r: (r.id, r.name))
[(14, 'Azure Interior'), (26, 'Brandon Freeman'), (33, 'Colleen
Diaz'), (27, 'Nicole Ford')]
```

The composition of a recordset

Recordsets are immutable, meaning that their values can't be directly modified. Instead, we can compose a new recordset based on existing ones. **Slice notation**, which is commonly used with Python lists, can be used on recordsets to extract a subset of the records. Here are a few examples:

- `rs[0]` and `rs[-1]` retrieve the first element and the last element, respectively.
- `rs[1:]` results in a copy of the recordset without the first element.
- `rs[:1]` returns the first element of the recordset.

> Tip
>
> For a fail-safe way to retrieve the first element of a recordset, use `rs[:1]` instead of `rs[0]`. The latter results in an error if `rs` is empty, whereas the former will just return an empty recordset in this case. Another option is to use the `first()` function from the `odoo.fields` module: `fields.first(rs)`.

Recordsets also support the following set operations:

- The `rs1 | rs2` operation is a *union* set operation and results in a recordset with all elements from both recordsets. This is a set-like operation and won't result in duplicate elements.

- For example, `self.env.user | self.env.user` returns a single record, such as `res.users(1,)`.

- The `rs1 & rs2` operation is an *intersection* set operation and results in a recordset with only the elements present in both recordsets.

- The `rs1 - rs2` operation is a *difference* set operation and results in a recordset with the `rs1` elements not present in `rs2`.

> **Tip**
>
> Recordsets also support the addition operation (+), however, it should be avoided. It has a different behavior from the union operation (|) and allows for duplicate elements in a recordset. However, this is rarely what we want. For example, `self.env.user + self.env.user` returns two records, such as `res.users(1, 1)`.

We can use these operations directly with a value assignment for shorter notation:

- The `self.author_ids |= author1` operation adds the `author1` record if it is not in the recordset.

- The `self.author_ids &= author1` operation keeps only the records also present in the `author1` recordset.

- The `self.author_ids -= author1` operation removes the specific `author1` record if it is present in the recordset.

Recordset accumulation

In some cases, we want to loop through some logic and accumulate records resulting from each iteration of the loop. The ORM way to accumulate a recordset is to start with an empty recordset and then add records to it. To get an empty recordset, create a reference to the model. For example, consider the following:

```python
Partner = self.env["res.partner"]
recs = self.env["res.partner"]
for i in range(3):
    rec = Partner.create({"name": "Partner %s" % i})
    recs |= rec
```

The previous code loops three times and on each loop it creates a new partner record before accumulating it to the `recs` recordset. As it is a recordset, the `recs` variable can be used in cases where recordsets are expected, such as assigning a value to a to-many field.

However, accumulating recordsets is not time-efficient and should be avoided inside loops. The reason for this is that Odoo recordsets are immutable objects and any operation on a recordset implies copying it to get the modified version. When appending a record to a recordset, the original recordset is not modified. Instead, a copy of it is made with the record appended to it. This copy operation consumes time, and the larger the recordset is, the longer it takes.

As a result, alternatives should be considered. For the preceding example, we could have accumulated all of the record data dictionaries in a Python list and then made a single `create()` call to create all of the records. This is possible because the `create()` method can accept a list of dictionaries.

So, the loop could look like this:

```
values = []
for i in range(3):
    value = {"name": "Partner %s" % i}
    values.append(value)
recs = self.env["res.partner"].create(values)
```

However, this solution won't work in all cases. Another option is to use a Python list to accumulate records. Python lists are mutable objects, and appending elements is an efficient operation for them. As Python lists are not actually recordsets, this option can't be used where a recordset is expected, for example, an assignment to a to-many field.

The following is an example of accumulating records to a Python list:

```
Partner = self.env["res.partner"]
recs = []
for i in range(3):
    rec = Partner.create({"name": "Partner %s" % i})
    recs.append(new_rec)
```

The previous examples illustrate a few techniques that can be used in loops to build recordsets from individual elements. However, there are many cases where the loop is not strictly needed and operations such as `mapped()` and `filtered()` can provide more efficient ways to achieve the desired aim.

Recordset comparisons

There are cases where we need to compare the content of a recordset to decide what further action is needed. Recordsets support the expected comparison operations.

To check if a `<rec>` record is an element of a `<my_recordset>` recordset, the following code can be used:

- `<rec> in <my_recordset>`
- `<rec> not in <my_recordset>`

Recordsets can also be compared to check if one is contained in another. To compare two recordsets, use `set1` and `set2`:

- Using `set1 <= set2` and `set1 < set2` returns `True` if all of the elements in `set1` are also in `set2`. The `<` operators return `False` if both recordsets have the same elements.

- Using `set1 >= set2` and `set1 > set2` returns `True` if all of the elements in `set2` are also in `set1`. The `>` operators return `False` if both recordsets have the same elements.

Transactions and low-level SQL

ORM methods that are called from a client run in a *transaction*. Transactions ensure correctness in the case of concurrent writes or failures. During a transaction, the data records used are locked, protecting them from other concurrent transactions and ensuring that they are not unexpectedly changed. In case of failure, all the transaction changes are rolled back, returning to the initial state.

Transaction support is provided by the PostgreSQL database. When an ORM method is called from a client, a new transaction is initiated. If an error occurs during the method execution, any changes that have been made are reverted. If the method execution completes with no errors, then the changes made are committed, making them effective and visible to all other transactions.

This is automatically handled for us, and we usually don't need to worry about it. However, in some advanced use cases, it might be useful to have control over the current transaction.

> **Changes in Odoo 13**
>
> Since Odoo 13, database write operations are not done while the method is running. Instead, they accumulate in a memory cache, and the actual database writing is delayed to the end of the execution of the method, which is performed by a `flush()` call that is invoked automatically at that point.

Controlling database transactions

There are cases where controlling the transaction can be useful and the `self.env.cr` database cursor can be used for this. An example of this is looping through records to perform an operation on each of them, where we want to skip the ones with operation errors without affecting the other ones.

For this, the object provides the following:

- `self.env.cr.commit()` commits the transaction's buffered write operations, making them effective in the database.

- `self.env.cr.rollback()` cancels the transaction's `write` operations since the last commit or all of them if no commit was made.

> **Tip**
>
> An Odoo `shell` session mimics a method execution context. This means that the database writes are not performed until `self.env.cr.commit()` is called.

Executing raw SQL

SQL can be run directly in the database by using the cursor `execute()` method. This takes a string with the SQL statement to run and a second optional argument with the values to use as parameters for the SQL.

The values parameter can be a tuple or a dict. When using a tuple, the parameters are replaced with `%s`, and when using a dict, they are replaced with `%(<name>)s`. Here are examples of both approaches:

```
>>> self.env.cr.execute("SELECT id, login FROM res_users WHERE
login=%s OR id=%s", ("demo", 1))
>>> self.env.cr.execute("SELECT id, login FROM res_users WHERE
login=%(login)s OR id=%(id)s", {"login": "demo", "id": 1})
```

Any of the previous instructions run the SQL, replacing the parameters and preparing a cursor with the results that needs to be fetched. More details on this can be found in the psycopg2 documentation at https://www.psycopg.org/docs/usage.html#query-parameters.

> **Caution!**
>
> With cr.execute(), we should not directly compose the SQL query concatenating parameters. Doing so is known to be a security risk that can be exploited through SQL injection attacks. Always use the %s placeholders with the second parameter to pass values.

To fetch the results, the fetchall() function can be used, returning the rows' tuples:

```
>>> self.env.cr.fetchall()
[(6, 'demo'), (1, '__system__')]
```

The dictfetchall() function can also be used to retrieve records as dicts:

```
>>> self.env.cr.dictfetchall()
[{'id': 6, 'login': 'demo'}, {'id': 1, 'login': '__system__'}]
```

> **Tip**
>
> The self.env.cr database cursor object is an Odoo-specific wrapper around the PostgreSQL library, psycopg2. This means that the psycopg2 documentation is helpful to understand how to fully use the object:
>
> https://www.psycopg.org/docs/cursor.html

It is also possible to run **data manipulation language (DML)** instructions, such as UPDATE and INSERT. The Odoo environment relies on a data cache, and it may become inconsistent with the database when these DML instructions are executed. For this reason, after running using raw DML, the environment cached should be invalidated by using self.env.cache.invalidate(fnames=None, ids=None).

fnames is a list with the names of the fields to invalidate and refresh. If this is not provided, all fields will be invalidated.

`ids` is a list with the record IDs to invalidate and refresh. If this is not provided, all will be invalidated.

> **Caution!**
>
> Executing SQL directly in the database bypasses the ORM validations and dependencies and can lead to inconsistent data. You should use it only if you're sure of what you are doing.

Summary

In this chapter, we learned how to work with model data to perform **CRUD** operations—that is, **creating**, **reading**, **updating**, and **deleting** data—and all the techniques needed to make use of and manipulate *recordsets*. This provides the foundation needed for us to implement our business logic and automation code.

To experiment with the ORM API, we used the Odoo interactive shell. We ran our commands in an environment accessible through `self.env`. The environment is similar to the one provided in the model method, and so it is a useful playground for exploring the Odoo API.

The environment allows us to query data from any Odoo model that is made available as a recordset. We learned about the different ways to create recordsets and then how to read the data provided, including special data types such as dates, binary values, and relational fields.

Another fundamental capability in Odoo is to write back data. In this chapter, we also learned how to create new records, write to existing records, and delete records.

We also looked at working with date and time values by using the Python built-in tools and a few additional helper functions included in the Odoo framework.

Recordsets can be manipulated to add elements, filter out records, reorder, or accumulate values, as well as to compare them or check for the inclusion of particular records. Any of these operations may be needed when implementing business logic, and this chapter presented the essential techniques for all of these.

Finally, in some cases, we may need to skip using the ORM model and use low-level SQL operations to directly access the database or have finer control over transactions. These allow us to address the occasional cases where the ORM model is not the best tool for the job.

With all these tools under our belt, we are ready for the next chapter, where we will add the business logic layer for our models and implement model methods that use the ORM API to automate actions.

Further reading

The official Odoo documentation for recordsets can be found at `https://www.odoo.com/documentation/15.0/developer/reference/backend/orm.html`.

8

Business Logic – Supporting Business Processes

In the previous chapters, we learned how to use models to build the application data structures, and then how to explore and interact with that data using the ORM API and recordsets.

In this chapter, we will put all this together to implement business logic patterns that are common in applications. We will learn about the several ways business logic can be triggered, as well as some common patterns that are used to support them. We will also learn about important development techniques, such as logging, debugging, and testing.

We'll cover the following topics in this chapter:

- Learning project – the book checkout module
- Ways to trigger business logic
- Understanding ORM method decorators for recordsets
- Exploring useful data model patterns
- Using the ORM built-in methods
- Adding onchange user interface logic
- The message and activity features
- Creating a wizard
- Raising exceptions
- Writing unit tests
- Using log messages
- Learning about the available developer tools

By the end of this chapter, you should be confident in designing and implementing business logic automation and know how to test and debug your code.

Technical requirements

In this chapter, we will create a new `library_checkout` add-on module. It depends on the `library_app` and `library_member` add-on modules, which we created in the previous chapters.

The code for these add-on modules can be found in this book's GitHub repository, at `https://github.com/PacktPublishing/Odoo-15-Development-Essentials-Fifth-Edition`, in the `ch08` directory.

Both of these add-on modules need to be available in the Odoo add-ons path so that they can be installed and used.

Learning project – the book checkout module

The master data structures for the library application are in place. Now, we want to add transactions to our system. We would like library members to be able to borrow books. This means we should keep track of book availability and returns.

Each book checkout has a life cycle, from the moment they are created to the moment when the books are returned. It is a simple workflow that can be represented as a Kanban board, where the several stages are presented as columns, and the work items from the left-hand column are sent to the right until they are completed.

This chapter focuses on the data model and business logic that are needed to support this feature.

The basic user interface will be discussed in *Chapter 10, Backend Views – Designing the User Interface*, while the Kanban views will be discussed in *Chapter 11, Kanban Views and Client-Side QWeb*. Let's quickly have a rundown of the data model.

Preparing the data model

The first thing we must do is plan the data model that's needed for the book checkout feature.

The **book checkout** model should have the following fields:

- **Library member** borrowing books (required)
- **Checkout date** (defaults to today)
- **Responsible person** for the checkout (defaults to the current user)
- **Checkout lines**, with the books requested (one or more)

To support the book checkout life cycle, we will also have the following:

- **Stage** of the request—draft, open, borrowed, returned, or canceled
- **Due date**, when the books are due to be returned
- **Returned date**, when the books were returned

We will start by creating the new `library_checkout` module and implementing an initial version of the library checkout model. This will not introduce anything new compared to the previous chapters but will provide the foundation to build the features that are relevant for this chapter.

Creating the module

The `library_checkout` module needs to be created, similar to what we did in the previous chapters. Follow these steps to do this:

1. Create a new `library_checkout` directory in the same directory as the other add-on modules of the library project. This is where the following files should be added.

2. Add the `__manifest__.py` file and ensure it has the following content:

```
{ "name": "Library Book Checkout",
    "description": "Members can borrow books from the
      library.",
    "author": "Daniel Reis",
    "depends": ["library_member"],
    "data": [
        "security/ir.model.access.csv",
        "views/library_menu.xml",
        "views/checkout_view.xml",
    ],
}
```

3. Add the main `__init__.py` file with the following line of code:

```
from . import models
```

4. Add the `models/__init__.py` file with the following line of code:

```
from . import library_checkout
```

5. Add the model definition file, `models/library_checkout.py`, as follows:

```
from odoo import fields, models


class Checkout(models.Model):
    _name = "library.checkout"
    _description = "Checkout Request"

    member_id = fields.Many2one(
        "library.member",
```

```
            required=True,
    )
    user_id = fields.Many2one(
        "res.users",
        "Librarian",
        default=lambda s: s.env.user,
    )
    request_date = fields.Date(
        default=lambda s: fields.Date.today(),
    )
```

Next, we should add the data files, including the access rule, the menu items, and some basic views so that the module can be used.

1. Add the access security configuration to the `security/ir.model.access.csv` file:

```
id,name,model_id:id,group_id:id,perm_read,perm_
write,perm_create,perm_unlink
checkout_user,Checkout User,model_library_
checkout,library_app.library_group_user,1,1,1,1
```

2. Next, the `views/library_menu.xml` file needs to be added for implementing the menu items:

```
<odoo>

  <record id="action_library_checkout"
          model="ir.actions.act_window">
    <field name="name">Checkouts</field>
    <field name="res_model">library.checkout</field>
    <field name="view_mode">tree,form</field>
  </record>

  <menuitem id="menu_library_checkout"
          name="Checkout"
          action="action_library_checkout"
          parent="library_app.menu_library"
  />

</odoo>
```

3. The views are implemented in the `views/checkout_view.xml` file:

```xml
<odoo>

    <record id="view_tree_checkout" model="ir.ui.view">
        <field name="name">Checkout Tree</field>
        <field name="model">library.checkout</field>
        <field name="arch" type="xml">
            <tree>
                <field name="request_date" />
                <field name="member_id" />
            </tree>
        </field>
    </record>

    <record id="view_form_checkout" model="ir.ui.view">
        <field name="name">Checkout Form</field>
        <field name="model">library.checkout</field>
        <field name="arch" type="xml">

            <form>
                <sheet>
                    <group>
                        <field name="member_id" />
                        <field name="request_date" />
                        <field name="user_id" />
                    </group>
                </sheet>
            </form>

        </field>
    </record>

</odoo>
```

Now that the module contains the preceding files, it can be installed in our development database:

Figure 8.1 – The initial Library Checkout feature

Now, we can start adding more interesting features.

Throughout this project, we will be adding pieces of business logic to different places to showcase the several possibilities that Odoo provides. The next section will discuss these options.

Exploring ways to trigger business logic

Once the data model is in place, business logic is needed to perform some automatic actions on it. Business logic can either be directly initiated by the user, with an action such as a button click, or it can be triggered automatically when an event occurs, such as a write on a record.

Much of this business logic will involve reading and writing on recordsets. The details and techniques for this were discussed in *Chapter 7, Recordsets – Working with Model Data*, where we provided the tools for the actual business logic implementation.

The next question is how the business logic should be triggered. This will depend on when and why the business logic should be triggered. Here is a summary of the several options.

Some business logic is tightly connected to the model field definitions. Some of the instances of **model definition-related business logic** are as follows:

- **Data validation rules**, to enforce conditions that the data should meet. These are methods that are decorated with @api.constrains.

- **Automatic computations**, which are implemented as fields – virtual or stored – that have their values computed by a method. These are methods that are decorated with @api.depends and assigned to the compute field attribute.

- **Default values**, which can be dynamically computed, are methods that are decorated with @api.model and assigned to the default field attribute.

This model definition logic was discussed in detail in *Chapter 6, Models – Structuring the Application Data*. Some examples can be found in the *Data model patterns* section. The *ORM method decorators for recordsets* section provides a recap of the several ORM decorators mentioned here.

We also have **model event-related business logic**, which is related to business workflows. It can be attached to the following record-related events:

- **Create, write, and unlink** business logic can be added to these events, for the cases where the other, more elegant approaches are not possible.

- **Onchange** logic can be applied to user interface views so that we have some field values that are changed as a consequence of changes being made to other fields.

For actions that are directly initiated by the user, the following options are available:

- A button view element for calling an object method. The button can be on a form or tree of the Kanban view.

- A server action, which is available from a menu item or in the Action context menu.

- A window action for opening a wizard form, where input can be collected from the user and a button will call the business logic. This allows for richer user interaction.

These techniques will be presented throughout this chapter. The supporting methods will often use API decorators, so it is important to understand the different available ones. For clarity, the next section provides an overview of them.

Understanding ORM method decorators for recordsets

The method definition can be preceded by an @, which applies a decorator to it. These decorators add specific behaviors for these methods and depending on the purpose of a method, different decorators can be used.

Decorators for computed fields and validation methods

A few decorators are useful for validation logic and computed fields. They are listed here:

- `@api.depends(fld1,...)` is used for computed field functions to identify what changes the (re)calculation should be triggered on. It must set values on the computed fields; otherwise, an error will be shown.

- `@api.constrains(fld1,...)` is used for model validation functions and performs checks for when any of the mentioned fields are changed. It should not write changes in the data. If the checks fail, an exception should be raised.

These were discussed in detail in *Chapter 6, Models – Structuring the Application Data*.

Another group of decorators affect the `self` recordset behavior and are relevant when you're implementing other kinds of business logic.

Decorators that affect the self recordset

By default, methods are expected to act on a recordset that's provided by the self `first` argument. The method code will usually include a `for` statement that loops through each of the records in the `self` recordset.

> **Changes in Odoo 14**
>
> The `@api.multi` decorator was removed from Odoo 14. In previous Odoo versions, it was used to explicitly signal that the decorated method expects a recordset in the `self` parameter. This is already the default behavior for methods, so its use is only for clarity. The `@api.one` decorator has been deprecated since Odoo 9 and was also removed in Odoo 14. It handled the record loop for you so that the method code would be called once for each record, and the `self` argument would always be a singleton. Since Odoo 14, both decorators must be removed from the code since they are not supported anymore.

In some cases, the method is expected to work at the class level and not on particular records, behaving like a **static method**. These methods are decorated with `@api.model` and, in this case, the `self` method parameter should be used as a reference to the model; it is not expected to contain records.

For example, the `create()` method uses `@api.model` – it does not expect records as input, only a values dictionary, which will be used to create and return a record. The methods that are used to calculate default values should also use the `@api.model` decorator.

Before we can go deeper into the business logic's implementation, we must add more depth to the data model and, in the process, provide examples of a couple of common data model patterns.

Exploring useful data model patterns

There are a few data structures that are often needed for models that represent business documents. These can be seen in several Odoo apps, such as **Sales Orders** or **Invoices**.

A common pattern is the header/lines data structure. It will be used for a checkout request so that you can have several books. Another pattern is to use states or stages. These two have differences, and we will discuss them and provide a reference implementation shortly.

Finally, the ORM API provides a few methods that are relevant for the user interface. These will also be discussed in this section.

Using header and lines models

A common need for form views is to have header-line data structures. For example, a sales order includes several lines for the ordered items. In the case of the checkout feature, a checkout request can have several request lines, one for each of the borrowed items.

With Odoo, it is simple to implement this. Two models are needed for a header-line form view – one for the document header and another for the document lines. The line model has a many-to-one field to identify the header it belongs to, while the header model has a one-to-many field listing the lines in that document.

The `library_checkout` module was already added to the checkout model, so now, we want to add the lines. Follow these steps to do so:

1. Edit the `models/library_checkout.py` file to add the one-to-many field for the checkout lines:

```
line_ids = fields.One2many(
    "library.checkout.line",
    "checkout_id",
    string="Borrowed Books",
)
```

2. Add the file for the new model to `models/__init__.py`, as follows:

```
from . import library_checkout
from . import library_checkout_line
```

3. Next, add the Python file for declaring the checkout lines model, `models/library_checkout_line.py`, with the following content:

```
from odoo import api, exceptions, fields, models


class CheckoutLine(models.Model):
    _name = "library.checkout.line"
    _description = "Checkout Request Line"

    checkout_id = fields.Many2one(
        "library.checkout",
        required=True,
    )
    book_id = fields.Many2one("library.book",
        required=True)
    note = fields.Char("Notes")
```

4. We must also add access security configuration. Edit the `security/ir.model.access.csv` file and add the following highlighted line:

```
id,name,model_id:id,group_id:id,perm_read,perm_
write,perm_create,perm_unlink
checkout_user,Checkout User,model_library_
checkout,library_app.library_group_user,1,1,1,1
checkout_line_user,Checkout Line User,model_library_
checkout,library_app.library_group_user,1,1,1,1
```

5. Next, we want to add the checkout lines to the form. We will be adding it as the first page of a notebook widget. Edit the `views/checkout_view.xml` file and, just before the `</sheet>` element, add the following code:

```xml
<notebook>
    <page name="lines">
        <field name="line_ids">
            <tree editable="bottom">
                <field name="book_id" />
                <field name="note" />
            </tree>
        </field>
    </page>
</notebook>
```

The Checkouts form will look as follows:

Figure 8.2 – The Checkouts form with the notebook widget

The line's one-to-many field displays a list view that's nested in the parent form view. By default, Odoo will look up a list view definition to use for rendering, which is typical for any list view. If none are found, a default one will be automatically generated.

It is also possible to declare specific views inside `<field>`. We did this in the preceding code. Inside the `line_ids` field element, there is a nested `<tree>` view definition that will be used for this form.

Using stages and states for document-centered workflows

In Odoo, we can implement workflows that are centered on documents. What we refer to as documents can be things such as sales orders, project tasks, or HR applicants. All of these are expected to follow a certain life cycle since they're created until they conclude. Each work item is recorded in a document that will progress through a list of possible stages until it is completed.

If we present these stages as columns in a board, and the documents as items in those columns, we get a Kanban board, providing a quick view of all the work in progress.

There are two approaches to implementing these progress steps – **states** and **stages**:

- **States** is a closed selection list of predefined options. This is convenient for implementing business rules since the possible states are fixed and known ahead of time. Models and views have special support for the `state` special field name, making it convenient to use. The closed states list is a disadvantage, in that it can't easily accommodate custom process steps.

- **Stages** is a flexible list of process steps that are implemented through a related stages model that can be configured to process specific needs. It is usually implemented using a `stage_id` field name. The list of available stages is easy to modify as you can remove, add, or reorder them. It has the disadvantage of not being reliable for process automation. Since the list of stages can be changed, automation rules can't rely on particular stage IDs or descriptions.

When we're designing the data model, we need to decide whether it should use stages or states. If triggering business logic is more important than the ability to configure the process steps, states should be preferred; otherwise, stages should be the preferred choice.

If you can't decide, there is an approach that can provide the best of both worlds: we can use stages and map each stage to a corresponding state. The list of process steps can easily be configured by users, and since each stage will be linked to some reliable state code, it can also be confidently used to automate business logic.

This combined approach will be used for the library checkout feature. To implement the checkout stages, we will add the `library.checkout.stage` model. The fields that are needed to describe a stage are as follows:

- **Name**, or title.

- **Sequence**, which is used to order the stage columns.

- **Fold**, to be used by the Kanban view to decide what columns should be folded by default. We usually want to set this on inactive item columns, such as *Done* or *Canceled*.

- **Active**, to allow archived or no-longer-used stages, in case the process is changed.

- **State**, a closed selection list, which is used to map each stage to a fixed state.

To implement the preceding fields, we should start adding the **Stages** model, including the model definition, views, menus, and access security:

1. Add the `models/library_checkout_stage.py` file and ensure it contains the following model definition code:

```python
from odoo import fields, models


class CheckoutStage(models.Model):
    _name = "library.checkout.stage"
    _description = "Checkout Stage"
    _order = "sequence"

    name = fields.Char()
    sequence = fields.Integer(default=10)
    fold = fields.Boolean()
    active = fields.Boolean(default=True)
    state = fields.Selection(
        [("new","Requested"),
         ("open","Borrowed"),
         ("done","Returned"),
         ("cancel", "Canceled")],
        default="new",
    )
```

The preceding code shouldn't be surprising to you. Stages have a logical sequence, so the order in which they are presented is important. This is ensured by _order="sequence". We can also see the state field mapping each stage to a basic state, which can be safely used by the business logic.

2. As usual, the new code file must be added to the models/__init__.py file, which should then look like this:

```
from . import library_checkout_stage
from . import library_checkout
from . import library_checkout_line
```

3. Access security rules are also needed. Stages contain setup data, and it should only be editable by the **Manager** user group. Regular users should have read-only access. For this, add the following highlighted lines to the security/ir.model.access.csv file:

```
id,name,model_id:id,group_id:id,perm_read,perm_
write,perm_create,perm_unlink
checkout_user,Checkout User,model_library_
checkout,library_app.library_group_user,1,1,1,1
checkout_line_user,Checkout Line
User,model_library_checkout,library_app.library_group_
user,1,1,1,1
checkout_stage_user,Checkout Stage User,model_library_
checkout_stage,library_app.library_group_user,1,0,0,0
checkout_stage_manager,Checkout Stage Manager,model_
library_checkout_stage,library_app.library_group_
manager,1,1,1,1
```

4. Next, a menu item is needed, to navigate to the stage's setup. This should be under the **Configurations** menu in the app. The library_app module does not provide one yet, so let's edit it to add this. Edit the library_app/views/library_menu.xml file and add the following XML:

```
<menuitem id="menu_library_configuration"
          name="Configuration"
          parent="menu_library"
/>
```

5. Now, the **Stages** menu item can be added under the **Configurations** menu. Edit the `library_checkout/views/library_menu.xml` file and add the following XML:

```xml
<record id="action_library_stage"
        model="ir.actions.act_window">
  <field name="name">Stages</field>
  <field name="res_model">
    library.checkout.stage</field>
  <field name="view_mode">tree,form</field>
</record>

<menuitem id="menu_library_stage"
          name="Stages"
          action="action_library_stage"
          parent=
            "library_app.menu_library_configuration"
/>
```

6. We need some stages to work with, so let's add some default data to the module. Create the `data/library_checkout_stage.xml` file with the following code:

```xml
<odoo noupdate="1">
  <record id="stage_new" model=
    "library.checkout.stage">
    <field name="name">Draft</field>
    <field name="sequence">10</field>
    <field name="state">new</field>
  </record>
  <record id="stage_open" model=
    "library.checkout.stage">
    <field name="name">Borrowed</field>
    <field name="sequence">20</field>
    <field name="state">open</field>
  </record>
  <record id="stage_done" model=
    "library.checkout.stage">
    <field name="name">Completed</field>
```

```xml
            <field name="sequence">90</field>
            <field name="state">done</field>
        </record>
        <record id="stage_cancel" model=
          "library.checkout.stage">
            <field name="name">Canceled</field>
            <field name="sequence">95</field>
            <field name="state">cancel</field>
        </record>
    </odoo>
```

7. Before this can take effect, it needs to be added to the `library_checkout/__manifest__.py` file, as follows:

```python
    "data": [
        "security/ir.model.access.csv",
        "views/library_menu.xml",
        "views/checkout_view.xml",
        "data/library_checkout_stage.xml",
    ],
```

The following screenshot shows what the Stages list view is expected to look like:

Figure 8.3 – The Stages list view

This takes care of all the components that are needed to add the Stages model to `library_checkout` and allow users to configure it.

Adding stage workflow support to models

Next, the stage field should be added to the library checkout model. For a proper user experience, two more things should be taken care of:

- The default stage to assign should be the first with a new state.

- When grouping by stage, all the available stages should be present, even if there are no checkouts in each of the stages.

These should be added to the `library_checkout/models/library_checkout.py` file, in the `Checkout` class.

The function for finding the default stage should return the record that will be used as the default value:

```python
@api.model
def _default_stage_id(self):
    Stage = self.env["library.checkout.stage"]
    return Stage.search([("state", "=", "new")],
        limit=1)
```

This returns the first record in the stage model. Since the stage model is ordered by sequence, it will return the one with the lowest sequence number.

When we're grouping by stages, we would like to see all the possible stages rather than only the ones with checkout records. The method that's used for this should return a recordset to use for the groups. In this case, it is appropriate to return all the active stages:

```python
@api.model
def _group_expand_stage_id(self, stages, domain,
    order):
    return stages.search([], order=order)
```

Finally, the `stage_id` field we wish to add to the checkout model can use the preceding methods for the `default` and `group_expand` attributes:

```python
stage_id = fields.Many2one(
    "library.checkout.stage",
    default=_default_stage_id,
    group_expand="_group_expand_stage_id")
state = fields.Selection(related="stage_id.state")
```

`stage_id` has a many-to-one relationship with the stages model. The default value is calculated by the `_default_stage_id` method function, and the groupby on `stage_id` will use the result of the `_group_expand_stage_id` method function.

> **Changes in Odoo 10**
>
> The `group_expand` field attribute was introduced in Odoo 10 and is not available in previous versions.

The `group_expand` parameter overrides the way grouping works on the field. The default behavior for grouping operations is to only see the stages that are being used; the stages with no checkout document won't be shown. But in the case of the `stage_id` field, we want to see all the available stages, even if some don't have any items.

The `_group_expand_stage_id()` helper function returns the list of group records that the grouping operation should use. In this case, it returns all the existing stages, regardless of having library checkouts in that stage or not.

> **Note**
>
> The `group_expand` attribute must be a string with a method name. This is unlike other attributes, such as `default`, which can be either strings or direct references to the method name.

The `state` field was also added. It simply makes the stage-related `state` field in this model available so that it can be used in views. This will use the special support for `state` that views have available.

Methods to support the user interface

The following methods are mostly used by the web client to render the user interface and perform basic interaction:

- `name_get()` computes the **display name**, which is the text that represents each record that's used on views to display related records. It returns a list of (ID, name) tuples, along with the ID. It is the default computation for the `display_name` value and can be extended to implement custom display representations, such as displaying an identifier code along with the record name.

- `name_search(name="", args=None, operator="ilike", limit=100)` performs a search on the display name. It is used on views when the user is typing in a relationship field to produce a list containing the suggested records that match the typed text. It returns a list of (ID, name) tuples.

- `name_create(name)` creates a new record that only has a name as input. It is used in Kanban views with `on_create="quick_create"`, where you can quickly create a related record by just providing its name. It can be extended to provide specific defaults for the new records that are created through this feature.

- `default_get([fields])` returns the default values for a new record to be created, as a dictionary. The default values may depend on variables, such as the current user or the session context. This can be extended to add additional default values.

- `fields_get()` is used to describe the model's field definitions.

- `fields_view_get()` is used by the web client to retrieve the structure of the UI view to render. It can be given the ID of the view as an argument, or the type of view we want using `view_type="form"`. For example, `self.fields_view_get(view_type="tree")` will return the tree view XML architecture to be rendered for the `self` model.

These built-in ORM models can be helpful as extension points to implement model-specific business logic.

The next section will discuss how business logic can be triggered by record operations, such as creating or writing on a record.

Using the ORM built-in methods

The model definition-related methods can do many things, but some business logic is not possible through them, so it needs to be attached to the ORM record writing operations.

ORM provides methods to perform **Create**, **Read**, **Update**, and **Delete** (**CRUD**) operations on our model data. Let's explore these write operations and how they can be extended to support custom logic.

To read data, the main methods that are provided are `search()` and `browse()`, as discussed in *Chapter 7, Recordsets – Working with Model Data*.

Methods for writing model data

The ORM provides three methods for the three basic write operations, shown as follows:

- `<Model>.create(values)` creates a new record on the model. It returns the created record. `values` can be a dictionary or a list of dictionaries for mass-creating records.

- `<Recordset>.write(values)` updates the recordset with the `values` dictionary. It returns nothing.
- `<Recordset>.unlink()` deletes the records from the database. It returns nothing.

The `values` argument is a dictionary that maps field names to values to write. These methods are decorated with `@api.multi`, except for the `create()` method, which is decorated with `@api.model`.

> **Changes in Odoo 12**
>
> Being able to use `create()` to access a list of dictionaries, instead of a single dictionary object, was introduced in Odoo 12. This also allows us to create records in batches. This capability is supported through the special `@api.model_create_multi` decorator.

In some cases, these methods need to be extended to run some specific business logic when they are triggered. This business logic can be run before or after the main method operations are executed.

Example of extending create()

Let's look at an example that makes use of this. We want to prevent new checkout records from being created directly in the `Borrowed` or `Returned` states. Usually, validations should be implemented in specific methods that are decorated with `@api.constrains`. But this particular case is tied to the create record event and is hard to implement as a regular validation.

Edit the `library_checkout/models/library_checkout.py` file and add the `create()` extension method:

```python
@api.model
def create(self, vals):
    # Code before create: should use the 'vals' dict
    new_record = super().create(vals)
    # Code after create: can use the 'new_record'
    # created
    if new_record.stage_id.state in ("open", "close"):
        raise exceptions.UserError(
            "State not allowed for new checkouts."
        )
    return new_record
```

The new record is created by the `super().create()` call. Before this, the new record is not available to use in the business logic – only the `values` dictionary can be used, or even changed, to force values on the to-be-created record.

The code after `super().create()` does have access to the new record that's been created and can use record features, such as accessing related records using dot-notation chains. The preceding example uses `new_record.stage_id.state` to access the state that corresponds to the new record stage. States are not user-configurable and provide a reliable list of values to use in business logic. So, we can look for `open` or `done` states and raise an error if any of them are found.

Example of extending write()

Let's look at another example. The `Checkout` model should keep track of the date when the books were borrowed, Checkout Date, and the date when they were returned, Close Date. This can't be done using computed fields. Instead, the `write()` method should be extended to detect changes on the checkout state and then update the dates that have been filed at the right moment: when changing into the `open` or `close` states.

Before we implement this logic, the two date fields must be created. Edit the `library_checkout/models/library_checkout.py` file and add the following code:

```
checkout_date = fields.Date(readonly=True)
close_date = fields.Date(readonly=True)
```

When a record is modified, the `checkout_date` and `close_date` fields should be set when the checkout record enters the appropriated states. For this, we will use a custom `write()` method, as follows:

```
def write(self, vals):
    # Code before write: 'self' has the old values
    if "stage_id" in vals:
        Stage = self.env["library.checkout.stage"]
        old_state = self.stage_id.state
        new_state = \
            Stage.browse(vals["stage_id"]).state
        if new_state != old_state and new_state == \
            "open":
            vals['checkout_date'] = fields.Date.today()
        if new_state != old_state and new_state == \
            "done":
```

```
            vals['close_date'] = fields.Date.today()
    super().write(vals)
    # Code after write: can use 'self' with the updated
    # values
    return True
```

In the preceding example, the extension code was added before the `super()` call; so, *before* the write operation is done on the `self` record. To know what change is about to be made to the record, we can inspect the `vals` parameter. The `stage_id` value in the `vals` dictionary is an ID number, not a record, so it needs to be browsed to get the corresponding record, and then read the corresponding `state`.

The old and new states are compared to trigger the date value update at the appropriate moment. Whenever possible, we prefer to change the values to write before the `super().write()` instruction and modify the `vals` dictionary instead of setting the field value directly. We'll see why in the next section.

Example of extending write() that sets values on fields

The previous code only modifies the values to use for the write; it does not assign values directly to the model fields. This is safe to do, but it may not be enough in some cases.

Assigning a model field value inside a `write()` method leads to an infinite recursion loop: the assignment triggers the write method again, which then repeats the assignment, triggering yet another write call. This will repeat until Python returns a recursion error.

There is a technique to avoid this recursion loop, making it possible for `write()` methods to set values on its record fields. The trick is to set a unique marker in the environment's `context` before setting the values, and only run the setting values code when that marker is not present.

An example will help make this clear. Let's rewrite the previous example so that the updates are done after calling `super()`, rather than before:

```
def write(self, vals):
    # Code before write: 'self' has the old values
    old_state = self.stage_id.state
    super().write(vals)
    # Code after write: can use 'self' with the updated
    # values
    new_state = self.stage_id.state
    if not self.env.context.get("_checkout_write"):
```

```
        if new_state != old_state and new_state == "open":
            self.with_context(
                _checkout_write=True).write(
                    {"checkout_date": fields.Date.today()})
        if new_state != old_state and new_state ==
            "done":
            self.with_context(
                _checkout_write=True).write(
                    {"close_date": fields.Date.today()})
    return True
```

With this technique, the extension code is guarded by an `if` statement and only runs if a specific marker is not found in the context. Furthermore, the additional `self.write()` operations use the `with_context` method to set that marker before doing the write. This combination ensures that the custom login inside the `if` statement runs only once and is not triggered on further `write()` calls, avoiding the infinite loop.

When (not) to extend the create() and write() methods

Extending the `create()` or `write()` methods should be carefully considered.

In most cases, some validation must be performed, or some value must be automatically computed when the record is saved. For these common cases, there are better options, as listed here:

- For field values that are automatically calculated based on other fields, use computed fields. For example, you should calculate a header total when the values of the lines are changed.

- For non-fixed field default values, use a function as the default field value. It will be evaluated and used to assign the default value.

- To have other field values change when some field is changed, use the `onchange` methods, if this is expected to be done on the user interface, or use the new **computed writable fields**, if this needs to be done at the server side. For example, when the user selects a customer, you can automatically set the price list to the customer's one, though this price list selection can be changed by the user later. When you're using the `onchange` methods, this only works on form view interaction, not on direct write calls, though computed writable fields work in both cases. The *Adding onchange user interface logic* section will provide more detail about this.

- For validations, use `constraint` functions. These are automatically triggered when the field value changes and are expected to raise errors if the validation conditions fail.

There are still cases where none of these options will work and extending `create()` or `write()` is needed, such as when the default values to set depend on the other fields of the record that's being created. In this case, a default value function won't work because it does not have access to the other field values of the new record.

Methods for data import and export

Data import and export, as discussed in *Chapter 5, Importing, Exporting, and Module Data*, is also available from the ORM API, through the following methods:

- `load([fields], [data])` is used to import data and is used by Odoo when importing CSV or spreadsheet data into Odoo. The first argument is the list of fields to import, and it maps directly to a CSV top row. The second argument is a list of records, where each record is a list of string values to parse and import. It maps directly to the CSV data rows and columns and implements the features of CSV data import, such as external identifiers support.

- `export_data([fields])` is used by the web client's Export function. It returns a dictionary with a `datas` key containing the data; that is, a list of rows. The field names can use the `.id` and `/id` suffixes that are used in CSV files, and the data is in a format that's compatible with an importable CSV file.

It is also possible to implement automation on the user interface, while the user is editing data. We'll learn about this in the next section.

Adding onchange user interface logic

It is possible to make changes to the web client view while the user is editing it. This mechanism is known as **onchange**. It is implemented through methods decorated with `@api.onchange`, and they are triggered by the user interface view when the user edits a value on a particular field.

Since Odoo 13, the same effect can be achieved by using a particular form of computed fields, called **computed writable fields**. This ORM improvement aims to avoid some limitations of the classic onchange mechanism, and in the long run, it should replace it completely.

Classic onchange methods

Onchange methods can change other field values in the form, perform a validation, show a message to the user, or set a domain filter in relation fields, limiting the available options.

The onchange method is called asynchronously and returns data that's being used by the web client to update the fields in the current view.

Onchange methods are linked to the triggering fields, which are passed as arguments to the `@api.onchange("fld1", "fld2", ...)` decorator.

> **Note**
>
> The `api.onchange` arguments do not support dot notation; for example, `"partner_id.name"`. If used, it will be ignored.

Inside the method, the `self` argument is a virtual record that contains the current form data. It is virtual because it can be a new or changed record that is still being edited and hasn't been saved to the database yet. If values are set on this `self` record, these will be changed on the user interface form. Notice that it doesn't write to database records; instead, it provides information so that you can change the data in the UI form.

> **Note**
>
> Other restrictions apply to onchange methods, as documented at `https://www.odoo.com/documentation/15.0/developer/reference/backend/orm.html#odoo.api.onchange`. Computed writable fields can be used as a full-featured alternative to onchanges. See the *The new onchange, with computed writable fields* section for more information.

No return value is needed, but a `dict` structure may be returned with a warning message to display in the user interface, or a domain filter to be set on form fields.

Let's work with an example. On the checkout form, when the library member is selected, the request date will be set to `today`. If the date changed, a warning message will be shown to the user, alerting them about it.

To implement this, edit the `library_checkout/models/library_checkout.py` file and add the following method:

```python
@api.onchange("member_id")
def onchange_member_id(self):
    today_date = fields.Date.today()
    if self.request_date != today_date:
        self.request_date = today_date
    return {
        "warning": {
            "title": "Changed Request Date",
            "message": "Request date changed to
                today!",
        }
    }
```

The previous onchange method is triggered when the member_id field is set on the user interface. The actual method name is not relevant, but the convention is for its name to begin with the onchange_ prefix.

Inside an onchange method, self represents a single virtual record containing all of the fields that have currently been set in the record being edited, and we can interact with them.

The method code checks whether the current request_date needs to be changed. If it does, request_date is set to today so that the user will see that change in the form. Then, a non-blocking warning message is returned to the user.

The onchange methods do not need to return anything, but they can return a dictionary containing a warning or a domain key, as follows:

- The warning key should describe a message to show in a dialog window, such as `{"title": "Message Title", "message": "Message Body"}`.

- The domain key can set or change the domain attribute of other fields. This allows you to build more user-friendly interfaces; having a to-many field only makes the options that make sense at that moment available. The value for the domain key looks like `{"user_id": [("email", "!=", False)]}`.

The new onchange, with computed writable fields

The classic onchange mechanism has a key role in the user experience that's provided by the Odoo framework. However, it has a few important limitations.

One is that it works disconnected from the server-side events. Onchange is only played when requested by the form view and is not called as a consequence of an actual `write()` value change. This forces the server-side business logic to explicitly replay the relevant onchange methods.

Another limitation is that onchange is attached to the triggering fields and not to the change-affected fields. In non-trivial cases, this becomes hard to extend and makes it difficult to track the source of the changes.

To address these issues, the Odoo framework expanded the computed field capabilities so that it can also address the onchange use case. We will call this technique **computed writable fields**. The classic onchange is still supported and used, but it is expected to be replaced by computed fields and become deprecated in future versions.

> **Changes in Odoo 13**
>
> Computed writable fields were introduced in Odoo 13 and are available for that version and later ones.

Computed writable fields have compute methods assigned to them, must be stored, and must have the **readonly=False** attribute.

Let's implement the previous onchange using this technique instead. This is how the `request_date` field definition should be changed:

```
request_date = fields.Date(
    default=lambda s: fields.Date.today(),
    compute="_compute_request_date_onchange",
    store=True,
    readonly=False,
)
```

This is a regular stored and writable field, but it has attached a compute method that can be triggered in particular conditions. For example, the computed method should be triggered when the `member_id` field changes.

This is the code for the compute method, _compute_request_date_onchange:

```python
@api.depends("member_id")
def _compute_request_date_onchange(self):
    today_date = fields.Date.today()
    if self.request_date != today_date:
        self.request_date = today_date
    return {
        "warning": {
            "title": "Changed Request Date",
            "message": "Request date changed to
                today!",
        }
    }
```

@api.depends works as usual for computed fields and declares the fields to watch for changes. The actual field list to provide is the same as the one that's used by the classic @api.onchange.

The method code can be very similar to the equivalent onchange method. In this particular case, it is identical. Note that the computed field is not ensured to be set a value on every method call. This only happens when some conditions are met. In this case, the original request date is different from today's date. This goes against regular computed field rules but is allowed for computed writable fields.

Particularly relevant to business processes is the ability to send emails or notify users. The next section discusses the features that Odoo provides for this.

The message and activity features

Odoo has global messaging and activity planning features available, all of which are provided by the **Discuss** application, and a mail technical name.

The messaging features are added by the mail.thread model and make a message widget on form views available, also known as *Chatter*. This widget allows you to log notes or send messages to other people. It also keeps a history of the messages that have been sent, and it is also used by automatic processes to log progress tracking messages.

The same app also provides activity management features through the mail.activity. mixin model. The activity widget can be added to the form view to allow users to schedule and track the history of activities.

Adding message and activity features

The mail module provides the `mail.thread` abstract class, which is used to add the messaging features to any model, and `mail.activity.mixin`, which does the same for the planned activity features. In *Chapter 4, Extending Modules*, we explained how to add these inherited features to models using the inheritance from mixin abstract classes.

Let's go through the necessary steps:

1. Add the `mail` module dependency to the `library_checkout` add-on module by editing the `'depends'` key in the `library_checkout/__manifest__.py` file, as follows:

    ```python
    "depends": ["library_member", "mail"],
    ```

2. To have the `library.checkout` model inherit from the message and activity abstract classes, edit the `library_checkout/models/library_checkout.py` files, as follows:

    ```python
    class Checkout(models.Model):
        _name = "library.checkout"
        _description = "Checkout Request"
        _inherit = ["mail.thread", "mail.activity.mixin"]
    ```

3. To add the message and activity fields to the checkout form view, edit the `library_checkout/` and `views/checkout_view.xml` files:

    ```xml
    <record id="view_form_checkout" model="ir.ui.view">
        <field name="name">Checkout Form</field>
        <field name="model">library.checkout</field>
        <field name="arch" type="xml">

        <form>
          <sheet>
            <group>
                <field name="member_id" />
                <field name="request_date" />
                <field name="user_id" />
    ```

```
            </group>
            <notebook>
              <page name="lines">
                <field name="line_ids">
                  <tree editable="bottom">
                    <field name="book_id" />
                    <field name="note" />
                  </tree>
                </field>
              </page>
            </notebook>
          </sheet>
          <div class="oe_chatter">
            <field name="message_follower_ids"
                   widget="mail_followers" />
            <field name="activity_ids"
                   widget="mail_activity"/>
            <field name="message_ids"
                   widget="mail_thread" />
          </div>
        </form>

      </field>
    </record>

</odoo>
```

Having done this, the checkout model will have the message and activity fields and their features available.

Message and activity fields and models

The message and activity features add new fields to the models that inherit the `mail.thread` and `mail.activity.mixin` classes, along with all the supporting models for these features. These are the basic data structures that have been added.

The `mail.thread` mixin class makes two new fields available:

- **Followers**: `message_follower_ids` has a one-to-many relationship with `mail.followers` and stores the message followers that should receive notifications. Followers can either be partners or channels. A **partner** represents a specific person or organization. A **channel** is not a particular person and instead represents a subscription list.

- **Messages**: `message_ids` has a one-to-many relationship with `mail.message` records and lists the record message history.

The `mail.activity.mixin` mixin class adds the following new field:

- **Activities**: `activity_ids` has a one-to-many relationship with `mail.activity` and stores activities that have been completed or planned.

Message subtypes

Messages can be assigned a **subtype**. Subtypes can identify particular events, such as a task being created or closed, and are useful for fine-tuning what notifications should be sent to whom.

Subtypes are stored in the `mail.message.subtype` model and can be configured in the **Settings | Technical | Email | Subtypes** menu.

The basic message subtypes that are available are as follows:

- **Discussions**, with the `mail.mt_comment` XML ID, are used for the messages that are sent through the **Send message** option in the message widget. Followers will be sent a message notification about this.

- **Note**, with the `mail.mt_note` XML ID, is used by the messages that are created with the **Log note** XML ID, which do not send out notifications.

- **Activities**, with the `mail.mt_activities` XML ID, are used for the messages that are created with the `Schedule activity` link. It is not intended to send a notification.

Apps can add their own subtypes, which are usually linked to relevant events. For example, the **Sales** app adds two subtypes: `Quotation sent` and `Sales Order Confirmed`. These are used by the app's business logic when you're logging these events in the message history.

Subtypes allow you to determine when notifications should be sent out and to whom. The followers menu, at the top right of the messages widget, allows you to add or remove followers, as well as selecting the particular subtypes they will receive notifications about. The following screenshot shows the subtype selection form for a specific follower – *Deco Addict*, in this case:

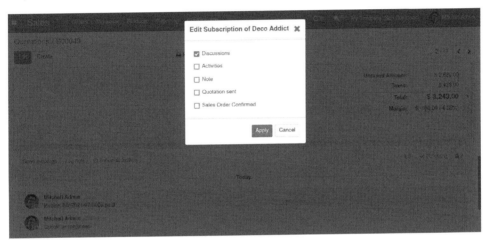

Figure 8.4 – Followers widget to select the active message subtypes

The subtype subscription flags can be edited manually, and their default value is configured on editing the **Subtype** definition to check the **Default** field. When it is set, the followers on new records will receive notifications by default.

Other than the built-in subtypes, add-on modules add their own subtypes. A subtype can be global or intended for a particular model. In the latter case, the subtype's `res_model` field identifies the model it applies to.

Posting messages

Module business logic can make use of the messaging system to send notifications to users.

The `message_post()` method is used to post a message. Here is an example:

```
self.message_post("Hello!")
```

The preceding code adds a simple text message but sends no notification to the followers. This is because, by default, messages are posted using **Log a Note**, with the `subtype="mail.mt_note"` parameter.

To have the message send a notification as well, the `mail.mt_comment` subtype should be used, as shown in the following example:

```
self.message_post(
    "Hello again!",
    subject="Hello",
    subtype='mail.mt_comment",
)
```

The message body is HTML, so we can include markup for text effects, such as `<b>` for bold text or `<i>` for italics.

The message body will be sanitized for security reasons, so some particular HTML elements may not make it to the final message.

Adding followers

Also useful from a business logic viewpoint is the ability to automatically add followers to a document so that they can then get the corresponding notifications. There are a few methods available to add followers, as follows:

- `message_subscribe(partner_ids=<list of int IDs>)` adds partners
- `message_subscribe(channel_ids=<list of int IDs>)` adds channels
- `message_subscribe_users(user_ids=<list of int IDs>)` adds users

The default subtypes will be applied to each subscriber. To force a user to subscribe to a specific list of subtypes, you can add the `subtype_ids=<list of int IDs>` attribute, which lists the specific subtypes to enable for the subscription. If this is used, it will also reset the existing follower-subscribed subtypes to the specified ones.

Creating a wizard

Wizards are user interface patterns that provide rich interaction for the user, usually to provide input for an automated process.

As an example, the `checkout` module will provide a wizard for library users to mass email borrowers. For example, they could select the oldest checkouts with borrowed books and send them all a message, requesting for the books to be returned.

Users start by going to the checkouts list view, selecting the checkout records to use, and then selecting a **Send Messages** option from the **Action** context menu. This will open the wizard form, allowing them to write the message subject and body. Clicking the **Send** button will send an email to each person that borrowed the selected checkouts.

The wizard model

A wizard displays a form view to the user, usually as a dialog window, with some fields to be filled in and buttons to trigger some business logic. These will then be used for the wizard's logic.

This is implemented using the same model/view architecture that's used for regular views, but the supporting model is based on `models.TransientModel` instead of `models.Model`. This type of model has a database representation too, which is used to store the wizard's state. The wizard data is temporary, to allow the wizard to complete its work. A scheduled job regularly cleans up the old data from the wizard database tables.

The `library_checkout/wizard/library_checkout_massmessage.py` file will create the model data structure that's needed for the user interaction: the list of checkout records to be notified, the message subject, and the message body.

Follow these steps to add the wizard to the `library_checkout` module:

1. First, edit the `library_checkout/__init__.py` file to import the code into the `wizard/` subdirectory, as follows:

    ```
    from . import models
    from . import wizard
    ```

2. Add the `wizard/__init__.py` file with the following line of code:

    ```
    from . import checkout_mass_message
    ```

3. Then, create the actual `wizard/checkout_mass_message.py` file, as follows:

```python
from odoo import api, exceptions, fields, models


class CheckoutMassMessage(models.TransientModel):
    _name = "library.checkout.massmessage"
    _description = "Send Message to Borrowers"


    checkout_ids = fields.Many2many(
        "library.checkout",
        string="Checkouts",
    )
    message_subject = fields.Char()
    message_body = fields.Html()
```

With that, we have prepared the basic data structures that are needed for the wizard.

Note that regular models shouldn't have relationship fields that use transient models.

The consequence of this is that transient models shouldn't have one-to-many relationships with regular models. The reason for this is that the one-to-many relationship on the transient model would require the regular model to have the inverse many-to-one relationship with the transient model, which would cause issues with automatically cleaning up transient records.

The alternative to this is to use a many-to-many relationship. Many-to-many relationships are stored in a dedicated table, and the rows in this table are automatically deleted when either side of the relationship is deleted.

The wizard's access security

Just like regular models, transient models also need access security rules to be defined on them. This is done in the same way as it is for regular modules – usually, in the `security/ir.model.access.csv` file.

Changes in Odoo 13

Up until Odoo 12, transient models did not need access security rules. This changed in Odoo 13, so now, transient models require access rules, just like regular models do.

To add ACLs for the wizard's model, edit the `security/ir.model.access.csv` file and add the following highlighted line:

```
id,name,model_id:id,group_id:id,perm_read,perm_write,perm_
create,perm_unlink
checkout_user,Checkout User,model_library_checkout,library_app.
library_group_user,1,1,1,1
checkout_line_user,Checkout Line
checkout_user,Checkout User,model_library_checkout,library_app.
library_group_user,1,1,1,1
checkout_stage_user,Checkout Stage User,model_library_checkout_
stage,library_app.library_group_user,1,0,0,0
checkout_stage_manager,Checkout Stage Manager,model_library_
checkout_stage,library_app.library_group_manager,1,1,1,1
checkout_massmessage_user,Checkout Mass Message User,model_
library_checkout_massmessage,library_app.library_group_
user,1,1,1,1
```

Adding one line is enough to add full access to the Library User group; no specific access rights are needed for the Library Manager group.

The wizard form

The wizard form views are defined in the same way as they are for regular models, except for two specific elements:

- A `<footer>` section can be used to replace the action buttons.
- A `special="cancel"` button is available to interrupt the wizard without performing any action.

The following is the content of the `wizard/checkout_mass_message_wizard_view.xml` file:

```
<odoo>

  <record id="view_form_checkout_message"
    model="ir.ui.view">
    <field name="name">Library Checkout Mass Message
      Wizard</field>
    <field name="model">
      library.checkout.massmessage</field>
```

```xml
<field name="arch" type="xml">

    <form>
      <group>
        <field name="message_subject" />
        <field name="message_body" />
        <field name="checkout_ids" />
      </group>
      <footer>
        <button type="object"
          name="button_send"
          string="Send Messages" />
        <button special="cancel"
          string="Cancel"
          class="btn-secondary" />
      </footer>
    </form>

  </field>
</record>

<record id="action_checkout_message"
        model="ir.actions.act_window">
  <field name="name">Send Messages</field>
  <field name="res_model">
    library.checkout.massmessage</field>
  <field name="view_mode">form</field>
  <field name="binding_model_id"
        ref="model_library_checkout" />
  <field name="binding_view_types">form,list</field>
  <field name="target">new</field>
</record>

</odoo>
```

The previous XML code adds two data records – one for the w.
another for the action to open the wizard.

The ir.actions.act_window window action record is made availab.
context menu using the binding_model_id field value.

Remember to add this file to the manifest file:

```
"data": [
    "security/ir.model.access.csv",
    "wizard/checkout_mass_message_wizard_view.xml",
    "views/library_menu.xml",
    "views/checkout_view.xml",
    "data/library_checkout_stage.xml",
],
```

The wizard form will look as follows:

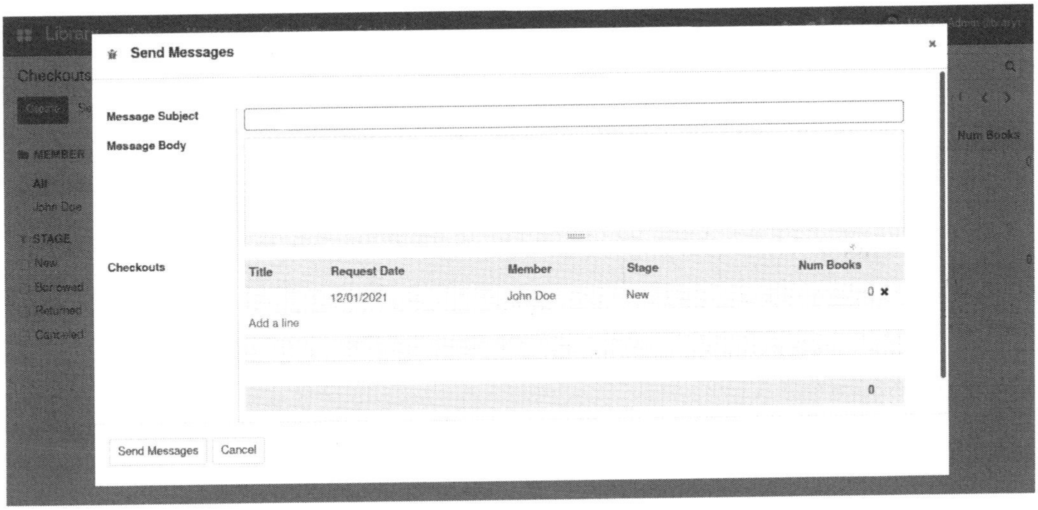

Figure 8.5 – The Send Messages wizard form

To open the wizard, the user should select one or more records on the checkout list view and choose the **Send Messages** option via the **Action** menu, which is available at the top of the list view.

form, but it is not capable of performing any
.th, we would like the wizard to present the list of
ut list view.

splays an empty form. It is not a record yet; this will
.on that's calling a method.

ιened, we have an empty record. The create()
.d yet; this will only happen when we press a button.
he initial values to be presented in a wizard form.

It is ι   lata on the empty form by setting default values on the
fields. defaυ.   .n ORM API method that's in charge of computing the default
values for a record. ιι ι.   ι extended to add custom logic, like so:

```
@api.model
def default_get(self, field_names):
    defaults_dict = super().default_get(field_names)
    # Add values to the defaults_dict here
    return defaults_dict
```

The preceding method function can be used to add the default value for the checkout_
ids field. But we still need to know how to access the list of records that will be selected
in the origin list view.

When you're navigating from a client window to the next, the web client stores some data
about the origin view in the environment's context. This data is as follows:

- Active_model, which is the technical name of the model

- Active_id, which is the ID of the form active record or the tree view's first
  record, if you're navigating from a list

- active_ids, which is a list that contains the selected records or just one element
  if you're navigating from a form

- active_domain, if the action is triggered from a form view

In this case, `active_ids` can be used to get the record IDs that have been selected in the list view and set the default value on the `checkout_ids` field. This is what the `default_get` method looks like:

```python
@api.model
def default_get(self, field_names):
    defaults_dict = super().default_get(field_names)
    checkout_ids = self.env.context["active_ids"]
    defaults_dict["checkout_ids"] = checkout_ids
    return defaults_dict
```

First, `super()` is used to call the framework's `default_get()` implementation, which returns a dictionary containing default values. Then, the `checkout_id` key is added to `defaults_dict`, with the `active_ids` value read from the environment's context.

With this, when the wizard form is opened, the `checkout_ids` field will be automatically populated with the records that have been selected. Next, the logic for the form's **Send Messages** button needs to be implemented.

Upon inspecting the form XML code, we can see that `button_send` is the name of the function that's called by the button. It should be defined in the `wizard/checkout_mass_message.py` file, as shown in the following code:

```python
def button_send(self):
    self.ensure_one()
    for checkout in self.checkout_ids:
        checkout.message_post(
            body=self.message_body,
            subject=self.message_subject,
            subtype='mail.mt_comment',
        )
    return True
```

The method is designed to work with a single record and would not work correctly if `self` was a recordset instead of a singleton. To make this explicit, `self.ensure_one()` is being used.

Here, `self` represents the wizard record data, which was created when the button was pressed. It contains the data that was entered on the wizard form. Validation is performed to ensure a message body text is provided by the user.

The `checkout_id` field is accessed, and a loop iterates through each of its records. For each checkout record, a message is posted using the `mail.thread` API. The `mail.mt_comment` subtype must be used for a notification email to be sent to the record followers. The message's `body` and `subject` are taken from the `self` record fields.

It is good practice for methods to always return something – the `True` value at the very least. The sole reason for this is that some XML-RPC clients don't support `None` values. When a Python function has no explicit `return`, it implicitly returns the `None` value. In practice, you may not be aware of the issue because the web client uses JSON-RPC, not XML-RPC, but it is still a good practice to follow.

Wizards are the most complex tools in our business logic toolbox and close out the list of techniques that will be presented in this chapter.

Business logic also involves testing if the right conditions are being met before or after running some operation. The next section explains how to trigger exceptions when this doesn't happen.

Raising exceptions

There are times where the inputs are inappropriate for the task to perform, and the code needs to warn the user about it and interrupt the program's execution with an error message. This is done by raising an exception. Odoo provides exception classes that should be used in these situations.

The most useful Odoo exceptions are as follows:

```
from odoo import exceptions
raise exceptions.ValidationError("Inconsistent data")
raise exceptions.UserError("Wrong input")
```

The `ValidationError` exception should be used for validations in Python code, such as the ones in `@api.constrains` decorated methods.

The `UserError` exception should be used in all other cases where some action should not be allowed because it goes against business logic.

As a general rule, all data manipulation that's done during method execution is done in a database transaction and rolled back when an exception occurs. This means that, when an exception is raised, all of the previous data changes are canceled.

Let's look at an example of using the wizard's `button_send` method. If we think about it, it doesn't make any sense to run the send message's logic if no checkout document was selected. And it doesn't make sense to send messages with no message body. Let's warn the user if any of these things happen.

To do so, edit the `button_send()` method and add the following highlighted code:

```python
    def button_send(self):
        self.ensure_one()
        if not self.checkout_ids:
            raise exceptions.UserError(
                "No Checkouts were selected."
            )
        if not self.message_body:
            raise exceptions.UserError(
                "A message body is required"
            )
        for checkout in self.checkout_ids:
            checkout.message_post(
                body=self.message_body,
                subject=self.message_subject,
                subtype='mail.mt_comment',
            )
        return True
```

When you're using exceptions, make sure that the `from odoo import exceptions` instruction is added to the top of the code file. Adding validations is as simple as checking that some conditions have been met and raising an exception if they haven't been.

The next section discusses the development tools that every Odoo developer should be familiar with. We will start with automated tests.

Writing unit tests

Automated tests are generally accepted as a best practice in software. They not only help ensure code is correctly implemented, but more importantly, they provide a safety net for future code changes or rewrites.

In the case of dynamic programming languages, such as Python, there is no compilation step and syntax errors can go unnoticed. Ensuring there's test code coverage is particularly important for detecting code writing mistakes, such as a mistyped identifier name.

These two goals provide a guiding light to test writing. One goal should be test coverage – writing test cases that run all your lines of code.

This alone will usually make good progress on the second goal, which is to verify the correctness of the code. This is because, after working on code coverage tests, we will surely have a great starting point to build additional test cases for non-trivial use cases.

> **Changes in Odoo 12**
>
> In earlier Odoo versions, tests could also be described using YAML data files. With Odoo 12, the YAML data file engine was removed, and this type of file is not supported anymore. The last piece of documentation on it is available at `https://doc.odoo.com/v6.0/contribute/15_guidelines/coding_guidelines_testing/`.

Next, we will learn how to add unit tests to a module and then run them.

Adding unit tests

Add-on module tests must be added to a `tests/` subdirectory. The test runner will automatically discover tests in the subdirectories with this particular name, and the module's top `__init__.py` file should *not* import them.

To add tests for the wizard logic that was created in the `library_checkout` add-on module, we will start by creating the `tests/__init__.py` file and importing the test files to be used. In this case, it should contain the following line of code:

```
from . import test_checkout_mass_message
```

Then, we must create the `tests/test_checkout_mass_message.py` file and ensure it has the basic skeleton for the unit test code:

```
from odoo import exceptions
from odoo.tests import common


class TestWizard(common.SingleTransactionCase):

    def setUp(self, *args, **kwargs):
        super(TestWizard, self).setUp(*args, **kwargs)
        # Add test setup code here...

    def test_01_button_send(self):
        """Send button should create messages on
            Checkouts"""
        # Add test code
```

Odoo provides a few classes to use for tests, as follows:

- `TransactionCase` uses a different transaction for each test, which is automatically rolled back at the end.

- `SingleTransactionCase` runs all the tests in a single transaction, which are only rolled back at the end of the last test. This can speed up tests significantly, but the individual tests need to be written in such a way that they are compatible.

These test classes are wrappers around the `unittest` test cases, which are part of the Python standard library. For more details on this, you can refer to the official documentation at `https://docs.python.org/3/library/unittest.html`.

The `setUp()` method is where test data is prepared and is usually stored as class attributes so that it is available to the test methods.

Tests are implemented as class methods, such as the `test_01_button_send()` example in the previous code. The test case method names must begin with the `test_` prefix. This is what allows them to be discovered by the test runner. Test methods are run in the order of the test function names.

The `docstring` method is printed to the server log when the tests are run and should be used to provide a short description of the test that's being performed.

Running tests

Once the tests have been written, it is time to run them. For that, you must upgrade or install the modules to test (-I or -u) and add the--test-enable option to the Odoo server command.

The command will look like this:

```
(env15) $ odoo -c library.conf --test-enable -u library_
checkout --stop-after-init
```

Only the installed or upgraded modules will be tested – that's why the -u option was used. If some dependencies need to be installed, their tests will run too. If you don't want this to happen, then install the new modules and then run the tests while upgrading (-u) the module to test.

Although the module contains testing code, this code doesn't test anything yet and should run successfully. If we take a closer look at the server log, there should be INFO messages reporting the test runs, similar to this:

```
INFO library odoo.modules.module: odoo.addons.library_checkout.
tests.test_checkout_mass_message running tests.
```

The test code skeleton is ready. Now, the actual testing code needs to be added. We should start with setting up the data.

Setting up tests

The first step when writing tests is to prepare the data to use. This is typically done in the setUp method. For our example, a checkout record is needed so that it can be used in the wizard tests.

It is convenient to perform the test actions as a specific user to also test that access control has been configured properly. This can be achieved using the sudo(<user>) model method. Recordsets carry that information with them, so after being created using sudo(), later operations in the same recordset will be performed using that same context.

This is the code for the setUp method:

```
from odoo import exceptions
from odoo.tests import common


class TestWizard(common.SingleTransactionCase):
```

```
    def setUp(self, *args, **kwargs):
        super().setUp(*args, **kwargs)
        # Setup test data
        admin_user = self.env.ref('base.user_admin')
        self.Checkout = self.env['library.checkout']\
            .with_user(admin_user)
        self.Wizard = self.env[
            'library.checkout.massmessage']\
            .with_user(admin_user)
        a_member = self.env['library.member']\
            .create({'partner_id':
                admin_user.partner_id.id})
        self.checkout0 = self.Checkout\
            .create({'member_id': a_member.id})
```

Now, we can use the `self.checkout0` record and the `self.Wizard` model for our tests.

Writing test cases

Now, let's expand the `test_button_test()` method that we saw in the initial skeleton to implement the tests.

A basic test runs some code on the tested object, gets a result, and then uses an `assert` statement to compare it with an expected result. The message posting logic does not return any value to check, so a different approach is needed.

The `button_send()` method adds a message to the message history. One way to check if this happened is to count the number of messages before and after running the method. The test code can count the number of messages before and after the wizard. The following code adds this:

```
    def test_01_button_send(self):
        """Send button creates messages on Checkouts"""
        count_before = len(self.checkout0.message_ids)
        # TODO: run wizard
        count_after = len(self.checkout0.message_ids)
        self.assertEqual(
            count_before + 1,
            count_after,
```

```
                "Expected one additional message in the
                Checkout.",
        )
```

The check for verifying whether the test succeeded or failed is the `self.assertEqual` statement. It compares the number of messages before and after running the wizard. It is expected to find one more message than it did previously. The last parameter provides an optional but recommended message that's printed when the test fails.

The `assertEqual` function is just one of the assert methods that's available. The appropriate assert function should be selected for the check to perform. The `unittest` documentation provides a good reference for all of the methods. It can be found at `https://docs.python.org/3/library/unittest.html#test-cases`.

Running the wizard is not straightforward, and the user interface workflow needs to be mimicked. Recall that the environment's context is used to pass data to the wizard, on the `active_ids` key. We must create a wizard record with the values that have been filled in the wizard form for the message subject and body and then run the `button_send` method.

The complete code looks like this:

```
def test_01_button_send(self):
    """Send button creates messages on Checkouts"""
    count_before = len(self.checkout0.message_ids)
    Wizard0 = self.Wizard\
        .with_context(active_ids=self.checkout0.ids)
    wizard0 = Wizard0.create({
        "message_subject": "Hello",
        "message_body": "This is a message.",
    })
    wizard0.button_send()
    count_after = len(self.checkout0.message_ids)
    self.assertEqual(
        count_before + 1,
        count_after,
        "Expected one additional message in the
        Checkout.",
    )
```

The `with_context` model method is used to add `active_ids` to the environment's context. Then, the `create()` method is used to create the wizard record and add the user-entered data. Finally, the `button_send` method is called.

More test cases are added with additional methods for the test class. Remember, with `TransactionCase` tests, a rollback is done at the end of each test and the operations that were performed in the previous test are reverted. With `SingleTransactionCase`, tests build each other up, and the test run sequence is important. Since tests are run in alphabetical order, the names that are chosen for the test methods are relevant. To make this clearer, it is a good practice to add a number at the beginning of the test method names, as we did in the preceding example.

Testing exceptions

In some cases, the code is expected to raise an exception, and that should also be tested. For example, we can test whether validation is being performed correctly.

Continuing with the wizard tests, validation is performed to check for an empty message body. A test can be added to check that this validation is done properly.

To check whether an exception has been raised, the corresponding code must be placed inside a `with self.assertRaises()` code block.

Another method should be added for this test, as follows:

```python
def test_02_button_send_empty_body(self):
    """Send button errors on empty body message"""
    Wizard0 = self.Wizard\
        .with_context(active_ids=self.checkout0.ids)
    wizard0 = Wizard0.create({})
    with self.assertRaises(exceptions.UserError) as e:
        wizard0.button_send()
```

If the `button_send()` method doesn't raise `UserException`, the test will fail. If it does raise that exception, the test will succeed. The exception that's raised is stored in the `e` variable, which could be inspected by additional method commands – for example, to verify the content of the error message.

Using log messages

Writing messages to the log file is useful for monitoring and auditing running systems. It can also help with code maintenance, making it easier to get debug information from running processes, without the need to change code.

To use logging in Odoo code, first, a logger object must be prepared. For this, add the following code lines at the top of the `library_checkout/wizard/checkout_mass_message.py` file:

```
import logging
_logger = logging.getLogger(__name__)
```

The `logging` Python standard library module is being used here. The `_logger` object is initialized using the name of the current code file, `__name__`. With this, the log messages will include information about the file that generated them.

There are several levels available for log messages. These are as follows:

```
_logger.debug('A DEBUG message')
_logger.info('An INFO message')
_logger.warning('A WARNING message')
_logger.error('An ERROR message')
```

We can now use the logger to write messages to the Odoo server log.

This log can be added to the `button_send` wizard method. Add the following instruction before the ending line; that is, `return True`:

```
        _logger.info(
            "Posted %d messages to the Checkouts: %s",
            len(self.checkout_ids),
            str(self.checkout_ids),
        )
```

With this code, when the wizard is used to send messages, a message similar to the following will be printed to the server log:

```
INFO library odoo.addons.library_checkout.wizard.checkout_mass_
message: Posted 2 messages to the Checkouts: [3, 4]
```

Notice that Python string interpolation – that is, using the % operator – was not used in the log message. More specifically, instead of _logger.info("Hello %s" % "World"), what was used was something like _logger.info("Hello %s", "World"). Not using interpolation means one less task for the code to perform at runtime, which makes logging more efficient. So, the variables should always be provided as additional log parameters.

The timestamps of server log messages always use UTC. This may come as a surprise and comes from the fact that the Odoo server internally handles all dates in UTC.

For debug-level log messages, _logger.debug() is used. As an example, add the following debug log message right after the checkout.message_post() instruction:

```
_logger.debug(
        "Message on %d to followers: %s",
        checkout.id,
        checkout.message_follower_ids)
```

By default, this won't print anything to the server log, since the default log level is INFO. The log level needs to be set to DEBUG for the debug messages to be printed to the log.

The Odoo --log-level command option sets the general log level. For example, adding --log-level=debug to the command line enables all debug log messages.

This can be fine-tuned and have a specific log level set only for particular modules. To enable debug messages only for this wizard code, use the --log-handler option. This can be used several times to set the log level for several modules.

For example, the Python module for the wizard is odoo.addons.library_checkout.wizard.checkout_mass_message, as shown in the INFO log messages. To set a debug log level for it, use the following command-line option:

```
--log-handler=
odoo.addons.library_checkout.wizard.checkout_mass_message:DEBUG
```

The complete reference to the Odoo server logging options can be found in the official documentation: https://www.odoo.com/documentation/15.0/developer/misc/other/cmdline.html.

> **Tip**
> If you want to get into the nitty-gritty details of Python logging, the official documentation is a good place to start: https://docs.python.org/3/library/logging.html.

Logging is a useful tool, but it's short when it comes to debugging. There are a few tools and techniques that are available to help developers with their work. We'll look at these in the next section.

Learning about the available developer tools

There are a few tools to ease developers' work. The web interface's **Developer Mode**, which we introduced earlier in this book, is one of them. A server developer mode option is also available that provides some developer-friendly features. It will be explained in more detail next. After that, we will discuss how to debug code on the server.

Server development options

The Odoo server provides a `--dev` option, which enables developer features to speed up the development cycle, such as the following:

- Entering the debugger when an exception is found in an add-on module. This is done by setting a debugger. `pdb` is the default one.

- Reloading Python code automatically when a Python code file is saved, avoiding a manual server restart. This can be enabled with the `reload` option.

- Reading view definitions directly from XML files, avoiding manual module upgrades. This can be enabled with the `xml` option.

- A Python debugging interface is used directly in the web browser. This can be enabled with the `werkzeug` option.

The `--dev` option accepts a comma-separated list of options. The `all` option can be used to conveniently enable all of these options using `--dev=all`.

When you're enabling a debugger, the Odoo server will use `pdb` by default, but other options can be used if they've been installed in your system. The supported alternatives are as follows:

- `ipdb`; see `https://pypi.org/project/ipdb` for details.

- `pudb`; see `https://pypi.org/project/pudb` for details.

- `wdb`; see `https://pypi.org/project/wdb` for details.

When you're editing Python code, the server needs to be restarted every time the code is changed so that the latest code is reloaded and used by Odoo. The `--dev=reload` option automates this reloading. When enabled, the Odoo server detects changes that have been made to code files and automatically triggers code reloading, making the code changes effective immediately.

For the code reload to work, the `watchdog` Python package is required. It can be installed with the following command:

```
(env15) $ pip3 install watchdog
```

The `--dev=all` server command option also enables `reload`, and it is what is used most of the time:

```
(env15) $ odoo -c library.conf --dev=all
```

Note that this is only useful for Python code changes. For other changes, such as changing the model's data structure, a module upgrade is needed; reloading it is not enough.

Debugging

A big part of a developer's work is debugging code. For this, it is convenient to be able to set breakpoints and run the code step by step.

Odoo is a server that runs Python code that waits for client requests, which are processed by the relevant server code, and then returns a response to the client. This means that Python code debugging is done on the server side. Breakpoints are activated in the server, pausing the server's execution on that line of code. So, the developer needs access to the terminal window running the server both to set breakpoints and to operate the debugger when those breakpoints are triggered.

The Python debugger

The simplest debugging tool that's available is the Python integrated debugger, `pdb`. However, other options are available that provide a richer user interface, closer to what sophisticated IDEs usually provide.

There are two ways a debugger prompt can be triggered.

One is when an unhandled exception is raised and the `--dev=all` option is enabled. The debugger will stop the code's execution at the instruction causing the exception. The developer can then inspect the variables and program state at that moment, to gain a better understanding of what is causing it.

The other way is to manually set a breakpoint by editing the code and adding the following line where the execution should pause:

```
import pdb; pdb.set_trace()
```

This does not require the `-dev` mode to be enabled. An Odoo server reload is needed for the changed code to be used. When the program execution reaches the `pdb.set_trace()` command, a `(pdb)` Python prompt will be shown in the server's terminal window, waiting for input.

The `(pdb)` prompt works as a Python shell and can run any expression or command in the current execution context. This means that the current variables can be inspected and even modified.

A few debugger-specific commands are also available. These are the most important commands that are available:

- `h` (help) displays a summary of the available `pdb` commands.
- `p` (print) evaluates and prints an expression.
- `pp` (pretty-print) is useful to print data structures, such as dictionaries or lists.
- `l` (list) lists the code around the instruction to be executed next.
- `n` (next) steps over to the next instruction.
- `s` (step) steps into the current instruction.
- `c` (continue) continues execution normally.
- `u` (up) moves up in the execution stack.
- `d` (down) moves down in the execution stack.
- `bt` (backtrace) shows the current execution stack.

The Python official documentation includes a complete description of the `pdb` commands: `https://docs.python.org/3/library/pdb.html#debugger-commands`.

A sample debugging session

To understand how to use the debugger's features, let's see what a debugging session looks like.

Start by adding a debugger breakpoint to the first line of the `button_send()` wizard method, as follows:

```
    def button_send(self):
        import pdb; pdb.set_trace()
        self.ensure_one()
        # ...
```

After performing a server reload, open the **Send Message** wizard form and click on the **Send Messages** button. This will trigger the `button_send()` method on the server, which will pause at the breakpoint. The web client will stay in a **Loading...** state while it is waiting for the server's response.

At that point, the terminal window where the server is running should display something similar to this:

```
> /home/daniel/work15/library/library_checkout/wizard
/checkout_mass_message.py(29)button_send()
-> self.ensure_one()
(Pdb)
```

This is the `pdb` debugger prompt, and the two previous lines provide information about where the Python code execution was paused. The first line shows the file, line number, and function name, while the second line is the code in that line that will be run next.

> **Tip**
> During a debug session, server log messages can creep in. Most of these are from the `werkzeug` module. They can be silenced by adding the `--log-handler=werkzeug:WARNING` option to the Odoo command. Another option is to lower the general log verbosity using `--log-level=warn`.

Typing h shows a quick reference of the available commands. Typing l shows the current line of code and the surrounding lines of code.

Typing n runs the current line of code and moves to the next one. Pressing *Enter* repeats the previous command.

The p debug command prints out the result of an expression, while pp does the same but formats the output to be more readable, especially the dict and list data structures. For example, to print the value for the checkout_ids field that's used in the wizard, type the following:

```
(pdb) self.checkout_ids
library.checkout(1,)
(Pdb)
```

The debug prompt can run Python commands and expressions. Any Python expressions are allowed, even variable assignments.

When you're done with a debugging session, type c to continue the normal program execution. In some cases, you may want to interrupt the execution, and q can be used to quit.

> **Tip**
>
> When you go back from the debugger to the terminal prompt, the terminal may look unresponsive, and any typed text won't be printed to the terminal. This can be solved by using the reset command; that is, by typing <enter>reset<enter>.

Alternative Python debuggers

While pdb has the advantage of being available out of the box, it can be quite terse. Fortunately, a few more comfortable options exist.

The IronPython debugger, ipdb, is a popular choice that uses the same commands as pdb but adds improvements such as tab completion and syntax highlighting for more comfortable usage. It can be installed with the following command:

```
$ pip3 install ipdb
```

To add a breakpoint, use the following command:

```
import ipdb; ipdb.set_trace()
```

Another alternative debugger is pudb. It also supports the same commands as pdb and works in text terminals, but it uses a window-like graphical display. Useful information, such as the variables in the current context and their values, is readily available on the screen in separate windows.

It can be installed either through the system package manager or through pip, as shown here:

```
$ sudo apt-get install python-pudb  # using Debian OS packages
$ pip3 install pudb  # or using pip, possibly in a virtualenv
```

A breakpoint can be added in a way similar to pdb:

```
import pudb; pudb.set_trace()
```

A short version is also available:

```
import pudb; pu.db
```

The preceding code can be typed faster and also provides the intended effect – to add a code execution breakpoint.

> **Note**
> Since Python 3.7, breakpoints can be simplified by using the breakpoint() function instead of pdb.set_trace(). Debugging libraries can overwrite the breakpoint() behavior to directly call them. However, at the time of writing, pudb and ipdb aren't doing this, so there is no benefit to using breakpoint() with them.

Printing messages and logging

Sometimes, we just need to inspect the values of some variables or check whether some code blocks are being executed. A Python print() instruction can do the job perfectly without stopping the flow of execution. Note that the printed text is sent to the standard output and won't be stored in the server log if it is being written to a file.

The print() function is only being used as a development aid and should not make its way to the final code, ready to be deployed. If the print statements can also help investigate issues in a production system, consider converting them into debug-level log messages.

Inspecting and killing running processes

There are also a few tricks that allow us to inspect running Odoo processes.

First, find the server instance's **process ID** (**PID**). This number is printed with each log message, right after the timestamp. Another way to find the PID is to run the following command in another terminal window:

```
$ ps ax | grep odoo
```

Here is a sample output:

```
 2650 pts/5   S+    0:00 grep --color=auto odoo
21688 pts/4   Sl+   0:05 python3 /home/daniel/work15/env15/bin/
odoo
```

The first column in the output is the PID of the processes. In this example, `21688` is the Odoo process PID.

Now that we know the process PID, signals can be sent to that Odoo server process. The `kill` command is used to send these signals. By default, `kill` sends a signal to terminate a process, but it can also send other, friendlier signals.

The Odoo server will print out the stack trace at the code currently being executed if it's sent a `SIGQUIT` or `-3` signal:

```
$ kill -3 <PID>
```

After sending `SIGQUIT`, the Odoo server log will display a stack trace. This can be useful for understanding what code was being executed at that point. This information is printed for each of the threads being used.

It is used by some code profiling approaches to track where the server is spending time and profile the code's execution. Some useful information on code profiling is given in the official documentation at `https://www.odoo.com/documentation/15.0/howtos/profilecode.html`.

Other signals we can send to the Odoo server process include `HUP`, to reload the server, and `INT` or `TERM` to force the server to shut down, as follows:

```
$ kill -HUP <PID>
```
```
$ kill -TERM <PID>
```

The HUP signal can be particularly useful for reloading the Odoo configuration without stopping the server.

Summary

In this chapter, we explored the various features of the ORM API and how to use them to create dynamic applications that react to users, which helps them avoid errors and automate tedious tasks.

The model validations and computed fields can cover a lot of use cases, but not all. We learned how to extend the API's create, write, and unlink methods to cover further use cases.

For rich user interaction, we used the `mail` core add-on mixins to add features for users to communicate about documents and plan activities on them. Wizards allow the application to dialogue with the user and gather the data that's needed to run particular processes. Exceptions allow the application to abort incorrect operations, informing the user of the problem and rolling back intermediate changes, keeping the system consistent.

We also discussed the tools that are available for developers to create and maintain their applications: logging messages, debugging tools, and unit tests.

In the next chapter, we will still be working with the ORM, but we will be looking at this from the point of view of an external application: we will be working with the Odoo server as a backend for storing data and running business processes.

Further reading

The following are the most relevant reference materials for the topics that were discussed in this chapter:

- ORM reference: `https://www.odoo.com/documentation/15.0/developer/reference/backend/orm.html`

- Message and activities features: `https://www.odoo.com/documentation/15.0/developer/reference/backend/mixins.html`

- Odoo tests reference: `https://www.odoo.com/documentation/15.0/developer/reference/backend/testing.html`

- Python `unittest` reference: `https://docs.python.org/3/library/unittest.html#module-unittest`

9
External API – Integrating with Other Systems

The Odoo server provides an external API that's used by its web client and is also available for other client applications. In this chapter, we'll learn how to use the Odoo external API to implement external applications that interact with an Odoo server by using it as a backend.

This can be used to write scripts to load or modify Odoo data, or to integrate with an Odoo existing business application, which is complementary and can't be replaced by an Odoo app.

We'll describe how to use OdooRPC calls, and then use that knowledge to build a simple command-line application for the *Library* Odoo app using Python.

The following topics will be covered in this chapter:

- Introducing the learning project – a client app to catalog books
- Setting up Python on the client machine
- Exploring the Odoo external API

- Implementing the client app's XML-RPC interface
- Implementing the client app's user interface
- Using the OdooRPC library

By the end of this chapter, you should have created a simple Python application that can use Odoo as a backend to query and store data.

Technical requirements

The code in this chapter requires the `library_app` Odoo module that we created in *Chapter 3, Your First Odoo Application*. The corresponding code can be found in this book's GitHub repository at `https://github.com/PacktPublishing/Odoo-15-Development-Essentials`.

The path to the Git clone repository should be in the Odoo add-ons path and the `library_app` module should be installed. The code examples will assume that the Odoo database you're working with is `library`, to be consistent with the installation instructions provided in *Chapter 2, Preparing the Development Environment*.

The code in this chapter can be found in the same repository, in the `ch09/client_app/` directory.

Introducing the learning project – a client app to catalog books

In this chapter, we will work on a simple client application to manage the library book catalog. It is a **command-line interface** (**CLI**) application that uses Odoo as its backend. The features that we will implement will be basic to keep the focus on the technology that's used to interact with the Odoo server.

This simple CLI application should be able to do the following:

- Search for and list books by title.
- Add new books to the catalog.
- Edit a book title.

The goal is to focus on how to use the Odoo external API, so we want to avoid introducing additional programming languages that you might not be familiar with. By introducing this constraint, the most sensible choice is to use Python to implement the client app. Still, once we understand the XML-RPC library for a particular language, the techniques to handle the RPC calls will also apply.

The application will be a Python script that expects specific commands to perform. Here is an example:

```
$ python3 library.py add "Moby-Dick"
$ python3 library.py list "moby"
3 Moby-Dick
$ python3 library.py set-title 3 "Moby Dick"
```

This example session demonstrates the client app being used to add, list, and modify book titles.

This client app will run using Python. Before we start looking at the code for the client app, we must make sure that Python is installed in the client machine.

Setting up Python on the client machine

The Odoo API can be accessed externally using two different protocols: XML-RPC and JSON-RPC. Any external program capable of implementing a client for one of these protocols will be able to interact with an Odoo server. To avoid introducing additional programming languages, we will use Python to explore the external API.

Until now, Python code was only being used on the server side. For the client app, Python code will run on the client, so the workstation may require additional setup.

To follow the examples in this chapter, the system you're using needs to be able to run Python 3 code. If you've followed the same development environment that's been used for the other chapters in this book, this might already be the case. However, if it isn't, we should make sure that Python is installed.

To make sure that Python 3 is installed in the development workstation, run the `python3 --version` command in a terminal window. If it is not installed, please refer to the official page to find the installation package for your system, at `https://www.python.org/downloads/`.

With Ubuntu, there's a good chance it is preinstalled on your system. If not, it can be installed with the following command:

```
$ sudo apt-get install python3 python3-pip
```

For Windows 10, it can be installed from the Microsoft Store.

Running `python3` in PowerShell will direct you to the corresponding download page.

If you are a Windows user and have installed Odoo with the all-in-one installer, you may be wondering why the Python interpreter is not already available for you. In this case, you'll need an additional installation. The short answer is that the Odoo all-in-one installer has an embedded Python interpreter that is not directly made available to the general system.

Now that Python has been installed and is available, it can be used to explore the Odoo external API.

Exploring the Odoo external API

Some familiarity with the Odoo external API should be gained before we implement the client app. The following sections explore the XML-RPC API using a *Python interpreter*.

Using XML-RPC to connect to the Odoo external API

The simplest way to access the Odoo server is by using XML-RPC. The `xmlrpc` library, from Python standard library, can be used for this.

Remember that the application being developed is a client that connects to a server. So, a running Odoo server instance is needed for the client to connect to. The code examples will assume that an Odoo server instance is running on the same machine, `http://localhost:8069`, but any reachable URL can be used if the server you wish to use is running on a different machine.

The Odoo `xmlrpc/2/common` endpoint exposes public methods, and these can be accessed without a login. These can be used to inspect the server version and check login credentials. Let's use the `xmlrpc` library to explore the `common` publicly available Odoo API.

First, start a Python 3 console and type the following:

```
>>> from xmlrpc import client
>>> srv = "http://localhost:8069"
>>> common = client.ServerProxy("%s/xmlrpc/2/common" % srv)
```

```
>>> common.version()
{'server_version': '15.0', 'server_version_info': [15, 0, 0,
'final', 0, ''], 'server_serie': '15.0', 'protocol_version': 1}
```

The preceding code imports the xmlrpc library and sets up a variable with the server address and listening port. This can be adapted to the specific URL of the Odoo server to connect to.

Next, an XML-RPC client object is created to access the server public services that are exposed at the /xmlrpc/2/common endpoint. You do not need to log in. One of the methods available there is version(), which is used to inspect the Odoo server version. It is a simple way to confirm that communication with the server is working.

Another useful public method is authenticate(). This method confirms that the username and password are accepted and returns the user ID that should be used in requests. Here is an example:

```
>>> db, user, password = "library", "admin", "admin"
>>> uid = common.authenticate(db, user, password, {})
>>> print(uid)
2
```

The authenticate() method expects four parameters: the database name, the username, the password, and the user agent. The previous code used variables to store these and then passed those variables as parameters.

> **Changes in Odoo 14**
>
> Odoo 14 supports API keys, and this may be required for Odoo API external access. API keys can be set on the user's **Preferences** form, in the **Account Security** tab. The XML-RPC usage is the same, except that the API key should be used as the password. More details are provided in the official documentation at https://www.odoo.com/documentation/15.0/developer/misc/api/odoo.html#api-keys.

The user agent environment should be used to provide some metadata about the client. It's mandatory, and should at least be an empty dictionary, { }.

If the authentication fails, a False value will be returned.

The common public endpoint is quite limited, so to gain access to the ORM API or another endpoint, the required authentication needs to be used.

Using XML-RPC to run server methods

To access the Odoo models and their methods, the `xmlrpc/2/object` endpoint needs to be used. The requests to this endpoint require login details.

This endpoint exposes a generic `execute_kw` method and receives the model's name, the method to call, and a list containing the parameters to pass to that method.

Here is an example of how `execute_kw` works. It calls the `search_count` method, which returns the number of records that match a domain filter:

```
>>> api = xmlrpc.client.ServerProxy('%s/xmlrpc/2/object' % srv)
>>> api.execute_kw(db, uid, password, "res.users", "search_count", [[]])
3
```

This code uses the `xmlrpc/2/endpoint` object to access the server API. The `execute_kw()` method is called using the following arguments:

- The name of the database to connect to
- The connection user ID
- The user password (or API key)
- The target model identifier
- The method to call
- A list of positional arguments
- An optional dictionary with keyword arguments (not used in this example)

All the model methods can be called, except for the ones prefixed with an underscore (_), which are considered private. Some methods might not work with the XML-RPC protocol if they return values that can't be sent through the XML-RPC protocol. This is the case for `browse()`, which returns a recordset object. Trying to use `browse()` through XML-RPC returns a `TypeError: cannot marshal objects` error. Instead of `browse()`, XML-RPC calls should use `read` or `search_read`, which return data in a format the XML-RPC protocol can send to the client.

Now, let's see how `search` and `read` can be used to query Odoo data.

Using the search and read API methods

The Odoo server-side code uses `browse` to query records. This can't be used by RPC clients because the recordset objects can't be transported through the RPC protocol. Instead, the `read` method should be used.

`read([<ids>, [<fields>])` is similar to the `browse` method, but instead of a recordset, it returns a list of records. Each record is a dictionary that contains the fields that have been requested and their data.

Let's see how `read()` can be used to retrieve data from Odoo:

```
>>> api = xmlrpc.client.ServerProxy("%s/xmlrpc/2/object" % srv)
>>> api.execute_kw(db, uid, password, "res.users", "read", [2,
["login", "name", "company_id"]])
[{'id': 2, 'login': 'admin', 'name': 'Mitchell Admin',
'company_id': [1, 'YourCompany']}]
```

The preceding example calls the `read` method of the `res.users` model with two positional arguments – the record ID 2 (a list of IDs could have been used instead) and the list of fields to retrieve, `["login", "name", "company_id"]`, and no keyword arguments.

The result is a list of dictionaries, where each dictionary is a record. The values of to-many fields follow a particular representation. They are a pair of values with the record ID and the record display name. For example, the `company_id` value that was returned previously was `[1, 'YourCompany']`.

The record IDs may not be known, and in that case, a search call is needed to find the record IDs that match a domain filter.

For example, if we wish to find the admin user, we can use `[("login", "=", "admin")]`. This RPC call is shown here:

```
>>> domain = [("login", "=", "admin")]
>>> api.execute_kw(db, uid, password, "res.users", "search",
[domain])
[2]
```

The result is a list with only one element, 2, which is the ID of the `admin` user.

A frequent action would be to use combinations of the `search` and `read` methods to find the ID for the records meeting a domain filter and then retrieve the data for them. For a client app, this means two round trips to the server. To simplify this, the `search_read` method is available, which can perform both operations in a single step.

Here is an example of search_read being used to find the admin user and return its name:

```
>>> api.execute_kw(db, uid, password, "res.users", "search_
read", [domain, ["login", "name"]])
[{'id': 2, 'login': 'admin', 'name': 'Mitchell Admin'}]
```

The search_read method is using two positional arguments: a list containing the domain filter, and a second list containing the fields to retrieve.

The arguments for search_read are as follows:

- domain: A list with a domain filter expression
- fields: A list with the names of the fields to retrieve
- offset: The number of records to skip or use for record pagination
- limit: The maximum number of records to return
- order: A string to be used by the database's ORDER BY clause

The fields argument is optional, both for read and search_read. If it's not provided, all the model fields will be retrieved. But this may cause expensive function field computation and a large amount of data being retrieved that is probably not needed. So, the recommendation is to provide an explicit list of fields.

The execute_kw call can use both positional and keyword arguments. Here is what the same call looks like when you're using keyword arguments instead of positional ones:

```
>>> api.execute_kw(db, uid, password, "res.users", "search_
read", [], {"domain": domain, "fields": ["login", "name"]})
```

search_read is the most used method to retrieve data, but there are more methods available to write data or trigger other business logic.

Calling other API methods

All the other model methods are exposed through RPC, except for the ones prefixed with an underscore, which are considered private. This means that create, write, and unlink can be called to modify data on the server.

Let's look at an example. The following code creates a new partner record, modifies it, reads it to confirm the modification was written, and finally deletes it:

```
>>> x = api.execute_kw(db, uid, password, "res.partner", "create",
[{'name': 'Packt Pub'}])
>>> print(x)
49
>>> api.execute_kw(db, uid, password, "res.partner", "write",
[[x], {'name': 'Packt Publishing'}])
True
>>> api.execute_kw(db, uid, password, "res.partner", "read",
[[x], ["name"]])
[{'id': 49, 'name': 'Packt Publishing'}]
>>> api.execute_kw(db, uid, password, "res.partner", "unlink",
[[x]])
True
>>> api.execute_kw(db, uid, password, "res.partner", "read",
[[x]])
[]
```

One limitation of the XML-RPC protocol is that it doesn't support None values. There's an XML-RPC extension that supports None values, but whether this is available will depend on the particular XML-RPC library being used by the client app. Methods that don't return anything may not be usable through XML-RPC, since they are implicitly returning None. This is why it is good practice for methods to always return something, at a True value. Another alternative is to use JSON-RPC instead. The OdooRPC library supports this protocol, and it will be used later in this chapter, in the *Using the OdooRPC library* section.

The Model methods that are prefixed with an underscore are considered private and aren't exposed through XML-RPC.

> **Tip**
> Often, client apps want to replicate manual user entry on an Odoo form. Calling the create() method might not be enough for this, because forms can automate some fields using onchange methods, which are triggered by the form's interaction, but not by create(). The solution is to create a custom method on the Odoo server, that uses create() and then runs the needed onchange methods.

It is worth repeating that the Odoo external API can be used by most programming languages. The official documentation provides examples for Ruby, PHP, and Java. This is available at https://www.odoo.com/documentation/15.0/webservices/odoo.html.

So far, we've seen how to call Odoo methods using the XML-RPC protocol. Now, we can use this to build the book catalog client application.

Implementing the client app XML-RPC interface

Let's start by implementing the Library book catalog client application.

This can be split into two files: one for the Odoo backend interface containing the server backend, library_xmlrpc.py, and another for the user interface, library.py. This will allow us to use alternative implementations for the backend interface.

Starting with the Odoo backend component, a LibraryAPI class will be used to set up the connection with the Odoo server that supports methods that are needed to interact with Odoo. The methods to implement are as follows:

- search_read(<title>) to search for book data by title
- create(<title>) to create a book with a specific title
- write(<id>, <title>) to update a book title using the book ID
- unlink(<id>) to delete a book using its ID

Choose a directory to host the application files in and create the library_xmlrpc.py file. Start by adding the class constructor, as follows:

```python
import xmlrpc.client


class LibraryAPI():

    def __init__(self, host, port, db, user, pwd):
        common = xmlrpc.client.ServerProxy(
            "http://%s:%d/xmlrpc/2/common" % (host, port))
        self.api = xmlrpc.client.ServerProxy(
            "http://%s:%d/xmlrpc/2/object" % (host, port))
        self.uid = common.authenticate(db, user, pwd, {})
```

```
        self.pwd = pwd
        self.db = db
        self.model = "library.book"
```

This class stores all of the information needed to execute calls on the target model: the API XML-RPC reference, `uid`, the password, the database name, and the model name.

The RPC calls to Odoo will all use the same `execute_kw` RPC method. A thin wrapper around it is added next, in the `_execute()` private method. This takes advantage of the object stored data to provide a smaller function signature, as shown in the following code block:

```
    def _execute(self, method, arg_list, kwarg_dict=None):
        return self.api.execute_kw(
            self.db, self.uid, self.pwd, self.model,
            method, arg_list, kwarg_dict or {})
```

This `_execute()` private method can now be used for less verbose implementations of the higher-level methods.

The first public method is the `search_read()` method. It will accept an optional string that's used to search book titles. If no title is given, all the records will be returned. This is the corresponding implementation:

```
    def search_read(self, title=None):
        domain = [("name", "ilike", title)] if title else
                 []
        fields = ["id", "name"]
        return self._execute("search_read", [domain,
            fields])
```

The `create()` method will create a new book with the given title and return the ID of the created record:

```
    def create(self, title):
        vals = {"name": title}
        return self._execute("create", [vals])
```

The `write()` method will have the new title and book ID as arguments and will perform a write operation on that book:

```python
def write(self, id, title):
    vals = {"name": title}
    return self._execute("write", [[id], vals])
```

Finally, the `unlink()` method is used to delete a book, given the corresponding ID:

```python
def unlink(self, id):
    return self._execute("unlink", [[id]])
```

We end the file with a small piece of test code that will be executed if we run the Python file, which can help test the methods that have been implemented, as shown here:

```python
if __name__ == "__main__":
    # Sample test configurations
    host, port, db = "localhost", 8069, "library"
    user, pwd = "admin", "admin"
    api = LibraryAPI(host, port, db, user, pwd)
    from pprint import pprint
    pprint(api.search_read())
```

If we run this Python script, we should see the content of our library books printed out:

```
$ python3 library_xmlrpc.py
[{'id': 1, 'name': 'Odoo Development Essentials 11'},
 {'id': 2, 'name': 'Odoo 11 Development Cookbook'},
 {'id': 3, 'name': 'Brave New World'}]
```

Now that we have a simple wrapper around our Odoo backend, let's deal with the command-line user interface.

Implementing the client app user interface

Our goal here was to learn how to write the interface between an external application and the Odoo server, and we did this in the previous section. But let's go the extra mile and build the user interface for this minimalistic client application.

To keep this as simple as possible, we will use a simple command-line user interface and additional dependencies will be avoided. This leaves us with Python's built-in features to implement command-line applications and the `ArgumentParser` library.

Now, alongside the `library_xmlrpc.py` file, create a new `library.py` file. This will import Python's command-line argument parser and then the `LibraryAPI` class, as shown in the following code:

```python
from argparse import ArgumentParser
from library_xmlrpc import LibraryAPI
```

Next, we must describe the commands that the argument parser will expect. There are four commands:

- `list` to search for and list books
- `add` to add a book
- `set` to update a book title
- `del` to delete a book

The command-line parser code for implementing the preceding commands is shown here:

```python
parser = ArgumentParser()
parser.add_argument(
    "command",
    choices=["list", "add", "set", "del"])
parser.add_argument("params", nargs="*")  # optional args
args = parser.parse_args()
```

The `args` object represents the command-line options given by the user. `args.command` is the command being used, while `args.params` holds the additional parameters to use for the command, if they've been given any.

If no or incorrect commands are given, the argument parser will handle that and will show the user what input is expected. A complete reference to `argparse` can be found in the official documentation at `https://docs.python.org/3/library/argparse.html`.

The next step is to perform the action that corresponds to the user command. We will start by creating a LibraryAPI instance. This requires Odoo connection details that, in this simple implementation, will be hardcoded, as shown here:

```
host, port, db = "localhost", 8069, "library"
user, pwd = "admin", "admin"
api = LibraryAPI(host, port, db, user, pwd)
```

The first line sets some fixed parameters for the server instance and database to connect to. In this case, the connection is to a local Odoo server, listening on the 8069 default port, to a library database. To connect to a different server and database, these parameters should be adapted accordingly.

New specific code to handle each command must be added. We will start with the list command, which returns a list of books:

```
if args.command == "list":
    title = args.params[:1]
    books = api.search_read(title)
    for book in books:
        print("%(id)d %(name)s" % book)
```

The LibraryAPI.search_read() method is being used in the preceding code to retrieve the list of book records. The returned list is then iterated to print out each element.

Next is the add command:

```
if args.command == "add":
    title = args.params[0]
    book_id = api.create(title)
    print("Book added with ID %d for title %s." % (
        book_id, title))
```

Since the hard work was already done in the LibraryAPI object, the implementation just needs to call the create() method and show the result to the end user.

The set command allows us to change the title of an existing book. It should have two parameters – the ID of the book and the new title:

```python
if args.command == "set":
    if len(args.params) != 2:
        print("set command requires a Title and ID.")
    else:
        book_id, title = int(args.params[0]),
            args.params[1]
        api.write(book_id, title)
        print("Title of Book ID %d set to %s." % (book_id,
            title))
```

Finally, there is the implementation for the del command, to delete a book record. This is not very different from the previous commands:

```python
if args.command == "del":
    book_id = int(args.params[0])
    api.unlink(book_id)
    print("Book with ID %s was deleted." % book_id)
```

The client application is done, and you can try it out using the commands of your choice. In particular, we should be able to run the example commands shown at the beginning of this chapter.

> **Tip**
>
> On a Linux system, library.py can be made executable by running the chmod +x library.py command and adding #!/usr/bin/env python3 to the first line of the file. After this, running ./library.py in the command line should work.

This is quite a basic application, and it is easy to think of a few ways to improve it. The point here was to build a minimum viable application using the Odoo RPC API.

Using the OdooRPC library

Another relevant client library to be considered is OdooRPC. It is a complete client library that uses the JSON-RPC protocol instead of XML-RPC. The Odoo official web client uses JSON-RPC as well, although XML-RPC is still also supported.

The OdooRPC library is now maintained under the Odoo Community Association umbrella. The source code repository can be found at https://github.com/OCA/odoorpc.

The OdooRPC library can be installed from PyPI using the following command:

```
$ pip3 install odoorpc
```

The OdooRPC library sets up a server connection when a new odoorpc.ODOO object is created. At this point, we should use the ODOO.login() method to create a user session. Just like on the server side, the session has an env attribute containing the session's environment, including the user ID, uid, and context.

The OdooRPC library can be used to provide an alternate implementation for the library_xmlrpc.py interface with the server. It should provide the same features but be implemented using JSON-RPC instead of XML-RPC.

To achieve this, a library_odoorpc.py Python module will be created that provides a drop-in replacement for the library_xmlrpc.py module. To do this, create a new library_odoorpc.py file alongside it that contains the following code:

```python
import odoorpc


class LibraryAPI():

    def __init__(self, host, port, db, user, pwd):
        self.api = odoorpc.ODOO(host, port=port)
        self.api.login(db, user, pwd)
        self.uid = self.api.env.uid
        self.model = "library.book"
        self.Model = self.api.env[self.model]

    def _execute(self, method, arg_list, kwarg_dict=None):
        return self.api.execute(
            self.model,
            method, *arg_list, **kwarg_dict)
```

The OdooRPC library implements the Model and Recordset objects, which mimic the behavior of their server-side counterparts. The goal is for the code that's using this library to be similar to the code that's used on the Odoo server side. The methods that are used by the client make use of this and store a reference to the library.book model object in the self.Model attribute, which is provided by the OdooRPC env["library.book"] call.

The _execute() method is implemented here as well; it allows us to compare it to the plain XML-RPC version. The OdooRPC library has the execute() method to run arbitrary Odoo model methods.

Next is the implementation for the search_read(), create(), write(), and unlink() client methods. In the same file, add these methods inside the LibraryAPI() class:

```python
    def search_read(self, title=None):
        domain = [("name", "ilike", title)] if title else
                 []
        fields = ["id", "name"]
        return self.Model.search_read(domain, fields)


    def create(self, title):
        vals = {"name": title}
        return self.Model.create(vals)


    def write(self, id, title):
        vals = {"name": title}
        self.Model.write(id, vals)


    def unlink(self, id):
        return self.Model.unlink(id)
```

Notice how this client code is similar to the Odoo server-side code.

This LibraryAPI object can be used as a drop-in replacement for library_xmlrpc.py. It can be used as the RPC connection layer by editing the library.py file and changing the from library_xmlrpc import LibraryAPI line to from library_odoorpc import LibraryAPI. Now, test drive the library.py client application; it should perform just like before!

Summary

The goal of this chapter was to learn how the external API works and what it is capable of. We started by exploring it with simple scripts using the Python XML-RPC client, though the external API can be used from any programming language. The official documentation provides code examples for Java, PHP, and Ruby.

Then, we learned how to use XML-RPC calls to search for and read data, and then how to call any other method. We can, for example, create, update, and delete records.

Next, we introduced the OdooRPC library. It provides a layer on top of the RPC base library (XML-RPC or JSON-RPC) to provide a local API that's similar to the API that can be found on the server side. This lowers the learning curve, reduces programming mistakes, and makes it easier to copy code between server and client code.

With this, we have finished the chapters dedicated to the programming API and business logic. Now, it's time to look at views and the user interface. In the next chapter, we will look at backend views in more detail and the user experience that can be provided out of the box by the web client.

Further reading

The following additional reference material may complement the topics described in this chapter:

- The official documentation on Odoo web services, including code examples for programming languages other than Python: https://www.odoo.com/documentation/15.0/developer/misc/api/odoo.html
- The OdooRPC documentation: https://pythonhosted.org/OdooRPC

Section 4: Views

Next is the view layer. We will discuss in detail the **graphical user interface** (**GUI**) using the models and business logic. The Odoo web client provides a rich set of components to design the GUI, but a web development framework is also available for flexible website development. QWeb templates play a big role in advanced web client views, reports, and website pages, and are introduced here.

In this section, the following chapters are included:

- *Chapter 10, Backend Views – Designing the User Interface*
- *Chapter 11, Kanban Views and Client-Side QWeb*
- *Chapter 12, Creating Printable PDF Reports with Server-Side QWeb*
- *Chapter 13, Creating Web and Portal Frontend Features*

10
Backend Views – Designing the User Interface

This chapter describes how to create views to implement the user interface for business applications. The Odoo user interface starts with the menu items and various actions being executed on menu clicks, so these are the first components we will learn about.

The most used view type is the *form view*, and there are a few elements we must learn about, from organizing the disposition of the elements in the view to understanding all the options that are available for fields and buttons.

Some other frequently used views include list views and search views. Finally, other view types are available that are useful for specific purposes, such as the pivot and graph views. An overview of these will be provided toward the end of this chapter.

The following topics will be covered in this chapter:

- Adding menu items
- Understanding window actions
- Exploring the form view's structure
- Using fields
- Using buttons
- Adding dynamic view elements
- Exploring list views
- Exploring search views
- Understanding the other available view types

By the end of this chapter, you should be familiar with all the Odoo view types and have the resources to use them. In particular, you will be confident with designing non-trivial form views and providing an adequate user experience.

Technical requirements

We'll continue working with the `library_checkout` add-on module. The model layer for it is already complete; now, it needs the view layer for the user interface.

The code in this chapter is based on the code that we created in *Chapter 8, Business Logic – Supporting Business Processes*. The necessary code can be found in this book's GitHub repository at `https://github.com/PacktPublishing/Odoo-15-Development-Essentials`, in the `ch10` directory.

Adding menu items

Menu items are the starting point for user interface navigation. They form a hierarchical structure, where the top-level items represent applications, and the level below is the application main menu. Further sub-menu levels can be added.

Menu items with no sub-menus are *actionable* and can trigger an action that tells the web client what to do, such as opening a view.

Menu items are stored in the `ir.ui.menu` model and can be browsed via the **Settings | Technical | User Interface | Menu Items** menu.

The `library_app` add-on module created a top-level menu for the library books, while the `library_checkout` add-on module added the menu items for the checkouts and checkout stages. These are both implemented in `library_checkout/views/library_menu.xml`.

This is the XML for the checkout menu item:

```
<menuitem id="menu_library_checkout"
          name="Checkout"
          action="action_library_checkout"
          parent="library_app.library_menu"
/>
```

The preceding code uses a `<menuitem>` shortcut element, which is an abbreviated way to create a menu record that's more convenient than a `<record model="ir.ui.menu">` element.

The most used `<menuitem>` attributes are as follows:

- `name` is the menu item's title and is present in the user interface.

- `action` is the XML ID of the action to run when clicking on the menu item.

- `parent` is the XML ID of the parent menu item. In this case, the parent was created in another module, so it needs to be referenced using the complete XML ID; that is, `<module>.<XML ID>`.

Some other attributes are also available:

- `sequence` sets a number to order the presentation of the menu items; for example, `sequence="10"`.

- `groups` is a comma-separated list of XML IDs of the security groups that have access to the menu item; for example, `groups="library_app.library_group_user,library_app.library_group_manager"`.

- `web_icon` is the path to the icon to use. It's only relevant for top-level menu items in the enterprise edition. The path value should follow the `web_icon="library_app,static/description/icon.png"` format.

Menu items can run an action, as identified by the `action` attribute, and in most cases, this will be a **window action**. The next section will explain how to create actions and what they are capable of.

Understanding window actions

A **window action** on a menu gives the web client instructions on what to do, such as opening a view, and can be used in menu items or buttons in views.

Window actions identify the model to use and the views to present in the user interface. They can also filter the available records using a `domain` filter and can set default values and filters using the `context` attribute.

Window actions are stored in the `ir.actions.act_window` model and can be browsed by going to the **Settings | Technical | Actions | Window Actions** menu.

The `library_checkout/views/library_menu.xml` file contains the definition for the window action that's used by the checkout menu item:

```xml
<record id="action_library_checkout"
        model="ir.actions.act_window">
    <field name="name">Checkouts</field>
    <field name="res_model">library.checkout</field>
    <field name="view_mode">tree,form</field>
</record>
```

A window action is an `ir.actions.act_window` record. The most important fields are as follows:

- `name` is the title that will be displayed on the view that's opened through the action.

- `res_model` is the identifier of the target model.

- `view_mode` is a comma-separated list of the view types to make available. The first in the list is the one to open by default.

The other relevant window actions fields are as follows:

- `target` defaults to `current` and opens the view inline in the main content area. If it's set to `new`, it will open the view in a pop-up dialog window; for example, `target="new"`.

- `context` sets context information on the target views, which can set default values or activate filters, among other things; for example, `<field name="context">{'default_user_id': uid}</field>`.

- `domain` is a domain expression that forces a filter for the records that can be browsed in the opened views; for example, `domain="[('user_id', '=', uid)]"`.

- `limit` is the number of records for each page in the list view; for example, `limit="80"`.

- `view_id` is a reference to a particular view to be used. It can't be used together with `view_mode`. It is often used together with `target="new"`, to open a particular form as a popup.

Changes in Odoo 13

Until Odoo 12, the `<act_window>` shortcut element could be used to create window actions. This was removed in Odoo 13. Now, window actions must be created using a `<record model="ir.actions.act_window">` element.

In this chapter, we will add view types for the `library.checkout` model. By doing so, we will showcase the other available view types, other than form and tree/list views.

The view types to be made available must be indicated by the window action. So, let's edit the `library_checkout/views/library_menu.xml` file to add the new view types, as highlighted in the following code:

```
<record id="action_library_checkout"
        model="ir.actions.act_window">
    <field name="name">Checkouts</field>
    <field name="res_model">library.checkout</field>
    <field name="view_mode"
        >tree,form,activity, calendar,graph,pivot</field>
</record>
```

These changes can't be made yet. The definitions of the corresponding view types should be implemented before they are added to the window action's `view_mode`.

Other than the menu items or view buttons, actions can also be used in the **Action** context menu, which is available near the search box. The next section explains this in detail.

Adding options to the Action context menu

Window actions can also be used from the **Action** menu button, available at the top of form views, and also in list views when records are selected:

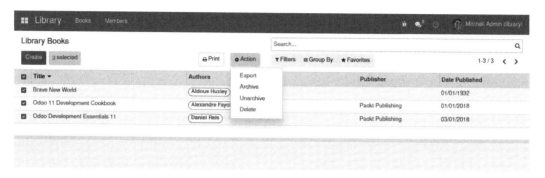

Figure 10.1 – The Action context menu

This menu is contextual because the action will apply to the record or records currently selected.

To have an action available in the **Action** menu, two more fields have to be set on the window action:

- `binding_model_id` is a reference to the model to use the action for; for example, `<field name="binding_model_id" ref="model_library_checkout" />`.

- `binding_view_types` can be used to limit the option's visibility to specific view types, such as `form` or `list`; for example, `<field name="binding_view_types">form,list</field>`.

An example of this has already been implemented in the `library_checkout` module, in the `wizard/checkout_mass_message_wizard_view.xml` file. This has been copied here for reference:

```xml
<record id="action_checkout_message"
        model="ir.actions.act_window">
    <field name="name">Send Messages</field>
    <field name="res_model">
    library.checkout.massmessage</field>
    <field name="view_mode">form</field>
    <field name="binding_model_id"
        ref="model_library_checkout" />
```

```
<field name="binding_view_types">form,list</field>
    <field name="target">new</field>
</record>
```

The settings that are related to binding to the **Action** menu are highlighted in the previous code.

The following screenshot illustrates the corresponding action menu item:

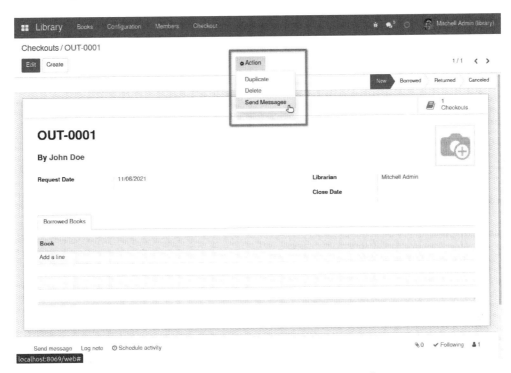

Figure 10.2 – The Send Message action menu options

> **Changes in Odoo 13**
> The action binding fields were changed in Odoo 13. Until Odoo 12,
> src_model set the binding and used the model identifier, library.
> checkout, for example. It is available in the form view, and it can also be
> made available in the list view by setting multi to true.

Once a window action has been triggered, the corresponding views are opened. The most used view types are form and list. The next section details how to create form views.

Exploring the form view structure

Form views are the main way users can interact with data records. Form views can either follow a simple layout or a business document layout, similar to a paper document. In this section, we'll learn how to design these business document views and how to use the elements and widgets that are available.

In *Chapter 8, Business Logic – Supporting Business Processes*, we created a library checkout model and prepared a basic form for it. We will revisit and enhance it in this section.

The following screenshot shows what the form view will look like when we're done:

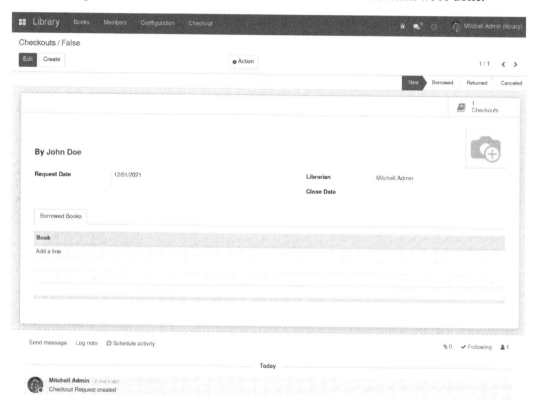

Figure 10.3 – The enhanced Checkouts form view

You can refer to this screenshot while we gradually add the different elements throughout this chapter.

Using business document views

Historically, organizations use paper forms to support their internal processes. Business application models support digital versions of these paper forms, and in the process, they can add automation and make operations more efficient.

For a more intuitive user interface, form views can mimic these paper documents, helping users to visualize processes they are used to running on paper forms.

For example, for the **Library** app, book checkouts are probably a process where a paper form has to be filled in. It is probably a good idea to let the checkout form have a layout that looks like a paper document.

A business document is a form that contains two elements: a <head> section and a <sheet> section. head contains buttons and widgets to control the document's business workflow, while sheet contains the actual document content. After the sheet section, we can also have the message and activity widgets.

To add this structure to the checkout form, start by editing the library_checkout/views/checkout_view.xml file and changing the form view record to the following basic skeleton:

```xml
<record id="view_form_checkout" model="ir.ui.view">
    <field name="model">library.checkout</field>
    <field name="arch" type="xml">

    <form>

        <header>
            <!-- To add buttons and status widget -->
        </header>

        <sheet>
            <!-- To add form content -->
        </sheet>

        <!-- Discuss widgets -->
        <div class="oe_chatter">
            <field name="message_follower_ids"
                    widget="mail_followers" />
            <field name="activity_ids"
```

```
                  widget="mail_activity" />
          <field name="message_ids"
                  widget="mail_thread" />
      </div>
    </form>

  </field>
</record>
```

The view name is optional and automatically generated if it's missing. So, for simplicity, the `<field name="name">` element was omitted from the preceding view record.

The `<head>` and `<sheet>` sections are empty for now, and will be expanded next.

The messaging section at the bottom uses the widgets provided by the `mail` add-on module, as explained in *Chapter 8, Business Logic – Supporting Business Processes*.

The first section to check is the form header.

Adding a header section

The header at the top usually features the steps that the document will move through in its life cycle and the related action buttons. These action buttons are regular form buttons, and the button for moving on will usually be highlighted, to help the user.

Adding header buttons

Let's start by adding a button to the currently empty header section.

While editing the `<header>` section in the form view, add a button to move a checkout to the `done` state:

```
<header>
  <field name="state" invisible="True" />
  <button name="button_done"
    type="object"
    string="Return Books"
    attrs="{'invisible':
      [('state', 'in', ['new', 'done', 'cancel'])]}"
    class="oe_highlight"
  />
</header>
```

By using the preceding code, the `Return Books` button is added to the header with `type="object"`, meaning that a model method is called. `name="button_done"` declares the method name to call.

`class="oe_highlight"` is used to highlight the button. When we have several buttons to choose from, the main or more usual course of action can be highlighted to help users.

The `attrs` attribute is used to have the button visible only in the states where it makes sense. It should be visible in the `open` state, so it should be set to invisible for the `new`, `done`, and `cancel` states.

The condition to do this uses the `state` field, which otherwise is not used on the form. For the `attrs` condition to work, the `state` field needs to be loaded into the web client. To ensure this, it was added as an invisible field.

In this particular case, the special `state` field name is being used, and the visibility condition to be implemented with `attrs` can be achieved with the simpler `states` attribute. The `states` attribute lists the states where the element will be visible.

By using `states` instead of `attrs`, the button will only be visible in the `open` state and will look like this:

```
<button name="button_done"
    type="object"
    string="Return Books"
    states="open"
    class="oe_highlight"
/>
```

The `attrs` and `states` element visibility features can also be used on other view elements, such as fields. We'll explore them in more detail later in this chapter.

For this button to work, the method that's being called must be implemented. For this, in the `library_checkout/models/library_checkout.py` file, add the following code to the `checkout` class:

```
def button_done(self):
    Stage = self.env["library.checkout.stage"]
    done_stage = Stage.search([("state", "=", "done")],
        limit=1)
    for checkout in self:
        checkout.stage_id = done_stage
    return True
```

First, the code looks up **Stages** to find the first record that matches the `done` state. It will be used to set the records to that stage.

The `self` recordset will usually be a single record, but the API allows it to be called for a multi-record recordset, so this possibility should be addressed. This can be done with a `for` loop on `self`. Then, for each record in the `self` recordset, the `stage_id` field must be set to the `done` stage.

Alongside the buttons, the header can feature a status bar widget to present the available *stages* or *states*.

Adding a status bar pipeline

Another helpful element in the header is a pipeline diagram presenting the process steps and where the current document is at. This can be based either on a *stages* or a *states* list. This pipeline widget can be clickable or not, in case we want the changes to only be made through buttons.

The status bar widget is added with a `<field>` element using the `statusbar` widget. The checkout model has the `stage_id` field that we will use:

```
<header>
  <field name="state" invisible="True" />
  <button name="do_clear_done" type="object"
    string="Clear Done"
    states="open,cancel"
    class="oe_highlight" />
  <field name="stage_id"
    widget="statusbar"
    options="{'clickable': True, 'fold_field': 'fold'}" />
</header>
```

The `statusbar` widget can be used either with a **state** selection field or a **stage** many-to-one field. These two kinds of fields can be found across several Odoo core modules.

The `clickable` option allows the user to change the document stage by clicking on the status bar. Having it enabled provides flexibility to the user. But there are also cases where we need more control over the workflow, and require the users to progress through the stages using only the available action buttons.

> **Changes in Odoo 12**
>
> Until Odoo 11, the clickable option was a field attribute, `<field widget="statusbar" clickable="True" />`. In Odoo 12, it was converted into a widget option, `<field widget="statusbar" options="{'clickable': True}" />`.

The `fold_field` option is used to allow less important stages, such as *canceled*, to be hidden (folded) in a **More** stage group. The stages to fold must have a boolean field identifying them. `fold_field` is set with the field name that's used for this. In this case, it is named `fold`.

Using states instead of stages

The **stage** is a many-to-one field that uses a supporting model to set up the steps of the process. It is flexible, can be configured by end users to fit their specific business process, and is perfect for supporting Kanban boards. The library checkouts model is using it.

The **state** is a closed selection list featuring fixed process steps, such as **New, In Progress**, and **Done**. It can be used in business logic since the available states can't change. But it can't be configured by end users.

Each of the approaches has pros and cons. It is possible to benefit from the best of both options by using stages and having each stage mapped into a state. The checkout model implemented this, adding a state field in the checkout stages model, which is also directly available in the checkout model through a related field.

If a model is using states only, the status bar pipeline can also be used, with the `statusbar` widget. However, the `fold_field` option is not available; instead, the `statusbar_visible` attribute can be used, listing the states to make visible.

Using the status bar with a state `field` looks like this:

```
<field name="state"
  widget="statusbar"
  options="{'clickable': True}"
  statusbar_visible="draft,open,done"
/>
```

Notice that the previous code is not used in the `library_checkout` module. Since it supports the more flexible stages, we prefer to use them on the user interface.

Now that we're are done with the header section, let's look at the main form section.

Designing the document sheet

The sheet canvas is the main area of the form and is where the actual data elements are placed. It is designed to look like an actual paper document.

Usually, a document sheet structure will contain the following areas:

- A document title at the top
- A button box at the top-right corner
- Document header data fields
- A notebook at the bottom, for additional fields that can be organized into tabs or pages

The document will often contain detailed lines of code. These are usually presented on the notebook's first page.

Here is the expected XML structure:

```xml
<sheet>
    <!-- Button box -->
    <div class="oe_button_box" name="button_box" />
    <!-- Header title -->
    <div class="oe_title" />
    <!-- Header fields -->
    <group />
    <!-- Notebook -->
    <notebook />
</sheet>
```

After the sheet, we usually have the Chatter widget, which contains the document followers, discussion messages, and planned activities.

Let's go through each of these areas. The button box will be discussed later, so next, we will discuss the header title.

Adding a header title

The header title will usually display the document's title in large letters. It may be followed by a subtitle and may also have an image next to it.

First, a couple of fields need to be added to the checkout model. A field needs to be used as the title, and an image needs to be used to represent the borrower. Edit the `library_checkout/models/library_checkout.py` file and add the following code:

```python
name = fields.Char(string="Title")
member_image = fields.Binary(related=
    "member_id.image_128")
```

The header title goes inside a `<div class="oe_title">` element. Regular HTML elements, such as `div`, `span`, `h1`, and `h3`, can be used.

In the following code, the `<sheet>` element has been expanded to include the title, plus some additional fields as subtitles:

```xml
<sheet>
  <div name="button_box" class="oe_button_box" />
  <field name="member_image" widget="image"
    class="oe_avatar" />
  <div class="oe_title">
    <label for="name" class="oe_edit_only"/>
    <h1><field name="name"/></h1>
    <h3>
      <span class="oe_read_only">By </span>
      <label for="member_id" class="oe_edit_only"/>
      <field name="member_id" class="oe_inline" />
    </h3>
  </div>
  <!-- More elements will be added from here... -->
</sheet>
```

The preceding XML render includes the following:

- A button box `<div>` element. It is empty now but can be used to add smart buttons.
- An image field, for `member_image`, using an avatar-like image widget.
- A `<div>` element containing the document title elements. Inside the title, there is the following:
  - A `<label>` for the `name` field, which is only visible in edit mode.
  - The `name` field, which is rendered as an HTML `<h1>` heading.
  - A `<h3>` subtitle heading containing the `member_id` field. This is only visible in read mode. The `<field>` tag uses `oe_inline` to let the HTML elements manage the text flow.

Fields outside a `<group>` element don't have labels rendered for them. The preceding XML has no `<group>` element, so labels need to be explicitly added.

After the title element, there will usually be header fields, organized into groups.

Organizing the form content using groups

The main content of the form should be organized using `<group>` tags.

The `<group>` tag inserts two columns in the canvas. Fields that are added inside a group use these two columns – the first for the field label and the second for the field value widget. Adding more fields to the group will stack them vertically as new fields are added in a new row.

A common pattern is to have two columns of fields, side by side. You can do this by adding two `<group>` tags nested into a top group.

Continuing with our form view, we'll use this to add the main content, after the title's `<div>` section:

```
<!-- More elements will be added from here... -->
<group name="group_top">
  <group name="group_col1">
    <field name="request_date" />
  </group>
  <group name="group_col2">
    <field name="close_date" />
```

```
        <field name="user_id" />
    </group>
</group>
```

The top `<group>` element creates two columns in the canvas. Each of the two nested `<group>` elements uses one of these columns. The first nested group uses the left column, while the second group takes the right column.

The `<group>` elements were assigned a `name`. This is not required but is recommended so that the module is easier to extend.

The `<group>` element can also have a `string` attribute, which is used to display title text for it.

> **Changes in Odoo 11**
>
> The `string` attribute cannot be used as an anchor for inheritance anymore. This is because the corresponding text can be translated, and this can break inherited/extension views. The `name` attribute should be used instead.

The following elements can be used to adjust the view layout:

- The `<newline>` element can be used to force a new line so that the next element is rendered in the next row's first column.
- The `<separator>` element can be added to add section titles. A title text can be set using the `string` attribute.

The `col` and `colspan` attributes provide additional control over the grid layout:

- The `col` attribute is used on `<group>` elements to customize the number of columns it contains. By default, a `<group>` element contains two columns, but that can be changed to any other number. Even numbers work better since, by default, each field that's added takes up two columns – one for the label and one for the value.
- The `colspan` attribute can be used on group-contained elements to set a specific number of columns they should take. By default, a field takes two columns.

The following code shows an alternative version of the top group element and uses `col="4"` to present the four fields in two columns:

```
<group name="group_top" col="4">
  <field name="request_date" />
  <field name="user_id" />
  <span colspan="2" />
  <field name="close_date" />
</group>
```

Notice that the order of the fields is different because the fields are placed from left to right, and then from top to bottom. The `<span colspan="2">` element was used to occupy the two first columns of the second row so that the `close_date` field takes the last two columns.

Some forms also feature a notebook section to organize the additional fields on different pages.

Adding tabbed notebooks

The notebook element is another way to organize the form's content. It is a container with multiple tabbed pages. These can be used to keep less-used data out of sight until it's needed or to organize a large number of fields by topic.

The checkout form will have a notebook element, and the first page will contain the list of borrowed books. For this, after the `<group name="group_top">` element, which we added in the previous section, include the following XML:

```
<notebook>
  <page name="page_lines" string="Borrowed Books">
    <field name="line_ids" />
  </page>
</notebook>
```

This notebook contains only one page. To add more, just include more `<page>` elements inside the `<notebook>` element. The page canvas does not render field labels by default. For that to happen, the fields should be placed inside a `<group>` section, just like for the form main canvas.

In this case, the one-to-many `line_ids` field was added inside the page, with no `<group>` element, so no label will be rendered for it.

The `page` element supports the following attributes:

- `string`, for the page title. This is required.
- `attrs` is a dictionary for mapping the `invisible` and `required` attribute values to the result of a domain expression.
- `accesskey`, an HTML access key.

This section discussed the typical layout for a form view, as well as the most important elements to use for this. The most important elements are the data fields. The next section discusses them in detail.

Using fields

Inside a form or list view, fields widgets are the way to present and edit data from model fields.

View fields have a few attributes available to them. Most of these attribute values have defaults that are taken from the model definition, but these can be overridden in the view.

Here is a quick reference for the common field attributes:

- `name` is the field name in the model and identifies the field that's being rendered by this element.
- `string` is the label text to be used. It overrides the model definition.
- `help` provides some tooltip help text that's shown when the mouse is hovered over the field.
- `placeholder` provides suggestion text to be displayed inside the field.
- `widget` sets a specific widget to be used to render the field. The available widgets will be discussed later in this section.
- `options` is a JSON data structure that's used to pass additional options to the widget. The values to use depend on the widget being used.
- `Class` is a comma-separated list of CSS classes to use for the field HTML rendering process.
- `nolabel="True"` prevents the automatic field label from being presented. It only makes sense for fields inside a `<group>` element and is often used along with a `<label for="...">` element.

- `invisible="True"` makes the field not visible, but its data is fetched from the server and is available on the form. Note that forms can't write on invisible fields.

- `readonly="True"` makes the field read-only on the form.

- `required="True"` makes the field mandatory on the form.

The following special attributes are only supported by specific field types:

- `password="True"` is used for text fields. It is displayed as a password field, masking the characters that are typed in.

- `filename` is used for binary fields and is the name of the model field to be used for the name of the uploaded file.

Two more topics are worth further discussion. One is how to have additional control of the field label's presentation, while the other is about using different web client widgets for a better user experience.

Modifying field labels

Fields won't automatically render labels unless they're inside a `<group>` element. In that case, labels will be explicitly suppressed using `nolabel="True"`.

Labels can be explicitly added using a `<label for="..."/>` element. This gives you more control over where to display field labels. The following code was used in the form title:

```
<label for="name" class="oe_edit_only" />
```

The `for` attribute identifies the field we should get the label text from. The optional `string` attribute can set specific text for the label. CSS classes can also be used. The previous code used the following:

- `class="oe_edit_only"` makes the element visible in edit mode only.

- `class="oe_read_only"` makes the element visible in read mode only.

This can be used to control how field labels are presented. How the field data is presented can also be adjusted using different widgets.

Choosing field widgets

Field content is presented using a web client widget. This can influence the way data is presented to the user, as well as the interaction when setting a value on the field.

Each field type is displayed using the appropriate default widget. However, additional alternative widgets may be available.

Text field widgets

For text fields, the following widgets can be used:

- `email` renders as an actionable `mailto` HTML link.

- `phone` renders as an actionable phone HTML link.

- `url` is used to format the text as a clickable URL.

- `html` is used to render the text as HTML content. In edit mode, it features a WYSIWYG editor to allow you to format the content without the need to use HTML syntax.

Numeric field widgets

For numeric fields, the following widgets are available:

- `handle` is specifically designed for sequence fields in list views and displays a handle to drag lines and reorganize their order.

- `float_time` formats a `float` field as hours and minutes.

- `monetary` displays a `float` field as a currency amount. It expects the currency that's used to be in a `currency_id` companion field. If the `currency` field has a different name, it can be set with `options="{'currency_field': '<field name>'}"`.

- `progressbar` represents a `float` as a percentage progress bar, which is useful for fields representing a completion rate.

- `percentage` and `percentpie` are other widgets that can be used with float fields.

Relation and selection field widgets

For relation and selection fields, the following widgets are available:

- `many2many_tags` displays values as a list of button-like labels.
- `many2many_checkboxes` displays the selectable values as a list of checkboxes.
- `selection` uses the `selection` field widget for a many-to-one field.
- `radio` displays the `selection` field options using radio buttons.
- `priority` represents the `selection` field as a list of clickable stars. The selection options are usually numeric digits.
- `state_selection` shows a traffic light button and is typically used for the Kanban state selection list. The `normal` state is gray, `done` is green, and any other state is represented in red.

> **Changes in Odoo 11**
>
> The `state_selection` widget was introduced in Odoo 11 and replaces the former `kanban_state_selection`, which has been deprecated.

Binary field widgets

For binary fields, the following widgets are available:

- `image` presents the binary data as an image.
- `pdf_viewer` presents the binary data in a PDF preview widget (introduced in Odoo 12).

Relation fields

The relation field widget allows you to search for and select a related record.

It also allows you to open the related record's form or navigate to the corresponding form and create new records on the fly, also known as **quick create**.

These features can be disabled using the `options` field attribute:

```
options="{'no_open': True, 'no_create': True}"
```

The `context` and `domain` field attributes are particularly useful in relational fields:

- `context` can set default values for related records that are created from the field.

- `domain` limits the selectable records. A common example is for a field to have the selection options depend on the value of another field that's present in the form.

To-many fields can also use the `mode` attribute to set the view types to use to display the records. A `tree` view is used by default, but other options include `form`, `kanban`, and `graph`. It can be a comma-separated list of view modes.

Relation fields can include inline specific view definitions to use. These are declared as nested view definitions, inside the `<field>` element. For example, the `line_ids` checkout can define a specific list and form views for these lines:

```
<notebook>
  <page name="page_lines" string="Borrowed Books" >
    <field name="line_ids">
      <tree>
        <field name="book_id" />
      </tree>
      <form>
        <field name="book_id" />
      </form>
    </field>
  </page>
</notebook>
```

The line list will use the inline `<tree>` definition provided. When you click on a line, a form dialog will appear and use the structure in the inline `<form>` definition.

We've seen everything that can be done with fields. The next most important view element is buttons, which are used to run actions.

Using buttons

Buttons allow the user to trigger actions, such as opening another view or running business logic in a server function. They were introduced previously in this chapter, when we discussed the form header, but they can also be added anywhere in form and list views.

Buttons support the following attributes:

- `string` is the button text label, or the HTML `alt` text when an icon is used.

- `type` is the type of action to perform. Possible values include `object`, to call a Python method, or `action`, to run a window action.

- `name` identifies the specific action to perform, according to the chosen type: either a model method name or the database ID of a window action to run. The `%(<xmlid>)d` formula can be used to translate an XML ID into the necessary database ID when the view is being loaded.

- `args` is used when `type="object"` is used to pass additional parameters to the method call.

- `context` sets the values on the context. This could be used in the called method or affect the view that's opened by the windows action.

- `confirm` is the text for a confirmation message box when the button is clicked. This is displayed before the action is run.

- `special="cancel"` is used on wizard forms to add a **Cancel** button, which is used for closing the form without performing any action.

- `icon` is an icon image to be shown in the button. The available icons are from the Font Awesome set and they should be specified using the corresponding CSS class, such as `icon="fa-question"`. For an icon reference, check out `https://fontawesome.com/`.

> **Changes in Odoo 11**
>
> Before Odoo 11, the button icons were images that originated from the GTK client library and were limited to the ones available in `addons/web/static/src/img/icons`.
>
> The workflow engine was deprecated and removed in Odoo 11. In previous versions, where workflows were supported, buttons could trigger workflow engine signals using `type="workflow"`. In this case, the `name` attribute was supposed to have a workflow signal name.

A particular kind of button that's found at the top right area of some forms is called a **smart button**. Let's have a closer look at it.

Using smart buttons

It's not uncommon for document forms to have a smart button area in the top-right section. Smart buttons are shown as rectangles with a statistic indicator that can be followed through when clicked.

The Odoo UI pattern is to have an invisible box for smart buttons. This button box is usually the first element in `<sheet>` and looks like this:

```
<div name="button_box" class="oe_button_box">
  <!-- Smart buttons will go here... -->
</div>
```

The container for the buttons is just a `div` element with the `oe_button_box` class. In Odoo versions before 11.0, the `oe_right` class may also be needed to ensure that the button box stays aligned to the right-hand side of the form.

For the library checkout module, a smart button will be added for the still open checkouts that are being made by this library member. The button should present a statistic with the count of those checkouts and, when clicked, should open a checkout list that contains those items.

For the button statistic, a computed field needs to be created in the `library.checkout` model, in the `library_checkout/models/library_checkout.py` file:

```python
count_checkouts = fields.Integer(
    compute="_compute_count_checkouts")


def _compute_count_checkouts(self):
    for checkout in self:
        domain = [
            ("member_id", "=", checkout.member_id.id),
            ("state", "not in", ["done", "cancel"]),
        ]
        checkout.count_checkouts = \
            self.search_count(domain)
```

The preceding computation loops through each checkout record to compute and runs a search query for that member, counting the number of open checkouts.

> **Tip**
> The preceding implementation goes against a performance principle: don't do record search operations inside loops.

For performance optimization, the search operation should be done in bulk, before the loop, and the result should be used inside the loop. An example of this implementation is shown next. This involves non-trivial code, so feel free to skip it if you feel it is too difficult to understand right now.

The `read_group()` method can be used to get the grouped data. It returns a list of `dict` rows, such as `[{'member_id_count': 1, 'member_id': (1, 'John Doe'), ...), ...]`. It is hard to look up a `member_id` in this data structure. This lookup can become a trivial operation if the list of rows is converted into a dictionary that's mapping a `member_id` to a record count.

Here is the alternative implementation, using these techniques:

```python
def _compute_count_checkouts(self):
    members = self.mapped("member_id")
    domain = [
        ("member_id", "in", members.ids),
        ("state", "not in ", ["done", "cancel"]),
    ]
    raw = self.read_group(domain, ["id:count"],
        ["member_id"])
    data = {
        x["member_id"][0]: x["member_id_count"] for
            x in raw
    }
    for checkout in self:
        checkout.count_checkouts = data.get(
            checkout.member_id.id, 0)
```

Now that there is a field computing the number to display, the smart button can be added to the view. Right at the top of the `<sheet>` section, replace the button box placeholder we added previously with the following code:

```
<div name="button_box" class="oe_button_box">
  <button type="action"
    name="%(action_library_checkout)d"
    class="oe_stat_button"
    icon="fa-book"
    domain="[('member_id', '=', member_id)]"
    context="{'default_member_id': member_id}"
  >
    <field name="count_checkouts"
      string="Checkouts"
      widget="statinfo" />
  </button>
</div>
```

The `button` element itself is a container, and fields for displaying statistics should be added inside it. These statistics are regular fields that use a specific `statinfo` widget. The number of open checkouts is presented using the `count_checkouts` field, inside the button definition.

The smart button must have the `class="oe_stat_button"` CSS style and should have an icon set with the `icon` attribute.

In this case, it contains `type="action"`, meaning that a button runs a *window action*, as identified by the `name` attribute. The `%(action_library_checkout)d` expression returns the database ID for the action to run. This *window action* opens the checkout list. To ensure only the relevant records are displayed there, the `domain` attribute is used. And if a new record is created on that view, it is convenient that the current member is set as a default value. This can be done using the `default_member_id` key in the `context` attribute.

For reference, these are the attributes that can be used with smart buttons:

- `class="oe_stat_button"` renders a rectangle instead of a regular button.
- `icon` sets the icon to use, as chosen from the *Font Awesome* set. Visit `http://fontawesome.com` to browse the available icons.

- `type` and `name` are the button type and the name of the action to trigger, respectively. For smart buttons, the type will usually be `action` for a *window action*, while `name` will be the ID of the action to execute. `"%(action-xmlid)d"` can be used to convert an XML ID into the needed database ID.

- `string` adds label text to the button. It wasn't used in the preceding code example because the field is providing a text label.

- `context` can be used to set default values on the target view, for new records that are created on the view that's being navigated from the button.

- `help` adds a help tooltip that's displayed when the mouse pointer hovers over the button.

Other than buttons and smart buttons, dynamic elements can be added to views to change the values or visibility of elements. This will be discussed in the next section.

Adding dynamic view elements

View elements can dynamically change their appearance or behavior, depending on the field values. Field values can be dynamically set values of domain filters on other form fields through the *onchange* mechanism. These features will be discussed next.

Using onchange events

The **onchange** mechanism allows us to trigger server logic while the user is modifying data on an unsaved form. For example, when setting the product field, a unit price on the same form can be automatically set.

In older Odoo versions, the onchange events were defined at the view level, but since Odoo 8, they are declared directly on the model layer, without the need for any specific view markup. This can be done with methods that use the `@api.onchange('field1', 'field2', ...)` decorator. It binds onchange logic to the declared fields. The onchange model methods were discussed in more detail in *Chapter 8, Business Logic – Supporting Business Processes*, and an example was discussed there.

The onchange mechanism also takes care of automatically recalculating the computed fields, reacting immediately to user input. Continuing with the previous example, if the price field is changed, a computed field with the total amount would also be automatically updated with the new price information.

Using dynamic attributes

View elements can have some attributes react to changes on field values; for example, to become visible or mandatory.

The following attributes can be used to control the visibility of view elements:

- `groups` make an element visible, depending on the security groups the current user belongs to. Only the members of the specified groups will see it. It expects a comma-separated list of group XML IDs.

- `states` make an element visible, depending on the record's `state` field. It expects a comma-separated list of state values. Of course, the model must have a `state` selection field.

- `attrs` can set both the invisible and required attributes based on certain conditions. It uses a dictionary, with `invisible`, `readonly`, and `required` as the possible keys. These keys map to a domain expression that evaluates to true or false.

Here is an example of using `attrs`. To have the `closed_date` field only visible in the `done` state, the following code can be used:

```
<field name="closed_date"
        attrs="{'invisible':[('state', 'not in',
          ['done'])]}"
/>
```

The `invisible` attribute is available in any element, not only fields. For example, it can also be used on notebook pages and `group` elements.

The `readonly` and `required` attributes are only available for data fields and allow us to implement basic client-side logic, such as making a field mandatory while depending on other record values, such as the state.

This closes our discussion of form views. However, there are still a few view types to explore. Next, we will discuss list/tree views.

Exploring list views

List views are probably the most used view type, closely followed by form views. List views present records as lines and data fields as columns. By default, they are read-only, but they can also be made editable.

The list view's basic definition is simple. It is a sequence of field elements inside a `<tree>` element. `library_checkout` already contains a simple list view, in the `views/checkout_view.xml` file, that looks like this:

```xml
<record id="view_tree_checkout" model="ir.ui.view">
  <field name="name">Checkout Tree</field>
  <field name="model">library.checkout</field>
  <field name="arch" type="xml">
    <tree>
      <field name="request_date" />
      <field name="member_id" />
    </tree>
  </field>
</record>
```

A list view can contain fields and buttons, and the attributes that are described for forms are also valid in list views.

Moving on from the basics, a few additional features can be used on list views. In the next section, we will introduce the new list header section.

Adding a list view header section

Similar to form views, list views can also have a header section, where buttons can be added to perform actions on the model. The syntax is the same as for views.

For example, there is a **Send Messages** option available in the **Action** menu. This is not directly visible to the users, and it can be made more visible as a header button.

Editing the tree view to add this button looks like this:

```xml
<tree>
  <header>
    <button type="action"
      name="%(action_checkout_messag)d"
      string="Send Messages"
```

```
    />
  <header>
  <field name="request_date" />
  <field name="member_id" />
</tree>
```

The button actions work similarly to the **Action** menu options. The buttons are only visible when list records are selected.

> **New in Odoo 14**
>
> The `<header>` element on list views was introduced in Odoo 14. This feature is not available in previous versions.

In terms of the list view's content, rows can use different colors to highlight specific conditions to the user, such as a late activity in red. The next section explains how to use such decorations.

Using line decoration

The following expanded version of the list adds a few additional fields, as well as some decorator attributes, to the `<tree>` root element:

```
<tree
   decoration-muted="state in ['done', 'cancel']"
   decoration-bf="state=='open'"
>
  <header>
    <button type="action"
      name="%(action_checkout_messag)d"
      string="Send Messages"
    />
  <header>
  <field name="state" invisible="True" />
  <field name="name" />
  <field name="request_date" />
  <field name="member_id" />
  <field name="stage_id" />
</tree>
```

The tree element is using two decoration attributes by using expressions with the state field. decoration-muted uses gray lines to show the done or canceled state. decoration-bf highlights the open state with bold lines.

The fields that are used in these expressions must be declared in a <field> element of the view to ensure that the necessary data is retrieved from the server. If it doesn't need to be displayed, it can have the invisible="1" attribute set on it.

The row's text color and font can change based on the evaluation of a Python expression. This can be done through the decoration-NAME attributes, which can be set with an expression to evaluate. The available attributes are as follows:

- decoration-bf sets the font to bold.
- decoration-it sets the font to italic.
- decoration-muted sets the text color to gray.
- decoration-primary sets the text color to a dark blue.
- decoration-success sets the text color to a light blue.
- decoration-warning sets the text color to yellow.
- decoration-danger sets the text color to red.

The preceding decoration names are based on the Bootstrap library. See https://getbootstrap.com/docs/3.3/css/#helper-classes for more details.

Other than the decoration attributes, a few others are available to control the behavior of the list view.

Other list view attributes

Some of the other relevant attributes of the tree element are as follows:

- default_order is used to set a specific sort order for the rows. Its value is a comma-separated list of field names that's compatible with a SQL ORDER BY clause.
- create, delete, and edit, if set to false (in lowercase), disable the corresponding action on the list view.
- editable makes records editable directly on the list view. Possible values include top and bottom; that is, the location where the new records will be added.

These attributes allow you to control the default row order and whether the record can be edited directly in the view.

One more relevant feature is the ability to calculate totals and subtotals for list view columns, as shown in the next section.

Adding column totals

List views also support column totals for numeric fields. Summary values can be displayed using one of the aggregation attributes that's available — sum, avg, min, or max.

The aggregation attribute that's used should be set with label text for the summary value.

For example, let's consider that the checkout model has added a field stating the number of borrowed books, num_books. To see the corresponding total sum on the list view, the following field element should be added:

```
<field name="num_books" sum="Num. Books" />
```

The num_books field counts the number of borrowed books in each checkout. It's a computed field, and we need to add it to the model:

```
num_books = fields.Integer(compute=
    "_compute_num_books")


@api.depends("line_ids")
def _compute_num_books(self):
    for book in self:
        book.num_books = len(book.line_ids)
```

The group subtotal is only available for stored fields. So, in the previous example, store=True needs to be added if group subtotals are an important feature for the library app users.

After form and list views, the next most important UI element is the search view, which lets us perform a default search and group by a filter.

Exploring search views

At the top right of the view, there is a search box with a few buttons underneath it, including **Filters** and **Group By**. When you're typing in the search box, you will see suggestions regarding the field to be searched.

The search options that are proposed are configured in the **search view**. The current search view can be inspected using the developer menu and by choosing the **Edit ControlPanelView** option.

Search views are defined through the `<search>` view type. It can provide the following types of elements:

- `<field>` elements to add filter options when typing in the search box.

- `<filter>` elements to add predefined filters under the **Filters** and **Group By** buttons.

- A `<searchpanel>` element, to include a navigation tree on the left-hand side of the user interface.

> **Changes in Odoo 13**
>
> The `<searchpanel>` widget for the list and Kanban views was introduced in Odoo 13 and is not available in earlier versions.

To add these search options to the `library_checkout` module, edit the `views/checkout_view.xml` file and add the following record:

```xml
<record id="view_filter_checkout" model="ir.ui.view">
  <field name="model">library.checkout</field>
  <field name="arch" type="xml">
    <search>
      <!-- Add content here -->
      <field name="name" />
    </search>
  </field>
</record>
```

Now, let's walk through each of the element types that can be added here. The `<field>` element will be explained next.

Understanding the <field> element

When typing in the search box, the user will see suggestions that will let them apply this search to particular fields. These options are defined using `<field>` elements.

For example, adding the following XML inside the `<search>` element will propose searching the text in additional fields:

```xml
<field name="name"/>
<field name="member_id"/>
<field name="user_id"/>
```

This code adds search result suggestions for the `title`, `member`, and `user` fields.

The search `<field>` elements can use the following attributes:

- `name` is the field name to be searched.
- `string` is the text label to use.
- `operator` can be used as a comparison operator that's different from the default one; that is, = for numeric fields and `ilike` for the other field types.
- `filter_domain` sets a specific domain expression to use for the search, providing one flexible alternative to the operator attribute. The searched text string is referred to in the expression as `self`. A trivial example is `filter_domain="[('name', 'ilike', self)]"`.
- `groups` makes searching on the field available only to users that belong to some security groups. It expects a comma-separated list of XML IDs.

These filters can be activated independently and will be joined by an `OR` logic operation. Blocks of filters separated with a `<separator/>` element will be joined by an `AND` logic operation.

This section provided a good summary of how `<field>` elements can be used. Now, let's learn about the `<filter>` elements that are available.

Understanding the <filter> element

Predefined options are available upon clicking the **Filter** and **Group By** buttons, under the search box. These can be clicked by users to apply their filter conditions.

> **Tip**
> Filter elements can also be used by window actions, which can activate them, by adding a `search_default_<filter name>: True` key to the context.

Filter options can be added with the `<filter>` element, along with a `domain` attribute setting for specific search conditions to use, through a domain filter. The following is an example:

```
<filter name="filter_not_done"
        string="To Return"
        domain="[('state','=','open')]"/>
<filter name="filter_my_checkouts"
```

```
                              string="My Checkouts"
                              domain="[('user_id','=',uid)]"/>
```

This adds two selectable filters. They will be available for selection in the **Filters** button, below the search box. The first filters the **To Return** checkouts, which are the ones in the open state. The second one filters the checkout where the current user is the responsible librarian, filtering user_id by the current user. This is available from the context uid key.

The filter element is also used to add options to the **Group By** button. Here is an example:

```
            <filter name="group_user"
                     string="By Member"
                     context="{'group_by': 'member_id'}"/>
```

This filter sets a group by context key with the field name to group by. In this case, it will group by member_id.

For the <filter> elements, the following attributes are available:

- name is an identifier to be used for later inheritance/extension or to be enabled using a window action context key. It is not mandatory, but it is good practice to always provide it.

- string is the label text to be displayed for the filter. It is mandatory.

- domain is the domain expression to be added to the current domain.

- context is a context dictionary to be added to the current context. It will usually be used to set the group_by key with the field name to group by.

- groups makes this element field available only for a list of security groups (XML IDs).

Upon adding the preceding code to the library_checkout module, the module will be upgraded. These filter and group by options will be available in the buttons near the search box.

Another search view element that's available is the search panel. We'll look at this in the next section.

Adding a search panel

Search views can also add a search panel, which will be visible on the left-hand side of the selected view. It lists the available values in a field. Clicking on a value filters the records by that value. By default, this search panel is only visible in the list and Kanban views, although this can be changed.

The following code adds a search panel to the library checkout view. Add the following XML inside the <search> view element:

```
<searchpanel>
    <field name="member_id" enable_counters="1" />
    <field name="stage_id" select="multi" />
</searchpanel>
```

The preceding code adds two fields to the search panel called members and stages. Each of them lists several available values, and clicking on these values applies the corresponding filter.

The <searchpanel> element has one attribute available, view_type, that can set the view types where the panel is to be made visible. By default, its value is view_type="tree,kanban".

The <field> elements inside <searchpanel> support a few attributes. Here is a selection of the most important ones:

- string sets specific label text to use.
- icon sets an icon to be presented.
- color sets the icon's color. It uses an HTML hex code, such as #8F3A84.
- select="multi" adds selection checkboxes, which allow the user to select multiple values. This is only available for many-to-one and many-to-many fields.
- groups sets a list XML IDs of the security groups that can see the search panel.
- enable_counters="1" adds a record number counter next to each value. Beware that this can have a performance impact on the view.
- limit sets the number of selected values that are allowed. The default is 200 and can be set to zero so that there's no limit.

> **Changes in Odoo 13**
> The search panel element was introduced in Odoo 13 and is not available in previous versions.

This is what the list view with the search panel looks like, after making these changes:

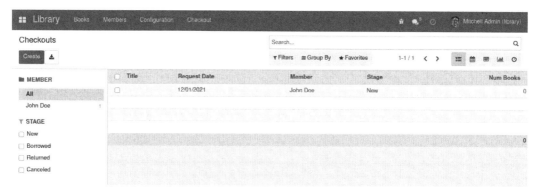

Figure 10.4 – List view with the search panel

The form, list, and search views are the most frequently used view types. But there are a few more view types that are available for designing our user interfaces. We'll look at these in the next section.

Understanding the other available view types

The form and list views are essential user interface components, but other than them, a few other specific view types can be used.

We're already familiar with the three basic views: form, tree, and search. Beyond these, the following view types are also available in Odoo Community Edition:

- kanban presents records as cards that can be organized in columns to create Kanban boards.

- activity presents a summary of scheduled activities.

- calendar present records in a calendar format.

- graph presents data as a graphical chart.

- pivot presents data as an interactive pivot table.

- qweb is used to declare QWeb templates to be used in reports, Kanban views, or web pages. However, this is not a web client-supported view type like forms and lists are.

Kanban views will be presented in depth in *Chapter 11, Kanban Views and Client-Side QWeb*, so they won't be addressed here.

> **Changes in Odoo 14**
>
> The `diagram` view type, which could be used to present relationships between records, was removed in Odoo 14. The last piece of documentation that's available for this, for Odoo 13, can be found at `https://www.odoo.com/documentation/13.0/developer/reference/addons/views.html#diagram`.

Odoo Enterprise Edition supports a few more views types:

- `dashboard`, which presents aggregate data using subviews, such as pivots and graphs.
- `cohort`, which is used to show how data changes over a certain period.
- `map`, which presents records in a map and can display routes between them.
- `Gantt`, which presents date scheduling information in a Gantt chart. This is commonly used in project management.
- `grid`, which presents data organized in a grid with rows and columns.

The official documentation provides good references to all of the views and their available attributes: `https://www.odoo.com/documentation/15.0/developer/reference/backend/views.html#view-types`.

> **Tip**
>
> Additional view types can be found as community add-on modules. Under the Odoo Community Association umbrella, web client extensions, including view types and widgets, can be found in the `https://github.com/OCA/web` GitHub repository. For example, the `web_timeline` add-on module provides a `timeline` view type, which is also capable of presenting scheduling information as Gantt charts. It is a Community Edition alternative to the `gantt` view type.

The following sections provide a brief explanation of the additional view types that are available in Odoo Community Edition.

Exploring the activity view

The activity view provides a summary of the scheduled activities. It is provided by the `mail` add-on module, so it needs to be installed for this view type to be available.

It can be enabled by adding the `activity` view type to the `view_mode` field of the window action. From the **Library | Checkouts** menu option, edit the `action_library_checkout` window action:

```
<field name="view_mode">tree,form,activity</field>
```

If no view definition exists, one will be automatically generated.

This is a simple definition that's equivalent to the default generated one:

```
<record id="view_activity_checkout" model="ir.ui.view">
  <field name="model">library.checkout</field>
  <field name="arch" type="xml">
    <activity string="Checkouts">
      <templates>
        <div t-name="activity-box">
          <div>
            <field name="ntame" />
          </div>
        </div>
      </templates>
    </activity>
  </field>
</record>
```

The HTML in the `<templates>` element is used to describe the record information.

Exploring the calendar view

This view type presents the records in a calendar that can be viewed using different periods: per year, month, week, or day.

This is a calendar view for the library checkouts that shows the items on a calendar according to their request date:

```xml
<record id="view_calendar_checkout" model="ir.ui.view">
  <field name="model">library.checkout</field>
  <field name="arch" type="xml">
    <calendar date_start="request_date"
              color="user_id">
      <field name="member_id" />
      <field name="stage_id" />
    </calendar>
  </field>
</record>
```

The following attributes are supported by the calendar view:

- `date_start` is the field for the start date (required).
- `date_stop` is the field for the end date (optional).
- `date_delay` in the field containing the duration in days. It is to be used instead of `date_end`.
- `all_day` provides the name of a Boolean field that is to be used to signal full-day events. In these events, the duration is ignored.
- `color` is the field that's used to color a group of calendar entries. Each distinct value in this field will be assigned a color, and all of its entries will have the same color.
- `mode` is the default display mode for the calendar. It can be either `day`, `week`, `month`, or `year`.
- `scales` is a comma-separated list of modes available. By default, they all are.
- `form_view_id` can provide the identifier for a specific form view to use when you're opening records from the calendar view.
- `event_open_popup="True"` opens the form view as a dialog window.

- `quick_add` lets you quickly create a new record. Only a description needs to be given by the user.

> **Changes in Odoo 11**
>
> The `display` calendar attribute was removed in Odoo 11. In previous versions, it could be used to customize the format of the calendar entry's title text; for example, `display="[name], Stage [stage_id]"`.

For this view to be available in the **Library | Checkouts** menu option, the view type needs to be added to the `view_mode` area of the corresponding window with the `action_library_checkout` identifier:

```
<field name="view_mode">tree,form,calendar</field>
```

After making this module upgrade and reloading the page, the calendar view should be available.

Exploring the pivot view

The data can also be seen in a pivot table; that is, a dynamic analysis matrix. For this, we have the pivot view.

The num_books field will be used in the pivot view to add the checkouts model. Data aggregations are only available for database stored fields; this is not the case for the num_books field. So, it needs to be modified to add the `store=True` attribute:

```
num_books = fields.Integer(
    compute="_compute_num_books",
    store=True)
```

To also add a pivot table to the library checkouts, use the following code:

```
<record id="view_pivot_checkout" model="ir.ui.view">
  <field name="model">library.checkout</field>
  <field name="arch" type="xml">
    <pivot>
      <field name="stage_id" type="col" />
      <field name="member_id" />
      <field name="request_date" interval="week" />
      <field name="num_books" type="measure" />
```

```
    </pivot>
  </field>
</record>
```

The graph and pivot views should contain field elements that describe the axes and measures to use. Most of the available attributes are common to both view types:

- `name` identifies the field to use in the graph, just like in other views.

- `type` is how the field will be used; that is, as a `row` group (default), `measure`, or `col` (only for pivot tables; it is used for column groups).

- `interval` is meaningful for date fields and is the time interval that's used to group time data by `day`, `week`, `month`, `quarter`, or `year`.

Other than these essential attributes, more are available and are documented at `https://www.odoo.com/documentation/15.0/developer/reference/backend/views.html#pivot`.

For this view to be available in the **Library | Checkouts** menu option, the view type needs to be added in the `view_mode` area of the `action_library_checkout` window action:

```
<field name="view_mode">tree,form,pivot</field>
```

After making this module upgrade and reloading the page, the calendar view should be available.

Exploring the graph view

Graph views present charts with data aggregations. The available charts include bar, line, and pie charts.

Here is an example of a graph view for the checkout model:

```
<record id="view_graph_checkout" model="ir.ui.view">
  <field name="model">library.checkout</field>
  <field name="arch" type="xml">
    <graph type="bar">
      <field name="stage_id" />
      <field name="num_books" type="measure" />
    </graph>
  </field>
</record>
```

The `graph` view element can have a `type` attribute that can be set to `bar` (the default), `pie`, or `line`. In the case of `bar`, the additional `stacked="True"` element can be used to make it a stacked bar chart.

The graph uses two types of fields:

- `type="row"` is the default and sets the criteria to aggregate values.
- `type="measure"` is used for the fields that are to be used as metrics – that is, the actual values being aggregated.

Most of the available graph view attributes are common to the pivot view type. The official documentation provides a good reference: `https://www.odoo.com/documentation/15.0/developer/reference/backend/views.html#reference-views-graph`.

For this view to be available in the **Library | Checkouts** menu option, the view type needs to be added to the `view_mode` area of the `action_library_checkout` window action:

```
<field name="view_mode">tree,form,graph</field>
```

After making this module upgrade and reloading the page, the calendar view should be available.

Summary

Well-designed views are key for a good user experience. Applications need to support the business logic, but an easy-to-use user interface is also important to help users navigate efficiently through the business processes and minimize errors.

The Odoo web client provides a rich set of tools to build such user interfaces. This includes a menu system, several view types, and different field widgets to choose from.

Adding menu items is the first step, and these use window actions to let the web client know what views should be presented.

Most of the user interaction will happen on form views, and it is important to understand all the elements that can be used there. We started by presenting the general structure that form views are expected to follow, as well as the elements to be added to each.

This includes the header section, the title fields, the other form fields, a possible notebook section with pages, and a final messaging area.

Record data is presented and modified using field elements. Details were presented on how to use them and the several options that can be used to adjust their presentation. Another important element is buttons, which allow us to navigate to other views or run server functions.

The next view type we discussed was the list view. While simpler than the form view, it is an important record navigation tool. The search view was also discussed and is useful for adding predefined filter and grouping options to the search box area. This is important for users to quickly access the data that's needed for their regular operations.

Finally, an overview was provided of the other view types available, such as the pivot, graph, and calendar views. There are used less often, but they still have an important role in specific cases.

In the next chapter, we'll learn more about a specific view type that we've not covered in this chapter: the Kanban view and the templating syntax that's used by it, QWeb.

Further reading

The following reference materials complement the topics that were described in this chapter:

- The official Odoo documentation:

  - On actions: `https://www.odoo.com/documentation/15.0/developer/reference/backend/actions.html`

  - On views: `https://www.odoo.com/documentation/15.0/developer/reference/backend/views.html`

- The Font Awesome icon index: `https://fontawesome.com/v4.7.0/icons/`

11
Kanban Views and Client-Side QWeb

Kanban views support lean processes, providing a visual representation of the work in progress and the status of each work item. This can be an important tool to streamline business processes.

This chapter introduces **kanban board** concepts, and how they are implemented in **Odoo** by using the kanban view type, stage columns, and kanban states.

Kanban views are powered by **QWeb** – the template engine used by Odoo. It is **XML**-based and used to generate **HTML** fragments and pages. It is also used for reports and website pages, so it is an important part of Odoo that developers should be familiar with.

In this chapter, we will show how to organize a kanban view in several areas, such as the title and main content, as well as how to use the QWeb syntax to apply the widgets and effects that are available.

The QWeb template language will be described in detail to provide a complete understanding of its features.

The later sections will explain how to extend the QWeb templates used in kanban views and present useful techniques for this. Here, you will learn how to add web assets that you intend to be used in these views, such as **CSS** and **JavaScript**.

The following topics will be covered in this chapter:

- Introducing kanban boards
- Designing kanban views
- Designing kanban cards
- Exploring the QWeb template language
- Extending kanban views
- Adding CSS and JavaScript assets

By the end of this chapter, you will understand kanban boards and be able to design your own kanban views.

Technical requirements

This chapter continues enhancing the `library_checkout` addon module from *Chapter 10, Backend Views – Designing the User Interface*. The corresponding code can be found in the `ch11/` directory of the **GitHub** repository at `https://github.com/PacktPublishing/Odoo-15-Development-Essentials`.

Introducing kanban boards

Kanban is a Japanese word literally meaning *billboard* and is associated with lean manufacturing. More recently, *kanban boards* have become popular in the software industry with the adoption of **agile** methodologies.

A kanban board provides a visual representation of a work queue. The board is organized into columns, which represent the *stages* of the work process. Work items are represented by *cards* placed on the appropriate column of the board. New work items start from the leftmost column and travel through the board until they reach the rightmost column, which represents the completed work.

The simplicity and visual impact of kanban boards make them a good tool to support simple business processes. A basic example of a kanban board has three columns: *To Do*, *Doing*, and *Done*, as shown in the following diagram:

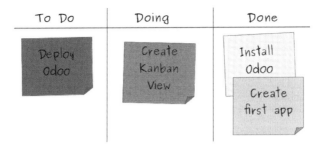

Figure 11.1 – An example of a kanban board

In many cases, a kanban board is a more effective way to manage a process when compared to heavier workflow engines.

Odoo supports kanban views – along with the classic list and form views – to support kanban boards. Now that we know what a kanban board is, let's learn how to use one.

Supporting kanban boards in Odoo

Browsing the Odoo apps, we can see two different ways to use kanban views. One is a simple *card list*, which is used in places such as contacts, products, employees, and apps. The other is a kanban board, which is organized in columns representing the steps of a process.

For simple card lists, a good example is the **Contacts** kanban view. The contact cards have an image on the left-hand side and a bold title in the main area, followed by a list of values:

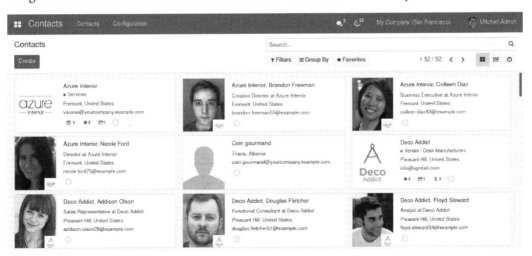

Figure 11.2 – The Contacts kanban view

While this contacts view uses a *kanban view*, it is not a *kanban board*.

Examples of kanban boards can be found on the *CRM* app's **Pipeline** page or on the **Project Tasks** page. An example of the **Pipeline** page is shown in *Figure 11.3*:

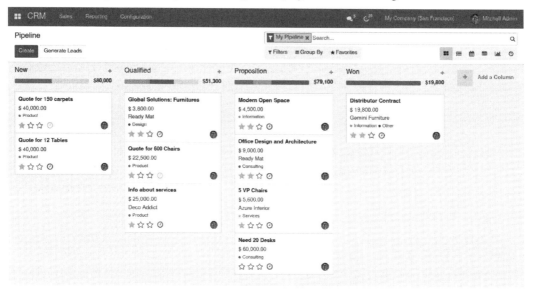

Figure 11.3 – The CRM Pipeline kanban board

The most important difference between this kanban board and the **Contacts** kanban view is the card organization in columns. This is done using the **Group By** feature, which is similar to what list views use. Usually, the grouping is done in a *stage* field. One very useful feature of kanban views is that they support dragging and dropping cards between columns, which automatically assigns the corresponding value to the field the view is grouped by.

The **CRM Pipeline** page cards have a bit more structure. The main card area also has a title, followed by a list of relevant information, as well as a footer area. In this footer area, we can see a priority widget on the left-hand side, followed by an activities indicator, and on the right-hand side, we can see a small image of the responsible user.

It's not visible in the figure shown in this chapter, but the cards also have an options menu on the top-right, which is shown when hovering the mouse pointer over it. This menu allows us to, for example, change a color indicator for the card.

Looking at the cards in both examples, we can see some differences. In fact, their design is quite flexible, and there isn't a single way to design a kanban card. But these two examples provide a starting point for your designs.

We will be using the more elaborate structure as a model for the cards on our checkouts kanban board.

Understanding kanban states

On a kanban board, work items start in the leftmost column, and while the work is in progress, they travel through the columns until reaching the rightmost column, which shows the completed items. This implies a *push strategy*, which means when work on a column is done, the work item is *pushed* to the next column.

A push strategy tends to lead to a build-up of work items in progress, which can be inefficient. Lean approaches advise using a *pull strategy* instead. Here, each stage *pulls* work from the previous one when it is ready to start the next work item.

Odoo supports the pull strategy with the use of kanban states. Each record work item has a kanban state field signaling its flow status: *In progress* (gray), *Blocked* (red), or *Ready* (green).

When the work needed in a stage is completed, instead of moving the card to the next column, it is marked as *Ready*. This gives a visual indication that the work item is ready to be pulled by the next stage. Additionally, if something is preventing the work from moving ahead, it can be marked as *Blocked*, giving a visual indication that help is needed to unblock this work item.

As an example, kanban states are used in the **Project Tasks** kanban view. In the following screenshot, we can see the kanban state *gray-red-green* indicator in the bottom-right of each card. Also, note the progress bar at the top of each column, which provides a visual indication of the items in each state:

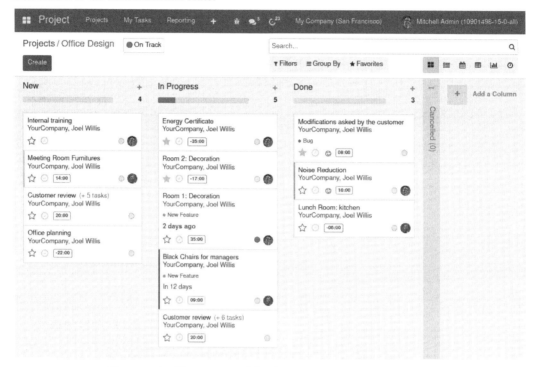

Figure 11.4 – The project task kanban view with the kanban states

The kanban state is meaningful in each stage, so it should be reset when an item moves to another stage.

You have now learned about the different views in a kanban board and what they look like. Now, we will move on to learning how to design them.

Designing kanban views

The book checkout process can use a kanban view to visualize the work in progress. In this case, the kanban board columns could represent the checkout stages, and each checkout could be represented by a card.

This is what the library checkout kanban view will look like when complete:

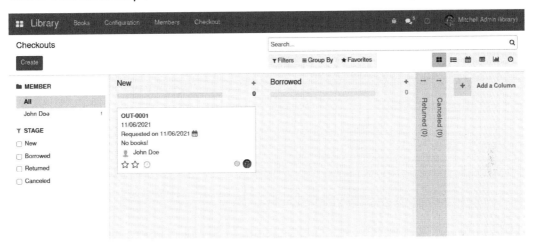

Figure 11.5 – Library checkouts kanban view

Form views mostly use Odoo-specific XML elements such as `<field>` and `<group>`. They also use some HTML elements such as `<h1>` or `<div>`, but their use is limited. Kanban views are quite the opposite. They are HTML-based and additionally support two Odoo-specific elements: `<field>` and `<button>`.

With kanban views, the final HTML presented in the web client is dynamically generated from QWeb templates. The QWeb engine processes special XML tags and attributes in the templates to produce the final HTML. This allows a lot of control of how the content is rendered, but it also makes the view design more complex.

As a kanban view design is so flexible, different design structures can be used. A good approach is to find an existing kanban view that would fit well with the use case at hand, inspect it, and use it as a reference.

Creating a minimal viable kanban view

Kanban views allow for a rich user interface and can quickly get complex. The first step in learning how to design kanban views is to create a minimum viable view.

To add a kanban view to the `library_checkout` module, follow these steps:

1. Add `kanban` in `view_mode` of the window action. To do this, edit the `views/library_menu.xml` file and update the value set in the `view_mode` field to match the following:

```xml
<record id="action_library_checkout"
        model="ir.actions.act_window">
    <field name="name">Checkouts</field>
    <field name="res_model">library.checkout</field>
    <field name="view_mode">
    kanban,tree,form,calendar,pivot,graph,activity
    </field>
</record>
```

In the previous code, `kanban` was added at the beginning of the list to have it as the default view type.

2. The new kanban view will be added in a new XML file, `views/checkout_kanban_view.xml`. So, add this file to the `__manifest__.py` module in the `data` key:

```python
"data": [
    "security/ir.model.access.csv",
    "views/library_menu.xml",
    "views/checkout_view.xml",
    "views/checkout_kanban_view.xml",
    "wizard/checkout_mass_message_wizard_view.xml"
    ,
    "data/stage_data.xml",
],
```

3. Finally, add the XML code for a minimal kanban view in the `views/checkout_kanban_view.xml` file by using the following code:

```xml
<odoo>
```

```
    <record id="library_checkout_kanban"
      model="ir.ui.view">
      <field name="model">library.checkout</field>
      <field name="arch" type="xml">

<kanban>
  <templates>
    <t t-name="kanban-box">
      <div>
        <field name="name" />
      </div>
    </t>
  </templates>
</kanban>

      </field>
    </record>

</odoo>
```

In the previous code, a kanban view is declared inside a `<kanban>` element. Kanban views are described using the QWeb template language. The templates are added inside a `<templates>` sub-element.

The main template for each kanban card is described in the `<t t-name="kanban-box">` element. This QWeb template is minimal. It is an HTML `<div>` element containing an Odoo-specific `<field>` widget, which is also used in form and tree views.

This provides a pretty basic *kanban view* XML structure to start building from. To be a *kanban board*, it needs to feature columns for each process stage.

Presenting kanban board columns

Kanban boards present the work items organized in columns, where each column is a stage in the process. New work items start on the left-hand columns and then travel through the columns until they arrive at the right-hand side, completed.

Kanban views present items in columns when grouping by a field. For a kanban board, the view should be grouped by a stage or state field – often, `stage_id` is used.

The `default_group_by` attribute sets a default column group for the kanban view. To have a kanban board for the book checkouts, edit the `<kanban>` element to look like this:

```
<kanban default_group_by="stage_id">
```

When opening this view, it will be grouped by stage by default (which is similar to *Figure 11.4*). The user is still able to change the applied **group by** by using the same `group_by` options used for list views.

Understanding kanban view attributes and elements

Kanban views support a few additional attributes to fine-tune their behavior.

The `<kanban>` top element supports these attributes:

- `default_group_by`: This sets the field to use for the default column groups.
- `default_order`: This sets a default order to use for the kanban items.
- `quick_create="false"`: This disables the `quick_create` option to create new items by providing just a title description, using the plus sign at the right-hand side of each column header. The `false` value is a JavaScript literal and must be in lowercase.
- `quick_create_view`: This can optionally be used to set a specific form view to use for the `quick_create` function. It should be set with the XML ID of the form view.
- `class`: This adds a CSS class to the root element of the rendered kanban view. A relevant class is `o_kanban_small_column`, which makes columns somewhat more compact than the default. Additional classes may be made available through the CSS assets provided by the module.
- `group_create`, `group_edit`, `group_delete`, and `quick_create_view`: These can be set to `false` to disable the corresponding action on the kanban columns. For example, `group_create="false"` removes the vertical **Add new column** bar on the right side of the screen.
- `records_draggable="false"`: This disables the ability to drag records between columns.

The `<kanban>` element can contain these elements:

- `<field>`: This is used to declare the fields used by the QWeb templates that need to be retrieved from the server. This is necessary when those fields are used in QWeb evaluation expressions. It is not needed for fields used in a template `<field>` element.

- `<progressbar>`: This element adds a progress bar widget on the group column headers.

- `<templates>`: This element is required where the kanban card QWeb templates are declared.

An example for the `<templates>` element can be seen in the minimal kanban view presented previously. An example of the `<progressbar>` element is provided next.

Adding a progress bar to group columns

A **progress bar** can show a total number for the column and a colored bar representing the column record sub-states. The CRM Pipeline page uses it to provide a summary for the lead activities, from **planned** to **overdue**. Another example is the use of kanban states, as used by the **Project Tasks** kanban board.

For this, first `kanban_state` needs to be added to the model, and then, it can be used in the view. To do so, apply the following steps:

1. Add the field to the `library.checkout` model, editing the `models/library_checkout.py` file as follows:

```python
# class Checkout(models.Model):
    kanban_state = fields.Selection(
        [("normal", "In Progress"),
         ("blocked", "Blocked"),
         ("done", "Ready for next stage")],
        "Kanban State",
        default="normal")
```

2. When changing the stage in the same file at the beginning of the `write()` method, add the business logic to reset `kanban_state`, as follows:

```python
    def write(self, vals):
        # reset kanban state when changing stage
        if "stage_id" in vals and "kanban_state"
          not in vals:
            vals["kanban_state"] = "normal"
        # Code before write ...
        # ...
        return True
```

This completes the model changes needed for the time being. Here, we are focusing on adding the progress bar – the kanban status widget will be added in a later section.

The `<progressbar>` element is one of the three element types allowed inside a `<kanban>` tag, along with `<field>` and `<templates>`.

To add it to the `<kanban>` view definition, edit the element to add the following highlighted code:

```
<kanban>
    <progressbar field="kanban_state"
    colors='{
        "done": "success",
        "blocked": "danger",
        "normal": "muted"}'
    sum_fields="num_books"
    />
    <templates>
        <t t-name="kanban-box">
            <div>
                <field name="name" />
            </div>
        </t>
    </templates>
</kanban>
```

The previous code adds the progress bar widget. The `field` attribute sets the model field to use, and the `colors` attribute maps the field values to the `"danger"`, `"warning"`, `"success"`, or `"muted"` colors.

By default, the column total indicator counts the number of items in each column. This can be changed to be the sum of the values in a model field. In the previous code, the optional `sum_fields` attribute was added to present the total number of books in each column's requests.

At this point, we have a functioning kanban view. However, the kanban cards can display richer features. The next section focuses on this, where we will further expand the templates used to render the kanban card content.

Designing kanban cards

The design of a kanban card is quite flexible and uses HTML that is produced from QWeb templates declared in the `<templates>` element.

The content area will often feature several other areas. Using the CRM Pipeline as a blueprint, the following sections can be found:

- A title section, with the lead short summary
- A content section, with the amount, customer name, and lead tags
- A left footer section, with the priority and activities widgets
- A right footer section, with the salesperson avatar
- A top-right menu button, which in this case, is visible on mouse hover

This section implements the previous kanban card structure, and it populates each section to showcase the most important features. The first step for designing kanban cards is to lay out the kanban card skeleton, which is described next.

> **Note**
>
> The proposed kanban skeleton, as well as certain CSS classes used, is based on the CRM Pipeline kanban view. Odoo modules can provide specific CSS classes and use them in the kanban card design. So, these can vary when inspecting the kanban view templates from different modules.

Organizing the kanban card layout

The kanban card minimal design will now be expanded to a skeleton including several areas, which we will now describe.

The kanban card is defined inside the `<templates>` section in an element with `t-name="kanban-box"`. This can be an HTML element or a QWeb `t-` directive. The definition created earlier in this chapter uses the neutral `<t>` QWeb element: `<t t-name="kanban-box">`.

Moving ahead, the kanban view template and the QWeb template should be edited to mark the areas to be worked on, as shown by the following code:

```
<kanban>
    <!-- Field list to ensure is loaded ... -->
```

```xml
<templates>

    <t t-name="kanban-box">
        <div class="oe_kanban_global_click">

            <div class="o_dropdown_kanban dropdown">
                <!-- Top-right drop down menu ... -->
            </div>

            <div class="oe_kanban_content">
                <div class="o_kanban_record_title">
                    <!-- Title area ... -->
                    <field name="name" />
                </div>
                <div class="o_kanban_record_body">
                    <!-- Other content area  ... -->
                </div>

                <div class="o_kanban_record_bottom">
                    <div class="oe_kanban_bottom_left">
                        <!-- Left side footer... -->
                    </div>
                    <div class="oe_kanban_bottom_right">
                        <!-- Right side footer... -->
                    </div>
                </div> <!-- o_kanban_record_bottom -->

                <div class="oe_clear"/>
            </div> <!-- oe_kanban_content -->
        </div> <!-- oe_kanban_global_click -->
    </t>
```

The previous QWeb template code provides a skeleton for all the areas usually seen in kanban cards.

When the t-name QWeb attribute is used in a <t> element, this element can have only one child element. This was the case in the preceding code, and the <div> child element must contain all the other kanban view elements.

It is worth noting that this overarching `<div>` element uses the `class="oe_kanban_global_click"` attribute. This makes the card clickable, and when the user does so, the corresponding form view will be opened in a similar way to what happens with list views.

The next task is to focus on each of the highlighted areas and add content to them.

Adding a title and other content fields

Now that we have a basic kanban card skeleton, the title and additional data can be added.

These will go inside the `<div class="oe_kanban_content">` element. The skeleton being used has sections for these: the `<div class="o_kanban_record_title">` and `<div class="o_kanban_record_body">` elements.

The following code expands this section to highlight the card title and add the checkout request date and the requesting library member ID:

```
<div class="o_kanban_record_title">
    <!-- Title area ... -->
    <strong><field name="name" /></strong>
</div>
<div class="o_kanban_record_body">
    <!-- Other content area ... -->
    <div><fields name="request_date" /></div>
    <div>
        <field name="member_id"
            widget="many2one_avatar"/>
    </div>

</div>
```

In this case, regular HTML elements can be used. For example, the `<strong>` element was used to highlight the title. Also, `<field>` elements can be used to render field values, which will be rendered using the appropriate formatting in a similar way to what happens in form views. In the previous code, `request_date` uses a `<field>` element, and so its content will be rendered using the Odoo-configured date format. It is wrapped in a `<div>` element so that there is a line break between several fields.

The `member_id` many-to-one object is also added by using a specific widget that presents the corresponding avatar image along with the name, `widget="many2one_avatar"`.

Now that we have added some basic data elements to the card, let's look at the drop-down menu area.

Adding the drop-down options menu

Kanban cards can have an options menu on the top-right corner. Common options include being able to edit or delete the record, set a color for the card, or run any action that can be called from a button.

The following is the baseline HTML code for the options menu to be added to the top of the oe_kanban_content element:

```
<div class="o_dropdown_kanban dropdown">
    <!-- Top-right drop down menu ... -->
    <a class="dropdown-toggle btn"
       role="button" data-toggle="dropdown"
       title="Dropdown menu" href="#">
       <span class="fa fa-ellipsis-v" />
    </a>
    <div class="dropdown-menu" role="menu">

        <!-- Edit menu option -->
        <t t-if="widget.editable">
          <a role="menuitem" type="edit"
             class="dropdown-item">Edit</a>
        </t>
        <!-- Delete menu option -->
        <t t-if="widget.deletable">
          <a role="menuitem" type="delete"
             class="dropdown-item">Delete</a>
        </t>

        <!-- Separator line -->
        <div role="separator" class=
          "dropdown-divider"/>

        <!-- Color picker option: -->
        <ul class="oe_kanban_colorpicker"
```

```
                data-field="color" />


        <!-- Set as Done menu option -->
        <a t-if="record.state != 'done'"
           role="menuitem" class="dropdown-item"
           name="button_done" type="object">Set
           as Done</a>


    </div>
</div>
```

Here, there are QWeb expressions using fields that may not be loaded into the view. In particular, the last `t-if` expression uses the record's `state` field. To ensure this field is available in the form, it should be added just after the `<kanban>` element:

```
<kanban>
    <!-- Field list to ensure is loaded ... -->
    <field name="state" />
```

Let's break down the drop-down menu code and look at the key elements added:

- The ellipsis icon, in an HTML anchor (`<a>`) element, to present the menu button.

- A `<div class="dropdown-menu" role="menu">` element, containing the menu options.

- The **Edit** menu item, which is an `<a>` element with `type="edit"`.

- The **Delete** menu item, which is an `<a>` element with `type="delete"`.

- A separator line, using `<div role="separator" class="dropdown-divider"/>`.

- A color picker menu option added with a `<ul class="oe_kanban_colorpicker" />` element. The `data-field` attribute sets the field used to store the picked color. This capability will be implemented in the next section, so it won't work right now.

- A menu item equivalent to a button click, added with an `<a>` element, featuring the same `name` and `type` attributes used in regular buttons. This particular one uses `name="button_done" type="object"`.

ms, such as **Edit** and **Delete**, are made available only if certain conditions
'one with the t-if QWeb directive. This and other QWeb directives are
detail later in this chapter in the *Exploring the QWeb template language*

...get global variable represents a KanbanRecord() JavaScript object, which
, responsible for the rendering of the current kanban card. Two particularly useful
properties are widget.editable and widget.deletable, which allow us to check
whether the corresponding actions are available.

Menu items can be added with additional <a> elements in a similar way to the **Set as
Done** option.

Menu items can be shown or hidden using a JavaScript expression that can use record
field values. For example, the **Set as Done** option can be set to only be displayed if the
state field is not set to done.

The color picker menu option uses a special widget that uses a color model field to store
the picked color. While the color selector is available, we did not add the feature to set the
card yet. Let's do this in the next section.

Adding a kanban card color indicator

Kanban cards can be set with a user-selected color. This colors a bar on the left side of the
card and can be useful to easily locate items.

The color to apply is selected using a color picker option on the card's menu. This is added
with a <ul class="oe_kanban_colorpicker" data-field="color"/>
element, as shown in the previous section. The data-field attribute sets the field to
use, which in this case is color.

To add a kanban color card indicator, complete the following steps:

1. Add the color field in the library.checkout model by editing the models/
   library_checkout.py file as follows:

   ```
   # class Checkout(models.Model):
   # ...
       color = fields.Integer()
   ```

   This is a regular integer field. The color picker widget maps the selectable color
   to numbers.

2. Now, the color field can be used to set a dynamic CSS style on the kanban cards though QWeb. First, add it to the fields to load by adding the following code:

```
<kanban>
  <!-- Field list to ensure is loaded ... -->
  <field name="color" />
  <field name="state" />
```

3. Finally, edit the kanban card top `<div>` element to add the dynamic color style, as shown in the following code:

```
<t t-name="kanban-box">
  <div t-attf-class="oe_kanban_global_click
    {{!selection_mode ? 'oe_kanban_color_' +
      kanban_getcolor(record.color.raw_value) :
    ''}}">
```

The preceding code uses `t-attf-class` to dynamically calculate a CSS class to apply. A JavaScript expression is declared in a `{{  }}` block to be evaluated and return a style to use, which depends on the `color` field value. This completes the steps to add a kanban color card indicator.

A few more widgets are available for kanban cards. The next sections show how to use them, where we will add them to the card footer section.

Adding priority and activity widgets

The priority widget is displayed as a list of stars that can be clicked to select a priority level. This widget is a `<field>` element with `widget="priority"`. The priority field is a `Selection` field, declaring the several priority levels available.

The `library.checkout` model needs to be modified to add a priority field. To do this, complete the following steps:

1. Edit the `models/library_checkout.py` file as follows:

```
# class Checkout(models.Model):
# ...
    priority = fields.Selection(
        [("0", "High"),
```

```
            ("1", "Very High"),
            ("2", "Critical")],
        default="0")
```

The activity widget is an indicator for the item's scheduled activities and is presented for the activities field (`<field name="activity_ids">`) with `widget="kanban_activity"`.

2. Now, the corresponding `<field>` elements need to be added to the kanban template on the left side. So, insert the priority widget:

```
<div class="oe_kanban_footer_left">
    <!-- Left side footer... -->
    <field name="priority" widget="priority"/>
    <field name="activity_ids"
        widget="kanban_activity"/>
</div>
```

The kanban card now has the priority and activity widgets added to the left side of the footer. Next, we will add a few more widgets to the right footer.

Adding kanban state and user avatar widgets

The kanban state widget presents a traffic light color for the item. It is a `<field>` element using `widget="kanban_state_selection"`.

For related user records, a specific widget is available for this: `widget="many2one_avatar_user"`.

Examples of both of these will be added to the kanban card right footer, as shown in the following code:

```
<div class="oe_kanban_footer_right">
    <!-- Right side footer... -->
    <field name="kanban_state"
        widget="kanban_state_selection" />
    <field name="user_id"
        widget="many2one_avatar_user" />
</div>
```

The kanban state is added using a `<field>` element with the `kanban_state_selection` widget.

The user avatar image is added with the `user_id` field, using the `widget="many2one_avatar_user"` widget.

One more important topic is using actions on kanban cards, which we will discuss in the following section.

Using actions in kanban view elements

In QWeb templates, the `<a>` tag for links can have a `type` attribute. This sets the type of action the link will perform so that links can act just like buttons in regular forms. So, in addition to the `<button>` elements, the `<a>` tags can also be used to run Odoo actions.

As is the case in form views, the action type can be set to `action` or `object` and should be accompanied by a `name` attribute that identifies the specific action to execute. Additionally, the following action types are also available:

- `open`: This opens the corresponding form view.
- `edit`: This opens the corresponding form view directly in edit mode.
- `delete`: This deletes the record and removes the item from the kanban view.

This completes our walkthrough of designing kanban views. Kanban views use the QWeb template language, and a few examples were used here. The next section takes a deep dive into QWeb.

Exploring the QWeb template language

The QWeb parser looks for special directives in the templates and replaces them with dynamically generated HTML. These directives are XML element attributes and can be used in any valid tag or element – for example, `<div>`, `<span>`, or `<field>`.

Sometimes, a QWeb directive needs to be used, but we don't want to place it in any of the XML elements in the template. For these cases, the `<t>` special element can be used. It can have QWeb directives such as `t-if` or `t-foreach`, but it is silent, and it won't have any effect on the final XML/HTML produced.

The QWeb directives frequently use evaluated expressions to produce different effects that depend on record values. The language used to evaluate these expressions depends on the environment where the QWeb is being executed. There are two different QWeb implementations: **client-side JavaScript** and **server-side Python**. Reports and website pages use the server-side Python implementation of QWeb.

Kanban views use the client-side JavaScript implementation. This means that the QWeb expression used in kanban views should be written using the JavaScript syntax, not Python.

When displaying a kanban view, the internal steps are roughly as follows:

1. Get the XML for the templates to render.
2. Call the server `read()` method to get the data for the fields used in the templates.
3. Locate the `kanban-box` template and parse it using QWeb to output the final HTML fragments.
4. Inject the HTML in the browser display (the **Document Object Model (DOM)**).

This is not meant to be technically exact. It's just a mind map that can be useful to understand how things work in kanban views.

Next, we'll learn about QWeb expression evaluation and explore the available QWeb directives, using examples that will enhance the checkout kanban card.

Understanding the QWeb JavaScript evaluation context

Many of the QWeb directives use expressions that are evaluated to produce some result. When used on the client side (as is the case for Kanban views), these expressions are written in JavaScript. They're evaluated in a context that has a few useful variables available.

A `record` object is available, representing the current record, with the fields requested from the server. The field values can be accessed using either the `raw_value` or `value` attributes:

- `raw_value`: This is the value returned by the `read()` server method, so it's more suitable for use in condition expressions.
- `value`: This is formatted according to the user settings and is meant to be used for display in the user interface. This is typically useful for date, datetime, float, monetary, and relational fields.

The QWeb evaluation context can also reference the JavaScript web client instance. To make use of that, a good understanding of the web client architecture is needed. In this chapter, we won't be able to go into detail regarding this. However, for reference purposes, the following identifiers are available in QWeb expression evaluation:

- `widget`: This is a reference to the current `KanbanRecord()` widget object and is responsible for the rendering of the current record into a kanban card. It exposes some helper functions we can use.

- `record`: This is a shortcut for `widget.record` and provides access to the fields available, using dot notation.

- `read_only_mode`: This indicates whether the current view is in read mode (and not in edit mode). It's a shortcut for `widget.view.options.read_only_mode`.

- `instance`: This is a reference to the full web client instance.

Since QWeb templates are written in XML files, there are limitations on the usage of some characters not accepted by the XML format (such as the lower than sign (<)). When these characters are needed – for example, to describe JavaScript expressions – escaped alternatives need to be used.

These are the alternative symbols that are available for inequality operations:

- `&lt;` is for less than (<).

- `&lt;=` is for less than or equal to (<=).

- `&gt;` is for greater than (>).

- `&gt;=` is for greater than or equal to (>=).

The preceding comparison symbols are not specific to Odoo and are part of the XML format standards.

The previous symbols can be used in QWeb evaluated expressions, and they are often used to calculate text to render for the `t-out` directive, which we will describe in the following section.

Using t-out to render values

The `<field>` element is available to render field values, with the advantage of Odoo taking care of properly formatting the output for us. But this has the limitation of only displaying the field content.

However, the `t-out` directive can render the result of a code expression as an HTML-escaped value:

```
<t t-out="'Requested on ${record.request_date.value}'" />
```

The preceding code renders the result of a JavaScript expression. The `record` represents the record retrieved from the Odoo server and provides access to the fields. The `value` property returns properly formatted content, as returned by a `<field>` element. The `raw_value` property returns the unformatted native value.

> **Changes in Odoo 15**
>
> The `t-out` directive was introduced in **Odoo 15**, and it replaces the discontinued `t-esc` directive, used until **Odoo 14**. The `t-raw` directive was also discontinued. This was previously used to render the raw value without escaping any HTML, and using it carries security risks.

Using t-set to assign values to variables

For more complex logic, the result of an expression can be stored into a variable to use later in the template. This is to be done using the `t-set` directive for the variable name to be set, followed by the `t-value` directive with the expression to calculate the value to be assigned.

As an example, the following code renders the title in red if the request has no lines yet. It uses a `red_or_black` variable for the CSS class to use, shown as follows:

```
<t t-set="red_or_black"
    t-value="record.num_books == 0 ? '' :
    'oe_kanban_text_red'"
/>
<strong t-att-class="red_or_black">
  <field name="name" />
</strong>
```

The previous example has a code expression using the num_books field, so we need to ensure it is loaded by adding a `<field name="num_books" />` element inside the `<kanban>` top element.

Variables can also be assigned HTML content, as in the following example:

```
<t t-set="calendar_sign">
  <i class="fa fa-calendar" title="Calendar" />
</t>
<t t-out="calendar_sign" />
```

The previous code assigns the HTML inside to the `calendar_sign` variable and then renders it using the `t-out` directive.

Using t-attf- for string substitution of dynamic attributes

Our kanban card is using the `t-attf-` QWeb directive to dynamically set a class in the top `<div>` element so that the card color depends on the `color` field value. For this, the `t-attf-` QWeb directive was used.

The `t-attf-` directive dynamically generates tag attributes using string substitution. This allows for parts of larger strings to be generated dynamically, such as URLs or CSS class names.

The directive looks for expression blocks that will be evaluated and replaced by the results. These are delimited either by `{{` and `}}` or by `#{` and `}`. The content of the blocks can be any valid JavaScript expression and can use any of the variables available for QWeb expressions, such as `record` and `widget`.

In this case, the `kanban_color()` JavaScript function was used. This is specifically provided to map color index numbers into the CSS class color names.

As an elaborate example, this directive will be used to dynamically change the color of the request date to be in red letters if the priority is high. For this, the `<field name="request_date"/>` element in the kanban card should be replaced with the following:

```
<div t-attf-class="oe_kanban_text_{{
  record.priority.raw_value &lt; '2'
  ? 'black' : 'red' }}">
  <field name="request_date"/>
</div>
```

This results in either `class="oe_kanban_text_red"` or `class="oe_kanban_text_black"`, depending on the priority value. This is evaluated dynamically – that means that when the user clicks on the priority widget to change it, the date color will immediately change.

Using t-att- for expressions calculated by dynamic attributes

The `t-att-` QWeb directive can dynamically generate an attribute value from an expression evaluation.

For example, the formatting effect from the previous section that used the `t-attf-` attribute could alternatively be implemented using `t-att-`. The following code shows this alternative implementation:

```
<div t-att-class="record.priority.raw_value &lt; '2'
    ? 'oe_kanban_text_black' : 'oe_kanban_text_red'">
  <field name="request_date"/>
</div>
```

When the expression evaluates to a false-equivalent value, the attribute is not rendered at all. This is important for special HTML attributes such as the `checked` input field.

Using t-foreach for loops

Iterating through loops is useful to repeat a particular HTML block. For this, the `t-foreach` directive is used with an expression returning an iterable value. It needs to be accompanied by a `t-as` directive, which sets the variable name for the iteration value.

This could be used to present the book titles requested in the checkout. This requires a loop on the `lines_ids` field.

Note that the accessible values for the `line_ids` elements are database IDs and not record objects. This can be confirmed by adding the following code in the `<!-- Other content area -->` area:

```
<div>
  <t t-foreach="record.line_ids.raw_value" t-as="line">
    <t t-out="line" />;
  </t>
</div>
```

The t-foreach directive accepts a JavaScript expression evaluating to a collection to iterate. record.<field>.value returns a representation of a string for the field value, and record.<field>.raw_value returns the database-stored values. For a to-many field, this is a list of IDS:

- The t-as directive sets the variable name to be used to refer to each iteration value.
- The t-out directive evaluates the provided expression – in this case, just the line variable name – and renders safely escaped HTML.

Presenting the record IDs is not very interesting. However, we do have a JavaScript function available to retrieve an image for an ID: kanban_image().

To use this, first, the checkout lines need to support an image. For this, the models/library_checkout_line.py file should be edited to add a field for the book cover image:

```
book_cover = fields.Binary(related="book_id.image")
```

Now, this field can be used in the kanban card:

```
<div>
  <t t-foreach="record.line_ids.raw_value" t-as="line">
    <t t-out="line" />;
    <img t-att-src="kanban_image(
      'library.checkout.line', 'book_cover', line)"
      class="oe_avatar" height="60" alt="Cover" />
  </t>
</div>
```

The previous code renders an image for the book title in each checkout line.

If there are many lines, this might be too much content for the kanban card. Since the t-foreach object is a JavaScript expression, it can use additional syntax to limit the number of the allowed cover thumbnails. JavaScript arrays have a slice() method to extract a subset of elements.

This can be used to limit the number to the first five elements by using the following variation of the for loop:

```
<t t-foreach="record.line_ids.raw_value.slice(0, 5)"
t-as="line>
```

The `for` loops have a few helper variables available. These variables are automatically generated and are prefixed by the variable name defined in `t-as`.

If `t-as="rec"` is used, where `rec` is set as the variable name, the helper variables would be as follows:

- `rec_index`: This is the iteration index, starting from zero.
- `rec_size`: This is the number of elements of the collection.
- `rec_first`: This is true on the first element of the iteration.
- `rec_last`: This is true on the last element of the iteration.
- `rec_even`: This is true on even indexes.
- `rec_odd`: This is true on odd indexes.
- `rec_parity`: This is either `odd` or `even`, depending on the current index.
- `rec_all`: This represents the object being iterated over.
- `rec_value`: This holds the value when iterating through a `{key:value}` dictionary (`rec` holds the key name).

For example, when presenting a list of comma-separated values, we would like to avoid a trailing comma. Avoiding rendering it on the last iteration is easy with the help of the `_last` loop variable. Here is an example of this:

```
<t t-foreach="record.line_ids.raw_value" t-as="rec">
  <t t-out="rec" />
  <t t-if="!rec_last">;</t>
</t>
```

The `rec_last` variable is `true` on the last record. Negating it with `!rec_last` enables printing the comma on all iterations except the last one.

Using t-if to apply conditions

The `t-if` directive expects an expression to be evaluated in JavaScript when rendering kanban views on the client side. The tag and its content will be rendered only if the condition evaluates to `true`.

In our example, it was used in the checkout kanban view to have menu options available depending on some conditions.

To take another example, we can display the checkout number of books borrowed, but only if the view has any lines. This can be confirmed by adding the following code in the `<!-- Other content area   -->` area:

```
<div> t-if="record.num_books.raw_value &gt; 0">
    <field name="num_books"/> books
</div>>
```

Here, we used a `t-if="<expression>"` attribute to render an element and its content only when the expression used evaluated to `true`. Notice that the condition expression uses the `&gt;` symbol instead of `>` to represent the greater-than operation.

The `else if` and `else` conditions are also supported with the `t-elif` and `t-else` directives. Here is an example of their use:

```
<div t-if="record.num_books.raw_value == 0">
    No books!
</div>
<div t-elif="record.num_books.raw_value == 1">
    One book
</div>
<div t-else="">
    <field name="num_books"/> books
</div>
```

These conditions are useful to render particular elements on particular cases.

Another useful feature is the ability to decompose templates into smaller reusable snippets that can be included using `t-call`. The following section explains how this works.

Using t-call to call and reuse templates

Instead of repeating the same HTML blocks over and over again, building blocks can be used to compose more complex user interface views. QWeb templates can be used as reusable HTML snippets that are inserted into other templates.

Reusable templates are defined inside the `<templates>` tag and identified by a top element with `t-name` other than `kanban-box`. These other templates can then be included using the `t-call` directive. This is true for the templates declared in the same kanban view, somewhere else in the same addon module, or even in a different addon.

As an example, the book cover list could be isolated in a reusable snippet. For this, another template can be added in the `<templates>` element after the `<t t-name="kanban-box">` node, as shown in the following example:

```
<t t-name="book_covers">
  <div>
    <t t-foreach="record.line_ids.raw_value" t-as="line">
      <t t-out="line" />;
      <img t-att-src="kanban_image(
        'library.checkout.line', 'book_cover', line)"
        class="oe_avatar" height="60" alt="Cover" />
    </t>
  </div>
</t>
```

Then, the `t-call` directive can be used to call this template in the `kanban-box` main template:

```
<t t-call="book_covers" />
```

To call templates defined in other addon modules, the `module.name` full identifier must be used, in a similar way to what happens with other views. For instance, this snippet can be referred to in another module using the `library_checkout.book_covers` full identifier.

The called template runs in the same context as the caller, so any variable names available in the caller are also available when processing the called template.

A more elegant alternative is to pass arguments to the called template. This is done by setting variables inside the `t-call` tag. These will be evaluated and made available in the sub-template context only, and they won't exist in the caller context.

As an example, the `books_cover` template could have an argument to set the maximum number of covers to display instead of being hardcoded in the sub-template. First, the `book_covers` template should be edited to replace the fixed limit with a variable, such as `limit`:

```
<t t-name="book_covers">
  <div>
    <t t-foreach="record.line_ids.raw_value.slice(0,
```

```
    limit)"
      t-as="line">
      <t t-out="line" />;
      <img t-att-src="kanban_image(
        'library.checkout.line', 'book_cover', line)"
        class="oe_avatar" height="60" alt="Cover" />
    </t>
  </div>
</t>
```

Now, `t-call` must set this variable using a nested `t-set` directive, as shown in the following code:

```
<t t-call="book_covers">
  <t t-set="limit" t-value="3" />
</t>
```

The entire content inside the `t-call` element is also available to the sub-template through the 0 magic variable. Instead of argument variables, an HTML code fragment could be added inside the `t-call` element, and then it could be used in the called template with `<t t-out="0" />`. This is especially useful for building layouts and combining/nesting QWeb templates in a modular way.

Using dictionaries and lists to dynamically set attributes

We've gone through the most important QWeb directives, but there are a few more to be aware of. Now, we'll give a short explanation of them.

Here, the `t-att-NAME` and `t-attf-NAME` style dynamic tag attributes were introduced. Additionally, the fixed `t-att` directive can be used. It accepts either a key-value dictionary mapping or a pair (that is, a two-element list).

For example, consider the following mapping:

```
<p t-att="{'class': 'oe_bold', 'name': 'Hello'}" />
```

The preceding code produces this result:

```
<p class="oe_bold" name="Hello" />
```

`t-att` can also work with a list or with pairs of values. For example, consider the following:

```
<p t-att="['class', 'oe_bold']" />
```

The preceding code produces this result:

```
<p class="oe_bold" />
```

These special ways to assign attributes to elements can be useful in cases where there is some server-side processing, and a resulting dictionary or list can be used on a single `t-att` element to be applied on a template element.

This completes a reasonable overview of the QWeb template language with a special focus on kanban view applications, although the QWeb language is also used on the server side – for example, it can be used for reports and website pages.

Not surprisingly, QWeb templates provide an extension mechanism. We will explore this in the next section.

Extending kanban views

The templates used in kanban views and reports can be extended in the same way other view types are extended: that is, declare the element to match, possibly using an XPath expression, and use the position attribute to set what the extensions should do (for example, add the new elements after of before the matched element). These techniques are explained in detail in *Chapter 4, Extending Modules*.

In practice, kanban views and QWeb templates are more complex than the regular form view, and matching the elements to extend can be tricky.

Using `<field>` elements as selectors can be difficult. It is common for the same field name to be included more than once in a kanban view: at the beginning, in the field list to load, and then again inside the kanban box template. Since the selector will match the first field element found, the modification won't be applied inside the template, as intended.

For example, the `//t[@t-name='kanban-box']//field[@name='name']` XPath expression locates any child elements matching `<t t-name="kanban-box">`, and then it finds any further child elements matching `<field name="name">`.

Another challenge is the frequent use of HTML elements with no clear identifier, such as `<div>` or `<span>`. In these cases, XPath expressions with non-trivial matching conditions are needed. For example, the `//div/t/img` XPath expression matches a `<div><t><img>` nested sequence of elements.

The following is an example that extends the Contacts kanban view:

```xml
<record id="res_partner_kanban_inherit" model="ir.ui.view">
  <field name="name">Contact Kanban modification</field>
  <field name="model">res.partner</field>
  <field name="inherit_id"
    ref="base.res_partner_kanban_view" />
  <field name="arch" type="xml">
    <xpath
     expr="//t[@t-name=
       'kanban-box']//field[@name='display_name']"
     position="before">
     <span>Name:</span>
    </xpath>
  </field>
</record>
```

In the previous example, XPath looks for a `<field name="display_name">` element inside a `<t t-name="kanban-box">` element. This rules out the same field element outside of the `<templates>` section.

For complex XPath expressions, some command-line tools can be helpful to explore the correct syntax to use.

The xmllint command-line utility – from the libxml2-utils **Debian/Ubuntu** package – has an --xpath option to perform queries on XML files. Here is an example of using it:

```
$ xmllint --xpath "//templates//field[@name='name']" library_
checkout/views/checkout_view.xml
```

Another option is the xpath command, from the libxml-xpath-perl Debian/Ubuntu package. Here is an example of using it:

```
$ xpath -e "//templates//field[@name='name']" library_checkout/
views/checkout_view.xml
```

These tools can be useful to quickly try and test XPath expressions on an XML file.

Until now, you have seen how to create and extend kanban views. However, these can make use of additional JavaScript and CSS assets for effects. The next section explains how to add these components.

Adding CSS and JavaScript assets

Kanban views are mostly HTML and make significant use of CSS classes. In this chapter, some standard CSS classes were introduced in the code examples, but modules can also provide their own CSS.

The generally used convention is to have the asset files inside the `/static/src` subdirectory.

Module web assets are declared in a `manifest` file in the `assets` key. This file is set with a dictionary that maps the assets bundle to be extended and the list of assets to add to it.

This provides the tool to add web assets to an Odoo module, such as CSS and JavaScript assets. These web asset files provide a structured way to better provide user interface elements for a richer user experience.

They can then be used in the module's QWeb templates, as discussed throughout the previous sections in this chapter.

Here is an example for the `library_checkout` addon module. Edit the `__manifest__.py` file to add the following:

```
"assets": {
    "web.assets_backend": {
        "library_checkout/static/src/css/checkout.css",
        "library_checkout/static/src/js/checkout.js",
    }
}
```

The previous code adds a CSS and JavaScript file to the `web.assets_backend` assets bundle.

The main asset bundles available are as follows:

- `web.assets_common`: This contains the assets common to the web client, website, and also the point of sale.
- `web.assets_backend`: This contains the assets specific to the backend web client.
- `web.assets_frontend`: This contains the assets to be made available for the public website.

The `assets` manifest key was introduced in Odoo 15. For previous Odoo versions, assets were declared using XML template inheritance. We will explain this next.

Adding assets before Odoo 15

In previous Odoo versions, assets were added using an XML file that extends the asset bundle. The XML file doing this was usually placed inside the `views/` module subdirectory.

The following example adds a CSS and JavaScript file to the `library_checkout` module. Add the `views/assets.xml` file with the following code:

```xml
<odoo>
  <template id="assets_backend"
    inherit_id="web.assets_backend"
    name="Library Checkout Kanban Assets" >
    <xpath expr="." position="inside">
      <link rel="stylesheet"
        href="/library_checkout/static/src/css/checkout.css"
      />
      <script type="text/javascript"
        src="/library_checkout/static/src/js/checkout.js">
      </script>
    </xpath>
  </template>
</odoo>
```

As usual, this code should also be added to the `data` key in the `__manifest__.py` descriptor file.

Summary

This chapter covered kanban views and demonstrated how they can act as a powerful user interface tool. By now, you should understand kanban boards, and you are equipped with the techniques needed to design kanban views.

In this chapter, you also explored the QWeb template language that powers kanban views. With the help of the examples in this chapter, you should now know how to use its features.

As is expected for Odoo, kanban views and QWeb templates can also be extended by other modules in a similar way to other view types. Having read this chapter, you know additional techniques to use this functionality on Kanban views.

Finally, we also discussed the use of CSS and JavaScript assets in advanced kanban views. We also looked at how these assets must be provided by the modules and must be added to the backend assets. You now know how to implement this.

The next chapter will continue exploring QWeb, but this time, we'll focus on the server side and see how to design printable reports.

Further reading

The following reference materials complement the topics discussed in this chapter:

- The official Odoo documentation on QWeb: `https://www.odoo.com/documentation/15.0/developer/reference/frontend/qweb.html`

- The **Bootstrap** CSS documentation: `https://getbootstrap.com/docs/4.1/getting-started/introduction/`

- The **Font Awesome** icon index: `https://fontawesome.com/v4.7.0/icons/`

12
Creating Printable PDF Reports with Server-Side QWeb

While a regular view can provide valuable information to users, there will be cases where a printed output is needed. Maybe it is a PDF document to be sent to a customer, or a paper document that is needed to support a physical process. To address these cases, Odoo apps support printed business reports. These are generated using QWeb and then exported to PDF documents, which can then be printed, emailed, or simply stored.

Being QWeb-based means that the same skills that can be used for Kanban views and web pages can be reused to design reports. Beyond QWeb, specific mechanisms are used, such as report actions, paper formats, and the variables that are available for QWeb report rendering.

In this chapter, examples will be used to illustrate how to structure and add content to a report. The usual report structure has a **header**, **details**, and **footer sections**. The content that can be added includes **field data**, including specific widgets such as images. Also common in reports is the need to present totals. All of these will be explained in detail in this chapter.

The following topics will be covered in this chapter:

- Installing wkhtmltopdf
- Creating business reports
- Designing report content
- Creating custom reports

By the end of this chapter, you will be familiar with all the steps needed to create Odoo reports, from report action to specific techniques that can be used on QWeb templates.

Technical requirements

This chapter expands the existing `library_app` add-on module, based on the code first created in *Chapter 3*, *Your First Odoo Application*. This chapter's code can be found in this book's GitHub repository at `https://github.com/PacktPublishing/Odoo-15-Development-Essentials` in the `ch12/` subdirectory.

Installing wkhtmltopdf

Odoo reports are just HTML pages that are then converted into PDF files. For this conversion, the `wkhtmltopdf` command-line tool is used. Its name stands for **Webkit HTML to PDF**.

For reports to be generated correctly, the recommended version of the `wkhtmltopdf` utility needs to be installed. Some versions of the `wkhtmltopdf` library are known to have issues, such as not printing page headers and footers, so we need to be picky about the version we use.

Since Odoo 10, version 0.12.5 is the officially recommended one. The most up-to-date Odoo information about `wkhtmltopdf` can be found at `https://github.com/odoo/odoo/wiki/Wkhtmltopdf`.

The packaged version provided by Debian or Ubuntu may not be appropriate. So, the recommendation is to directly download and install the correct package. The download links can be found at `https://github.com/wkhtmltopdf/wkhtmltopdf/releases/tag/0.12.5`.

To install the correct version of `wkhtmltopdf`, follow these steps:

1. First, make sure that there isn't an incorrect version already installed on the system by inputting the following command:

    ```
    $ wkhtmltopdf --version
    ```

2. If the preceding command reports a version other than the recommended one, it should be uninstalled. To do so, on a Debian/Ubuntu system, input the following command:

    ```
    $ sudo apt-get remove --purge wkhtmltopdf
    ```

3. Next, you need to download the appropriate package for your system and install it. Check the release page for the correct download link. At the time of the Odoo 15 release, Ubuntu 20.04 LTS *Focal Fossa* is the latest long-term support version. For a 64-bit architecture, install the `wkhtmltox_0.12.5-1.focal_amd64.deb` package. The download command to use in this case is as follows:

    ```
    $ wget "https://github.com/wkhtmltopdf/wkhtmltopdf/
    releases/download/0.12.5/wkhtmltox_0.12.5-1.focal_amd64.
    deb" -O /tmp/wkhtml.deb
    ```

4. Next, install the downloaded package with the following command:

    ```
    $ sudo dpkg -i /tmp/wkhtml.deb
    ```

    This may display an error because of missing dependencies. In that case, the following command can be used to fix this:

    ```
    $ sudo apt-get -f install
    ```

5. Finally, verify that the `wkhtmltopdf` library is correctly installed with the intended version number with the following command:

    ```
    $ wkhtmltopdf --version
    wkhtmltopdf 0.12.5 (with patched qt)
    ```

With this, you have successfully installed the correct version of `wkhtmltopdf` and now the Odoo server log won't display the **You need Wkhtmltopdf to print a pdf version of the report** information message during the startup sequence.

Now that you know how to download and install a suitable version of the `wkhtmltopdf` tool, let's look at how to create business reports.

Creating business reports

It would be helpful for the Library app to print out a report containing the book catalog. This report should list the book titles, along with details such as **publisher**, **publishing date**, and **authors**.

We will implement this throughout this chapter, and in the process showcase the several techniques involved in implementing Odoo reports. The report will be added to the existing `library_app` module.

The convention is to have report files in a `/reports` subdirectory, so a `reports/library_book_report.xml` data file will be added. As usual, when adding data files, remember to also declare them in the `data` key of the `__manifest__.py` file.

To be able to run a report, the first thing we must add is the report action.

Adding the report action

The **report action** triggers the execution of a report, similarly to how window actions trigger web client view presentations. A report action is a record in the `ir.actions.report` XML model, and it can be inspected by using the **Settings | Technical | Actions | Reports** menu option.

> **Changes in Odoo 14**
>
> Odoo 14 deprecated the `<report>` shortcut tag for report actions. A `<record model=""ir.actions.report">` element should be used instead.

To add the report action and trigger the execution of the report, edit the `reports/library_book_report.xml` file, as follows:

```
<odoo>
  <record id="action_library_book_report"
          model="ir.actions.report">
    <field name="name">Book Catalog</field>
    <field name="model">library.book</field>
    <field name="report_type">qweb-pdf</field>
    <field name="report_name">
      library_app.book_catalog</field>
    <field name="binding_model_id"
      ref="model_library_book" />
```

```
        <field name="binding_type">report</field>
    </record>
</odoo>
```

This report action makes this report available at the top of the **Library Books** view, on the **Print** button, next to the **Action** button:

Figure 12.1 – The Print context button

This marks the first step of having a report available to users.

The essential fields that were used in the previous code are as follows:

- `name` is the report action's title.

- `model` is the technical name of the report's base model.

- `report_type` is the type of document to generate. The options are `qweb-pdf`, `qweb-html`, or `qweb-text`.

- `report_name` is the XML ID of the QWeb template to be used to generate the report's content. Unlike other identifier references, it must be a complete reference that includes the module name; that is, `<module_name>.<identifier_name>`.

> **Tip**
> While working on report development, setting `report_type` to `qweb-html` allows you to inspect the HTML result that's generated by the QWeb template, and it also makes it easier to troubleshoot issues. When you've done this, it can be changed back to `qweb-pdf`.

The following fields are not required to add the report action, but are needed for the report to be presented in the **Print** menu, next to the **Action** menu:

- `binding_model_id` is a many-to-one field for identifying the model where the report print option should be available.
- `binding_type` should be set to `report`.

The other optional fields are as follows:

- `print_report_name` is a Python expression that's used to provide the report's title and filename. The `object` variable is available and represents the current record.
- `attachment` is a Python expression where you have to generate the attachment filename. The `object` variable is available and represents the current record. When set, the generated report is stored as an attachment.
- `attachment_use`, when set to `True`, means that new report generations reopen the stored original report instead of regenerating it.
- `paperformat_id` is a many-to-one field for the paper format to use. Paper formats include the page size and the portrait or landscape orientation.
- `groups_id` is a many-to-many field with the security groups that can use the report.
- `multi`, when set to `True`, means that the report is not available in the form view.

These actions won't work right now since the referenced QWeb template is missing. We'll deal with this in the following sections.

Using a QWeb report template for per-record documents

Odoo reports are generated using QWeb templates. QWeb generates HTML that can then be converted into a PDF document. QWeb directives and flow controls can be used as usual, but specific containers should be used to ensure proper page formatting.

The following example provides a minimum viable template for a QWeb report. Add the following code to the `reports/library_book_report.xml` file, just after the report action element that we added in the previous section:

```
<template id="book_catalog">
  <t t-call="web.html_container">
```

```
<t t-call="web.external_layout">

    <t t-foreach="docs" t-as="o">
        <div class="page">
            <!-- Report content -->
        </div>
    </t>


    </t>
    </t>
</template>
```

The most important elements here are the t-call directives that are using standard report structures. The web.html_container template does the basic setup to support an HTML document. The web.external_layout template handles the report header and footer using the corresponding company setup. The web.internal_layout template can be used as an alternative, featuring only a basic header; it's better suited for internal use reports.

> **Changed Since Odoo 11**
>
> In Odoo 11, the report layouts moved from the report module to the web module. Previous Odoo versions used report.external_layout or report.internal_layout references. Starting with Odoo 11, these need to be changed to web.<...> references.

The docs variable represents the base record set to generate the report. The report will typically use a t-foreach QWeb directive to iterate through each record. The previous report template generates a report header and footer for each record.

Notice that, since reports are just QWeb templates, inheritance can be applied, just like in the other views. QWeb templates that are used in reports can be extended using regular template inheritance – that is, using *XPath* expressions – as we will discuss next.

Using a QWeb report template for record listings

In the case of the book catalog, there is a single report document, with a header and a footer, containing a line or section for each record.

So, the report template needs to be adjusted for this, as shown in the following code:

```
<template id="book_catalog">
  <t t-call="web.html_container">
    <t t-call="web.external_layout">

      <div class="page">
        <!-- Report header content -->
        <t t-foreach="docs" t-as="o">
          <!-- Report row content -->
        </t>
        <!-- Report footer content -->
      </div> <!-- page -->

    </t>
  </t>
</template>
```

In the previous code, the `<div class="page">` element was moved before `<t t-foreach="docs">` so that a single report header and footer are printed, and the individual records will print additional content inside the same document.

Now that we have the basic report template, we can customize the report layout, which we will do next.

Choosing a report layout

The report layout can be customized by users. This will be applied to the report, so long as it uses `external_layout`.

The options for this are available from the **Settings | General Settings** menu, in the **Companies | Document Layout** section, as shown in the following screenshot:

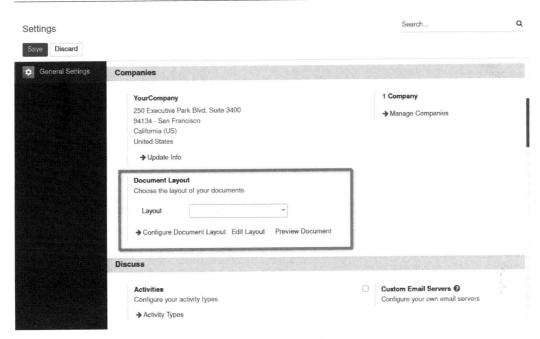

Figure 12.2 – Document layout configuration options

Here, the **Configure Document Layout** button opens a report template configurator, provides a few layout options, and allows you to make selections regarding the company logo, colors, or text font.

The selected layout can be set on the settings **Layout** field, and **Edit Layout** opens the corresponding view form, allowing you to directly customize the layout's QWeb XML definition.

Now that you know how to set up the general report layout, let's look at how to work with page formats.

Setting a paper format

Odoo proposes a few page formats out of the box, including European *A4* and *US Letter*. Additional page formats can be added, including those for specific page orientations.

Paper formats are stored in the `report.paperformat` model. The existing formats can be inspected using the **Settings | Technical | Reporting | Paper Format** menu option.

For the book catalog report, a **landscape orientation** will be used, and a new page format will be added for this.

To add the **A4 Landscape** paper format, add the following data record at the beginning of the `reports/library_book_report.xml` file:

```xml
<record id="paperformat_euro_landscape" model="report.
paperformat">
    <field name="name">A4 Landscape</field>
    <field name="format">A4</field>
    <field name="orientation">Landscape</field>
    <field name="margin_top">40</field>
    <field name="margin_bottom">32</field>
    <field name="margin_left">7</field>
    <field name="margin_right">7</field>
    <field name="header_line" eval="False" />
    <field name="header_spacing">35</field>
    <field name="dpi">90</field>
</record>
```

This is a copy of the European A4 format, defined by the `base` module, in the `data/report_paperformat_data.xml` file, with the orientation changed from portrait to landscape.

This paper format can now be used for reports. The default paper format is defined in the company setup, but reports can set specific paper formats to be used. This can be done using the `paperfomat_id` field in the report action.

The report action can be edited to add this field:

```xml
<record id="action_library_book_report"
        model="ir.actions.report">
    <field name="name">Book Catalog</field>
    <field name="model">library.book</field>
    <field name="report_type">qweb-pdf</field>
    <field name="report_name">
      library_app.book_catalog</field>
    <field name="paperformat_id"
      ref="paperformat_euro_landscape" />
</record>
```

With the basic skeleton for the report in place, it is time to start designing the report content.

Designing report content

The report content is written in HTML and makes use of Bootstrap 4 to help design the report's layout. Bootstrap is widely used in web development.

> **Tip**
> A complete reference can be found at `http://getbootstrap.com`.

Unlike Kanban views, the report QWeb templates are rendered on the server side and use the Python QWeb implementation. So, there are some differences to be aware of, compared to the JavaScript QWeb implementation. QWeb expressions are evaluated using Python syntax, not JavaScript.

Understanding the report rendering context

The server-side context where expressions are evaluated is also different from the client-side context that's used for Kanban views. On a report template, the following variables are available:

- `docs` is an iterable collection with the records to render the report for.
- `doc_ids` is a list of the IDs of the records to render the report for.
- `doc_model` identifies the model of the records; for example, `library.book`.
- `user` is the record for the user running the report.
- `res_company` is the record for the current user's company.
- `website` is the record for the current website, if any. This could be `None`.
- `web_base_url` is the base address of the Odoo server.
- `time` is a reference to Python's `time` library.
- `context_timestamp` is a function that takes a datetime object in UTC and converts it into the user's time zone.
- These values and Python libraries can be used in code expressions inside the template. For example, to print out the current user, we could use the following command:

```
<span t-out="user.name" />
```

The `docs` value is particularly important since it contains the data to be used for the report.

Now that you know how to access the data for the report, the next step is to add the report content.

Adding the report content

With the basic QWeb template, including its header, details, and footer, in place, you can now add content to it.

Here is the XML you must use to render the report header. It should be placed inside the `<div class="page">` node and before the `<t t-foreach=...>` element:

```xml
<div class="page">

    <!-- Report header content -->
    <div class="container">
        <div class="row bg-primary">
            <div class="col-3">Title</div>
            <div class="col-2">Publisher</div>
            <div class="col-2">Date</div>
            <div class="col-3">Publisher Address</div>
            <div class="col-2">Authors</div>
        </div>

        <t t-foreach="docs" t-as="o">
            <div class="row">
                <!-- Report row content -->
            </div>
        </t>

        <!-- Report footer content -->

    </div> <!-- container -->
</div> <!-- page -->
```

This content layout uses the Bootstrap 4 grid system, which was added with the `<div class="container">` element. Bootstrap has a grid layout with 12 available columns. More details on Bootstrap can be found at `https://getbootstrap.com/docs/4.1/layout/grid`.

> **Changes in Odoo 12**
>
> Odoo used Bootstrap 3 until Odoo 11 and started using Boc
> Odoo 12. Bootstrap 4 is not backward compatible with Boot
> on the changes from Bootstrap 3 to Bootstrap 4, see the Odc
> this topic: `https://github.com/odoo/odoo/wil`
> `tricks:-BS3-to-BS4.`

The previous code adds a header row with column titles. After t
loop to iterate through each record and render a row for each.

Next, the focus will be on rendering the row for each record – in
book in the catalog.

Rows are added using a `<div class="row">` element. A row contains cells, and each
cell can span several columns so that the row takes up 12 columns. Each cell is added
using a `<div class="col-N">` element, where N is the number of columns it spans.
For example, `<div class="col-3">Title</div>` is a cell spanning three columns.

The QWeb template rendering is done on the server side, and record set objects are used.
So, **dot notation** can be used to access fields from related data records. For example,
`o.name` gets the value of the `name` field from the `o` record. And it is easy to follow
relational fields to access their data. For example, `o.publisher_id.email` gets the
`email` field from the partner record referenced by the `publisher_id` field. Notice that
this is not possible in client-side rendered QWeb views, such as web client Kanban views.

To add the content for each record row, add the following XML inside the `<div
class="row">` element:

```xml
<!-- Report Row Content -->
<div class="row">
  <div class="col-3">
    <h4><span t-field="o.name" /></h4>
  </div>
  <div class="col-2">
    <span t-field="o.publisher_id" />
  </div>
  <div class="col-2">
    <span t-field="o.date_published"
          t-options="{'widget': 'date'}" />
  </div>
  <div class="col-3">
```

```
      t-field="o.publisher_id"
        t-options='{
          "widget": "contact",
          "fields": ["address", "email", "phone",
            "website"], "no_marker": true}' />
    </div>
    <div class="col-2">
      <!-- Render Authors -->
    </div>
  </div>
```

In the previous code, the t-field attributes are being used to render field data.

The t-options attribute can also be used to provide additional options for the field rendering, such as the widget to use.

Let's have a closer look at the field widgets and their options.

Using field widgets

In the template, field values are rendered using the t-field attribute. This can be complemented with the t-options attribute so that you can use a specific widget to render the field content.

t-options is set with a dictionary-like data structure. The widget key can be used to represent the field data.

In the previous example code, "widget": "contact" is used to present an address. It was used to render the publishing company's address, o.publisher_id. The no_marker="true" option was used to disable some pictograms and the contact widget, which are displayed by default.

> **Changes in Odoo 11**
>
> The t-options attribute was introduced in Odoo 11, replacing the
> t-field-options attribute that was used in previous Odoo versions.

For example, assuming that doc represents a particular record, rendering a date field value looks like this:

```
<span t-field="doc.date_published" t-options="{'widget':
'date'}" />
```

The reference documentation for the supported widgets and options can be found at
`https://www.odoo.com/documentation/15.0/developer/reference/`
`frontend/javascript_reference.html#field-widgets`.

> **Tip**
> Documentation is not always up to date, and additional details may be found
> regarding the corresponding source code. The place to look is `https://`
> `github.com/odoo/odoo/blob/15.0/odoo/addons/base/`
> `models/ir_qweb_fields.py`. Look for classes that inherit from
> `ir.qweb.field`. The `get_available_options()` methods give
> insight into the supported options.

With that, we've added the QWeb XML code to render the row for each book. However,
the `authors` column is missing. The next section will add the author names, along with
their images, illustrating how to add image content to a report.

Rendering images

The last column of the report features should present the list of authors, along with
their avatars. The avatar image can be presented using the `t-field` attribute and the
`image` widget.

In the last column, add the following code:

```
<!-- Render authors -->
<ul class="list-unstyled">
  <t t-foreach="o.author_ids" t-as="author">
    <span t-field="author.image_128"
      t-options="{'widget': 'image',
        'style': 'max-width: 32px'}" />
    <span t-field="author.name" />
  </t>
</ul>
```

In the previous code, there is a loop on the values to the `author_ids` many-to-many
field. For each author, you must render the image in the `image_128` partner field using
the `image` widget.

With that, you have added the header and details rows. The next few sections will work on
the report footer, which is presented at the end of the report, and in the process introduce
report totals.

Calculating totals

A common need in reports is to provide **totals**. In some cases, the model has fields computing these, and the report just needs to use them. In other cases, the totals might have to be computed by the report.

As an example, the Book Catalog report will present the total number of books and authors in a final row.

For this, a last row should be added after the closing tag of the `<t t-foreach="docs">` element, to present the report totals.

To do so, add the footer content with the following XML:

```
<!-- Report footer content -->
<div class="row">
  <div class="col-3">
    <t t-out="len(docs)" /> Books
  </div>
  <div class="col-7" />
  <div class="col-2">
    <t t-out="len(docs.mapped('author_ids'))" /> Authors
  <div>
</div>
```

The `len()` Python function is used to count the number of elements in a collection. Similarly, totals can also be computed using `sum()` over a list of values. For example, the following list comprehension computes a total amount:

```
<t t-out="sum([x.amount for x in docs])" />
```

This list comprehension is a loop on the `docs` variable and returns a list of values stating the `amount` value of each record.

Your last low with the report's total is created. However, there are cases where grand totals are not enough, and running totals are needed. The next section will show you how to accumulate the values for these running totals.

Calculating running totals

In some cases, the report needs to perform computations throughout its iterations – for example, to keep a **running total**, with the total sum up to the current record. This kind of logic can be implemented in QWeb using a variable to accumulate values on each record iteration.

To illustrate this, you can compute the accumulated number of authors. Start by initializing the variable, just before the t-foreach loop on the docs record set, using the following code:

```
<!-- Running total: initialize variable -->
<t t-set="missing_count" t-value="0" />
```

Then, inside the loop, add the record's number of authors to the variable. Do this right after presenting the list of authors, and also print out the current total on every line:

```
<!-- Running total: increment and present -->
<t t-set="missing_count"
    t-value=" missing_count + int(not o.publisher_id)" />
<p>(accum. <t t-out="missing_count"/>)</p>
```

The previous code can be added to any of the report cells – for example, in the *Publisher* column cell.

With that, you have added all the report content, including report totals. Another feature that you can use on reports is **multilingual support**. This is supported in Odoo and the next section explains how to use it.

Enabling language translation in reports

The Odoo user interface uses the language selected by the current user. In some cases, a report might need to change this to a particular language. For example, a document might be better printed using the customer language, rather than the user's selected language.

In QWeb, the t-call directive, which is used to render a template, can be followed by the t-lang attribute, with an expression evaluation of the language to use. It should evaluate to a language code, such as es or en_US, and is usually an expression with the field where the language to use can be found.

To showcase this, the *Library* app will include a version of the *Book Catalog* report using the library's base language, not the user's language. The library language will be the one that's set on the company partner record.

For this, the existing `book_catalog` template can be reused. It should be called from another template, and that call can set the language to use for the rendering process.

In the `reports/library_book_report.xml` file, add the following two record elements:

```
<record id="action_library_book_report_native"
        model="ir.actions.report">
  <field name="name">Native Language Book Catalog</field>
  <field name="model">library.book</field>
  <field name="report_type">qweb-pdf</field>
  <field name="report_name">
    library_app.book_catalog_native</field>
  <field name="binding_model_id"
    ref="model_library_book" />
  <field name="binding_type">report</field>
  <field name="paperformat_id"
    ref="paperformat_euro_landscape" />
</record>

<template id="book_catalog_native">
  <t t-call="library_app.book_catalog"
    t-lang="res_company.parter_id.lang" />
</template>
```

The first record adds the *Native Language Book Catalog* report action, which uses the `library_app.book_catalog_native` template to render the report.

The second record adds the report template. It is a single QWeb element that uses `t-call` to render the `book_catalog` template and `t-lang` to set the language to be used.

The expression that's used to find the language value is `res_company.parter_id.lang`. The `res_company` variable is one of the many that's available in any report and is the active company. Companies have a related partner record, `partner_id`, and partners have a field to store the language in, called `lang`.

The reports being worked on are based on a record set, such as `Books`. But there are cases where the data to be used needs specific computation. The next section describes options to handle these cases.

After completing this step, the final book catalog report example should look as follows:

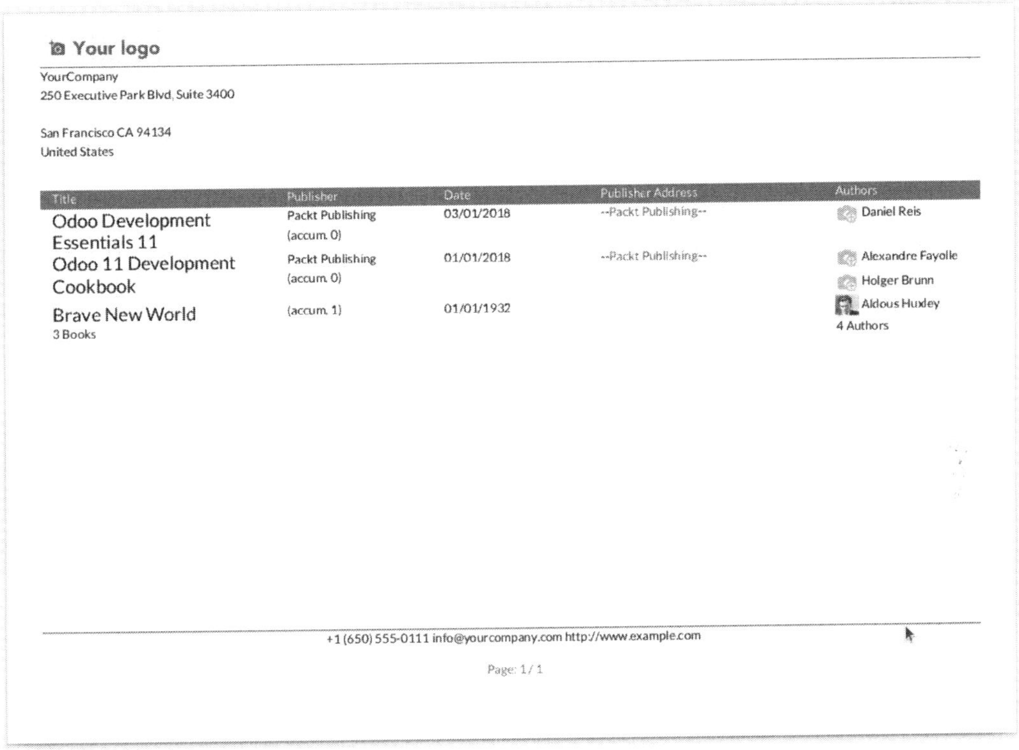

Figure 12.3 – The final book catalog report

The essential elements for building printable reports in Odoo were covered throughout this section. Going further, advanced reports can use specific logic to build the data to be used in the report. The next section discusses how to do this.

Creating custom reports

By default, a report is rendered for the selected records and is available in the rendering context through the `docs` variable. In some cases, it is useful to prepare arbitrary data structures to be used in the report. This is possible using **custom reports**.

A custom report can add whatever data that's needed to the report rendering context. This is done using an abstract model with a specific name, following the naming convention of `report.<module>.<report-name>`.

This model should implement a `_get_report_values()` method, which returns a dictionary with the variables to add to the rendering context.

As an example, a *Books by Publisher* custom report will be added to the *Library* app. It will show the books that have been published by each publisher. The following screenshot shows an example of the report's output:

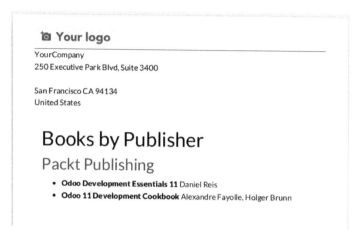

Figure 12.4 – Example of the Books by Publisher custom report

The report will be available in the *Contacts* list. One or more partners can be selected, and the report will present the titles published by each, if any. It can also be run from the publisher's form, as shown in the following screenshot:

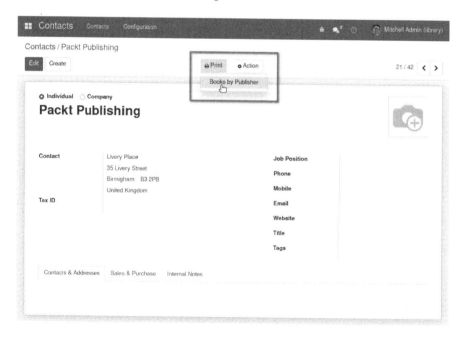

Figure 12.5 – Print menu option for the Books by Publisher report

This report implementation can be split into two steps. The first is the business logic for preparing the data to be used by the report, while the second is the QWeb template for the report layout.

The next section explains how to prepare the report data.

Preparing custom report data

A custom report can use data that's been prepared by specific business logic, instead of simply using the record set that's been selected by the user.

This can be done using an abstract model while following a specific name convention, that implements a _get_report_values() method, to return a dictionary with the variables to be used by the report template.

To implement this as a custom report, add the reports/library_publisher_report.py file with the following code:

```python
from odoo import api, models


class PublisherReport(models.AbstractModel):
    _name = "report.library_app.publisher_report"

    @api.model
    def _get_report_values(self, docids, data=None):
        domain = [("publisher_id", "in", docids)]
        books = self.env["library.book"].search(domain)
        publishers = books.mapped("publisher_id")
        publisher_books = [
            (pub,
                books.filtered(lambda book:
                    book.publisher_id == pub))
            for pub in publishers
        ]
        docargs = {
            "publisher_books": publisher_books,
        }
        return docargs
```

For this file to be loaded by the module, it is also necessary to do the following:

- Add the reports/__init__.py file with a from . import library_ publisher_report line.

- Add a from . import reports line to the top of the __init__.py file.

The model is an AbstractModel, meaning that it has no database representation and holds no data. The data to be used for rendering will be computed by specific business logic.

The report template identifier name will be publisher_report, so the model name should be report.library_app.publisher_report.

The model has an @api.model decorated method named _get_report_values. The docids argument is a list of the numeric IDs selected to print the report. The base model to run the report is res.partner, so these will be partner IDs.

The method uses specific business logic to find the books from the selected publishers and groups them by publisher. The result is in the publisher_books variable, which is a list of pairs, along with the publisher records and a record set of book records; that is, [(res.partner(1), library.book(1, 2, 3)].

_get_report_values returns a dictionary with a publisher_books key that returns this data structure. This key will be available as a variable in the report template and can be iterated in a loop.

Now that the custom report data has been prepared, the next step is to add the QWeb report template.

Adding the report template

The next step is to create the QWeb template that's used to render the report. This template is similar to what is done for regular reports. An XML file is needed, along with the report action and the report QWeb template. The only difference is that, instead of the docs context variable, this template will have context variables available as whatever key/ values are returned by the _get_report_values method.

To implement the report action and template, add the reports/library_ publisher_report.xml file with the following code:

```
<odoo>

    <record id="action_publisher_report" model=
      "ir.actions.report">
```

```
    <field name="name">Books by Publisher</field>
    <field name="model">res.partner</field>
    <field name="report_type">qweb-pdf</field>
    <field name="report_name">
      library_app.publisher_report</field>
    <field name="binding_model_id"
      ref="base.model_res_partner" />
    <field name="binding_type">report</field>
  </record>

  <template id="publisher_report">
    <t t-call="web.html_container">
      <t t-call="web.external_layout">
        <div class="page">
          <div class="container">

            <h1>Books by Publisher</h1>
            <t t-out="res_company" />
            <t t-foreach="publisher_books" t-as="group">
              <h2 t-field="group[0].name" />
              <ul>
                <t t-foreach="group[1]" t-as="book">
                  <li>
                    <b><span t-field="book.name" /></b>
                    <span t-field="book.author_ids" />
                  </li>
                </t>
              </ul>
            </t>
```

```
                    </div>
                </div>
            </t>
        </t>
    </template>

</odoo>
```

The previous XML includes two records – one for adding the *Books by Publisher* report action and another for adding the `publisher_report` report template.

When running this report, the report engine will try finding a `report.library_app.publisher_report` model. If it exists, as is the case here, the `_get_report_values()` method is used to add variables to the rendering context.

The QWeb template can then use the `publisher_books` variable to access the added data. It is a list containing a **tuple** for each publisher. The first tuple element, `group[0]`, is the publisher record that's used on the group header, while the second tuple element, `group[1]`, is the record set containing the published books, presented using a second for loop.

Remember to also reference this XML file in the `__manifest__.py` module. Having done this, once the `library_app` module has been upgraded and the Odoo web browser page has been reloaded, you will have the *Books by Publisher* report available in the `Print` context menu, when records are selected in the *Contacts* list.

Summary

In this chapter, you learned about the essential techniques to create and add custom Odoo reports. Installing the recommended version of the `wkhtmltopdf` utility is important to ensure the reports are rendered correctly. You learned that reports are run through report actions, which provide the basic information needed to render them. These may include the paper format to be used and you now know how to do so.

The next thing you learned about is report design, which can be implemented with QWeb templates. Knowledge of QWeb, HTML, and Bootstrap is needed for this, as you have been made aware of. In some cases, reports need specific business logic to prepare the data to use. For this, you learned how to create custom report models, along with the techniques to use them.

Printable reports can be important parts of a business application, as they are often needed as a simple way to send information to external parties or to support physical processes in the warehouse or shop floor. This chapter provided you with the tools and techniques to implement this kind of requirement. Now, you can ensure that your business application doesn't fall short of your user's needs.

In the next chapter, we will continue to use QWeb, this time to build website pages. Web controllers will also be explained, which allow richer features to be used on Odoo web pages.

Further reading

This additional reference material complements the topics described in this chapter.

Relevant Odoo official documentation:

- QWeb Reports: `https://www.odoo.com/documentation/15.0/developer/reference/backend/reports.html`

- QWeb Templates: `https://www.odoo.com/documentation/15.0/developer/reference/frontend/qweb.html`

- Bootstrap 4 official documentation: `https://getbootstrap.com/docs/4.1`

Other relevant resources:

- The Odoo Community Association hosts a project dedicated to the enhanced report feature at `https://github.com/OCA/reporting-engine`.

- Bootstrap additional learning resources from Packt Publishing can be found at `https://www.packtpub.com/tech/bootstrap`.

13
Creating Web and Portal Frontend Features

Odoo is a business application framework, providing all the tools necessary to quickly build apps. A uniform web client provides the business user interface. But organizations are not isolated from the world. Being able to also interact with external users is needed to support efficient processes. For this, Odoo supports a web interface.

The internal user web client is sometimes referred to as the **backend**, and the external user interface as the **frontend**. The frontend provides **portal features**, accessible to portal user logins. It also provides public features, accessible without the need for a login, referred as **website features**.

The portal complements backend apps, providing self-service features to external users, such as viewing and paying for their orders, or submitting a support ticket.

The website features are built on top of the Odoo **Content Management System (CMS)**, which allows you to build web pages, including easy-to-use *drag and drop* web page design tools. Additional website features are provided as **modules**, such as blogs, online jobs, or e-commerce.

In this chapter, you will learn how to develop frontend add-on modules, leveraging the website features provided by Odoo, while discussing the following topics:

- Introducing the library portal learning project
- Creating a frontend web page
- Learning about web controllers
- Adding portal features

By the end of this chapter, you will have learned how to use web controllers and QWeb templates to create dynamic web pages, integrated into the Odoo frontend. Additionally, you will learn how to leverage the Odoo portal module, adding your features to it.

Technical requirements

The work in this chapter requires the `library_checkout` add-on module, last edited in *Chapter 11, Kanban Views and Client-Side QWeb*. The add-on module and its dependencies code can be found in the Git repository at `https://github.com/PacktPublishing/Odoo-15-Development-Essentials`. The code in this chapter can be found in the same repository.

Introducing the library portal learning project

To learn about Odoo web page development, a new project will be used. The library app can use self-service features for library members. Members can be assigned a user login to have access to their book checkout requests.

The `library_portal` add-on module will be created for these portal self-service features.

The first file to add is the manifest, `library_portal/__manifest__.py`, which you can create with the following code:

```
{
    "name": "Library Portal",
    "description": "Portal for library members",
    "author": "Daniel Reis",
    "license": "AGPL-3",
    "depends": [
        "library_checkout", "portal"
    ],
```

```
    "data": [
        "security/library_security.xml",
        "security/ir.model.access.csv",
        "views/checkout_portal_templates.xml",
    ],
}
```

The module depends on `library_checkout` to extend its features. It also depends on the `portal` module, providing the foundation for portal features. The `website` module provides CMS features, and can also be used for web page development. However, the `portal` modules can provide essential frontend features without the need to have the *Website* app installed.

The `data` key lists three XML files to be used. The first two are security related, and give portal users the access needed to be able to view the checkout requests. The last XML file will have the QWeb templates for the portal user interface.

An empty `library_portal/__init__.py` file is also needed for the module directory to be a valid Python module, as required by the Odoo framework.

Now that the new module has the essential files, the next step is to add the basic components needed to have a functioning web page.

Creating a frontend web page

To get started with the basics of Odoo web development, a simple web page will be created. To do this, two components are needed: a **web controller**, triggered when a particular URL is accessed, and a **QWeb template**, to generate the HTML to be presented by that URL.

The web page used to showcase this is a book catalog, a simple list of the books in the library. The book catalog page will be accessible at `http://localhost:8069/library/catalog`.

The following screenshot provides an example of what should be seen:

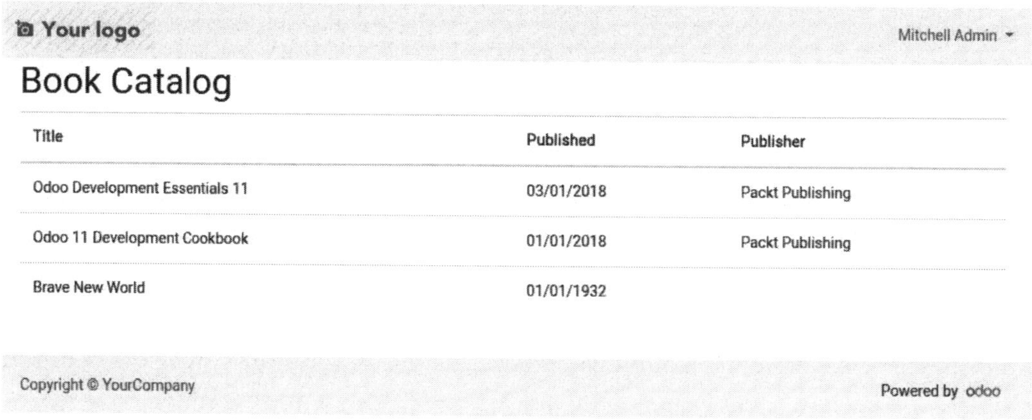
Your logo
Mitchell Admin
Book Catalog
Title
Published
Publisher
Odoo Development Essentials 11
03/01/2018
Packt Publishing
Odoo 11 Development Cookbook
01/01/2018
Packt Publishing
Brave New World
01/01/1932
Copyright © YourCompany
Powered by odoo

Figure 13.1 – Book catalog frontend web page

The first step is to add the web controller, which we will do in the next section.

Adding a web controller

Web controllers are Python objects, used to implement web features. They can link URL paths to an object method, so that when that URL is accessed, the method is executed.

For example, for the `http://localhost:8069/library/catalog` URL, the accessed path is `/library/catalog`.

A URL path, sometimes also called an **endpoint**, can be assigned to a server function. This is called **routing**. In Odoo, routes are declared with the `@http.route` method decorator in an `http.Controller` object.

To create the route for `/library/catalog`, perform the following steps:

1. The controller Python code will be added in the `controllers` subdirectory. In the `library_portal` module directory, edit the `__init__.py` file to import that subdirectory:

```
from . import controllers
```

2. Add the `controllers/__init__.py` file to import the Python file with the controller code, which will be in a `main.py` file:

```
from . import main
```

3. Add the actual controller file, `controllers/main.py`, with the following code:

```python
from odoo import http


class Main(http.Controller):

    @http.route("/library/catalog",
        auth="public", website=True)
    def catalog(self, **kwargs):
        Book = http.request.env["library.book"]
        books = Book.sudo().search([])
        return http.request.render(
            "library_portal.book_catalog",
                {"books": books},
        )
```

Having done these steps, the controller component is done, and is able to process requests for the `/library/catalog` route.

The `odoo.http` module provides the Odoo web-related features. The web controllers, responsible for page rendering, should be objects inheriting from the `odoo.http.Controller` class. The actual name used for the class is not important. In the previous code, the controller class name is `Main()`.

The `catalog()` method, in the `Main()` class, is decorated with `@http.route`, binding it to one or more URL routes. Here, the `catalog()` method is triggered by the `/library/catalog` route. It also uses the `auth="public"` argument, meaning that this route is accessible without requiring authentication. And the `website=true` argument means that this page will use the web frontend layout, and ensures some needed additional variables are made available.

> **Note**
> Using `website=True` does not require the *Website* app to be installed. It also works with base Odoo frontend web pages.

These `catalog()` route method is expected to do some processing and then return the HTML page to the user's web browser.

The `http.request` object is automatically set with the web request, and has available the `.env` attribute, to access the Odoo environment. This can be used to instantiate Odoo models. The example code does this to access the `library.book` model and then build a record set with all books available.

The route method runs as the user who is logged in, or as the Public special user if no user is logged in and the route allows public access. Since the Public user has very limited access, `sudo()` might be needed to ensure that the data to be presented can be retrieved.

The final line returns the result of `http.request.render()`. This prepares a QWeb template to be rendered. The two arguments are the template XML ID, `library_portal.book_catalog` in this case, and a dictionary with the variables to make available to the QWeb rendering context. In this case, a `books` variable is made available, set with a books record set.

> **Note**
>
> The `http.request.render()` function returns a Odoo `http.response` object, containing the instructions on what to render. The actual processing of the QWeb template into HTML is delayed until all web controller code is run and the response is ready to be sent to the client. This allows for the route method to be extended and, for example, the `qcontext` attribute, holding the dictionary to be used for the QWeb rendering, to be modified.

The controller is ready, but the QWeb template used needs to be created before it can work. The next section takes care of that.

Adding a QWeb template

QWeb templates are XML snippets containing HTML code and QWeb directives that can dynamically modify the output depending on conditions. The book catalog web page needs a QWeb template to render the HTML to be presented.

To add the `library_portal.book_catalog` QWeb template, perform the following steps:

1. A new XML data file, `views/main_templates.xml`, will be used to declare the template. Add that to the `__manifest__.py` module file, in the `data` key:

```
"data": [
    "views/main_templates.xml",
]
```

2. Add the XML data file with the QWeb template, `views/main_templates.xml`:

```xml
<odoo>
<template id="book_catalog" name="Book List">
  <t t-call="web.frontend_layout">
    <t t-set="title">Book Catalog</t>
      <div class="oe_structure">
        <div class="container">

            <h1 class="h1-book-catalog">
              Book Catalog</h1>
            <table class="table">
              <thead>
                <tr>
                  <th scope="col">Title</th>
                  <th scope="col">Published</th>
                  <th scope="col">Publisher</th>
                </tr>
              </thead>
              <tbody>

          <t t-foreach="books" t-as="book">
            <tr scope="row">
              <td><span t-field="book.name" /></td>
              <td><span t-field="book.date_published"
                  /></td>
              <td><span t-field="book.publisher_id"
                  /></td>
            </tr>
          </t>

              </tbody>
            </table>

        </div>
      </div>
    </t>
```

```
    </template>
    </odoo>
```

This completes the steps needed to get the QWeb template ready.

The previous code declares the `book_catalog` template. It is a Bootstrap table, with three columns. The `<thead>` section declares the columns headers, and the `<t t-foreach>` QWeb directive renders a table row for each book in the `books` record set.

> **Note**
>
> QWeb templates are XML. The XML language has stricter rules than regular HTML, which, for example, tolerates opening tags that are not closed. This is not allowed in XML, and therefore in QWeb templates. To be precise, QWeb templates follow the XHTML requirements.

Important in this template is the first directive, `<t t-call="web.frontend_layout">`. This is what makes the template HTML be rendered as an Odoo frontend web page, including page headers and footers. For this layout to be used, the controller route must include the `website=True` argument.

> **Tip**
>
> The website data passed into the QWeb evaluation context is set by the `_prepare_qcontext` method of the `ir.ui.view` model. For example, the `website` module adds variables to it, in the `models/ir_ui_view.py` file.

`<t t-set="title">` is also noteworthy. It is used by the frontend layout to set the browser tab title.

When we have both the controller and the QWeb template in place, once the `library_portal` module is installed or upgraded, opening `http://localhost:8069/library/catalog` with a web browser should display a table with the library's books.

These are the key components used to implement frontend web pages. Note that the *Website* app can be used to have more frontend features available, but is not required.

Being a web page, it may also need to use additional assets. The next section explains this.

Adding CSS and JavaScript assets

When designing web pages, the HTML code is often complemented with CSS or JavaScript, which are best provided as additional assets.

Assets to load are declared in the head section of the page. Odoo has specific QWeb templates in charge of loading assets. In particular, the `web.assets_backend` and `web.assets_frontend` provide the assets needed specifically for backend web client and frontend web pages. `web.assets_common` provides assets common to both.

To have additional assets loaded, the appropriate template needs to be extended.

For example, in the book catalog page, the title could be presented using a larger font size. This can be done by declaring a style in a CSS file, which is then used in the `<h1>` element. In fact, the book catalog QWeb template is already using `<h1 class="h1-book-catalog">`, applying a custom style.

To add this custom style, perform the following steps:

1. Create the `static/src/css/library.css` file with the following content:

    ```css
    .h1-book-catalog {
        font-size: 62px;
    }
    ```

2. This CSS must be loaded by frontend web pages. For this, the `web.assets_frontend` template should be extended. Add to the `__manifest__.py` file the following code:

    ```python
    "assets": {
        "web.assets_backend": {
            "library_portal/static/src/css/
            library.css",
        }
    }
    ```

This describes how a module can add web assets. These assets will usually be `.js`, `.css`, or `.scss` files.

> **Changes in Odoo 15**
>
> Web assets were previously added using an XML file, extending an QWeb template, such as `web.assets_backend` or `web.assets_frontend`. An example for this is provided in *Chapter 11*, *Kanban Views and Client-Side QWeb*, in the *Adding CSS and JavaScript assets* section.

The basics for creating a frontend web page have been described, and involve three key components: web controllers, QWeb templates, and web assets.

QWeb templates and their syntax have been thoroughly described in *Chapter 11, Kanban Views and Client-Side QWeb*, and *Chapter 12, Creating Printable PDF Reports with Server-Side QWeb*.

But web controllers are worth more attention, and a deeper description of their features. The following section will provide this.

Understanding web controllers

Web controllers are the server-side components responsible for responding when an Odoo web path is accessed, usually triggering the rendering of a web page.

A web path, such as `/library/catalog`, is assigned to a route, triggering a **controller method**. The method code can access details of the web request through the `request` object, and the result is a `response` object, with the details to return to the client.

Declaring routes

The `http.route` decorator is used to assign a method to a web path. These are the arguments available:

- `route`, usually provided as a positional argument, is a string, or a list of strings, with the paths to map. Method arguments can be extracted from the path. The syntax to express these arguments is detailed in the next section.

- `type`, to specify the type of request. By default, this is `http`, and can also be set to `json`.

- `auth` is the authentication type required. It can be one of `user`, `public`, or `none`. The `user` option requires a login to allow access, `public` allows anonymous access, through the public user, and `none` is useful in special cases, where an Odoo database is not needed, such as authentication endpoints.

These are the arguments that can be used on `route` decorators. The next section explains the syntax to extract values from the main argument, to be passed to the decorated method.

Extracting argument values from the route string

The **route strings** can specify arguments to extract, following the format `<type:name>`. For example, `<int:partner_id>` extracts an integer value, and passes it to the method as the `partner_id` keyword argument. Record instances are also supported, using the `model(<model name>)` syntax. For example, `<model('res.partner'):partner>` extracts a partner record, passed to the method with the `partner` keyword argument.

> **Note**
>
> More information on route path formatting can be found in the
> official Werkzeug documentation at `https://werkzeug.`
> `palletsprojects.com/routing/`.

The URL parameters are passed to the decorated method as keyword arguments. These
parameters are after the ? character in a GET request, or submitted by a POST request. For
example, the `http://localhost:8069/mypage`**?x=1&y=2** URL has two parameters,
x set to 1 and y set to 2.

> **Tip**
>
> Adding to routed methods the `**kw` generic keyword argument capture
> prevents it from erroring if an unexpected argument is added to the URL. For
> example, without it, accessing `http://localhost:8069/library/`
> `catalog`**?some_param=1** would return an error page. With `**kw` on
> the method arguments, it would be captured in the kw variable, and could be
> ignored by the method code.

The routed method return value can be any of the following:

- A **falsy** value, resulting in a *204 No Content* HTTP code response.
- A text string, used to return a response with that text as the HTML content.
- A `response` object, usually created with the `render()` method.

Next, let's learn how the `request` object can be used in a routed method.

Using the request object

A `request` object is automatically instanced when a client web request is made to the
Odoo server. It is made available by importing `odoo.http.request`.

The following are the most important attributes provided by this object:

- `env` is an Odoo `Environment` object, similar to what `self.env` provides in
  regular model methods.
- `context` is a dictionary-like `Mapping` object with the execution context. It is
  similar to model method context.
- `cr` is a PostgreSQL cursor object for the Odoo database.
- `db` is the database name.

- `session` is an object storing the session details, including authentication.

- `params` stores the request parameters. It is usually not useful, since the parameters are already provided as arguments to the method.

- `csrf_token(time_limit=None)` is a method to generate a CSRF token for the current session. The `time_limit` is the token validity period in seconds. The default, `None`, makes it valid for the whole session duration. This attribute is used, for example, to set a CSRF token for HTML forms.

For `http` type requests, the following methods are also available:

- `make_response(data, headers=None, cookies=None)` can be used to craft non-HTML responses.

- `not_found(description=None)` returns a *404 Not Found* HTTP code.

- `render(template, qcontext=None, lazy=True, **kw)` returns a QWeb template to render. The actual template rendering is delayed until the final dispatch to the client, and so it can be modified by inheriting methods.

Request objects provide a way to access the Odoo environment and all the information about the request made by the client. The next relevant object to understand is the `response`, to be sent back to the client initiating the request.

Using the response object

The `response` object is used to dispatch the final HTTP message to send to the client. When extending routed methods, it might be the case that the `response` returned by the parent `super()` method needs modifications.

The following is available on the `response` object:

- `template` is the name of the template to render.

- `qcontext` is a dictionary with the data to make available for the template rendering.

- `uid` is an integer with the ID of the user rendering the template. If not set, the current user running the method code is used.

- `render()` is the same rendering method also available in the `request` object.

- `flatten()` forces the rendering of the template.

The response object also supports the parameters provided by the parent library, `werkzeug.wrappers.Response`. The corresponding documentation can be found at `https://werkzeug.palletsprojects.com/wrappers/#werkzeug.wrappers.Response`.

You now have a good idea about the web development components. Odoo also provides a portal useful to interact with external users and the next section explains how to add features to it.

Adding portal features

The Odoo portal feature make information available to interact with external users. Different apps can add features to the portal. For example, the **Sales** app adds the ability for customers to check their orders, and even pay for them.

Portal users need to be created, providing access to the portal. This is done on the corresponding contact record in the **Action** context menu, with the **Grant portal access** option, as shown in *Figure 13.2*:

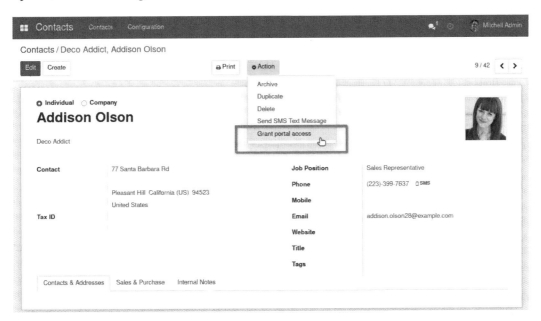

Figure 13.2 – The Grant portal access option on a contact record

Once the user goes through the sign-up process, they can log in to Odoo and see a **My Account** option when clicking on the username in the top right corner. This option opens the portal home page, presenting a summary of all the documents available to the user.

The documents available depend on the apps installed. *Figure 13.3* shows an example of what the portal home page looks like:

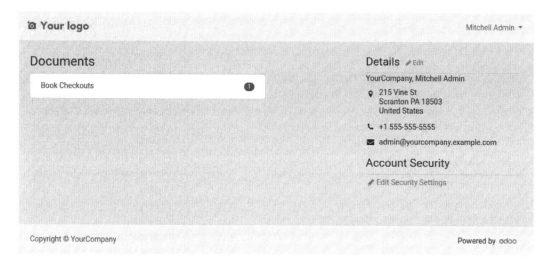

Figure 13.3 – Portal page with book checkouts feature

The `library_portal` module adds the **Book Checkouts** item to the portal **Documents**, as seen in *Figure 13.3*. This is the result of what will be implemented in this section.

The work for this will be split into three parts: access security, controllers, and QWeb templates. Each of the following sections will address one of these steps. You will start by setting the portal access security configuration.

Configuring access security for the portal users

Before portal users can access app data, the necessary access rights need to be given to the portal user group, `base.group_portal group`.

In the case of the library app, portal users should be given read-only access to the book, member, checkout, and stage models. Furthermore, each portal user should only be able to see their own member record and checkouts. For this, both access rights and record rules need to be added.

To configure the access security for portal users, perform the following steps:

1. Create the `security/ir.model.access.csv` file, adding read access to the library models, with the following content:

```
id,name,model_id:id,group_id:id,perm_read,perm_
write,perm_create,perm_unlink
access_book_portal,Book Portal Access,library_app.model_
library_book,base.group_portal,1,0,0,0
access_member_portal,Member Portal Access,library_member.
model_library_member,base.group_portal,1,0,0,0
access_stage_portal,Checkout Stage Portal Access,library_
checkout.model_library_checkout_stage,base.group_
portal,1,0,0,0
access_checkout_portal,Checkout Portal Access,library_
checkout.model_library_checkout,base.group_portal,1,0,0,0
access_checkout_portal_line,Checkout Portal Line
Access,library_checkout.model_library_checkout_line,base.
group_portal,1,0,0,0
```

2. Create the `security/library_security.xml` file with **record rules**, limiting the records portal that users will be able to access:

```xml
<odoo>
  <data noupdate="1">
    <record id="member_portal_rule" model="ir.rule">
      <field name="name">
        Library Member Portal Access</field>
      <field name="model_id"
             ref=
               "library_member.model_library_member"/>
      <field name="domain_force"
        >[('partner_id', '=',
        user.partner_id.id)]</field>
      <field name="groups"
        eval="[(4,ref('base.group_portal'))]"/>
    </record>

    <record id="checkout_portal_rule" model="ir.rule">
      <field name="name">
```

```
                Library Checkout Portal Access</field>
            <field name="model_id"
             ref=
                "library_checkout.model_library_checkout"/>
            <field name="domain_force"
              >[('member_id.partner_id', '=',
                user.partner_id.id)]</field>
            <field name="groups"
                eval="[(4,ref('base.group_portal'))]"/>
        </record>
    </data>
</odoo>
```

3. Finally, add these data files to the `data` key in the module `__manifest__.py` file:

```
"data": [
    "security/ir.model.access.csv",
    "security/library_security.xml",
    "views/assets.xml",
    "views/main_templates.xml",
],
```

The record rules created apply filters based on the current user partner record, `user.partner_id.id`. The members are filtered using the `partner_id` field, and the checkouts are filtered using the `member_id.partner_id` field.

After this, and a module upgrade, portal users will have the access rights needed to use the library portal pages.

> **Tip**
>
> It is often the case that web controllers avoid the need to have access rights added, by using `sudo()` to get elevated access, which is sure to have access to the data. While convenient, the usage of `sudo()` should be carefully considered, and avoided if possible. It is more secure to implement access security on the model layer, using ACLs and record rules, instead of relying on the controller logic for that.

Having the necessary access rights configured, the next step is to add the checkouts item to the portal main list.

Adding a portal document type to the main list

Accessing the portal **My Account** page shows several document types available, such as **sales orders** and **invoices**, and the number of items for each.

The `library_portal` module should add the **Book Checkouts** option to the **My Account** page. Perform the following steps for that:

1. Edit the `controllers/__init__.py` file to import the Python file with the controller code, which will be in the `portal.py` file:

```
from . import main
from . import portal
```

2. Add the controller file, `controllers/portal.py`, with the following code:

```
from odoo.http import route, request
from odoo.addons.portal.controllers import portal

class CustomerPortal(portal.CustomerPortal):
    def _prepare_home_portal_values(self, counters):
        values = super()
            ._prepare_home_portal_values(counters)
        if "book_checkout_count" in counters:
            count =
            request.env[
            "library.checkout"].search_count([])
            values["book_checkout_count"] = count
        return values
```

This extends the `CustomerPortal` controller, provided by the `portal` Odoo module. The previous code extends the `_prepare_home_portal_values()` method, responsible for calculating the document counters. It adds the `book_checkout_count` key to the result values, set with the checkout count.

3. Add the QWeb template file, `views/portal_templates.py`, with the following code:

```
<odoo>
    <template id="portal_my_home"
        inherit_id="portal.portal_my_home"
        name="Show Book Checkouts" priority="100"
```

```
             customize_show="True">
             <xpath expr="//div[hasclass('o_portal_docs')]"
                 position="inside">
               <t t-call="portal.portal_docs_entry">
                 <t t-set="title">Book Checkouts</t>
                 <t t-set="url"
                     t-value="'/my/book-checkouts'"/>
                 <t t-set="placeholder_count"
                     t-value="'book_checkout_count'"/>
               </t>
             </xpath>
           </template>
       </odoo>
```

This extends the `portal.portal_my_home` template, responsible for rendering the **My Account** page. The `portal.portal_docs_entry` template should be used to render each document item. It uses three variables: the `title`, the `url` to navigate to when clicked, and the `placeholder_count`, with the counter identifier provided by the `_prepare_home_portal_values` function.

4. Finally, add the new data file to `__manifest__.py`:

```
    "data": [
      "security/library_security.xml",
      "security/ir.model.access.csv",
      "views/assets.xml",
      "views/main_templates.xml",
      "views/portal_templates.xml",
    ],
```

The previous steps add the **Book Checkouts** option to the document list in the **My Account** page. Clicking on it will navigate to the `/my/book-checkouts` page, but this hasn't been implemented yet. The next section will do this in a portal-friendly way.

Adding a portal document list page

The **My Account** home page lists the various document types available. Clicking the document type link should open the list of documents available.

Figure 13.4 shows what the document list page should look like:

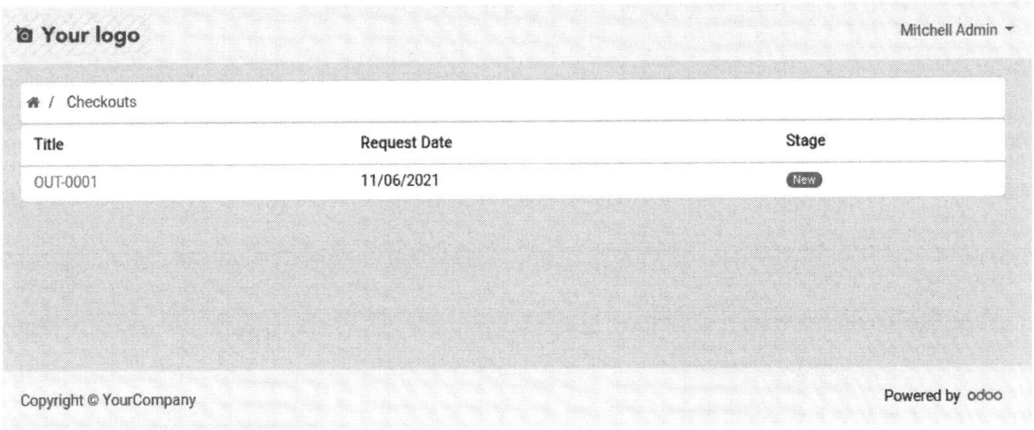

Figure 13.4 – Portal document list page for book checkouts

The portal provides base features to be used for these document list pages, such as record paging, filters, and sort options.

The previous example showed how to add a document type to the portal home page. Next, the document list needs to be implemented. Continuing with the code from the previous section, two steps are needed:

1. Edit the controller file, `controllers/portal.py`, to add the code for the `/my/book-checkouts` route, which will render the `my_book_checkouts` template.

2. Edit the QWeb template file, `views/portal_templates.py`, to add the `my_book_checkouts` template for the book checkout list page.

The code to add to `controllers/portal.py` is the following:

```
@route(
    ["/my/book-checkouts", "/my/book-checkouts/
        page/<int:page>"],
    auth="user",
    website=True,
)
def my_book_checkouts(self, page=1, **kw):
    Checkout = request.env["library.checkout"]
    domain = []
    # Prepare pager data
    checkout_count = Checkout.search_count(domain)
```

```
pager_data = portal.pager(
    url="/my/book_checkouts",
    total=checkout_count,
    page=page,
    step=self._items_per_page,
)
# Recordset according to pager and domain filter
checkouts = Checkout.search(
    domain,
    limit=self._items_per_page,
    offset=pager_data["offset"],
)
# Prepare template values and render
values = self._prepare_portal_layout_values()
values.update(
    {
        "checkouts": checkouts,
        "page_name": "book-checkouts",
        "default_url": "/my/book-checkouts",
        "pager": pager_data,
    }
)
return request.render(
    "library_portal.my_book_checkouts",
    values
)
```

The previous code adds a route for the /my/book-checkouts and /my/book-checkouts/page/ paths. The first is the one used by default, and the second allows navigating through the record pages.

The method code is organized into three sections:

- The first code section prepares the pager_data variable, used by the template to render the page navigation links. It uses a pager() function from the portal module, responsible for preparing this data.

- The second code section creates the record set to be used, `checkouts`. It does so using the domain filter and pager data set previously.

- The third and last code section prepares the `values` dictionary and renders the QWeb template. The values are initialized using the portal-provided `_prepare_portal_layout_values()` function, and then additional data keys are set, including the pager data. The record set to use is also set in the values, in this case in the `checkouts` data key.

> **Tip**
> The portal pages can also have support for user-selected sort order and filters. A good example of this is the portal **Tasks**, implemented by the *Project* app. Inspecting the corresponding controllers and QWeb templates can provide further guidance to add this to other portal pages.

You have added the controller code, now let's add the QWeb template with the following code:

```
<template id="my_book_checkouts" name=
    "My Book Checkouts">
  <t t-call="portal.portal_layout">
    <t t-if="checkouts" t-call="portal.portal_table">
      <thead>
        <tr>
          <th>Title</th>
          <th>Request Date</th>
          <th>Stage</th>
        </tr>
      </thead>
      <tbody>
        <tr t-foreach="checkouts" t-as="doc">
          <td>
            <a t-attf-href=
              "/my/book-checkout/{{slug(doc)}}">
              <span t-field="doc.name"/>
            </a>
          </td>
          <td>
            <span t-field="doc.request_date"/>
```

```
            </td>
            <td>
               <span t-field="doc.stage_id.name"
                     class="badge badge-pill badge-info"/>
            </td>
          </tr>
        </tbody>
      </t>
   <t t-else="">
      <div class="alert alert-warning" role="alert">
      There are no book checkouts.
      </div>
   </t>
  </t>
</template>
```

The previous code declares the my_book_checkouts QWeb template. It starts by calling the portal page template, portal.portal_layout.

Then, if there are records to render, it prepares an HTML table from them, calling the portal.portal_table template.

Next, the template adds the table header and body. The table body uses a for-loop on the checkouts record set to render each row.

Noteworthy is the <a> link on each record name. When rendering the checkout title, the t-attf directive is used to generate the link to open the corresponding detail. The special slug() function is used to generate a human-readable identifier for each record.

The link won't work for now, since the document detail page has not been implemented yet. The next section will do that.

Adding a portal document detail page

The portal has a home page, from which the user can navigate to document lists, and then open specific documents. A specific book checkout can be accessed with the /my/book-checkout/<id> path.

The previous sections implemented the home page and document list features. To complete the portal, the document detail page should be implemented. Continuing with the code from the previous section, two steps are needed:

1. Edit the controller file, `controllers/portal.py`, to add the code for the `/my/book-checkout` route, rendering the `book_checkout` template.

2. Edit the QWeb template file, `views/portal_templates.py`, to add the `book_checkout` template for the book checkout list page.

The code for the book checkout page controller is straightforward and brings nothing new. It is the following:

```python
@route(
    ["/my/book-checkout/
        <model('library.checkout'):doc>"],
    auth="user",
    website=True,
)
def portal_my_project(self, doc=None, **kw):
    return request.render(
        "library_portal.book_checkout",
        {"doc": doc},
    )
```

The previous code adds a route for the `/my/book-checkout/<id>` path, which translates the `<id>` into a `library.checkout` record. This record is used as a method argument, captured by the `doc` variable name.

Since the `doc` variable contains the checkout record to use, the method only needs to render the QWeb template for it, `library_portal.book_checkout`.

The code to use for the QWeb template is the following:

```xml
<template id="book_checkout" name="Checkout Form">
  <t t-call="portal.portal_layout">
    <t t-call="portal.portal_record_layout">
      <t t-set="card_header">
        <div class="row">
          <div class="col">
            <h5 class="text-truncate"
```

```
                  t-field="doc.name" />
          </div>
          <div class="col text-right">
              <span t-field="doc.stage_id.name"
                    class="badge badge-pill badge-info"
                    title="Current stage"/>
          </div>
      </div>
    </t>
    <t t-set="card_body">
    <!-- Member details -->
    <div class="row">
      <strong>Member</strong>
    </div>
    <div class="row">
        <div t-if="doc.member_id.image_1024"
             class="col flex-grow-0">
<img class="rounded-circle mt-1 o_portal_contact_img"
  t-att-src="image_data_uri(doc.member_id.image_1024)"
  alt="Contact"/>
        </div>
        <div class="col pl-sm-0">
            <address t-field="doc.member_id"
                     t-options='{
                         "widget": "contact",
                         "fields": ["name", "email",
                           "phone"]
                     }' />
        </div>
    </div>
    <!-- Checkout books -->
    <div class="row">
      <strong>Borrowed books</strong>
    </div>
    <div class="row">
      <div class="col">
```

```
        <ul>
            <li t-foreach="doc.line_ids" t-as="line">
                <span t-field=
                    "line.book_id.display_name" />
            </li>
        </ul>
        </div>
    </div>
    </t>
    </t>
</t>
</template>
```

The previous code created the `book_checkout` QWeb template. Again, it starts by calling the portal page template, `portal.portal_layout`.

Then, the document details template, `portal.portal_record_layout`, is called to prepare the detail content. It uses the following two QWeb variables, which should be set:

- `card_header` sets the HTML to use for the header.
- `card_body` sets the HTML to use for the document details.

This HTML adds rows with the content. Two particular elements are noteworthy:

- The `<img>` element, adding an image from a data field
- The `<address>` element, rendering an address for a partner record

The current implementation is missing a nice usability feature, the **breadcrumb** allowing users to navigate back through the links to the portal main page. The next section shows how to add this.

Adding a portal breadcrumb

Portal pages support a breadcrumb, on the top region of the page. By default, a home icon is available, allowing users to quickly navigate back to the main page. As the user navigates to the document list, and then to a particular document, these selections can be added to the breadcrumb.

The Odoo portal breadcrumb is added by the `portal.portal_breadcrumbs` template. It should be extended to add the specific navigation steps for particular document types.

To have the book checkout breadcrumb, edit the `views/portal_templates.py` file to add the following template:

```
<template id="portal_layout"
          name="Portal breadcrumb: book checkout"
          inherit_id="portal.portal_breadcrumbs">
    <xpath expr="//ol[hasclass('o_portal_submenu')]"
           position="inside">
        <li t-if="page_name == 'book-checkouts' or doc"
            class="col-lg-2"
            t-attf-class="breadcrumb-item
                          #{'active ' if not doc else ''}">
            <a t-if="doc"
               t-attf-href="/my/book-checkouts?{{
               keep_query() }}">
               Checkouts
            </a>
            <t t-else="">Checkouts</t>
        </li>
        <li t-if="doc" class="breadcrumb-item
            active text-truncate
                          col-8 col-lg-10">
            <t t-esc="doc.name"/>
        </li>
    </xpath>
</template>
```

The template in the previous code extends the `portal.portal_breadcrumbs` template. It extends the `<ol>` element with the `o_portal_submenu` class, adding breadcrumb `<li>` elements to it.

The extension adds two possible elements: one for the **Checkouts** document list, and another for a particular book checkout. The breadcrumb is included in all portal pages, and these added elements should be conditionally rendered, only if they make sense for the current page.

The previous sections guided you through the various steps needed to add new features to the Odoo portal, enabling external users to interact with Odoo.

Summary

Frontend web pages allow Odoo to also provide features to external users. This can be used to display generic information to the public, or give personalized information to portal users. The frontend web features are the foundation of the Odoo CMS, provided by the *Website* app, and for frontend features such as e-commerce.

In this chapter, you understood the technical components that are at the core of frontend web features, web controllers, and QWeb templates. Web controllers implement routes, triggered when accessing certain URL paths called routes, and running any specific business logic needed. QWeb templates receive data prepared by the web controller and render HTML output with the help of the QWeb templating engine.

You now know how to use these components to implement a public web page integrated with the Odoo frontend, including the usage of your own web assets. You also know how to leverage the essentials of the Odoo portal to provide self-service features to your external users.

This chapter completes your journey through the various components in the Odoo framework. The models are the central element around which other components are built up. The Odoo base module provides a few essential models developers should be familiar with. The next chapter takes on the task of providing an overview of these.

Further reading

These are additional reference materials that complement the topics discussed in this chapter, found in the official Odoo documentation:

- Web controllers: `https://www.odoo.com/documentation/15.0/developer/reference/backend/http.html`

- QWeb language: `https://www.odoo.com/documentation/15.0/developer/reference/frontend/qweb.html`

- JavaScript API reference: `https://www.odoo.com/documentation/15.0/developer/reference/frontend/javascript_reference.html`

- Bootstrap documentation: `https://getbootstrap.com/docs/4.1/getting-started/introduction`

Additional Bootstrap learning resources can be found on the Packt Publishing technical page: `https://www.packtpub.com/tech/Bootstrap`.

Section 5: Deployment and Maintenance

Finally, the fifth part covers deployment and maintenance practices. Some special considerations need to be taken into account when deploying for production use, such as configuring a reverse proxy between the Odoo service and the network. An additional reference chapter is included, providing an overview of the Odoo base key models.

In this section, the following chapters are included:

- *Chapter 14, Understanding Odoo Built-In Models*
- *Chapter 15, Deploying and Maintaining Production Instances*

14
Understanding Odoo Built-In Models

When a new database is created, an initial data model is populated, providing basic entities that can be used for **Odoo Apps**. This chapter identifies the most relevant basic entities and explains how to inspect them from the **user interface** (**UI**), as well as what their role is.

While this understanding is not indispensable for you to be able to develop Odoo apps, it will provide a solid base to understand the Odoo framework core concepts and help to leverage the technical menu to address more complex requirements or issues.

The following topics are discussed in this chapter:

- Understanding the contacts data model
- Understanding the users and companies data model
- Understanding the security-related information repository
- Understanding the database structure models
- Understanding the UI-related repository
- Understanding the configuration properties and company parameters
- Understanding the messaging data model

By the end of this chapter, you will be able to use the technical menu to inspect the most relevant internal data record of the Odoo framework, helping you with issue analysis and resolution.

Throughout the chapter, simplified **entity-relationship diagrams** (**ERDs**) are presented, allowing you to visualize how the core models are interrelated and thus have a deeper understanding of how these can be used in your business applications.

Technical requirements

To follow this chapter, you will only need admin access to an Odoo 15 instance and to enable the developer mode in the **Settings** | **Technical** menu. To follow the contacts data model section, the **Contacts** app must be installed, and to follow the messaging data model section, the **Discuss** app must be installed.

Understanding the contacts data model

Resource models carry the `res.` prefix on their technical **identifiers** (**IDs**). They hold Odoo's basic master data, such as users, companies, and currencies.

A central model for Odoo is the **Partner** model, also called **Contact**, with a technical name of `res.partner`. It is used anywhere an address, person, or organization needs to be represented. Examples are customers, suppliers, contact persons, invoicing or shipping addresses, employees, and applicants. It is also used to complement the contact data for users and configured companies.

While the `res.partner` model is provided by the Odoo base module and requires no specific app to be installed, to have the corresponding menus available, the **Contacts** app needs to be installed. These are the relevant **Contact** related models:

- **Bank**, or `res.bank`, holds bank identification data, as it turns out to be hard to do business without having a bank involved somehow. Bank data can be browsed from the **Contacts** | **Configuration** | **Bank Accounts** | **Banks** menu option.

- **Bank Account**, or `res.partner.bank`, holds bank account details. Bank accounts are related to a `res.partner` and, not surprisingly, also reference the `res.bank` bank they are related to. Bank accounts can be browsed at **Contacts** | **Configuration** | **Bank Accounts** | **Banks Accounts**.

- **Industry**, or `res.partner.industry`, is a high-level list of economic activities. It is populated with NACE codes. **NACE**, the **Nomenclature of Economic Activities**, is the European statistical classification of economic activities. The list can be found at **Contacts** | **Configuration** | **Industries**.

- **Country**, or `res.country`, lists the world countries and includes useful data such as the two-digit **International Organization for Standardization (ISO)** code, the phone-calling prefix number, or the currency used. The list is automatically populated when a new database is created and is used by the `res.partner` model. The country list can be browsed at **Contacts | Configuration | Localization | Countries**.

- **Country State**, or `res.country.state`, lists country states and similar administrative regions. The list is populated by default, and the data can be seen at **Contacts | Configuration | Localization | Feb. States**.

- **Country Group**, or `res.country.group`, allows us to define country groups. The default groups provided by Odoo are Europe, **Single Euro Payments Area (SEPA)** Countries, and South America. Other groups can be added per need, at **Contacts | Configuration | Localization | Country Groups**.

- **Currencies**, or `res.currency`, contains a currency list, relevant when multi-currency is enabled. The list is pre-populated by Odoo, and the relevant currencies should be set as `active`. The menu option to access the list is in the **Invoicing/Accounting** app (if **multi-currency** is enabled), in the corresponding **Configuration | Accounting | Currencies** menu option.

The following diagram provides a high-level overview of these models and their relations:

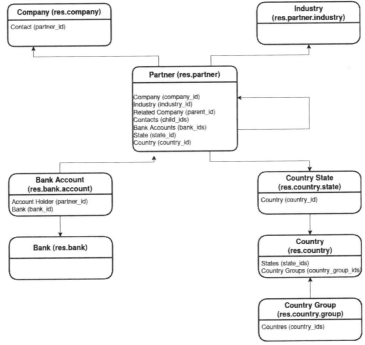

Figure 14.1 – Contacts data model

> **Note**
>
> The data model diagrams provided here are simplified ERDs. Part of the simplification is replacing the *crow's foot* notation, which may not be familiar to many of you, with simple arrows. An **arrow** represents a many-to-one relation. A **bidirectional arrow** represents a many-to-many relation. Dotted lines represent soft relations that don't use a database ID or a database **foreign key (FK)**. Model names use the singular form, as is the convention for ERDs, even if the Odoo model's name may use the plural form.

Other resource models are the users and companies, described in the next section.

Understanding the users and companies data model

Users and companies are central elements of the Odoo data model. They can be accessed in the **Settings | Users & Companies** menu. The menu options available are listed here:

- **User**, or res.users, stores the system users. These have an implicit partner record in the partner_id field, where the name, email, image, and other contact details are stored.

- **Access Group**, or res.group, stores the security access groups. This menu is only available with the developer mode enabled. Users belonging to a group will be granted that group's privileges. Groups can inherit other groups, meaning that they will also provide the privileges from these inherited groups.

- **Company**, or res.company, stores the organization's details and the company-specific configurations. It has an implicit partner record, holding the address and contact details, stored in the partner_id field. A default company is provided on new databases, with the base.main_company **Extensible Markup Language (XML)** ID.

The following diagram provides a high-level view of relations between these models:

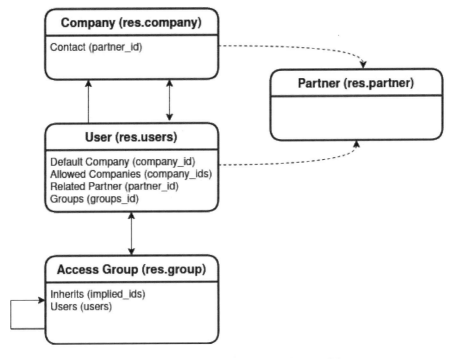

Figure 14.2 – Users and companies data model

The user and access group models are the foundation for the Odoo access security definitions. The next section details these models, accessible from the **Technical** menu.

Understanding the security-related information repository

Odoo users are granted access to features through access groups. These access groups hold the definitions of the privileges access they provide. The most relevant access models are listed here:

- **User**, or res.users, are the Odoo system users.

- **Access Group**, or res.group, are the access groups. Users belong to one or more groups, and each group grants certain privileges.

- **Model Access**, or ir.model.access, grants a group **create-read-update-delete** (**CRUD**) privileges on a model.

- **Rule**, or `ir.rule`, grants a group CRUD privileges on a subset of the model records, defined by a domain expression. For example, with regular access rights, you can grant write access, and then a record rule can limit certain records to be read-only.

The following diagram provides a simplified view of this part of the data model:

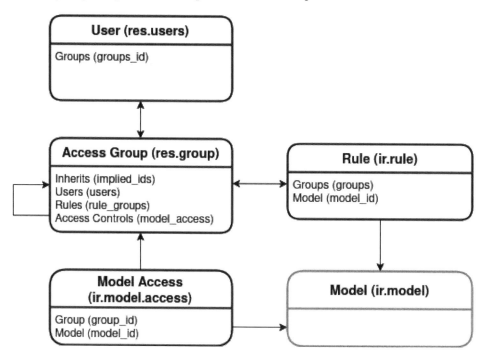

Figure 14.3 – Security-related data model

You have learned about the data model for users, access groups, partners, and access rights, which all have a close connection between them. In the next section, you will continue further improving your understanding of the database structure definition, such as models and fields.

Understanding the database structure models

The information repository (`ir.`) models describe the Odoo internal configuration, such as models, fields, and UI. These definitions can be accessed under the **Settings | Technical** menu.

The data models-related information repository can be found using the **Settings | Technical | Database Structure** menu. Following the most relevant option in that menu, we have these settings:

- **Decimal Accuracy**, or `decimal.precision`, is used to configure the number of precision digits for different use cases, such as product prices.

- **Model**, or `ir.model`, describes the Odoo installed data models that most of the time map to a database table where the data is stored. It is useful to find the model's XML ID, using the developer menu **View Metadata** option. The **In Apps** field is also useful for finding out the modules involved in the model data structure definition.

- **Field**, or `ir.model.field`, stores the model fields defined in the database. This list can be accessed using the **Settings | Technical | Database Structure | Fields** menu, or the developer menu **View Fields** option.

- **Attachment**, or `ir.attachment`, is the model used to store attachment files. It is a single storage place used across Odoo.

The **Settings | Technical | Sequences & Identifiers** menu includes models related to data record IDs and contains the following settings:

- **External Identifiers**, or `ir.model.data`, is where external IDs, also known as XML IDs are stored. They map ID names that are database instance-agnostic to database instance-specific ID keys. They are accessible at **Settings | Technical | Sequences & Identifiers | External Identifiers**.

- **Sequence**, or `ir.sequence`, describes the automatic number assignment sequences used—for example, on **sales orders** or **stock transfers**.

The following diagram presents a high-level view of the relations between these models:

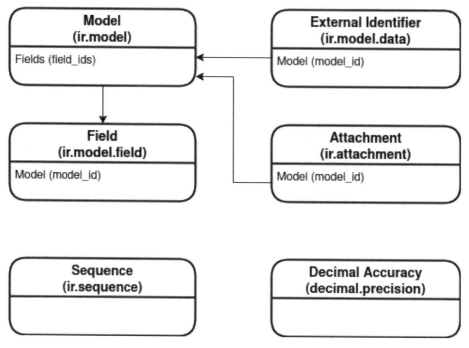

Figure 14.4 – Database structure data model

You have learned about the key models used to hold the Odoo model definition. Next, we have the presentation layer definition, discussed in the next section.

Understanding the UI-related information repository

UI elements, such as menus and views, are stored in information repository models. The corresponding data can be accessed through the **Settings | Technical | User Interface** menu. The most relevant options found there are listed here:

- **Menu**, or `ir.ui.menu`, defines the menu options. These form a hierarchy tree, and the leaf items can trigger an **Action**, then often provide instructions to display the composition of views.

- **Views**, or `ir.ui.view`, stores the view definitions and their extensions. View types include form, list, Kanban, and QWeb (both for reports and for web page templates).

Under the **Settings | Technical | Actions** menu, you can find a definition for these UI elements. The most relevant options are listed here:

- **Action**, or `ir.actions.actions`, is the base model that other action types derive from. Usually, you won't need to deal with it directly.

- **Reports**, or `ir.actions.report`, are actions to print a report. They will have related QWeb views, providing the report definition, used to generate the report **HyperText Markup Language** (**HTML**) that can then be converted to a **Portable Desktop Format** (**PDF**) format.

- **Window Action**, or `ir.actions.act_window`, is used to present the composition of a view and is probably the most frequently used action type. The simplest view composition is a list view and a form view.

- **Server Action**, or `ir.actions.server`, is used to run a server process, such as creating or modifying a record, sending an email, or even running Python code.

The following diagram provides a simplified view of the previous models and their relations:

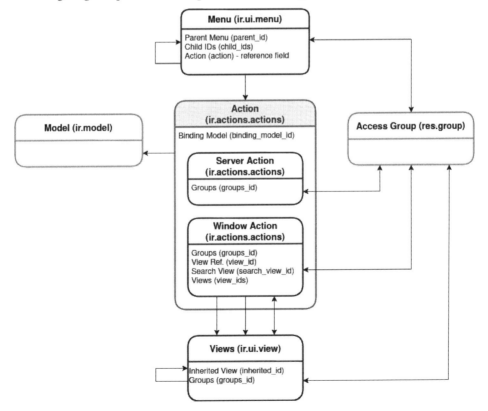

Figure 14.5 – Actions and UI data model

With this section, you should have gained a better understanding of the several elements relevant to defining the Odoo UI and how to use the technical menu to inspect them. In the next section, you will be introduced to the technical models used for global configuration parameters and for company-dependent data.

Understanding the configuration properties and company parameters

Another important menu in the technical options is **Settings | Technical | User Parameters**. You can find two options there: **System Parameters** and **Company Properties**.

System Parameters, or `ir.config_parameter`, stores global configuration options. Some are defaults that can be adjusted, while others are set when some options are selected in the **General Settings** option. It is a simple key/value list—for example, the `web.base.url` option stores the Odoo server **Uniform Resource Locator** (**URL**) and can be used to create links in email templates.

Company Properties, or `ir.property`, is where data for multi-company fields is stored. Some fields can have different values depending on the active company. These are also known as **property fields**.

For example, the partner fields **Account Receivable** (`property_account_receivable_id`), relevant for customers, and **Account Payable** (`property_account_payable_id`), relevant for suppliers, are both property fields.

Since the same field name can hold different values, depending on the active company, it can be a regular database file. That is where the `ir.property` model comes in as the place where these values can be stored.

This model has the following fields:

- **Name**: The field's technical name, such as `property_account_receivable_id`.
- **Field**: A relation with the corresponding `ir.model.fields` record.
- **Type**: The field type, such as `Float` or `Many2one`.
- **Resource**: A reference to the record this value corresponds to. For example, `res.partner,62` means a reference for the `res.partner` record with database ID 62.
- **Company**: The company this value is valid for.

- **Value**: The value this field has for this company, allowing for different companies to give different values. If the field is relational, the reference is encoded in a similar way as the **Resource** field—for example, `account.account,813` for a chart of accounts with ID 813.

> **Tip**
>
> The **Resource** field is optional. If blank, it is used as the default value for new records in that company. This is used for the case of the **Account Receivable** and **Account Payable** fields used as an example here.

Understanding the relevance of these company properties and parameters can be useful for advanced configuration tweaks, such as adjusting the public web URL to be used or defining a multi-company field default value. The next section will continue the technical menu exploration journey, this time covering message-related models.

Understanding messaging data models

A relevant technical area you might need to work with is the messaging-related models used by the Chatter widget found in many forms. These features are provided by the **Discuss** module with a technical name of `mail`, so it needs to be installed before the following menu items are available.

The relevant technical models can be found in the **Settings | Technical | Discuss** menu. The most important options found there are listed here:

- **Message**, or `mail.message`, stores each message. It is related to a *resource*, a particular record in a model, through the **Mail Thread** abstract model.

- **Message Subtype**, or `mail.message.subtype`, is used for each message. The basic subtypes are **Note**, for internal discussions, **Discussion,** for outside messages, and **Activities**, for scheduled activities. These are available for any model. Other subtypes, usually model-specific, can be added to identify different events. This allows the configuring of default subscriptions, deciding which events should trigger notifications to which followers.

- **Tracking Values**, or `mail.tracking.value`, stores the field values change log for tracked fields. For a field to be tracked, check the **Enable Ordered Tracking** field checkbox, or on a model Python definition, set the `tracked=True` field attribute. These changelogs are presented in the Chatter message, and so the tracking values are linked to a Chatter message.

- **Activities**, or `mail.activity`, stores the individual activities for a record. The **Activity Mixin** abstract adds other models the ability to link to activities, similarly to what **Mail Thread** does for messages.

- **Activity Type**, or `mail.activity.type`, are the configurable activity types, such as **Email**, **Call**, **Meeting**, or **Todo**.

- **Followers**, or `mail.followers`, stores a list of followers for each message thread. Each follower record also has a list of subtypes it has subscribed to. Whenever a new message with any of these subtypes is added, the follower will get a notification.

> **Tip**
>
> Data access and changelogs are important features in some environments with strict control policies. An alternative to the out-of-the-box tracking feature is the **Audit Log** community module. You can find it at `https://odoo-community.org/shop/product/audit-log-533`.

The following diagram provides a high-level view of these models and their relations:

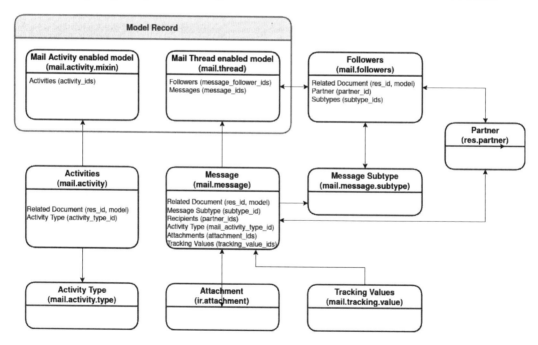

Figure 14.6 – Message and activity data model

Most of the time, you would use a few handpicked **application programming interface (API)** methods to create messages and activities and will not need to delve into the details on how the corresponding data is stored.

For some advanced cases, having a good understanding of the underlying data model can be valuable. In particular, understanding message subtypes and follower subscriptions to them can be useful for fine-grained control of notifications. This completes our overview of the Odoo framework's most important technical models.

Summary

In this chapter, you learned about the internal structures of the Odoo framework, provided by information repository (`ir`) and resource (`res`) models.

The **Contacts** model is central for storing all people and address data in Odoo, and installing the **Contacts** app adds the UI for this model and related data. Understanding how company contacts can have child contacts and addresses is important to effectively use Odoo. The **Users & Companies** menu, from the **Settings** app, was also discussed, to introduce **Users**, **Access Groups**, and **Companies**. The role of **Access Groups** to grant access privileges to **Users** is a key idea here. The remaining relevant elements are exposed in the **Technical** menu of the **Settings** app. Let's review some key ideas here addressed in the chapter.

Starting from the top of the menu, the **Discuss** submenu holds the message and activities data model, and a key idea is how subtypes are used to control automatic notifications. The **Actions** menu exposes the actions used in menu items and the context menu, and is used to present views, print reports, or execute code in the server. The **User Interface** menu introduces the **Menu Items** that make use of the **Actions**, as well as the **Views** menu option, used to hold both backend views and frontend HTML templates. Next in the menu is the **Database Structure** submenu. Here, the models used to describe all the Odoo data structures are available. These are referenced in multiple places during app development, such as in view definitions or model extensions. Closely related to models are the **Security** definitions, granting members of access groups access privileges to read or write to models, or specific record domains in a model.

While not every single technical menu option was reviewed, the most relevant ones were presented and should provide a solid understating of the data structures underlying the `base` and `mail` modules. Your journey through the Odoo development horizon is close to an end. Now that you have all the tools and skills to develop your business applications, the final piece missing is to deploy them and make them available for the end users.

The Odoo project's last mile is to deploy our work for real usage. Installing Odoo for a production environment has additional requirements when compared to a development installation. The next chapter will guide you through the setup of an Odoo production installation, avoiding the most common pitfalls.

15
Deploying and Maintaining Production Instances

In this chapter, you'll learn the basics of preparing an Odoo server for use in a production environment.

Setting up and maintaining servers is a non-trivial topic in itself and should be done by specialists. The information given here is not enough to ensure an average user can create a resilient and secure environment that hosts sensitive data and services.

The goal of this chapter is to introduce the most important configuration aspects and the best practices specific to Odoo deployments. This will help system administrators prepare their Odoo server hosts.

You will start by setting up the host system, and then you will install the Odoo prerequisites and Odoo itself. **Ubuntu** is a popular choice for cloud servers, and it will be used here. Then, the Odoo configuration file needs to be prepared. Until this point, the setup is similar to the one used for the development environment.

Next, Odoo needs to be configured as a system service so that it is automatically started when the server starts.

For servers hosted on a public cloud, Odoo should be served through **HTTPS**. For this, you will learn how to install and configure an **Nginx** reverse proxy by using a self-signed certificate.

The final section discusses how to perform server upgrades and prepare a staging environment that will allow us to perform dry-runs before the actual updates are applied.

The topics discussed in this chapter are as follows:

- Preparing the host system
- Installing Odoo from source code
- Configuring Odoo
- Setting up Odoo as a system service
- Setting up an Nginx reverse proxy
- Configuring and enforcing HTTPS
- Maintaining the Odoo service and modules

By the end of this chapter, you will be able to set up a reasonably secure Odoo server that is good enough for low-profile production use. However, the recipes given in this chapter aren't the only valid way to deploy Odoo – other approaches are also possible.

Technical requirements

To follow this chapter, you will need a clean Ubuntu 20.04 server – for example, a **virtual private server** (**VPS**) hosted on the cloud.

The code and scripts used in this chapter can be found in the `ch15/` directory of the **GitHub** repository at `https://github.com/PacktPublishing/Odoo-15-Development-Essentials`.

Preparing the host system

Odoo is usually deployed on **Debian**-based **Linux** systems. Ubuntu is a popular choice, and the latest **long-term support** (**LTS**) version is 20.04 **Focal Fossa**.

Other Linux distributions can also be used. The **CentOS/Red Hat Enterprise Linux** (**RHEL**) system is also popular in corporate circles.

The installation process requires elevated access, using the root superuser or the sudo command. When using a Debian distribution, the default login is root, which has administration access, and the command prompt shows #. On Ubuntu systems, the root account is disabled. Instead, the initial user is configured during the installation process and is a **sudoer**, meaning that the user is allowed to use the sudo command to elevate access and run commands with the root privileges.

Before starting the Odoo installation, the host system dependencies must be installed, and a specific user should be created to run the Odoo service.

The next section explains the required system dependencies on a Debian system.

Installing the system dependencies

When running Odoo from the source, some dependencies need to be installed in the system.

Before starting, it is a good practice to update the package index and then perform an upgrade to ensure that all installed programs are up to date, as follows:

```
$ sudo apt update
$ sudo apt upgrade -y
```

Next, the **PostgreSQL** database can be installed. Our user should be made a database superuser so that they have administration access to the database. These are the commands for this:

```
$ sudo apt install postgresql -y
$ sudo su -c "createuser -s $USER" postgres
```

> **Note**
> Odoo can use an existing PostgreSQL database, which is installed in its own server. If this is the case, the PostgreSQL service does not need to be installed in the Odoo server and the corresponding connection details should be set in the Odoo configuration file.

These are the Debian dependencies required to run Odoo:

```
$ sudo apt install git python3-dev python3-pip \
python3-wheel python3-venv -y
$ sudo apt install build-essential libpq-dev libxslt-dev \
libzip-dev libldap2-dev libsasl2-dev libssl-dev
```

To have report printing capabilities, wkhtmltox must be installed. The recommended version for Odoo 10 and later is 0.12.5-1. The download links can be found at https://github.com/wkhtmltopdf/wkhtmltopdf/releases/tag/0.12.5. The Ubuntu **code names** are **bionic** for version 18.04 and **focal** for version 20.04.

The following commands perform this installation for Ubuntu 20.04 Focal:

```
$ wget "https://github.com/wkhtmltopdf/wkhtmltopdf\
/releases""/download/0.12.5/\
wkhtmltox_0.12.5-1.focal_amd64.deb" \
-O /tmp/wkhtml.deb
$ sudo dpkg -i /tmp/wkhtml.deb
$ sudo apt-get -fy install  # Fix dependency errors
```

The package installation may report missing dependencies errors. In this case, the last command will force the installation of those dependencies and correctly complete the installation.

Next, you will create a system user to be used for the Odoo processes.

Preparing a dedicated system user

A good security practice is to run Odoo using a dedicated user, who has no special privileges on the host system.

A popular choice for this username is odoo. This is the command to create it:

```
$ sudo adduser --home=/opt/odoo --disabled-password \
--gecos "Odoo" odoo
```

Linux system users can have a home directory. For the Odoo user, this is a convenient place to store the Odoo files. A popular choice for this is /opt/odoo. The --home option used automatically creates this directory and sets it as the odoo user home.

This user does not have access to the PostgreSQL database yet. The following commands add that access and create the database for it to initialize the Odoo production environment:

```
$ sudo su -c "createuser odoo" postgres
$ createdb --owner=odoo odoo-prod
```

Here, `odoo` is the username and `odoo-prod` is the name of the database to support our Odoo instance. The `odoo` user was made the owner of the `odoo-prod` database. This means that it has *create and drop* privileges over that database, including the ability to drop it.

> **Tip**
>
> To run, Odoo does not require elevated privileges to the database being used. These may only be needed for some maintenance operations, such as installing or upgrading modules. So, for improved security, the Odoo system user can be a non-owner database user. Note that in this case, the maintenance should be done running Odoo with a different user than the owner of the database.

To start a session with the Odoo system user, use the following command:

```
$ sudo su - odoo
$ exit
```

This will be used to run installation steps as the Odoo user. When done, the `exit` command terminates that session and returns to the original user.

In the next section, we will continue with the installation of the Odoo code and **Python** dependencies in the `/opt/odoo` directory.

Installing Odoo from source code

While Odoo provides Debian/Ubuntu and CentOS/RHEL system packages, installing from source code is a popular option due to the flexibility and control it provides.

Using source code provides better control over what is deployed and makes it easier to manage changes and fixes once in production. For example, it allows us to tie the deployment process to a Git workflow.

At this point, the Odoo system dependencies are already installed, and the database is ready to use. Now, the Odoo source code can be downloaded and installed, along with the required Python dependencies.

Let's see how to download the Odoo source code.

Downloading the Odoo source code

Sooner or later, your server will need upgrades and patches. A version control repository can be of great help when this time comes. We use `git` to get our code from a repository, just like we did when installing the development environment.

Next, we'll impersonate the `odoo` user and download the code into its home directory, as follows:

```
$ sudo su - odoo
$ git clone https://github.com/odoo/odoo.git \
/opt/odoo/odoo15 \
-b 15.0 --depth=1
```

The `-b` option ensures that we get the right branch, and the `--depth=1` option retrieves only the latest code revision, ignoring the (long) change history and making the download smaller and faster.

> **Tip**
> **Git** is an important tool to manage code versions of your Odoo deployments. If you're not familiar with Git, it is worth learning more about it. A good starting point is `http://git-scm.com/doc`.

Custom modules will usually also be managed with Git and should also be cloned to the production server. For example, the following code will add the library custom modules into the `/opt/odoo/odoo15/library` directory:

```
$ git clone https://github.com/PacktPublishing/Odoo-15-
Development-Essentials/opt/odoo/library
```

The Odoo source code is available on the server, but it can't run yet because the required Python dependencies are not installed yet. Let's install these in the next section.

Installing the Python dependencies

Once the Odoo source code is downloaded, the Python packages required by Odoo should be installed.

Many of them also have Debian or Ubuntu system packages. The official Odoo installation package for Debian uses them, and the dependency package names can be found in the Odoo source code in the `debian/control` file: `https://github.com/odoo/odoo/blob/15.0/debian/control`.

These Python dependencies can also be installed directly from the **Python Package Index (PyPI)**. Doing this using a Python **virtual environment** provides better protection from changes being made to the host system.

The following commands create a virtual environment, activate it, and then install Odoo from source, along with all the required Python dependencies:

```
$ python3 -m venv /opt/odoo/env15
$ source /opt/odoo/env15/bin/activate
(env15) $ pip install -r /opt/odoo/odoo15/requirements.txt
(env15) $ pip install -e /opt/odoo/odoo15
```

And Odoo should be ready now. Any of the following commands can be used to confirm this:

```
(env15) $ odoo --version
Odoo Server 15.0
(env15) $ /opt/odoo/odoo15/odoo-bin --version
Odoo Server 15.0
$ /opt/odoo/env15/bin/python3 /opt/odoo/odoo15/odoo-bin
--version
Odoo Server 15.0
$ /opt/odoo/env15/bin/odoo --version
Odoo Server 15.0
```

Let's understand these commands one by one:

- The first command relies on the `odoo` command made available by `pip install -e /opt/odoo/odoo15`.

- The second command does not rely on the `odoo` command, and it directly calls the Odoo start script, `/opt/odoo/odoo15/odoo-bin`.

- The third command does not need the virtual environment to be activated beforehand, as it uses the corresponding Python executable directly, which has the same effect.

- The final command does the same in a more compact way. It uses directly the odoo command available in that virtual environment. This can be useful for some scripts.

Odoo is now ready to run. The next step is to take care of the configuration file to use, which we will explain in the following section.

Configuring Odoo

Once Odoo is installed, the configuration file to be used by the production service needs to be prepared.

The next sub-section provides guidance on how to do this.

Setting up the configuration file

Configuration files are expected to be in the /etc system directory. So, the Odoo production configuration file will be stored at /etc/odoo/odoo.conf.

To make it easier to see all of the available options, a default configuration file can be generated. This should be done by the user that will run the service.

If not done yet, create a session for the odoo user and activate the virtual environment:

```
$ sudo su - odoo
$ python3 -m venv /opt/odoo/env15
```

Now, the following command can be used to create a default configuration file:

```
(env15) $ odoo -c /opt/odoo/odoo.conf --save --stop-after-init
```

In the previous command, the -c option sets the location of the configuration file. If not given, it defaults to ~/.odoorc. The --save option writes the options to it. If the file does not exist, it will be created with all default options. If it already exists, it will be updated with the options used in the command.

The following commands set a few important options for it:

```
(env15) $ odoo -c /opt/odoo/odoo.conf --save \
--stop-after-init \
-d odoo-prod --db-filter="^odoo-prod$" \
--without-demo=all --proxy-mode
```

The options set are as follows:

- `-d`: This is the default database to use.
- `--db-filter`: This is a regular expression filtering the databases available for the Odoo service. The expression used makes available only the `odoo-prod` database.
- `--without-demo=all`: This disables demonstration data so that the Odoo initialized databases start clean.
- `--proxy-mode`: This enables the proxy mode, meaning that Odoo should expect requests forwarded from a reverse proxy.

The next step is to copy this default file to the `/etc` directory and set the necessary access rights so that the Odoo user can read it:

```
$ exit  # exit from the odoo user session
$ sudo mkdir /etc/odoo
$ sudo cp /opt/odoo/odoo.conf /etc/odoo/odoo.conf
$ sudo chown -R odoo /etc/odoo
$ sudo chmod u=r,g=rw,o=r /etc/odoo/odoo.conf  # for extra
hardening
```

The last command ensures that the user running the Odoo process can read but can't change the configuration file, thereby providing better security.

The Odoo log file directory also needs to be created and given access to the `odoo` user. This should go inside the `/var/log` directory. The following commands do this:

```
$ sudo mkdir /var/log/odoo
$ sudo chown odoo /var/log/odoo
```

Finally, the Odoo configuration file should be edited to ensure that a few important parameters are correctly configured. For example, the following command opens the file using the `nano` editor:

```
$ sudo nano /etc/odoo/odoo.conf
```

These are the suggested values for some of the most important parameters:

```
[options]
addons_path = /opt/odoo/odoo15/odoo/addons,/opt/odoo/odoo15/
addons,/opt/odoo/library
admin_passwd = StrongRandomPassword
db_name = odoo-prod
dbfilter = ^odoo-prod$
http_interface = 127.0.0.1
http_port = 8069
limit_time_cpu = 600
limit_time_real = 1200
list_db = False
logfile = /var/log/odoo/odoo-server.log
proxy_mode = True
without_demo = all
workers = 6
```

Let's explain them in detail:

- addons_path: This is a comma-separated list of the paths where add-on modules will be looked up. It's read from left to right, with the leftmost directories considered a higher priority.

- admin_passwd: This is the master password used to access the web client database management functions. It's critical to set this with a strong password or, even better, to set it to False to deactivate the function.

- db_name: This is the database instance to initialize during the server startup sequence.

- dbfilter: This is a filter for the databases to be made accessible. It's a Python-interpreted regex expression. For the user not to be prompted to select a database and for unauthenticated URLs to work properly, it should be set with ^dbname$, for example, dbfilter=^odoo-prod$. It supports the %h and %d placeholders, which are replaced by the HTTP request hostname and subdomain name.

- http_interface: This is the TCP/IP address Odoo will listen to. By default, it is 0.0.0.0, meaning all addresses. For a deployment behind a reverse proxy, this can be set to the reverse proxy address so that only requests from there are considered. Use 127.0.0.1 if the reverse proxy is in the same server as the Odoo service.

- `http_port`: This is the port number at which the server will listen. By default, port `8069` is used.

- `limit_time_cpu`/`limit_time_real`: This sets CPU time limits for the workers. The default settings, `60` and `120`, may be too low, and it could be convenient to increase them.

- `list_db = False`: This blocks database listing, both at the **remote procedure calls** (**RPCs**)-level and in the UI, and it blocks the database management screens and the underlying RPC functions.

- `logfile`: This is where the server log should be written. For system services, the expected location is somewhere inside `/var/log`. If left empty, the log prints to standard output instead.

- `proxy_mode`: This should be set to `True` when Odoo is accessed behind a reverse proxy, as we will be doing.

- `without_demo`: This should be set to `all` in production environments so that new databases don't have demo data on them.

- `workers`: This, with a value of two or more, enables the multiprocessing mode. We'll discuss this in more detail shortly.

From a security point of view, the `admin_passwd` and `list_db=False` options are particularly important. They block web access to the database management features and should be set in any production or internet-facing Odoo server.

> **Tip**
> The `openssl rand -base64 32` command can be used to generate a random password in the command line. Change the `32` number to whatever password size you prefer.

The following parameters can also be helpful:

- `data_dir`: This is the path where session data and attachment files are stored; remember to keep backups of this directory.

- `http_interface`: This sets the addresses that will be listened to. By default, it listens to `0.0.0.0`, but when using a reverse proxy, it can be set to `127.0.0.1` in order to respond to local requests only.

We can check the effect of the configuration made by running the Odoo manually, as follows:

```
$ sudo su - odoo
$ source /opt/odoo/env15/bin/activate
$ odoo -c /etc/odoo/odoo.conf
```

The last command will not display any output to the console, as log messages are being written to the log file instead of to the standard output.

To follow the log for a running Odoo server, the `tail` command can be used:

```
$ tail -f /var/log/odoo/odoo-server.log
```

This can be done from a different terminal window while the manual command is running in the original terminal.

To run multiple terminal sessions on the same terminal window, you can use **multiplexing** applications such as `tmux` or **GNU** `screen`. Ubuntu also has available the **Byobu** utility, which is a wrapper for `tmux` or `screen`. For more details, see `https://help.ubuntu.com/community/Byobu`.

> **Note**
>
> Unfortunately, the `logfile` configuration option can't be unset directly from the Odoo command. If we want to temporarily send the log output back to the standard output, the best solution is to use a copy of the configuration file without the `logfile` option set.

It may be the case that the `odoo-prod` database has not been initialized by Odoo and that this needs to be done manually. In this case, the initialization can be done by installing the `base` module:

```
$ /opt/odoo/env15/bin/odoo -c /etc/odoo/odoo.conf -i base \
--stop-after-init
```

At this point, the Odoo configuration should be ready. Before continuing, it is worth learning more about the multiprocessing workers in Odoo.

Understanding multiprocessing workers

A production instance is expected to handle a significant workload. By default, the server runs one process and can use only one CPU core for processing due to the Python language **Global Interpreter Lock (GIL)**. However, a multiprocessing mode is available so that concurrent requests can be handled, allowing us to take advantage of multiple cores.

The `workers=N` option sets the number of worker processes to use. As a guideline, it can be set to `1+2*P`, where P is the number of processor cores. Finding the best setting might involve some experimentation by using different numbers and checking how busy the server processors are. Having PostgreSQL running on the same machine also has an impact on this, and this will reduce the number of workers that should be enabled.

It is better to set workers that are too high for the load rather than too low. The minimum should be six, due to the parallel connections used by most browsers. The maximum is generally limited by the amount of RAM on the machine, as each worker will consume some server memory. As a rule of thumb for normal usage patterns, the Odoo server should be able to handle `(1+2*P)*6` simultaneous users, where P is the number of processors.

There are a few `limit-` configuration parameters that can be used to tune workers. Workers are recycled when they reach these limits, where the corresponding process is stopped and a new one is started. This protects the server from memory leaks and particular processes overloading the server resources.

The official documentation provides additional advice on how to tune the worker parameters. It can be found at `https://www.odoo.com/documentation/15.0/setup/deploy.html#builtin-server`.

At this point, Odoo is installed, configured, and ready to run. The next step is to have it running as an unattended system service. Let's look at this in detail in the next section.

Setting up Odoo as a system service

Odoo should run as a system service so that it is automatically started when the system boots and runs unattended, not requiring a user session.

In Debian/Ubuntu systems, the `init` system is responsible for starting services. Historically, Debian and its derived operating systems used `sysvinit`. This has changed, and recent Debian/Ubuntu systems use `systemd`. This is true for Ubuntu 16.04 and later.

To confirm that `systemd` is used in your system, try the following command:

```
$ man init
```

This command opens the documentation for the current `init` system in use, so you can check what is being used. At the top of the manual page, you should see `SYSTEMD` mentioned.

Let's continue with the `systemd` service configuration.

Creating a systemd service

If the operating system is recent – such as Debian 8 and Ubuntu 16.04 or later – `systemd` should be the `init` system being used.

To add a new service to the system, simply create a file describing it. Create a `/lib/systemd/system/odoo.service` file with the following content:

```
[Unit]
Description=Odoo Open Source ERP and CRM
After=network.target


[Service]
Type=simple
User=odoo
Group=odoo
ExecStart=/opt/odoo/env/bin/odoo -c /etc/odoo/odoo.conf --log-file=/var/log/odoo/odoo-server.log
KillMode=mixed


[Install]
WantedBy=multi-user.target
```

This service configuration file is based on the sample provided in the Odoo source code, which can be found at `https://github.com/odoo/odoo/blob/15.0/debian/odoo.service`. The `ExecStart` option should be adjusted to the specific paths to use in this system.

Next, the new service can be registered with the following command:

```
$ sudo systemctl enable odoo.service
```

To start this new service, run the following:

```
$ sudo systemctl start odoo
```

To check its status, use the following:

```
$ sudo systemctl status odoo
```

And it can be stopped using the following command:

```
$ sudo systemctl stop odoo
```

When running Odoo as a system service, it is useful to confirm that the client can access it. Let's see how that can be done from the command line.

Checking the Odoo service from the command line

To confirm that the Odoo service is up and responsive, we can check that it is responding to requests. We should be able to get a response from it and see no errors in the log file.

We can check whether Odoo is responding to HTTP requests inside the server by using the following command:

```
$ curl http://localhost:8069
<!DOCTYPE HTML PUBLIC "-//W3C//DTD HTML 3.2 Final//EN">
<title>Redirecting...</title>
<h1>Redirecting...</h1>
<p>You should be redirected automatically to target URL: <a
href="/web">/web</a>.  If not click the link.
```

In addition, to see what is in the `log` file, use the following command:

```
$ less /var/log/odoo/odoo-server.log
```

To follow what is being added to the log file live, `tail -f` can be used, as follows:

```
$ tail -f /var/log/odoo/odoo-server.log
```

Odoo is now installed and running as a service. Next, the setup can be improved by adding a reverse proxy. The next section explains this.

Setting up an Nginx reverse proxy

While Odoo itself can serve web pages, it is recommended to have a reverse proxy in front of it. A reverse proxy receives the traffic from the clients and then forwards it to the Odoo servers responding to them. Doing this has several benefits.

On the security side, it can provide the following:

- Handle (and enforce) HTTPS protocols to encrypt traffic.
- Hide the internal network characteristics.
- Act as an application firewall, limiting the URLs accepted for processing.

On the performance side, it can provide the following:

- Cache static content, avoiding burdening the Odoo services with these requests and thereby reducing their load.
- Compress content to speed up loading time.
- Act as a load balancer, distributing load between several Odoo services.

There are several options that can serve as a reverse proxy. Historically, **Apache** has been a popular choice. In recent years, Nginx has become widely used and is referred to in the Odoo official documentation. In our example, Nginx will be used for a reverse proxy, and the presented security and performance features will be implemented with it.

First, Nginx should be installed and set to be listening on the default HTTP port. It is possible that this port is already being used by another installed service. To ensure that the port is free and available, use the following command, which should result in an error:

```
$ curl http://localhost
curl: (7) Failed to connect to localhost port 80: Connection
refused
```

If it does not return the previous error message, an installed service is using port 80 and should be disabled or uninstalled.

For example, if an Apache server is installed, use the `sudo service apache2 stop` command to stop it, or even uninstall it with the `sudo apt remove apache2` command.

With port 80 free, Nginx can be installed and configured. The following command installs Nginx:

```
$ sudo apt-get install nginx
$ sudo service nginx start  # start nginx, if not already
started
```

To confirm that nginx is working correctly, visit the server address with a browser or with the curl http://localhost command in the server. This should return a **Welcome to nginx** page.

The Nginx configuration files are stored at /etc/nginx/available-sites/ and are activated by adding them to /etc/nginx/enabled-sites/, which is usually done with a symbolic link to the file in the available sites directory.

To prepare for the Odoo Nginx configuration, the default configuration should be removed and an Odoo configuration file added, as follows:

```
$ sudo rm /etc/nginx/sites-enabled/default
$ sudo touch /etc/nginx/sites-available/odoo
$ sudo ln -s /etc/nginx/sites-available/odoo \
/etc/nginx/sites-enabled/odoo
```

Next, using an editor such as nano or vi, edit the configuration file as follows:

```
$ sudo nano /etc/nginx/sites-available/odoo
```

The following example provides a basic Nginx configuration for Odoo:

```
upstream odoo {
    server 127.0.0.1:8069;
}
upstream odoochat {
    server 127.0.0.1:8072;
}
server {
    listen 80;
    server_name odoo.mycompany.com;
    proxy_read_timeout 720s;
    proxy_connect_timeout 720s;
    proxy_send_timeout 720s;
```

```
# Add Headers for odoo proxy mode
proxy_set_header X-Forwarded-Host  $host;
proxy_set_header X-Forwarded-For   $proxy_add_x_
  forwarded_for;
proxy_set_header X-Forwarded-Proto $scheme;
proxy_set_header X-Real-IP         $remote_addr;

# log
access_log /var/log/nginx/odoo.access.log;
error_log /var/log/nginx/odoo.error.log;

# Redirect longpoll requests to odoo longpolling port
location /longpolling {
  proxy_pass http://odoochat;
}

# Redirect requests to odoo backend server
location / {
  proxy_redirect off;
  proxy_pass http://odoo;
}

# common gzip
gzip_types text/css text/scss text/plain text/xml
  application/xml application/json application/javascript;
gzip on;
}
```

At the top of the configuration file, there are the upstream configuration sections. These point to the Odoo service, which is listening on ports 8069 and 8072 by default. The 8069 port serves the web client and RPC requests, and 8072 serves the long polling requests used by instant messaging features.

The `server` configuration section defines what happens to the traffic received on the `80` default HTTP port. Here, it is redirected to upstream Odoo services with the `proxy_pass` configuration directive. Any traffic for the `/longpolling` address is passed on to the `odoochat` upstream, and the `/` remaining traffic is passed on to the `odoo` upstream.

A few `proxy_set_header` directives add information to the request header to let the Odoo backend service know that it is being proxied.

> **Tip**
>
> For security reasons, it is important for Odoo to ensure that the `proxy_mode` parameter is set to `True`. The reason for this is that with Nginx, all requests hitting Odoo are coming from the Nginx server instead of the original remote IP address. Setting the `X-Forwarded-For` header in the proxy and enabling `--proxy-mode` allows Odoo to be aware of the original source of the request. Note that enabling `--proxy-mode` without forcing the header at the proxy level allows malicious clients to spoof their request address.

At the end of the configuration file, a couple of `gzip`-related directives can be found. These enable the compression of some files, thereby improving performance.

Once edited and saved, the Nginx configuration can be verified for correctness with the following command:

```
$ sudo nginx -t
nginx: the configuration file /etc/nginx/nginx.conf syntax is
ok
nginx: configuration file /etc/nginx/nginx.conf test is
successful
```

Now, the Nginx service can reload the new configuration, using one of the following commands, depending on the `init` system used:

```
$ sudo /etc/init.d/nginx reload
$ sudo systemctl reload nginx  # using systemd
$ sudo service nginx reload  # on Ubuntu systems
```

This will have Nginx reload the configuration used without interrupting the service, as would have happened if `restart` was used instead of `reload`.

To be properly secured, Odoo should be accessed through HTTPS. The next section will address this.

Configuring and enforcing HTTPS

Web traffic should not travel through the internet in plain text. When exposing the Odoo server on a network, HTTPS should be used to encrypt the traffic.

In some cases, it might be acceptable to use a self-signed certificate. Keep in mind that using a self-signed certificate provides limited security. While it allows for traffic to be encrypted, it has some security limitations, such as not being able to prevent man-in-the-middle attacks, or not being able to present security warnings on recent web browsers.

A more robust solution is to use a certificate signed by a recognized authority. This is particularly important when running e-commerce websites. Another option is to use a **Let's Encrypt** certificate, and the **Certbot** program automates getting SSL certificates for it. See `https://certbot.eff.org/instructions` to learn more.

Next, we will see how to create a self-signed certificate, in case this is the preferred choice.

Creating a self-signed SSL certificate

A certificate needs to be installed on Nginx to enable SSL. We can either have one provided by a certificate authority or generate a self-signed one.

To create a self-signed certificate, use these commands:

```
$ sudo mkdir /etc/ssl/nginx && cd /etc/ssl/nginx
$ sudo openssl req -x509 -newkey rsa:2048 \
-keyout server.key -out server.crt -days 365 -nodes
$ sudo chmod a-wx *            # make files read only
$ sudo chown www-data:root *   # access only to www-data group
```

The preceding code creates an `/etc/ssl/nginx` directory and a passwordless SSL certificate. When running the `openssl` command, the user will be asked for some additional information, and then a certificate and key files will be generated. Finally, the ownership of these files is given to the `www-data` user, which is used to run the web server.

With an SSL certificate ready to be used, the next step is to install it on the Nginx service.

Configuring HTTPS access on Nginx

To enforce HTTPS, an SSL certificate is needed. The Nginx service will use it to encrypt the traffic between the server and the web browser.

For this, the Odoo Nginx configuration file needs to be revisited. Edit it to replace the `server` directive with the following:

```
server {
   listen 80;
   rewrite ^(.*) https://$host$1 permanent;
}
```

With this change, requests for the `http://` address are converted into `https://` equivalent addresses, ensuring that the non-secure transport is not used by accident.

The HTTPS service still needs to be configured. This can be done by adding the following `server` directive to the configuration:

```
# odoo server
upstream odoo {
   server 127.0.0.1:8069;
}
upstream odoochat {
   server 127.0.0.1:8072;
}

# http -> https
server {
   listen 80;
   server_name odoo.mycompany.com;
   rewrite ^(.*) https://$host$1 permanent;
}

server {
   listen 443;
   server_name odoo.mycompany.com;
   proxy_read_timeout 720s;
   proxy_connect_timeout 720s;
   proxy_send_timeout 720s;

   # Add Headers for odoo proxy mode
   proxy_set_header X-Forwarded-Host $host;
```

```
proxy_set_header X-Forwarded-For $proxy_add_x_for
  warded_for;
proxy_set_header X-Forwarded-Proto $scheme;
proxy_set_header X-Real-IP $remote_addr;

# SSL parameters
ssl on;
ssl_certificate /etc/ssl/nginx/server.crt;
ssl_certificate_key /etc/ssl/nginx/server.key;
ssl_session_timeout 30m;
ssl_protocols TLSv1.2;
ssl_ciphers ECDHE-ECDSA-AES128-GCM-SHA256:ECDHE-RSA-
  AES128-GCM-SHA256:ECDHE-ECDSA-AES256-GCM-SHA384:ECDHE-
  RSA-AES256-GCM-SHA384:ECDHE-ECDSA-CHACHA20-
  POLY1305:ECDHE-RSA-CHACHA20-POLY1305:DHE-RSA-AES128-
  GCM-SHA256:DHE-RSA-AES256-GCM-SHA384;
ssl_prefer_server_ciphers off;

# log
access_log /var/log/nginx/odoo.access.log;
error_log /var/log/nginx/odoo.error.log;

# Redirect longpoll requests to odoo longpolling port
location /longpolling {
  proxy_pass http://odoochat;
}

# Redirect requests to odoo backend server
location / {
  proxy_redirect off;
  proxy_pass http://odoo;
}

# common gzip
gzip_types text/css text/scss text/plain text/xml
```

```
        application/xml application/json application/javascript;
    gzip on;
}
```

This additional `server` directive listens to the HTTPS port and uses the certificate files at `/etc/ssl/nginx/` to encrypt the traffic.

> **Note**
> The Nginx configuration proposed here is based on the official documentation found at `https://www.odoo.com/documentation/15.0/administration/install/deploy.html#https`.

Once this configuration is reloaded, Odoo should work through HTTPS only, as shown in the following commands:

```
$ sudo nginx -t
nginx: the configuration file /etc/nginx/nginx.conf syntax is
ok
nginx: configuration file /etc/nginx/nginx.conf test is
successful
$ sudo service nginx reload  # or: sudo systemctl reload nginx
* Reloading nginx configuration nginx
...done.
$ curl -k https://localhost
```

Encrypting the web traffic is not the only thing Nginx can do for us. It can also help to reduce the load on the Odoo upstream service. Let's look at this in detail in the next section.

Caching static content

Nginx can cache the static files served – this means that later requests for the cached files are served directly from Nginx and don't need to be requested by the upstream Odoo service.

This not only improves response time but also improves the Odoo service capacity to serve more users, as it is now focused on responding to dynamic requests.

To enable static content caching, add the following section to the Nginx configuration file after the `# comming gzip` directives:

```
    # cache static data
    location ~* /web/static/ {
        proxy_cache_valid 200 60m;
```

```
    proxy_buffering on;
    expires 864000;
    proxy_pass http://odoo;
}
```

With this configuration, static data is cached for 60 minutes. Odoo static content is defined as any file served from the `/web/static` path.

At this point, the server should be fully functional, with Nginx handling requests through HTTPS and then handing them over to the Odoo service for processing.

The Odoo service will require maintenance and updates, so the next section discusses how to do this.

Maintaining the Odoo service and modules

Once the Odoo server is up and running, it is expected for some maintenance to be needed – for example, installing or updating modules.

These actions involve some risk for the production system, and it is best to test them in a staging environment before applying in production. Let's start with a basic recipe to create a staging environment.

Creating a staging environment

The staging environment should be a copy of the production system and ideally should have its own dedicated server.

A simplification, which is safe enough for most cases, is to have the staging environment in the same server as the production system.

To create a copy of the `odoo-prod` production database as the `odoo-stage` database, use the following commands:

```
$ dropdb odoo-stage
$ createdb --owner=odoo odoo-stage
$ pg_dump odoo-prod | psql -d odoo-stage
$ sudo su - odoo
$ cd ~/.local/share/Odoo/filestore/
$ cp -r odoo-prod odoo-stage
$ exit
```

Note that some configurations are copied over, such as the connections to email servers, and you may want to have additional commands disabling them. The specific actions needed to do this depend on the database setup, but it's likely they can be automated by a script. For this, it is good to know that the `psql` command can be used to run SQL directly from the command line, for example, `psql -d odoo-stage -c "<SQL command>"`.

> **Tip**
>
> A database copy can be made in a much faster way using the following command:
>
> `$ createdb --owner=odoo --template=odoo-prod odoo-stage.`
>
> The caveat here is that in order for it to run, there can't be any open connections to the `odoo-prod` database, so the Odoo production server needs to be stopped before the command can be used.

Now that we have a copy of the production database for staging, the next step is to create a copy of the source to be used. This can be in a subdirectory called `/opt/odoo/stage`, for example.

The following shell commands copy the relevant files and create the staging environment:

```
$ sudo su - odoo
$ mkdir /opt/odoo/stage
$ cp -r /opt/odoo/odoo15/ /opt/odoo/stage/
$ cp -r /opt/odoo/library/ /opt/odoo/stage/   # custom code
$ python3 -m venv /opt/odoo/env-stage
$ source /opt/odoo/env-stage/bin/activate
(env-stage) $ pip install -r \
/opt/odoo/stage/odoo15/requirements.txt
(env-stage) $ pip install -e /opt/odoo/stage/odoo15
(env-stage) $ exit
```

Finally, a specific Odoo configuration file should be prepared for the staging environment, as the path to the files used is different. The HTTP ports used should also be changed so that the staging environment can run at the same time as the main production service.

This staging environment can now be used for testing purposes. So, the next section describes how a production update would be applied.

Updating Odoo source code

Odoo and custom module code will usually have versions managed through Git.

To get the latest Odoo source code from the GitHub repository, use the `git pull` command. Before doing that, the `git tag` command can be used to create a tag for the current commit being used so that it's easier to revert the code update, as follows:

```
$ sudo su - odoo
$ cd /opt/odoo/odoo15
$ git tag --force 15-last-prod
$ git pull
$ exit
```

For code changes to take effect, the Odoo service should be restarted. For data file changes to take effect, an upgrade to the modules is needed.

> **Tip**
>
> As a general rule, changes to Odoo stable versions are considered code fixes, and it's therefore not often worth the risk of performing module upgrades. If you need to perform a module upgrade, however, this can be achieved using the `-u <module>` additional option (or `-u base`), which upgrades all modules.

We can test the actions using the staging database before applying them in the production database, as follows:

```
$ source /opt/odoo/env15/bin/activate
(env15) $ odoo -c /etc/odoo/odoo.conf -d odoo-stage \
--http-port=8080 -u library  # modules to updgrade
(env15) $ exit
```

This Odoo staging server was configured to listen on port `8080`. We can navigate there with our web browser to check whether the upgraded code works correctly.

If something goes wrong, we can revert the code to an earlier version with the following commands:

```
$ sudo su - odoo
$ cd /opt/odoo/odoo15
$ git checkout 15-last-prod
$ exit
```

If everything works as expected, it should be safe to perform an upgrade on the production service, which is usually done by restarting it. If you want to perform an actual module upgrade, the suggested approach is to stop the server, run the upgrade, and then restart the service, as follows:

```
$ sudo service odoo stop
$ sudo su -c "/opt/odoo/env15/bin/odoo -c /etc/odoo/odoo.conf" \
" -u base --stop-after-init" odoo
$ sudo service odoo start
```

Making a backup of the database before running an upgrade is also advised.

In this section, you learned how to create a staging environment alongside the main Odoo environment to be used for testing. Updates to Odoo code or to custom modules can be tried on the staging environment before applying them in the production system. This allows us to identify and correct any issues you might find with the upgrades ahead of time.

Summary

In this chapter, we learned about the additional steps required for setting up and running Odoo on a Debian-based production server. We looked at the most important settings in the configuration file, and we learned how to take advantage of the multiprocessing mode.

For improved security and scalability, we also learned how to use Nginx as a reverse proxy in front of Odoo server processes and how to configure it to use HTTPS-encrypted traffic.

Finally, some advice was provided on how to create a staging environment and perform updates to Odoo code or custom modules.

This covers the essentials of what's needed to run an Odoo server and provide a reasonably stable and secure service to your users. We can now use it to host our library management system!

Further reading

To learn more about Odoo, you should take a look at the official documentation at `https://www.odoo.com/documentation`. Some topics are covered in more detail there, and you'll find topics not covered in this book.

There are also other published books on Odoo that you might find useful. **Packt Publishing** has a few in its catalog, and in particular, *Odoo Development Cookbook* provides more advanced material on topics not discussed in this book. At the time of writing, the last edition available was for Odoo 14, which is available at `https://www.packtpub.com/product/odoo-14-development-cookbook-fourth-edition/9781800200319`.

Finally, Odoo is an open source product with a vibrant community. Getting involved, asking questions, and contributing is a great way not only to learn but also to build a business network. With this in mind, we should also mention the **Odoo Community Association (OCA)**, which promotes collaboration and quality open source code. You can learn more about it at `https://odoo-community.org/` or `https://github.com/OCA`.

Enjoy your Odoo journey!

Index

D

W

X

Y

Packt>

Other Books You May Enjoy

If you enjoyed this book, you may be interested in these other books by Packt:

Odoo 14 Development Cookbook - Fourth Edition

Parth Gajjar, Alexandre Fayolle, Holger Brunn, Daniel Reis

ISBN: 9781800200319

- Build beautiful websites with Odoo CMS using dynamic building blocks
- Get to grips with advanced concepts such as caching, prefetching, debugging
- Modify backend JavaScript components and POS applications with the new OWL framework
- Connect and access any object in Odoo via Remote Procedure Calls (RPC)
- Manage, deploy, and test an Odoo instance with Odoo.sh
- Configure IoT Box to add and upgrade Point of Sale (POS) hardware
- Find out how to implement in-app purchase services

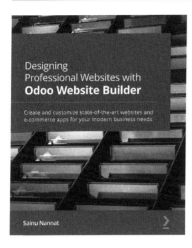

Designing Professional Websites with Odoo Website Builder

Sainu Nannat

ISBN: 9781801078122

- Find out how to implement structure blocks while developing a website
- Work with dynamic content blocks and inner content blocks in the Odoo website builder
- Use an HTML, CSS, or JS editor in the Odoo website builder to customize applications
- Create and design a blog with the Odoo website builder
- Build a fully functional e-commerce website and a discussion forum using the Odoo website builder
- Track visitors on the website and understand the live chat tool and its functionality

Packt is searching for authors like you

If you're interested in becoming an author for Packt, please visit `authors.packtpub.com` and apply today. We have worked with thousands of developers and tech professionals, just like you, to help them share their insight with the global tech community. You can make a general application, apply for a specific hot topic that we are recruiting an author for, or submit your own idea.

Share Your Thoughts

Now you've finished *Odoo 15 Development Essentials*, we'd love to hear your thoughts! Scan the QR code below to go straight to the Amazon review page for this book and share your feedback or leave a review on the site that you purchased it from.

`https://packt.link/r/1800200064`

Your review is important to us and the tech community and will help us make sure we're delivering excellent quality content.

Printed in Great Britain
by Amazon